MICROSOFT® OFFICE 97
FOR
WINDOWS®
FOR
DUMMIES®

MORE

MICROSOFT® OFFICE 97 FOR WINDOWS® FOR DUMMIES®

by Wallace Wang

IDG BOOKS
WORLDWIDE™

IDG Books Worldwide, Inc.
An International Data Group Company

Foster City, CA ♦ Chicago, IL ♦ Indianapolis, IN ♦ Southlake, TX

MORE Microsoft® Office 97 For Windows® For Dummies®

Published by
IDG Books Worldwide, Inc.
An International Data Group Company
919 E. Hillsdale Blvd.
Suite 400
Foster City, CA 94404
http://www.idgbooks.com (IDG Books Worldwide Web site)
http://www.dummies.com (Dummies Press Web site)

Library of Congress Catalog Card No.: 97-70734

ISBN: 0-7645-0136-4

Printed in the United States of America

10 9 8 7 6 5 4 3 2 1

1E/RW/QW/ZX/IN

Distributed in the United States by IDG Books Worldwide, Inc.

Distributed by Macmillan Canada for Canada; by Transworld Publishers Limited in the United Kingdom; by IDG Norge Books for Norway; by IDG Sweden Books for Sweden; by Woodslane Pty. Ltd. for Australia; by Woodslane Enterprises Ltd. for New Zealand; by Longman Singapore Publishers Ltd. for Singapore, Malaysia, Thailand, and Indonesia; by Simron Pty. Ltd. for South Africa; by Toppan Company Ltd. for Japan; by Distribuidora Cuspide for Argentina; by Livraria Cultura for Brazil; by Ediciencia S.A. for Ecuador; by Addison-Wesley Publishing Company for Korea; by Ediciones ZETA S.C.R. Ltda. for Peru; by WS Computer Publishing Corporation, Inc., for the Philippines; by Unalis Corporation for Taiwan; by Contemporanea de Ediciones for Venezuela; by Computer Book & Magazine Store for Puerto Rico; by Express Computer Distributors for the Caribbean and West Indies. Authorized Sales Agent: Anthony Rudkin Associates for the Middle East and North Africa.

For general information on IDG Books Worldwide's books in the U.S., please call our Consumer Customer Service department at 800-762-2974. For reseller information, including discounts and premium sales, please call our Reseller Customer Service department at 800-434-3422.

For information on where to purchase IDG Books Worldwide's books outside the U.S., please contact our International Sales department at 415-655-3200 or fax 415-655-3295.

For information on foreign language translations, please contact our Foreign & Subsidiary Rights department at 415-655-3021 or fax 415-655-3281.

For sales inquiries and special prices for bulk quantities, please contact our Sales department at 415-655-3200 or write to the address above.

For information on using IDG Books Worldwide's books in the classroom or for ordering examination copies, please contact our Educational Sales department at 800-434-2086 or fax 817-251-8174.

For press review copies, author interviews, or other publicity information, please contact our Public Relations department at 415-655-3000 or fax 415-655-3299.

For authorization to photocopy items for corporate, personal, or educational use, please contact Copyright Clearance Center, 222 Rosewood Drive, Danvers, MA 01923, or fax 508-750-4470.

is a trademark under exclusive license to IDG Books Worldwide, Inc., from International Data Group, Inc.

About the Author

Very few people really care who writes these computer books. If you're reading this in a bookstore right now, take a look at the other computer books on the shelves and you're sure to find more than a dozen that don't even display the author's name on the cover. Whether this is out of disregard for the author as a human being or out of complete embarrassment to have an actual person's name associated with a corporate entity more interested in hiring faceless legions of co-authors in a sweat shop assembly line to write individual chapters of a book so none of them can lay claim to the bulk of the book's generated royalties is a matter that only each individual book publisher can answer with any degree of accuracy.

In the event that you managed to read the above sentence without losing your place given the lack of punctuation marks to help organize your train of thought, then you must really be curious to learn more about the author of this book. So to avoid disappointing any faithful readers who have made it up to this point, the author's introduction officially begins with the next paragraph.

A couple of my favorite satirical songs that I listened to while writing this book included "Christmas at Ground Zero" by Weird Al Yankovic and "So Long Mom (A Song for World War III)" by Tom Lehrer. While taking a break from writing this book, I read *Tobermory,* a short story by Saki about a talking cat that points out the individual flaws of guests at a house party to the extent that the partygoers later conspire to kill the cat for speaking out. In addition, I also read a comic skit called "Martin LeSoeur, Reconteur" by Bob Elliot and Ray Goulding about a world-famous story-teller who can't remember the ending to one of his stories — and when he finally remembers the ending, he can't recall any part of the beginning.

Finally, I spent the greater portion of April 17, 1997, on a Thursday evening writing the "About the Author" section, the "Dedication" section, and the "Acknowledgments" section. If you ever purchase any of my other books published by IDG Books Worldwide, you'll notice that I vary the information provided on these pages just so you don't see the same tired text recycled over and over again. I get bored of seeing the same dry descriptions found in other publishers' books, so I hope you appreciate the time I spend and the effort I go through to make my books singularly unique in this regard.

Thanks for reading this far, and if you ever need to reach me to ask me a question about this book or anything else on your mind, feel free to drop me a line at 70334.3672@compuserve.com, bothekat@aol.com, bo_the_cat@msn.com, or bothecat@prodigy.net.

ABOUT IDG BOOKS WORLDWIDE

Welcome to the world of IDG Books Worldwide.

IDG Books Worldwide, Inc., is a subsidiary of International Data Group, the world's largest publisher of computer-related information and the leading global provider of information services on information technology. IDG was founded more than 25 years ago and now employs more than 8,500 people worldwide. IDG publishes more than 275 computer publications in over 75 countries (see listing below). More than 60 million people read one or more IDG publications each month.

Launched in 1990, IDG Books Worldwide is today the #1 publisher of best-selling computer books in the United States. We are proud to have received eight awards from the Computer Press Association in recognition of editorial excellence and three from *Computer Currents'* First Annual Readers' Choice Awards. Our best-selling *...For Dummies*® series has more than 30 million copies in print with translations in 30 languages. IDG Books Worldwide, through a joint venture with IDG's Hi-Tech Beijing, became the first U.S. publisher to publish a computer book in the People's Republic of China. In record time, IDG Books Worldwide has become the first choice for millions of readers around the world who want to learn how to better manage their businesses.

Our mission is simple: Every one of our books is designed to bring extra value and skill-building instructions to the reader. Our books are written by experts who understand and care about our readers. The knowledge base of our editorial staff comes from years of experience in publishing, education, and journalism — experience we use to produce books for the '90s. In short, we care about books, so we attract the best people. We devote special attention to details such as audience, interior design, use of icons, and illustrations. And because we use an efficient process of authoring, editing, and desktop publishing our books electronically, we can spend more time ensuring superior content and spend less time on the technicalities of making books.

You can count on our commitment to deliver high-quality books at competitive prices on topics you want to read about. At IDG Books Worldwide, we continue in the IDG tradition of delivering quality for more than 25 years. You'll find no better book on a subject than one from IDG Books Worldwide.

John Kilcullen
CEO
IDG Books Worldwide, Inc.

Steven Berkowitz
President and Publisher
IDG Books Worldwide, Inc.

Eighth Annual Computer Press Awards ≥1992

Ninth Annual Computer Press Awards ≥1993

Tenth Annual Computer Press Awards ≥1994

Eleventh Annual Computer Press Awards ≥1995

IDG Books Worldwide, Inc., is a subsidiary of International Data Group, the world's largest publisher of computer-related information and the leading global provider of information services on information technology. International Data Group publishes over 275 computer publications in over 75 countries. Sixty million people read one or more International Data Group publications each month. International Data Group's publications include: **ARGENTINA:** Buyer's Guide, Computerworld Argentina, PC World Argentina; **AUSTRALIA:** Australian Macworld, Australian PC World, Australian Reseller News, Computerworld, IT Casebook, Network World, Publish, Webmaster; **AUSTRIA:** Computerwelt Osterreich, Networks Austria, PC Tip Austria; **BANGLADESH:** PC World Bangladesh; **BELARUS:** PC World Belarus; **BELGIUM:** Data News; **BRAZIL:** Annuario de Informática, Computerworld, Connections, Macworld, PC Player, PC World, Publish, Reseller News, Supergamepower; **BULGARIA:** Computerworld Bulgaria, Network World Bulgaria, PC & MacWorld Bulgaria; **CANADA:** CIO Canada, Client/Server World, ComputerWorld Canada, InfoWorld Canada, NetworkWorld Canada, WebWorld; **CHILE:** Computerworld Chile, PC World Chile; **COLOMBIA:** Computerworld Colombia, PC World Colombia; **COSTA RICA:** PC World Centro America; **THE CZECH AND SLOVAK REPUBLICS:** Computerworld Czechoslovakia, Macworld Czech Republic, PC World Czechoslovakia; **DENMARK:** Communications World Danmark, Computerworld Danmark, Macworld Danmark, PC World Danmark, Techworld Danmark; **DOMINICAN REPUBLIC:** PC World Republica Dominicana; **ECUADOR:** PC World Ecuador; **EGYPT:** Computerworld Middle East, PC World Middle East; **EL SALVADOR:** PC World Centro America; **FINLAND:** MikroPC, Tietoverkko, Tietoviikko; **FRANCE:** Distributique, Hebdo, Info PC, Le Monde Informatique, Macworld, Reseaux & Telecoms, WebMaster France; **GERMANY:** Computer Partner, Computerwoche, Computerwoche Extra, Computerwoche FOCUS, Global Online, Macwelt, PC Welt; **GREECE:** Amiga Computing, GamePro Greece, Multimedia World; **GUATEMALA:** PC World Centro America; **HONDURAS:** PC World Centro America; **HONG KONG:** Computerworld Hong Kong, PC World Hong Kong, Publish in Asia; **HUNGARY:** ABCD CD-ROM, Computerworld Szamitastechnika, Internetto online Magazine, PC World Hungary, PC-X Magazin Hungary; **ICELAND:** Tolvuheimur PC World Island; **INDIA:** Information Communications World, Information Systems Computerworld, PC World India, Publish in Asia; **INDONESIA:** InfoKomputer PC World, Komputek Computerworld, Publish in Asia; **IRELAND:** ComputerScope, PC Live!; **ISRAEL:** Macworld Israel, People & Computers/Computerworld; **ITALY:** Computerworld Italia, Macworld Italia, Networking Italia, PC World Italia; **JAPAN:** DTP World, Macworld Japan, Nikkei Personal Computing, OS/2 World Japan, SunWorld Japan, Windows NT World, Windows World Japan; **KENYA:** PC World East African; **KOREA:** Hi-Tech Information, Macworld Korea, PC World Korea; **MACEDONIA:** PC World Macedonia; **MALAYSIA:** Computerworld Malaysia, PC World Malaysia, Publish in Asia; **MALTA:** PC World Malta; **MEXICO:** Computerworld Mexico, PC World Mexico; **MYANMAR:** PC World Myanmar; **NETHERLANDS:** Computer! Totaal, LAN Internetworking Magazine, LAN World Buyers Guide, Macworld Netherlands, Net, WebWereld; **NEW ZEALAND:** Absolute Beginners Guide and Plain & Simple Series, Computer Buyer, Computer Industry Directory, Computerworld New Zealand, MTB, Network World, PC World New Zealand; **NICARAGUA:** PC World Centro America; **NORWAY:** Computerworld Norge, CW Rapport, Datamagasinet, Financial Rapport, Kursguide Norge, Macworld Norge, Multimediaworld Norge, PC World Ekspress Norge, PC World Nettverk, PC World Norge, PC World ProduktGuide Norge; **PAKISTAN:** Computerworld Pakistan; **PANAMA:** PC World Panama; **PEOPLE'S REPUBLIC OF CHINA:** China Computer Users, China Computerworld, China InfoWorld, China Telecom World Weekly, Computer & Communication, Electronic Design China, Electronics Today, Electronics Weekly, Game Software, PC World China, Popular Computer Week, Software Weekly, Software World, Telecom World; **PERU:** Computerworld Peru, PC World Profesional Peru, PC World SoHo Peru; **PHILIPPINES:** Click!, Computerworld Philippines, PC World Philippines, Publish in Asia; **POLAND:** Computerworld Poland, Computerworld Special Report Poland, Cyber, Macworld Poland, Networld Poland, PC World Komputer; **PORTUGAL:** Cerebro/PC World, Computerworld/Correio Informatico, Dealer World Portugal, Mac*In/PC*In Portugal, Multimedia World; **PUERTO RICO:** PC World Puerto Rico; **ROMANIA:** Computerworld Romania, PC World Romania, Telecom Romania; **RUSSIA:** Computerworld Russia, Mir PK, Publish, Seti; **SINGAPORE:** Computerworld Singapore, PC World Singapore, Publish in Asia; **SLOVENIA:** Monitor; **SOUTH AFRICA:** Computing SA, Network World SA, Software World SA; **SPAIN:** Communicaciones World España, Computerworld España, Dealer World España, Macworld España, PC World España; **SRI LANKA:** Infolink PC World; **SWEDEN:** CAP&Design, Computer Sweden, Corporate Computing Sweden, Internetworld Sweden, it.branschen, Macworld Sweden, MaxiData Sweden, MikroDatorn, Natverk & Kommunikation, PCaktiv, Windows World Sweden; **SWITZERLAND:** Computerworld Schweiz, Macworld Schweiz, PCtip; **TAIWAN:** Computerworld Taiwan, Macworld Taiwan, NEW ViSiON/Publish, PC World Taiwan, Windows World Taiwan; **THAILAND:** Publish in Asia, Thai Computerworld; **TURKEY:** Computerworld Turkiye, Macworld Turkiye, Network World Turkiye, PC World Turkiye; **UKRAINE:** Computerworld Kiev, Multimedia World Ukraine, PC World Ukraine; **UNITED KINGDOM:** Acorn User UK, Amiga Action UK, Amiga Computing UK, Apple Talk UK, Computing, Macworld, Parents and Computers UK, PC Advisor, PC Home, PSX Pro, The WEB; **UNITED STATES:** Cable in the Classroom, CIO Magazine, Computerworld, DOS World, Federal Computer Week, GamePro Magazine, InfoWorld, I-Way, Macworld, Network World, PC Games, PC World, Publish, Video Event, THE WEB Magazine, and WebMaster; online webzines: JavaWorld, NetscapeWorld, and SunWorld Online; **URUGUAY:** InfoWorld Uruguay; **VENEZUELA:** Computerworld Venezuela, PC World Venezuela; and **VIETNAM:** PC World Vietnam. 3/24/97

Dedication

This book is dedicated to Matt Wagner and Bill Gladstone of Waterside Productions. Without their excellent negotiating skills, I might still be yet another starving stand-up comedian no one has ever heard of before. (Of course, as a stand-up comedian, most people still haven't heard of me, but at least with these books more people have been given access to my sense of humor in writing.)

Another big round of heart-felt warmth and thanks goes to Fred Burns, Ron Clark, Frank Manzano, Pete Balistreri, Karen Rontowski, Dante, Chris "the Zooman" Clobber, and Leo Fontaine of The Comedy Store in La Jolla, California. These guys didn't help with this book one bit, so I really don't know why I'm thanking them at all.

More thanks go out to the following comedians whose humor has inspired, enlightened, and entertained me during the writing of this book: Bill Hicks, George Wallace, Jeff Wayne, Dennis Miller, Tom Lehrer, Paula Poundstone, George Carlin, Jay Leno, Barry Crimmins, Jimmy Tingle, David Letterman, Robert Klein, and Will Durst. These people didn't help me write this book either, but at least they made me laugh a lot while I was doing all the hard work.

Final thanks go to Cassandra the Wife, Bo the Cat, Scraps the Cat, Tasha the Cat, and the person who first invented the tradition of the Dedication page for pure ego-gratification on the part of the author. Without the invention of the Dedication page, these paragraphs could never have been written and you would look rather silly right now just staring at a blank piece of paper.

Publisher's Acknowledgments

We're proud of this book; please send us your comments about it by using the IDG Books Worldwide Registration Card at the back of the book or by e-mailing us at feedback/dummies@idgbooks.com. Some of the people who helped bring this book to market include the following:

Acquisitions, Development, and Editorial

Project Editor: Nancy DelFavero

Acquisitions Editor: Michael Kelly, Quality Control Manager

Copy Editor: Susan Christophersen

Technical Editor: Kevin McCarter

Editorial Manager: Mary C. Corder

Editorial Assistants: Chris H. Collins, Darren Meiss

Production

Project Coordinator: E. Shawn Aylsworth

Layout and Graphics: Drew Moore, Mark C. Owens, Brent Savage

Proofreaders: Arielle Carole Mennelle, Carrie Voorhis, Christine D. Berman, Joel K. Draper, Robert Springer

Indexer: Steve Rath

Special Help

Michael Bolinger, Copy Editor
Diana Conover, Lead Copy Editor
Stephanie Koutek, Proof Editor
Shannon Ross, Project Editor
Tina Sims, Copy Editor

General and Administrative

IDG Books Worldwide, Inc.: John Kilcullen, CEO; Steven Berkowitz, President and Publisher

IDG Books Technology Publishing: Brenda McLaughlin, Senior Vice President and Group Publisher

Dummies Technology Press and Dummies Editorial: Diane Graves Steele, Vice President and Associate Publisher; Judith A. Taylor, Product Marketing Manager; Kristin A. Cocks, Editorial Director

Dummies Trade Press: Kathleen A. Welton, Vice President and Publisher; Stacy S. Collins, Product Marketing Manager

IDG Books Production for Dummies Press: Beth Jenkins, Production Director; Cindy L. Phipps, Supervisor of Project Coordination, Production Proofreading, and Indexing; Kathie S. Schutte, Supervisor of Page Layout; Shelley Lea, Supervisor of Graphics and Design; Debbie J. Gates, Production Systems Specialist; Tony Augsburger, Supervisor of Reprints and Bluelines; Leslie Popplewell, Media Archive Coordinator

Dummies Packaging and Book Design: Patti Sandez, Packaging Specialist; Lance Kayser, Packaging Assistant; Kavish + Kavish, Cover Design

◆

The publisher would like to give special thanks to Patrick J. McGovern, without whom this book would not have been possible.

◆

Author's Acknowledgments

Special thanks go to Nancy DelFavero (the project editor), Susan Christopherson (the copy editor), and Kevin McCarter (the technical reviewer) for making sure this book is as accurate as possible. While other authors often boast that "I assume all responsibility for any errors that may have crept into this book," I don't.

If you find any mistakes in this book that causes you to lose millions of dollars, I absolve myself of complete responsibility and liability. If you get a paper cut turning the pages of this book, don't sue me. If someone uses this book as a weapon against you, again, it's no fault of mine. If you use this book in a manner inappropriate for its intended use and hurt yourself terribly, keep those lawyers away because I can't afford outrageous legal fees to defend myself from anyone trying to turn the legal system into a national lottery.

By continuing to read this paragraph, you agree to hold myself, the publisher, the bookstore, your computer's manufacturer, and the local utility company that provides electricity to power your PC completely blameless in the event that anything goes wrong that might even be remotely connected to the purchase and use of this book. If you agree that people shouldn't twist the laws for personal gain to the detriment of the entire legal system, then this book is heartily and cheerfully acknowledged to you and your family. Feel free to write your name in the blank space in this page and forge my autograph if necessary to lend greater perceived value to your personal copy of this book.

Contents at a Glance

Cartoons at a Glance

By Rich Tennant • Fax: 508-546-7747 • E-mail: the5wave@tiac.net

Table of Contents

Introduction

● ●

*T*ake a look at most computer program manuals (or even most computer books), and and you'll notice a striking difference between this book and all the rest. Almost every computer book or manual organizes its explanations according to the way the program works, not the way you work.

Focusing on menu commands forces you to learn how the program works, which is like learning to drive by focusing on how your transmission works. Most people don't care how a transmission works, just as long as it works. Likewise, most people don't care about the particular order of menu commands as long as they know how to use them to get something done.

So instead of displaying endless dialog boxes or pull-down menu commands and exhaustively explaining what each command does, this book describes how to accomplish certain tasks and then explains how to use various menu commands to get the job done. After you get familiar with using various commands, you'll have the confidence that you need to start experimenting with Microsoft Office 97 on your own.

This book won't make you a Microsoft Office 97 expert overnight, but it will show you how to take full advantage of each program that makes up Microsoft Office 97. Just pick through the tips and tricks that interest you, and you'll gradually understand more about the programs and features that you use the most. Within a short time, you'll know enough about Microsoft Office 97 to work faster, more efficiently, and more productively than ever before (unless, of course, you don't want to).

Who Should Buy This Book

Everyone should buy this book, because this sentence says so and the publisher couldn't print this if it weren't true. But you will probably be especially inclined to use this book if you have, or are planning to buy, Microsoft Office 97. You can use this book to guide you through the mental land mines of frustration that accompany the task of learning any new computer program.

If you're not already familiar with the basics of Microsoft Office 97, first grab a copy of my book *Microsoft Office 97 For Windows For Dummies* (IDG Books Worldwide, Inc.). Make sure that you get that particular book, easily spotted by its bright yellow and black cover. Accept no substitutes or cheap imitations!

When you're familiar with the basics, such as starting Microsoft Office 97 and saving data, you can make maximum use of this book, which shows you the more advanced techniques buried inside Microsoft Office 97. You'll soon discover how to harness the power of Microsoft Office 97 to get your work done faster and easier than ever before, regardless of your previous experience with computers.

How This Book Is Organized

This book is organized using paper, glue, and ink. The text itself is organized into several parts, where each part covers a specific program in Microsoft Office 97. Whenever you need help (or just want to look like you're doing something at work while you're really flipping through the cartoons), browse through this book, find the part that covers the topic you're looking for, zip through the pithy and poignant text, and then toss the book aside and get back to work before your boss catches you goofing off.

Part I: Customizing Microsoft Office 97

Microsoft Office 97 is a brand-new program, which also means that any files you create using Microsoft Office 97 won't be compatible with previous versions of Microsoft Office right away. In case you want to share your files with other people, this part explains how to convert your files into a format that others can use as well.

This part of the book also explains how to customize your toolbars in Microsoft Office 97 so that you can get rid of those silly icons that make no sense to you and replace them with your own silly icons that do make sense to you.

Part II: Power Writing with Microsoft Word 97

Whether you write letters, memos, newsletters, novels, or ransom notes, you'll find that Microsoft Word 97 provides a feature to make your task easier. This part of the book reveals various time-saving shortcuts so that you can spend your time being creative instead of wrestling with the program's limitations (known in the advertising brochures as "features").

Part III: Number Crunching with Microsoft Excel 97

Besides calculating a result of numbers and formulas you type into a spreadsheet, Excel 97 can create maps from your data, automate your spreadsheets with macros, and even help you check your formulas to make sure that the answers you're getting actually make sense.

Part IV: The Microsoft PowerPoint 97 Dog-and-Pony Show

Although looks aren't everything, they can often help you win million-dollar roles in bad TV shows that people will joke about years from now. Because looks really are important, PowerPoint 97 helps you create pretty presentations to dazzle the competition and pacify your supervisors when you should really be working and doing something productive.

Part V: Getting Connected with Microsoft Outlook 97

Like everyone else, you would probably love to be more organized so that you could accomplish the tasks that really mean something to you. Unfortunately, most of us have to work, which gobbles up most of our precious time. To help you plan your time more effectively, use Microsoft Outlook 97 to turn your $2,000 computer into a $49.95 electronic organizer.

By using Microsoft Outlook 97 daily, you can plan dreams for the future, set goals for turning your dreams into reality, schedule tasks for reaching your goals, and eventually live the type of life that you really want to live rather than settle for endless days of mediocrity that provide the main source of revenue for psychiatrists all over the world.

Part VI: Storing Stuff in Microsoft Access 97

If you're using the Professional edition of Microsoft Office 97, you get to play around with a bonus program called Microsoft Access 97, which is a special database program that lets you store names, addresses, phone numbers, part numbers, invoices, or any other type of information that you think you may need at a future date. (Storing the names of valuable business contacts is wise. Storing your report cards from third grade probably is not.)

By letting you decide how you want to store, organize, and display information, Access 97 gives you the power to create your own custom programs to track inventory, print reports, or store customer names and addresses.

How to Use This Book

You can use this book as a reference, a tutorial, a weapon, or a shield (it's thick enough). Don't feel the need to read every page of this book. Instead, just browse through the parts that interest you and ignore the rest.

Although you aren't likely to use *every* program in Microsoft Office 97, take some time to browse through the parts of the book that describe the programs you don't use very often. Fooling around with spreadsheets may seem dull if you're not an accountant or engineer, but by playing around with them you just might find a way to make them useful in your own personal life or business. You paid for Microsoft Office 97, so you may as well try all its programs. At the very least, you can just erase the programs that you don't use off your hard disk and never bother with them again.

How much do you need to know?

As long as you know how to turn on a computer and use a mouse, you should be able to follow the instructions in this book with no major, trauma-inducing problems. If you find Windows 95 to be somewhat of a strange beast to master, however, you may want to get a copy of *Windows 95 For Dummies* by Andy Rathbone (published by IDG Books Worldwide, Inc.).

Conventions

To avoid later confusion (because computers do such a good job of sowing confusion without anyone's help), be sure that you understand the following terms:

- When you look at the screen, you may see two items: a *cursor* (which appears as a vertical, blinking line) and an *I-beam pointer* (which sometimes appears as a white arrow when you move it over certain parts of the screen).

  The blinking cursor moves whenever you use the keyboard, such as typing a letter or number, or pressing one of the four (up, down, left, right) arrow keys. The I-beam pointer moves whenever you move the mouse.

- *Clicking* means pressing the left mouse button once and letting go. Clicking is how you activate icons in the toolbar, for example.

- *Double-clicking* means pressing the left mouse button twice in rapid succession. Double-clicking typically activates a command.

- *Dragging* selects items that you want to move, delete, or format. To drag, place the I-beam pointer to the left of the item that you want to select, hold down the left mouse button, and move the mouse in the desired direction. When you release the mouse button, Windows 95 selects that item. You can tell when an item is selected because it appears in white against a black background.

- *Right-clicking* means clicking the mouse button to the right. (Some mice have three buttons, so ignore the middle button for now.) Right-clicking usually displays a shortcut menu on the screen.

Icons used in this book

This icon highlights information that can be helpful (as long as you don't forget it, of course).

This icon marks certain steps or procedures that can save you time when you use Microsoft Office 97.

Watch out! This icon warns you of potential trouble that you may run into while using Microsoft Office 97.

This icon highlights detailed information that's nice to know but not essential for using Microsoft Office 97.

Choosing commands in Microsoft Office 97

Microsoft Office 97 gives you two ways to choose commands:

- Clicking the mouse on an icon or menu command

- Pressing a keystroke combination such as Ctrl+S (which means hold down the Ctrl key, press the S key, and then release both keys simultaneously)

Most keyboard shortcuts involve holding down the Ctrl or Alt key (typically located to the left and right of the spacebar on your keyboard) in combination with one of the function keys (the keys labeled F1, F2, F3, and so on) or a letter key (A, B, C, and so on).

Use the method that you like best. Some people use the mouse, some use the keyboard, some use both, and some just hire another person to do all their hard work for them, instead.

Your first tip

 Don't be afraid to experiment, fool around, or play with any of the multitude of commands available in Microsoft Office. Anytime you choose a command by mistake, tell Microsoft Office 97 to take it back by pressing Ctrl+Z (hold down the Ctrl key, press the Z key, and let go of both keys at the same time).

Now that you know how to undo commands, feel free to pick a command at random, just to see what happens. Then press Ctrl+Z to return your data to normal. By freely experimenting with Microsoft Office 97 and keeping the handy Ctrl+Z keystroke ready at all times, you can teach yourself how to use many features of Microsoft Office 97 practically all by yourself, using the same method by which most people learn best, anyway: trial and error.

Getting Started

Now that you have a copy of Microsoft Office 97 on your computer (you did pay for it, didn't you?), you're ready to start using the advanced features that Microsoft buried in the most obscure places. But don't worry. As you pick up various tips and tricks from this book, you'll soon see that Microsoft Office 97 really can make you more productive with your computer in ways that you may never have dreamed about until now. So what are you waiting for? Stop reading this paragraph and turn the page.

Part I

Customizing
Microsoft Office 97

Look, all I said was, "FTC for Mr. Gates," and this nerdy guy with big glasses comes out and tells me he's not afraid of me, I can investigate him all I want, and he'll see me in court with his attorneys.

In this part . . .

*N*othing corrupts so completely as complete power. So, rather than unleash your pent-up frustrations on an innocent coworker, take your megalomaniac dreams out by controlling Microsoft Office 97 instead.

This part of the book explains how to customize the toolbars for every program in Microsoft Office 97. It also provides tips for saving Office 97 files for other people to use who haven't bought a copy of Microsoft Office 97 for their own computer which would help keep Bill Gates and his family the unofficial royalty of Seattle and the software world.

Chapter 1

Staying Compatible with the Rest of the World

In This Chapter

▶ Keeping Word 97 compatible

▶ Using Excel 97 with other files

▶ Making PowerPoint 97 work with older versions

▶ Transferring files into Outlook 97

▶ Importing and exporting data with Access 97

*A*lthough Microsoft Office 97 comes loaded with fancy new features, it can have one serious drawback. Every Microsoft Office 97 program saves its data in a totally different file format than previous versions of Microsoft Office.

If you write a letter using Word 97 and give it to someone using Word 6.0, guess what? Your friend (or coworker) using Word 6.0 won't be able to edit or even view anything that you write using Word 97. Word 97 can edit any files created by Word 6.0, however. In other words, newer programs (such as Word 97 or Excel 97) can use files created by older versions of the same program (such as Word 6.0 or Excel 5.0), but older versions can't use anything created by Microsoft Office 97.

So, if you're using Microsoft Office 97 but your friends and coworkers still insist on using the older versions of Microsoft Office, you have two solutions:

✔ Force everyone to use Microsoft Office 97.

✔ Make your copy of Microsoft Office 97 compatible with everyone else's software.

Unless you're a boss who can force everyone in the company to switch to Microsoft Office 97 en masse, chances are that you'll have to share your Microsoft Office 97 files with people who still insist on using Word 6.0, Excel 5.0, WordPerfect, PowerPoint 4.0, or Lotus 1-2-3.

Why programs have such odd version numbers

In the early days of the computer industry when companies released a new program, they called it version 1.0. Because version 1.0 of a program was brand new (and likely to be bug-ridden), many people avoided buying a program until version 2.0 arrived.

As a slick marketing trick to convince customers to buy their programs, companies started naming their programs with any version number they wanted. So, instead of calling a new program version 1.0, companies often gave their program a higher version number, such as version 2.0 or version 3.0, to convince customers that this particular version had already been battle-tested in the market.

Like other software companies, Microsoft also skipped version numbers along the way for

their convenience. When they first slapped together Microsoft Office, each program had a different version number. To avoid confusion, Microsoft tried to maintain the same version numbers for all of their programs. As a result, Microsoft Word skipped from version 2.0 to 5.0 to keep up with Microsoft Excel, which jumped from version 4.0 to 5.0.

When Microsoft released Microsoft Office 95, they gave each program version 7.0. Now with Microsoft Office 97, every program has dumped version numbers in favor of year abbreviations such as Word 97 and PowerPoint 97. (If Microsoft releases a new version of Microsoft Office in the year 2000, we can look forward to using Word 00 or Outlook 00.)

Microsoft's Web site (http://www.microsoft.com) contains several free programs that can convert your Word 97 or Excel 97 files into other file formats such as Word 6.0 or Excel 5.0 files.

Keeping Word 97 Compatible

Files created by Word 97 can be edited only by Word 97. If you want to share your Word 97 files with other people, you have two options:

- Save a second copy of your Word 97 file in a different file format.
- Make Word 97 save all files in a different file format.

Table 1-1 lists all the different file formats that you can use.

Table 1-1	File Formats Used by Various Programs
File format type	*Used by this program*
Word document	Microsoft Word 97
Word 6.0/95	Microsoft Word 7.0 and Microsoft Word 6.0
Word 2.*x* for Windows	Microsoft Word 2.0
WordPerfect 5.*x* for Windows	Any version of WordPerfect for Windows below 6.0 such as version 5.1 or 5.2
WordPerfect 5.1 for DOS	DOS version of WordPerfect 5.1
WordPerfect 5.0	DOS or Windows version of WordPerfect 5.0
Works 4.0 for Windows	Microsoft Works 4.0 for Windows
Works 3.0 for Windows	Microsoft Works 3.0 for Windows
Windows Write	Microsoft Write
HTML Document	Any HTML editor or browser such as Microsoft FrontPage or Netscape Navigator
Unicode Text	Any Windows 95 word processor
Rich Text Format	Any word processor capable of reading Rich Text Format (RTF)
MS-DOS Text	Any Windows or DOS word processor
MS-DOS Text with Line Breaks	Any Windows or DOS word processor
Text Only	Any word processor (including those designed for the Macintosh, Amiga, UNIX, or OS/2)
Text Only with Line Breaks	Any word processor (including those designed for the Macintosh, Amiga, UNIX, or OS/2)

If you need to share your Word 97 files with someone else only occasionally, using the Save As option is easier. To use the Save As option, load the Word 97 file that you want to share and follow these steps:

1. **Choose File⇨Save As.**

   A Save As dialog box appears, as shown in Figure 1-1.

2. **Click in the Save as type list box and choose a file format to use, such as Word 6.0/95.**

3. **Type a new name for your File name text box.**

4. **Click on Save.**

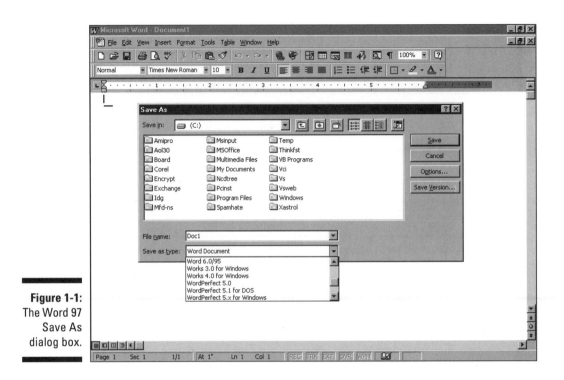

Figure 1-1:
The Word 97
Save As
dialog box.

If you need to share files with others on a regular basis, choosing the Save As command every time you want to save a file can be a real pain in the neck. Computers are already good enough at causing frustration on their own, therefore you'll be happy to know of a second way to save your Word 97 files so that you can share them with other people.

To pick a file format for Word 97 to use all the time (unless you tell it otherwise), follow these steps:

1. Choose Tools⇨Options.

An Options dialog box appears.

2. Click on the Save tab, as shown in Figure 1-2.

3. Click in the Save Word files as list box and choose a file format (such as Word 6.0/95).

4. Click on OK.

To make Word 97 compatible with the previous version of Microsoft Word 95 (found in Microsoft Office 95) and Microsoft Word 6.0 (found in Microsoft Office 4.3), choose Word 6.0/95 as the file format in Step 3.

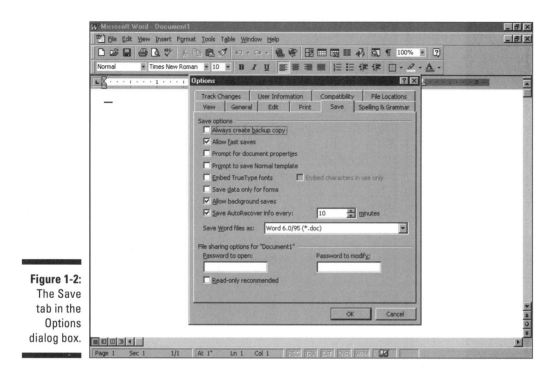

Figure 1-2:
The Save
tab in the
Options
dialog box.

Using Excel 97 with Other Files

Excel 97 can save data in its own file format or in another file format so that
you can share the file with other people who don't use Excel 97. If you want
to share your Excel 97 files with other people, your only option is to use the
Save As command to save your file in a different file format. Table 1-2 lists
the most common file formats that you may need.

Table 1-2	File Formats for Saving an Excel 97 File
File format type	*Used by this program*
Microsoft Excel Workbook	Microsoft Excel 97
Microsoft Excel 7.0 & 5.0/95 Workbook	Microsoft Excel 97, Microsoft Excel 7.0, and Microsoft Excel 5.0
Microsoft Excel 5.0/95 Workbook	Microsoft Excel 7.0 and Microsoft Excel 5.0
Microsoft Excel 4.0 Workbook	Microsoft Excel 4.0
Microsoft Excel 4.0 Worksheet	Microsoft Excel 4.0

(continued)

Table 1-2 *(continued)*

File format type	Used by this program
Microsoft Excel 3.0 Worksheet	Microsoft Excel 3.0
Microsoft Excel 2.1 Worksheet	Microsoft Excel 2.1
WK4 (1-2-3)	Lotus 1-2-3 version 4.0
WK3 (1-2-3)	Lotus 1-2-3 version 3.0
WK1 (1-2-3)	Lotus 1-2-3 version 2.0
WKS (1-2-3)	Lotus 1-2-3 version 1A
WQ1 (Quattro Pro/DOS)	Quattro Pro for DOS
DBF4 (dBASE IV)	DBASE IV
DBF 3 (dBASE III Plus)	DBASE III Plus
DBF 2 (dBASE II)	DBASE II
DIF (Data Interchange Format) SYLK (Symbolic Link)	Most other spreadsheets. DIF and SYLK were "standards" once used by many programs.
CSV (Comma delimited)	Most other spreadsheets including Macintosh and OS/2 spreadsheets
HTML	Any HTML editor or browser such as Microsoft FrontPage or Netscape Navigator
Text	Any program

To use the Save As option, load the Excel 97 file that you want to share and follow these steps:

1. **Choose File⇨Save As.**

   A Save As dialog box appears, as shown in Figure 1-3.

2. **Click in the Save as type list box and choose a file format to use, such as Microsoft Excel 7.0 & 5.0/95 Workbook.**

3. **Type a new name for your File name text box.**

4. **Click on Save.**

If you want to create a file that can be shared between Excel 97 and Excel 7.0 (or Excel 5.0), save your files in the Microsoft Excel 7.0 & 5.0/95 Workbook file format.

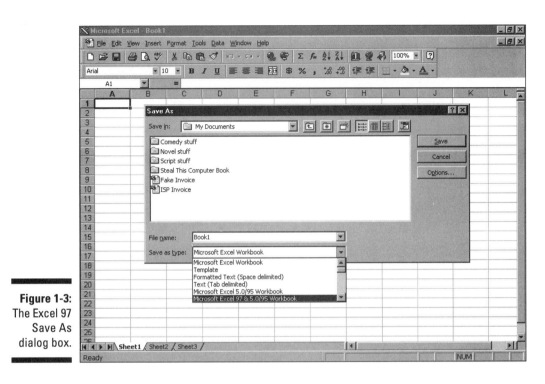

Figure 1-3:
The Excel 97
Save As
dialog box.

Making PowerPoint 97 Compatible

Whereas both Word 97 and Excel 97 can share files with a variety of programs sold by competing software publishers, PowerPoint 97 is a bit less open when it comes to sharing files.

If you're using PowerPoint 97 but your coworkers are using rival presentation programs such as Freelance Graphics or Harvard Graphics, guess what? PowerPoint 97 won't know how to use a Freelance Graphics file. Unless you can convert your Freelance Graphics files into a PowerPoint file format, you can't use a Freelance Graphics file in PowerPoint 97.

Basically, PowerPoint 97 can share files only with older versions of PowerPoint. So, if you want to share your PowerPoint 97 files with someone using an older version of PowerPoint, you have two options:

- ✔ Use the Save As command to save individual files to a different file format.
- ✔ Force PowerPoint 97 to save all files in a different file format.

Table 1-3 lists all the different file formats that you can use to save your PowerPoint presentation.

PowerPoint 97 can also save your presentation as one or more graphics files. By saving your presentation slides as a GIF or JPEG file, you can easily import those files into another program. Just remember that when you save a PowerPoint 97 presentation into a graphics file such as Windows Metafile or GIF, your presentation becomes a series of separate graphics instead of a single integrated presentation.

Table 1-3	File Formats for Saving a PowerPoint 97 File
File format type	*Used by this program*
Presentation	Microsoft PowerPoint 97
PowerPoint 95 & 97 Presentation	Microsoft PowerPoint 7.0 and Microsoft PowerPoint 4.0
PowerPoint 95	Microsoft PowerPoint 7.0
PowerPoint 4.0	Microsoft PowerPoint 4.0
PowerPoint 3.0	Microsoft PowerPoint 3.0

If you need to share your PowerPoint 97 files with someone just periodically, using the Save As option is easier. To use the Save As option, load the PowerPoint 97 file that you want to share and follow these steps:

1. **Choose File⇨Save As.**

   A Save As dialog box appears, as shown in Figure 1-4.

2. **Click in the Save as type list box and choose a file format to use, such as PowerPoint 95 & 97 Presentation.**

3. **Type a new name for your File name text box.**

4. **Click on Save.**

If you want to create a file that can be shared between PowerPoint 97 and PowerPoint 7.0 (or PowerPoint 4.0), save your files in the PowerPoint 95 & 97 Presentation file format.

If you need to share PowerPoint 97 files with others on a regular basis, you can make PowerPoint 97 always save files in a different file format.

To pick a file format for PowerPoint 97 to use all the time, follow these steps:

1. **Choose Tools⇨Options.**

   An Options dialog box appears.

2. **Click on the Save tab, as shown in Figure 1-5.**

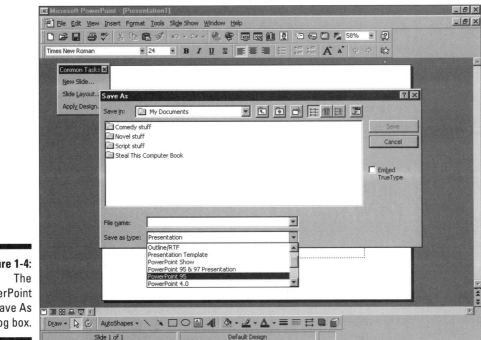

Figure 1-4:
The
PowerPoint
97 Save As
dialog box.

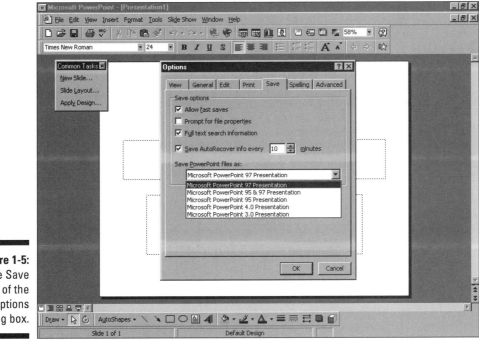

Figure 1-5:
The Save
tab of the
Options
dialog box.

   3. **Click the Save <u>W</u>ord files as list box and choose a file format (such as Microsoft PowerPoint 95 & 97 Presentation).**

   4. **Click on OK.**

To make PowerPoint 97 compatible with the previous version of Microsoft PowerPoint 95 (found in Microsoft Office 95) and Microsoft PowerPoint 4.0 (found in Microsoft Office 4.3), choose Microsoft PowerPoint 95 & 97 Presentation as the file format in Step 3.

Transferring Files in and out of Outlook 97

If you've been storing names, address, phone numbers, e-mail, and appointments using a non-Microsoft product, shame on you. As punishment, you won't be able to transfer your valuable information into Microsoft Outlook 97 without a lot of struggling.

To transfer data stored in other programs such as Sidekick or Lotus Organizer, you may need to download a special converter program available on Microsoft's Web site at http://www.microsoft.com.

Bringing files into Outlook 97

For those of you who have information trapped in the old Microsoft Schedule+ program (which is part of the old Microsoft Office 95), Microsoft blesses your loyalty by allowing you to transfer all your Schedule+ files into Microsoft Outlook 97 without much hassle.

If you have data stored in another program, you can save it as a dBASE, comma, or tab-delimited text file and then stuff it into Microsoft Outlook 97. If you have no idea what the previous sentence is even trying to tell you, then just pretend that you never read it and you'll sleep much easier.

To stuff files from another program into Microsoft Outlook 97, follow these steps:

   1. **Choose <u>F</u>ile⇨<u>I</u>mport and Export.**

      An Import and Export Wizard dialog box appears, as shown in Figure 1-6.

   2. **Click on Import from Schedule+ or another program or file and then click on <u>N</u>ext.**

      An Import a File dialog box appears, as shown in Figure 1-7.

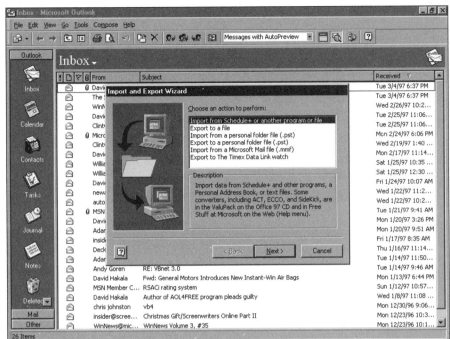

Figure 1-6:
The Import
and Export
Wizard
dialog box.

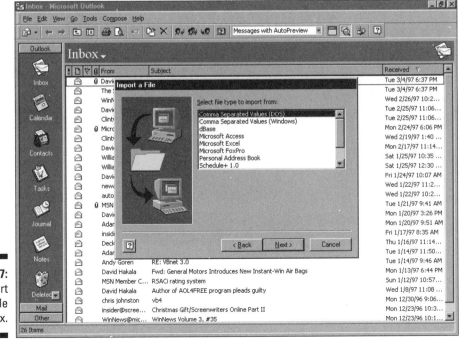

Figure 1-7:
The Import
a File
dialog box.

3. Click on a file format (such as Microsoft Schedule+ 7.0) and click on Next.

A different Import a File dialog box appears, as shown in Figure 1-8.

4. Click on Browse.

A Browse dialog box appears.

5. Click on the file that you want to import and then click on OK.

Still another Import a File dialog box appears, as shown in Figure 1-9.

6. Click where you want to store the data (such as the Inbox or Contacts) and click on Next.

Another Import a File dialog box appears, telling you what's going to happen next, as shown in Figure 1-10.

7. Click in the check box next to the action displayed in the Import a File dialog box.

(For greater control over how Microsoft Outlook 97 stores your data, click on the Map Custom Fields button.)

8. Click on Finish.

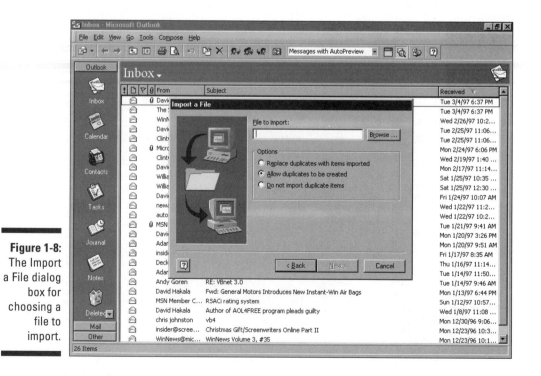

Figure 1-8:
The Import a File dialog box for choosing a file to import.

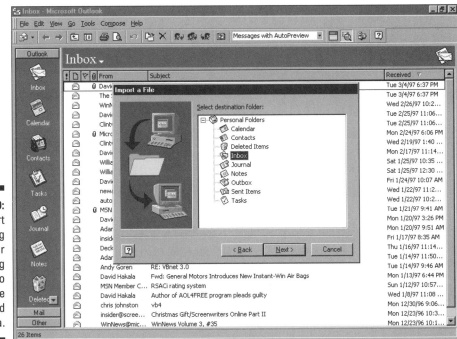

Figure 1-9:
The Import
a File dialog
box for
choosing
where to
store the
imported
data.

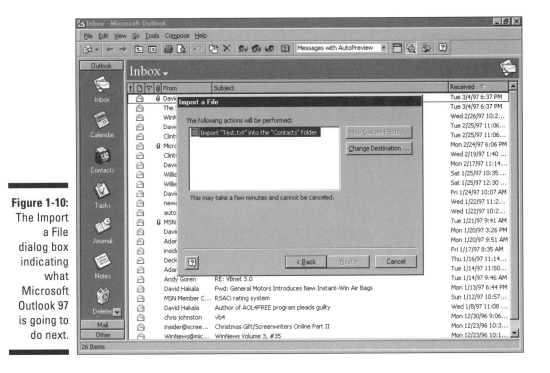

Figure 1-10:
The Import
a File
dialog box
indicating
what
Microsoft
Outlook 97
is going to
do next.

Saving Outlook 97 data into another file

To save your Microsoft Outlook 97 data into another file format, follow these steps:

1. **Choose File⇨Import and Export.**

   An Import and Export Wizard dialog box appears (see Figure 1-6).

2. **Click on Export to a file and then click on Next.**

   An Export to a File dialog box appears, shown in Figure 1-11, asking you what data you want to export from Microsoft Outlook 97.

3. **Click on a folder (such as Inbox or Contacts) and then click on Next.**

   Another Export to a File dialog box appears as shown in Figure 1-12, asking for a file format to use.

4. **Click on one of the following file formats:**

   • **Comma Separated Values** — Creates an ASCII text file where data is separated by commas such as: Name, Address, Phone.

   • **dBase** — Creates a dBASE database.

Figure 1-11:
The Export to a File dialog box for choosing what type of data to save in another file.

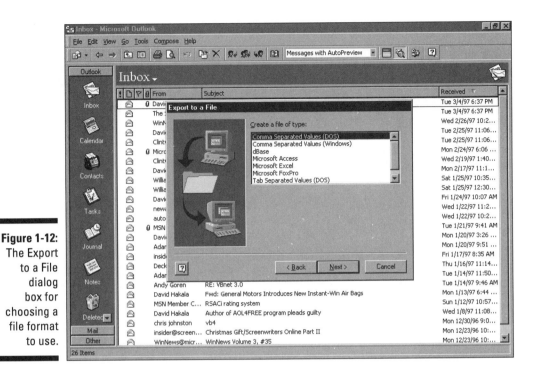

Figure 1-12:
The Export
to a File
dialog
box for
choosing a
file format
to use.

- **Microsoft Access** — Creates a Microsoft Access database.

- **Microsoft Excel** — Creates a Microsoft Excel worksheet.

- **Microsoft FoxPro** — Creates a Microsoft FoxPro database.

- **Tab Separated Values** — Creates an ASCII text file in which data is separated by tabs such as: Name   Address   Phone.

5. Click on Next.

Another Export to a file dialog box appears, shown in Figure 1-13, asking what you want to name your newly created file.

6. Click on the Browse button.

A Browse dialog box appears.

7. Type a file name in the File Name text box and click on OK.

8. Click on Next.

Another Export to a File dialog box appears, shown in Figure 1-14, telling you what's going to happen next.

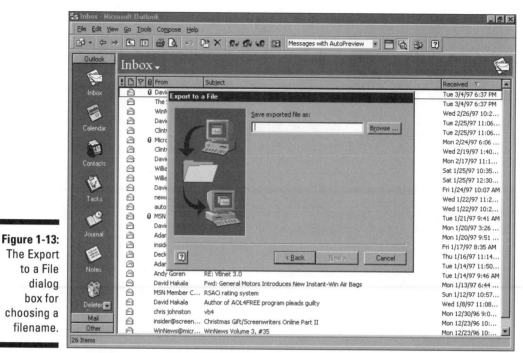

Figure 1-13:
The Export
to a File
dialog
box for
choosing a
filename.

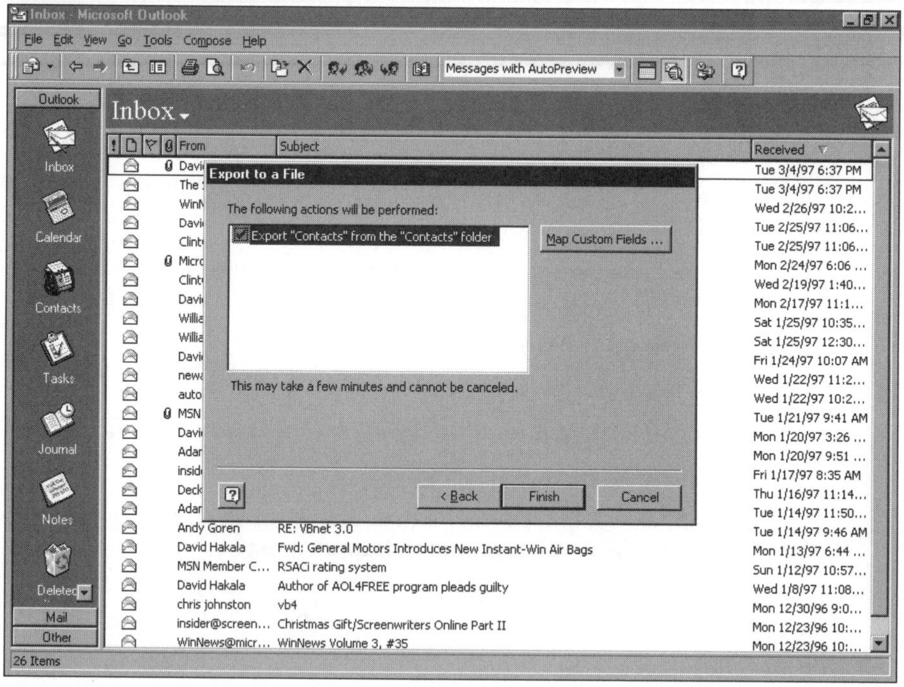

Figure 1-14:
The Export
to a File
dialog box
telling you
what's
going to
happen
next.

9. **Make sure that a check box appears next to the action displayed in the Export to a File dialog box.**

   (For greater control over how Microsoft Outlook 97 exports your data, click on the Map Custom Fields button.)

10. **Click on Finish.**

Microsoft Outlook 97 tries its best to export data into a different file format, but don't be surprised if you have to edit the newly exported file to make it suitable for displaying within another program such as Microsoft Excel or Microsoft Access.

Importing and Exporting Data with Access 97

If you have data trapped within another database program such as dBASE, FoxPro, or Paradox, you'll be happy to know that two ways exist for you to use this data within Microsoft Access 97:

- ✔ Convert a foreign database file into a Microsoft Access 97 file.
- ✔ Attach a foreign database file to a Microsoft Access 97 file.

If you want to stop using another database program (such as dBASE III Plus) and plan to use Microsoft Access 97 exclusively, your best bet is to convert all your older database files into a new Microsoft Access 97 file.

If you switched to Microsoft Access 97 but your less-forward-thinking friends or coworkers insist on using another database program, just attach the other database program's file to a Microsoft Access 97 file. Attaching another database file to an Access 97 file means that you can edit that file using either Access 97 or the program that created the database file (such as dBASE III Plus).

Converting a foreign database file into Access 97

If you're switching from another database program to Access 97, you should convert your older database files into an Access 97 file. Then you can junk your other database program and use Access 97 exclusively.

When you convert another database file, Access 97 turns the other database file into an Access 97 table within an existing Access 97 file. After converting a database file into an Access 97 table, you should delete the old database file to keep from mixing up two separate copies of the same data.

To convert a different database file into an Access 97 table, load an existing Access 97 database file and follow these steps:

1. **Choose File⇨Get External Data⇨Import.**

   An Import dialog box appears, as shown in Figure 1-15.

2. **Click in the Files of type list box and choose a file type (such as Paradox or dBASE 5).**

3. **Click on the database file that you want to convert and then click on Import.**

   Access 97 displays a dialog box to let you know that it successfully converted the file into an Access 97 file.

4. **Click on OK.**

5. **Click on Close to remove the Import dialog box.**

6. **Choose Window⇨Database.**

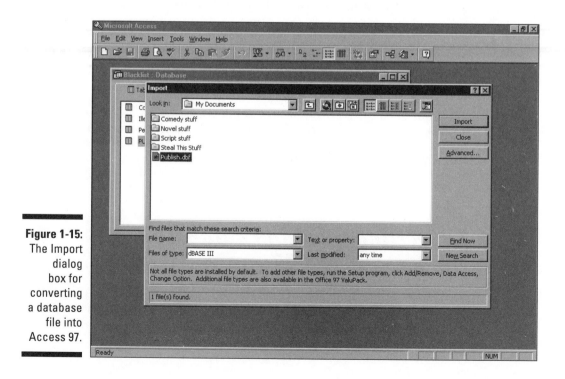

Figure 1-15:
The Import dialog box for converting a database file into Access 97.

The Database window appears.

7. Click on the Tables tab.

Access 97 displays your newly imported database file as an Access 97 table, as shown in Figure 1-16.

Attaching a foreign database to an Access 97 file

To use another database file within Access 97 without converting it, load an existing Access 97 database file and follow these steps:

1. Choose File⇨Get External Data⇨Link Tables.

A Link dialog box appears, which looks similar to the Import dialog box (refer to Figure 1-15).

2. Click in the Files of type list box and choose a file type (such as Microsoft FoxPro or dBASE III).

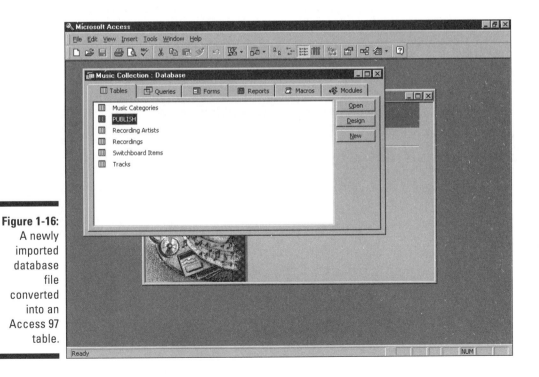

Figure 1-16:
A newly imported database file converted into an Access 97 table.

3. **Click on the database file you want to attach and click on Link.**

Access 97 displays a dialog box to let you know that it successfully converted the file into an Access 97 file.

4. **Click on OK.**

5. **Click on Close to remove the Link dialog box.**

6. **Choose Window⇨Database.**

The Database window appears.

7. **Click on the Tables tab.**

Access 97 displays your newly linked database file as an Access 97 table, as shown in Figure 1-17.

Saving an Access 97 file to a foreign database file

Just in case you have to share your Access 97 files with people too stubborn to switch to using Access 97 themselves, you may have to save your Access 97 data as a different database file.

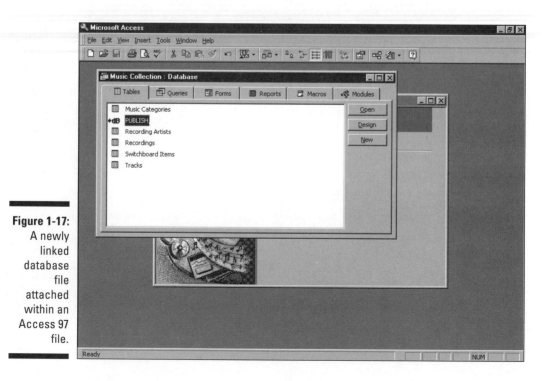

Figure 1-17:
A newly linked database file attached within an Access 97 file.

If you need to share Access 97 data with someone using a different database file, save your data as another database file and then link that same file back to your Access 97 file. Be sure to delete the original data stored within Access 97 so that you don't have two copies of the same information in the same Access 97 file.

To save an Access 97 table to a different database file, load the Access 97 file containing the data that you want to save in another database file format and follow these steps:

1. **Choose Window⇨Database.**

   The Database window appears.

2. **Click on the Tables tab and then click on the table that you want to convert to a different database file.**

3. **Choose File⇨Save As/Export.**

   A Save As dialog box appears, as shown in Figure 1-18.

4. **Click on OK.**

   A Save Table dialog box appears, as shown in Figure 1-19.

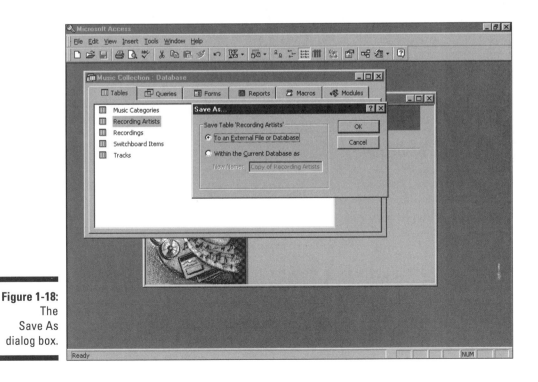

Figure 1-18: The Save As dialog box.

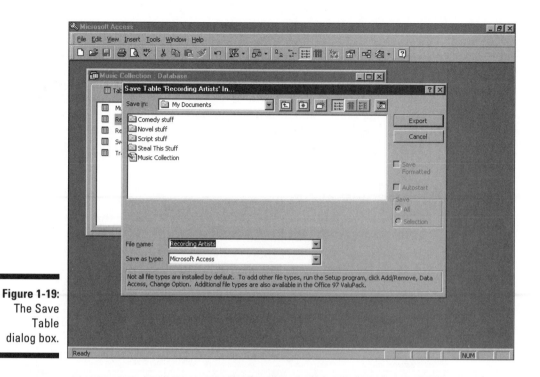

Figure 1-19:
The Save
Table
dialog box.

5. **Click in the Save as type list box and choose a file format (such as Paradox 4 or Microsoft FoxPro 2.6).**

6. **Type a name in the File name text box.**

7. **Click on Export.**

   Access 97 silently converts your chosen Access 97 table into a foreign database file.

Chapter 2

Customizing Office 97 Toolbars

● ●

In This Chapter

▶ Displaying and hiding toolbars

▶ Customizing your toolbars

▶ Making your own toolbars

▶ Changing the size of toolbar icons

● ●

*T*he Microsoft Office 97 pull-down menus contain every possible command that you could ever hope to use in Word 97, Excel 97, PowerPoint 97, Outlook 97, or Access 97. But pull-down menus can be as clumsy to use as most computer manuals, so Microsoft Office 97 offers toolbars as a quicker alternative.

Toolbars are shortcuts that allow you to click on an icon to choose a command instead of wading through ugly pull-down menus. Although Microsoft has created default toolbars for every program in Microsoft Office 97, you might want to modify the appearance of your toolbars for your own personal needs.

Manipulating Your Toolbars

Every Microsoft Office 97 program can display toolbars in one of three ways, as shown in Figure 2-1:

✔ **Hidden:** The toolbar is not visible (which is pretty much the definition of "hidden").

✔ **Docked:** The toolbar hugs one side of the screen such as the top or left side.

✔ **Floating:** The toolbar hovers in the middle of the screen like a piece of dirt on your monitor.

Docked toolbar   Floating toolbar

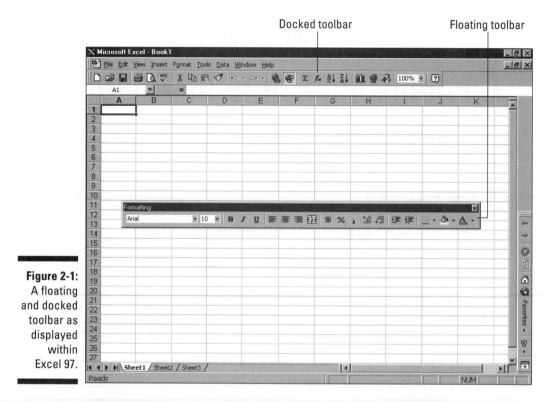

Figure 2-1:
A floating
and docked
toolbar as
displayed
within
Excel 97.

Hiding (and displaying) a toolbar

Each Microsoft Office 97 program offers several toolbars; Word 97 gives you the choice of displaying up to 18 different toolbars. Needless to say, if you try to display that many toolbars simultaneously, you won't have room left on the screen to do any useful work.

Rather than bombard you with more toolbars than you might care to see at any given time, you can selectively choose which toolbars to show (or hide).

To display (or hide) a toolbar, follow these steps:

1. **Choose Tools⇨Customize.**

   A Customize dialog box appears, as shown in Figure 2-2.

2. **Click on the Toolbars tab.**

   A list of available toolbars appears.

3. **Make sure that a check box appears in front of the toolbar that you want to display.**

   If you want to hide a toolbar, make its check box appear blank.

4. **Click on OK.**

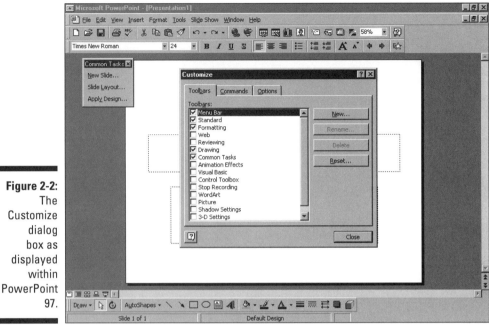

In case you want to know the long way to make the Customize dialog box appear, you can also choose View➪Toolbars➪Customize.

To make a toolbar appear or disappear in Outlook 97, you just have to choose View➪Toolbars and click on the toolbar that you want to make visible or invisible.

Docking and "floating" a toolbar

Depending on the particular toolbar, some toolbars appear "docked" (usually smashed flat against the top of the screen, right below the pull-down menus) or "floating" (usually covering whatever you happen to be working on at the time).

Making a floating toolbar

To turn a docked toolbar into a floating toolbar, follow these steps:

1. **Move the mouse pointer directly over a vertical border that divides the toolbar icons into sections, as shown in Figure 2-3.**

2. **Double-click on the left mouse button.**

   The docked toolbar magically turns into a floating toolbar, as shown in Figure 2-4.

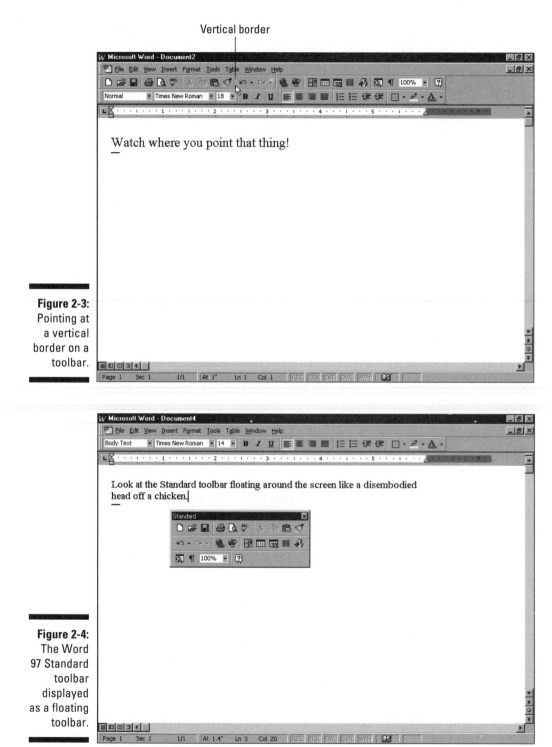

Figure 2-3:
Pointing at
a vertical
border on a
toolbar.

Figure 2-4:
The Word
97 Standard
toolbar
displayed
as a floating
toolbar.

Resizing and moving a floating toolbar

Because floating toolbars just hang around like unwanted guests, you may want to move them out of the way or change their shape into something skinnier or squarer.

To move a floating toolbar, follow these steps:

1. **Move the mouse pointer directly over the title bar of the floating toolbar.**

2. **Hold down the left mouse button and drag the mouse.**

   The new location of the toolbar appears as a gray rectangle, as shown in Figure 2-5.

3. **Release the left mouse button when you're happy with the new location of the floating toolbar.**

Rather than move a floating toolbar, you might just want to change its shape. To resize a floating toolbar, follow these steps:

1. **Move the mouse pointer directly to one edge of the floating toolbar until the mouse pointer turns into a double-pointing arrow.**

2. **Hold down the left mouse button and drag the mouse.**

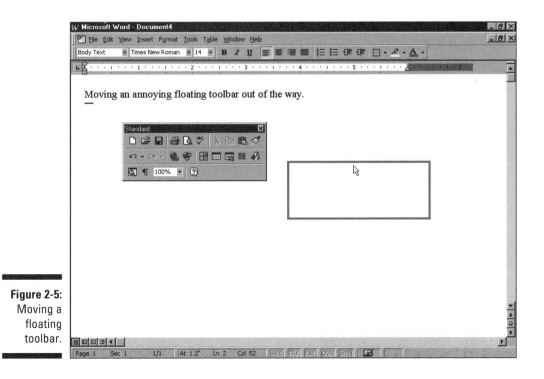

Figure 2-5:
Moving a
floating
toolbar.

The new shape of the floating toolbar appears as a gray rectangle, as shown in Figure 2-6.

3. Release the left mouse button when you're happy with the shape of the floating toolbar.

Docking a floating toolbar

Floating toolbars can often get in the way, so you might want to dock a floating toolbar to one side of the screen.

To dock a floating toolbar to the top, side, or bottom of the screen, follow these steps:

1. Move the mouse pointer directly over the title bar of the floating toolbar that you want to dock.

2. Hold down the left mouse button and drag the mouse to the top, side, or bottom of the screen until the floating toolbar turns into an extremely narrow gray rectangle, as shown to the left in Figure 2-7.

3. Release the left mouse button.

Your floating toolbar now appears docked to the side (or bottom) of the screen, as shown in Figure 2-8.

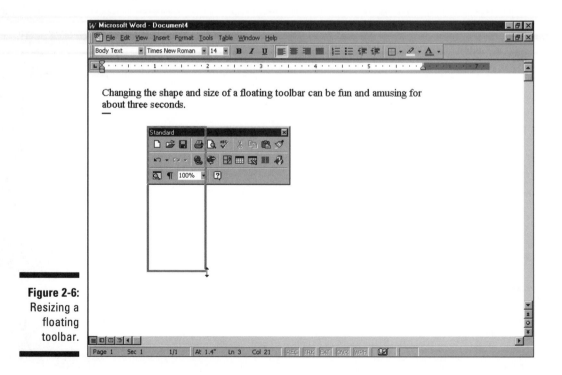

Figure 2-6:
Resizing a floating toolbar.

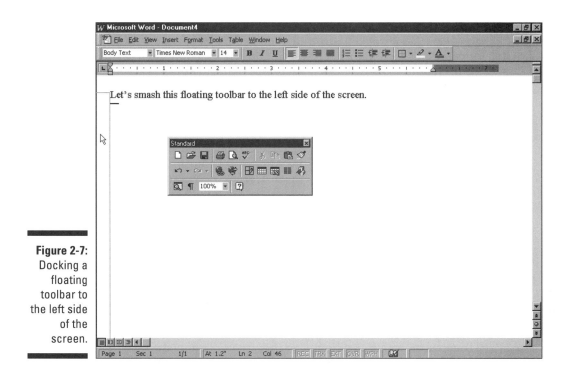

Figure 2-7:
Docking a floating toolbar to the left side of the screen.

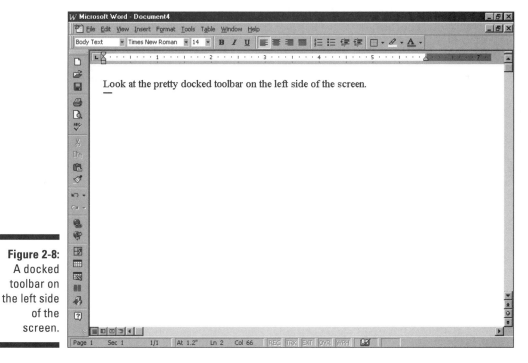

Figure 2-8:
A docked toolbar on the left side of the screen.

If you double-click on the title bar of a floating toolbar, it immediately docks itself in its last docked position. For example, if you dock a toolbar to the right of the screen, turn it into a floating toolbar, and then double-click on its title bar, the toolbar docks itself to the right side of the screen again.

Customizing Toolbars

Docking and floating the existing Microsoft Office 97 toolbars can be amusing and give you a feeling of power over your computer, if only for a brief moment in time. Those of you who like the thought of customizing your programs will be happy to know that you can change the icons that appear on each toolbar.

Rearranging icons on a toolbar

Just in case you don't like the order of the icons on your toolbars, feel free to rearrange them any way you like.

To move an icon to a different part of the toolbar, make sure that the toolbar appears as either a docked or floating toolbar and then follow these steps:

1. **Move the mouse pointer over the icon that you want to move on the toolbar.**

2. **Hold down the Alt key and the left mouse button simultaneously, while dragging the mouse until a black I-beam icon appears in the location where you want to move the toolbar (see Figure 2-9).**

3. **Release the Alt key and the left mouse button.**

   Your chosen icon appears in the location where the black I-beam icon appeared on the toolbar.

You can even move icons from one toolbar to another toolbar if you want.

Copying an icon on a toolbar

If you have a particular fondness for a specific toolbar icon, Microsoft Office 97 gives you the option of copying an icon so that you can put it on a different toolbar or in a different location on the same toolbar.

To copy a toolbar icon, make sure that the toolbar appears as either a docked or floating toolbar; then, follow these steps:

I-beam icon

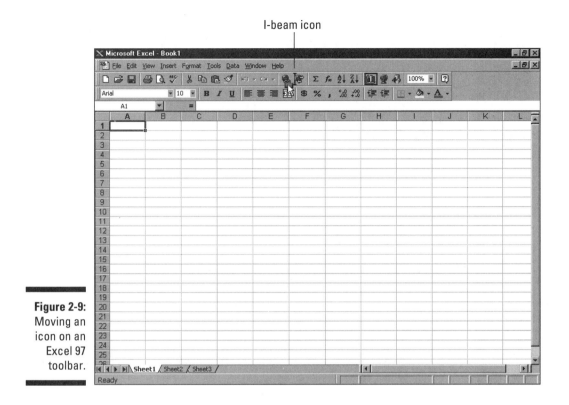

Figure 2-9:
Moving an
icon on an
Excel 97
toolbar.

1. **Move the mouse pointer over the icon that you want to copy from the toolbar.**

2. **Simultaneously hold down the Ctrl key, the Alt key, and the left mouse button (and keep holding them until Step 3). Drag the mouse so that a black I-beam icon appears in a different location on the same toolbar or on a different toolbar (see Figure 2-9).**

3. **Release the Ctrl key, the Alt key, and the left mouse button.**

   Your chosen icon disappears off the toolbar.

Deleting icons from a toolbar

Although Microsoft's millionaire programmers tried to design Microsoft Office 97's toolbars to display the most commonly used commands as icons, you may never use certain icons. Instead of allowing those seldom-used icons to taunt you with their presence, you can delete them from the toolbar.

To delete an icon from a toolbar, make sure that the toolbar appears as either a docked or floating toolbar; then, follow these steps:

1. **Move the mouse pointer over the icon that you want to delete from the toolbar.**

2. **Hold down the Alt key and left mouse button simultaneously while dragging the mouse so that the icon appears off the toolbar, as shown in Figure 2-10.**

3. **Release the Alt key and the left mouse button.**

   Your chosen icon disappears off the toolbar.

Adding icons on a toolbar

Sometimes a toolbar doesn't offer all the commands that you use most often. Instead of suffering in silence, you can actually add your own icons to a toolbar so that you can put your favorite commands on any toolbar you want.

Microsoft Outlook 97 won't let you add icons to any of its toolbars. So there.

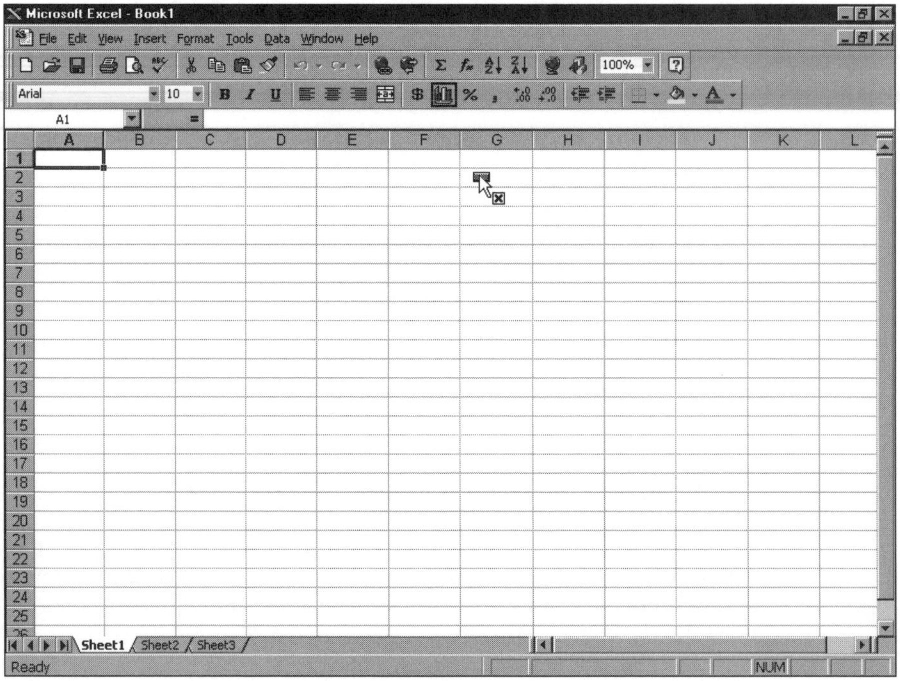

Figure 2-10:
Deleting an icon off an Excel 97 toolbar.

To add an icon to a toolbar, make sure that the toolbar appears either as a docked or floating toolbar; then, follow these steps:

1. **Choose Tools⇨Customize.**

   A Customize dialog box appears (see Figure 2-2 shown previously).

2. **Click on the Commands tab, as shown in Figure 2-11.**

3. **In the Categories list box, click on a category for the command that you want to add to a toolbar.**

   For example, if you want to add a command that appears in the Edit category, click on Edit in the Categories list box.

4. **Move the mouse pointer over the command that you want to put on a toolbar (such as the Find or Open command).**

5. **Hold down the left mouse button and drag the mouse over the displayed toolbar where you want to add the icon, as shown in Figure 2-12.**

   A black I-beam icon appears to show you where the icon will appear on the toolbar.

6. **Release the left mouse button.**

7. **Click on Close to remove the Customize dialog box.**

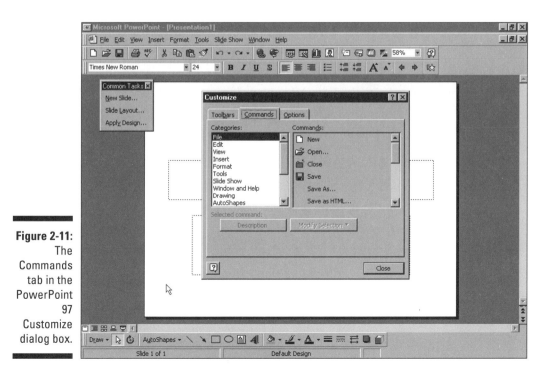

Figure 2-11:
The Commands tab in the PowerPoint 97 Customize dialog box.

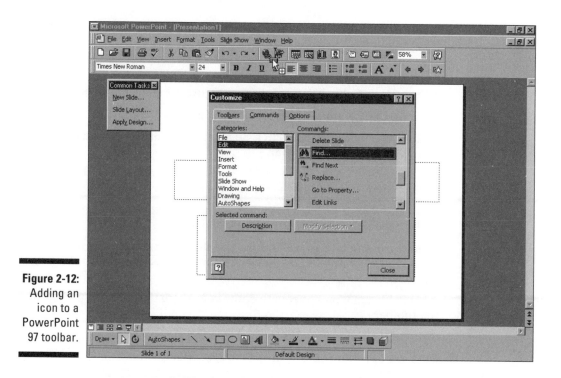

Figure 2-12:
Adding an
icon to a
PowerPoint
97 toolbar.

Resetting a toolbar

You can rearrange, delete, add, or copy icons from all your different
toolbars, which can result in your toolbars looking unrecognizable to
anybody else. Fortunately, you can always reset your toolbars to their
original appearance at any time.

To reset a toolbar, follow these steps:

1. **Choose Tools⇨Customize.**

   The Customize dialog box appears (refer back to Figure 2-2).

2. **Click on the toolbar that you want to reset and then click on Reset.**

   A Reset Toolbar dialog box appears.

3. **Click on OK.**

4. **Click on Close to remove the Customize dialog box.**

Rolling Your Own Toolbars

Modifying the existing toolbars can help you personalize your programs, but if you want to get really creative, you can create your own toolbars and load them up with the commands that you need most often.

Creating a brand new toolbar

To create a toolbar of your very own, follow these steps:

1. **Choose Tools⇨Customize.**

   The Customize dialog box appears (see Figure 2-2).

2. **Click on the Toolbars tab.**

3. **Click on New.**

   A New Toolbar dialog box appears, as shown in Figure 2-13.

4. **Type a name for your toolbar in the Toolbar name text box.**

5. **Click in the Make toolbar available to list box and click on the template or document in which you want to save the toolbar.**

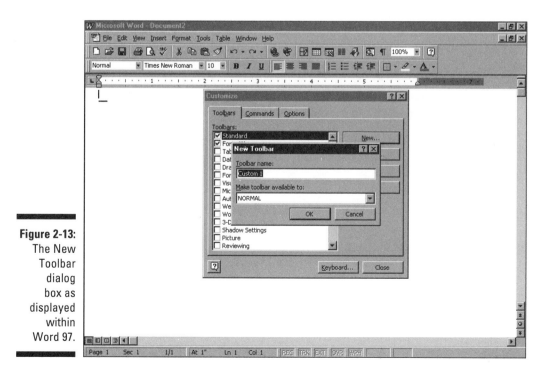

Figure 2-13:
The New Toolbar dialog box as displayed within Word 97.

For example, if you want your newly created toolbar to appear only in a certain document, click on that document name in the list box.

6. **Click on OK.**

Your new toolbar appears as an empty floating toolbar.

7. **Click on the Commands tab in the Customize list box.**

8. **In the Categories list box, click on a category for the command that you want to add to a toolbar.**

For example, if you want to add a command that appears in the Edit category, click on Edit in the Categories list box.

9. **Move the mouse pointer over the command that you want to put on a toolbar (such as the Find or Open command).**

10. **Hold down the left mouse button and drag the mouse over your displayed toolbar where you want to add the icon.**

A black I-beam icon appears to show you where the icon will appear on the toolbar.

11. **Release the left mouse button.**

Repeat Steps 8 through 11 for each icon that you want to add to your toolbar.

12. **Click on Close to remove the Customize dialog box when you're done.**

Deleting a toolbar that you created

If you've created your own toolbars, you may want to delete them off the face of the earth in case you never need them again.

You can delete only toolbars that you've created. You can never delete any toolbars that Microsoft's wealthy programmers have created for you, so don't even try.

To delete a toolbar that you have already created, follow these steps:

1. **Choose Tools⇨Customize.**

The Customize dialog box appears (refer to Figure 2-2).

2. **Click on the Toolbars tab.**

3. **Click on the toolbar that you want to delete.**

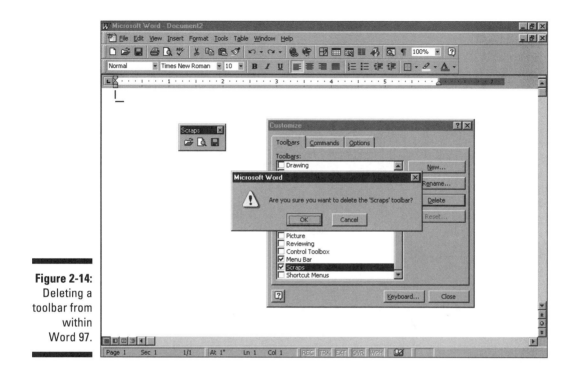

Figure 2-14:
Deleting a
toolbar from
within
Word 97.

4. Click on Delete.

A dialog box appears, shown in Figure 2-14, asking whether you really want to delete your toolbar.

5. Click on OK.

6. Click on Close to remove the Customize dialog box.

Changing the Size of Your Toolbar Icons

To many people, the icons on the toolbars look just big enough to be recognizable but small enough so you don't understand what the heck they're supposed to represent. If you'd rather make your toolbar icons bigger so that they're easier to see, this is how to do it:

1. Choose Tools⇨Customize.

A Customize dialog box appears (refer to Figure 2-2).

2. Click on the Options tab.

3. Click in the Large icons check box.

Your toolbar icons immediately mutate in size right before your eyes, as shown in Figure 2-15.

4. Click on Close.

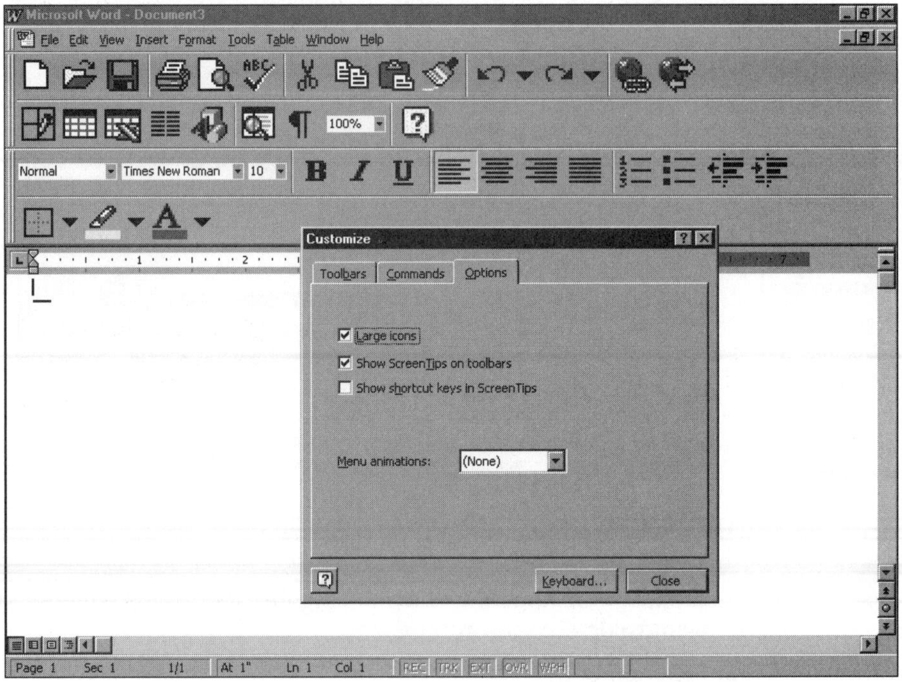

Figure 2-15: Unnaturally large icons displayed in the toolbar.

Part II
Power Writing with Microsoft Word 97

The 5th Wave   By Rich Tennant

MOUSE PADS THAT NEVER MADE IT

The Road-Kill Pad

The Chia-Pad

The Plastic Vomit Pad

The Pad-Thai

In this part . . .

Aside from playing games, most people use computers so they can write with a word processor (provided that they can get their computer to work in the first place). Fortunately, Microsoft Word 97 provides plenty of time-saving shortcuts, such as macros (which can automate your writing), templates (so that you don't have to waste time formatting your documents yourself), and features to automatically generate an index or table of contents.

As usual, Microsoft tried (emphasis on *tried*) to make these advanced features of Word 97 accessible to everyone, but you're likely to get confused trying to find out about them from the sparse documentation and help screens of Word 97. So feel free to dig through this part of the book to master the secrets yourself.

Chapter 3

Making Menus and Keystroke Shortcuts

In This Chapter

▶ Customizing your menus

▶ Renaming menu titles

▶ Making keystroke shortcuts

*T*he pull-down menus in Microsoft Word 97 contain every available command. Unfortunately, digging through crowded menus can often make a program seem harder to use. So, in an effort to please everyone, Microsoft Word 97 gives you the ability to add, delete, rename, or even create your own pull-down menus.

In another gesture of benevolence, Microsoft Word 97 also lets you assign keystroke shortcuts to your most commonly used commands. Instead of digging through a pull-down menu every time you want to choose a command, you can press a strange keystroke combination, such as Ctrl+F11. By assigning your own keystroke shortcuts to specific commands, you can make Microsoft Word 97 even easier to use than before.

Customizing Pull-Down Menus

Microsoft Office 97's pull-down menus can offer so many commands that you may be more confused than helped. To simplify (or complicate) Microsoft Word 97, you may want to add, delete, or rearrange the pull-down menus to suit your own peculiar taste.

If you modify the pull-down menus in your version of Microsoft Word 97, other people may have trouble using your copy of Microsoft Word 97. Depending on your situation, this can be extremely troublesome or just highly amusing.

Rearranging commands on a pull-down menu

You might not like the order of the commands on your pull-down menus, so feel free to move them around them anyway you like.

To move a command to a new location or to a different pull-down menu altogether, follow these steps:

1. **Choose Tools⇨Customize.**

   The Customize dialog box appears.

2. **Click on a pull-down menu title.**

   A black border appears around the menu title, as shown in Figure 3-1.

Figure 3-1:
Moving a command on a pull-down menu.

3. **Move the mouse pointer over the menu command that you want to move.**

4. **Hold down the left mouse button and drag the mouse to a new location.**

   A black line appears to show the new location of the command if you release the left mouse button.

5. **Release the left mouse button when you're happy with the position of the command.**

Copying a pull-down menu command

If you use a particular command often, you can have it appear in two or more pull-down menus. To copy a menu command, follow these steps:

1. **Choose Tools⇨Customize.**

   The Customize dialog box appears.

2. **Click on a pull-down menu title and then move the mouse pointer over the menu command that you want to copy.**

3. **Simultaneously hold down the Ctrl key and the left mouse button while dragging the mouse to another location.**

   A black line appears to show where the copy of the command will appear if you let go of the left mouse button.

4. **Release the Ctrl key and the left mouse button when you're happy with the position of the command.**

Deleting commands off a pull-down menu

Not all commands that appear on a pull-down menu may be useful. To avoid cluttering up your menus, take a few moments and yank off those commands that you don't want to see anymore.

To delete a command off a pull-down menu, follow these steps:

1. **Choose Tools⇨Customize.**

   The Customize dialog box appears.

2. **Click on a pull-down menu title and then move the mouse pointer over the menu command that you want to delete.**

3. **Hold down the left mouse button and drag the mouse anywhere off the pull-down menu.**

4. **Release the left mouse button.**

   Your chosen menu command no longer appears on the pull-down menu.

Changing your menu command icons

To provide a visual relationship between specific menu commands and those cryptic little icons that appear on the toolbars, Microsoft Word 97 displays icons within the pull-down menus themselves. For example, if you click on the File menu, you'll notice that the icons that appear next to the Open and New commands also appear on the Standard toolbar.

Removing menu icons

In case you don't like icons cluttering up your pull-down menus, you can get rid of them by following these steps:

1. **Choose Tools⇨Customize.**

   The Customize dialog box appears.

2. **Click on a pull-down menu title and then move the mouse pointer over the menu command displaying the icon that you want to delete.**

3. **Click on the right mouse button.**

   A pop-up menu appears, as shown in Figure 3-2.

4. **Click on Text Only (in Menus).**

5. **Click on Close in the Customize dialog box.**

Choosing a new menu icon

In case you think that the icons currently representing your menu commands don't make any sense, pick your own icons instead. To choose a new icon for a menu command, follow these steps:

1. **Choose Tools⇨Customize.**

   The Customize dialog box appears.

2. **Click on a pull-down menu title and then move the mouse pointer over a menu command.**

3. **Click on the right mouse button.**

   A pop-up menu appears (refer to Figure 3-2).

4. **Click on Change Button Image.**

   Another pop-up menu appears, as shown in Figure 3-3.

Figure 3-2:
The right
mouse
button pop-
up menu for
editing your
menu
commands.

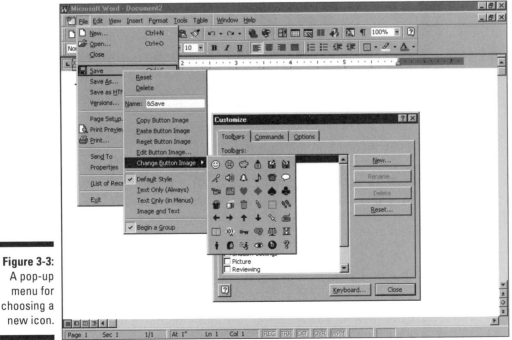

Figure 3-3:
A pop-up
menu for
choosing a
new icon.

5. Click on a new icon that you want to represent your menu command.

6. Click on Close in the Customize dialog box.

Changing an icon in a pull-down menu doesn't change that same icon in a toolbar.

You can also use the preceding steps to add an icon to a menu command that doesn't have an icon next to it.

Editing a menu icon

For those with an artistic bent, Microsoft Word 97 gives you the power to edit an icon and draw a new one if you like. To edit or draw an icon for a menu, follow these steps:

1. Choose Tools⇨Customize.

The Customize dialog box appears.

2. Click on a pull-down menu title and then move the mouse pointer over the menu command displaying the icon that you want to edit.

3. Click on the right mouse button.

A pop-up menu appears (refer to Figure 3-2).

4. Click on Edit Button Image.

A Button Editor window appears, as shown in Figure 3-4.

5. Click on a color in the Colors group.

6. Click on the icon in the Picture box with the left mouse button to draw your chosen color.

Click in the Erase box to draw the default background color of your icon. (This erases whatever color is already there.)

7. Click on OK when you're done drawing or modifying your icon.

8. Click on Close in the Customize dialog box.

Resetting a menu icon

Naturally, if you mess up the icons that appear in your pull-down menus, you may want to restore them to their appearance before you got too creative (or too careless). To reset your menu icons to their original appearance, follow these steps:

1. Choose Tools⇨Customize.

The Customize dialog box appears.

2. Click on a pull-down menu title and then move the mouse pointer over the menu command displaying the icon that you want to reset.

Picture box   Colors group   Erase box

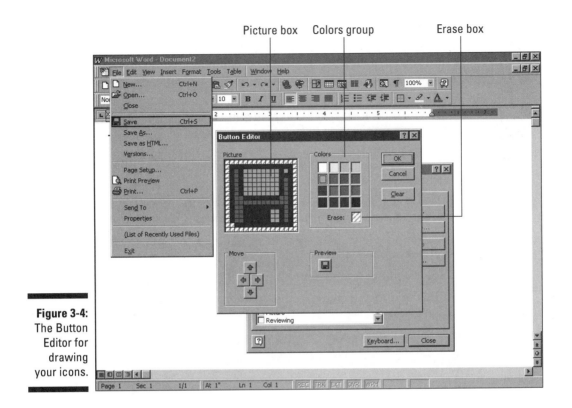

Figure 3-4:
The Button
Editor for
drawing
your icons.

3. Click on the right mouse button.

A pop-up menu appears (refer back to Figure 3-2).

4. Click on Reset Button Image.

5. Click on Close in the Customize dialog box.

Adding commands to a pull-down menu

Sometimes a pull-down menu may not provide all the commands that you
need. Fortunately, you can always add new commands to a pull-down menu
anytime you want, just to exercise your free will or mess up somebody else's
copy of Word 97.

To add a command to a pull-down menu, follow these steps:

1. Choose Tools⇨Customize.

A Customize dialog box appears.

2. Click on the Commands tab.

3. **Click on the pull-down menu title where you want to add your new command (such as the File or Window menu).**

4. **In the Categories list box of the Customize dialog box, click on a category for the command that you want to add to a pull-down menu.**

   For example, if you want to add a command that appears in the Edit category, click on Edit in the Categories list box (in Figure 3-5 the category Web is selected).

5. **Move the mouse pointer over the command that you want to put on the menu (such as the Find or Open command, or in this case, a Search the Web command).**

6. **Hold down the left mouse button and drag the mouse to the pull-down menu where you want to add the command, as shown in Figure 3-5.**

   A black I-beam icon appears to show you where the command will appear on the menu.

7. **Release the left mouse button.**

8. **Click on Close to remove the Customize dialog box.**

Figure 3-5:
Adding a
command
to a pull-
down menu.

Renaming a pull-down menu title or command

Although Word 97 uses standard pull-down menu titles such as File, View, and Window, you might want more descriptive titles instead. For maximum flexibility, you can rename both your menu titles (the ones that appear at the top of the screen) and your menu commands (the ones that appear within a pull-down menu).

Renaming pull-down menu titles

To rename a pull-down menu title, follow these steps:

1. **Choose Tools⇨Customize.**

   The Customize dialog box appears.

2. **Move the mouse pointer over the pull-down menu title that you want to rename and then click on the right mouse button.**

   A pop-up menu appears, as shown in Figure 3-6.

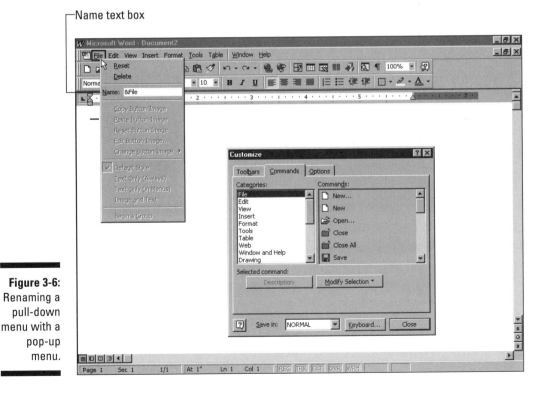

Figure 3-6:
Renaming a pull-down menu with a pop-up menu.

3. **Click in the Name text box and type a new name for your pull-down menu.**

   To underline a letter in your menu title, put an ampersand character (&) in front of the letter. For example, &Stuff would appear on the pull-down menu as Stuff.

4. **Click on Close to make the Customize dialog box go away.**

Renaming commands on a pull-down menu

To rename a command on a pull-down menu, follow these steps:

1. **Choose Tools⇨Customize.**

   The Customize dialog box appears.

2. **Click on the pull-down menu title containing the command that you want to rename; then, move the mouse pointer over the command that you want to rename.**

3. **Click on the right mouse button.**

   A pop-up menu appears.

4. **Click in the Name text box and type a new name for your pull-down command.**

   To underline a letter in your menu command, put an ampersand character (&) in front of the letter. For example, &Kill File would appear on the pull-down menu as Kill File.

5. **Click on Close to make the Customize dialog box go away.**

Resetting a pull-down menu

Rearranging your pull-down menus can be fun and mind-expanding, but you may want to restore your pull-down menus to their original appearance in case you want your copy of Word 97 to look like everybody else's copy.

Resetting a pull-down menu wipes out any modifications that you may have made. Therefore, choose this command only if deleting modifications is what you truly want to do.

To reset a menu, follow these steps:

1. **Choose Tools⇨Customize.**

   The Customize dialog box appears.

2. **Move the mouse pointer over the pull-down menu title that you want to reset and click the right mouse button.**

   A pop-up menu appears (refer to Figure 3-6).

3. **Click on Reset.**

4. **Click on Close to remove the Customize dialog box.**

Making Keystroke Shortcuts

If you use a particular command often enough, you may want a faster way of choosing it than taking your hands off the keyboard and reaching for the mouse each time. To give touch-typists an additional edge over their counterparts who rely on the mouse to do everything, Microsoft Word 97 lets you assign your own keystroke shortcuts to any Word 97 command.

For example, if you don't like the idea of choosing the Print Preview command by clicking on the Print Preview icon on the toolbar or choosing Print Preview from the File menu, give it a keystroke shortcut such as F12 instead. Then, just press F12 every time you want to choose the Print Preview command.

Assigning keystroke shortcuts

To assign your own keystrokes to a command, follow these steps:

1. **Choose Tools⇨Customize.**

   The Customize dialog box appears.

2. **Click on the Toolbars tab.**

3. **Click on the Keyboard button.**

   A Customize Keyboard dialog box appears, as shown in Figure 3-7.

4. **Click in the Categories list box and choose a category such as File or Edit.**

5. **Click in the Commands list box and choose a command to which you want to assign a keystroke shortcut.**

6. **Click in the Press new shortcut key box.**

7. **Press the key combination that you want to assign as your shortcut, such as Ctrl+F11.**

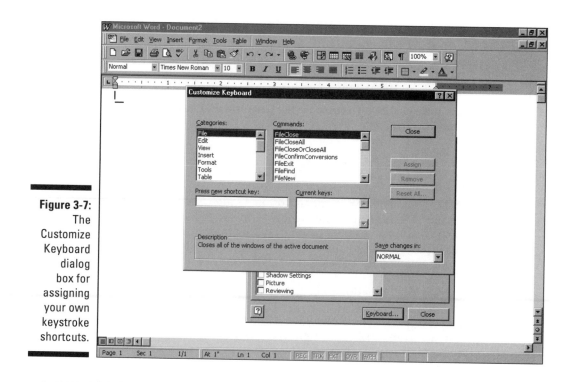

Figure 3-7:
The
Customize
Keyboard
dialog
box for
assigning
your own
keystroke
shortcuts.

8. Click on Assign.

9. Click on Close to make the Customize Keyboard dialog box go away.

10. Click on Close to make the Customize dialog box disappear.

You should choose keystroke shortcuts that are easy to remember and press. For example, Ctrl+E is much easier to press and remember than Alt+Shift+F2. Just remember that most of the simpler keystrokes have already been assigned to commonly used commands such as Save (Ctrl+S) or Print (Ctrl+P).

Word 97 actually gives you two ways to assign your keystroke shortcuts:

✔ Whenever anyone tries to use your copy of Word 97

✔ Just in the current document that you're editing

Unless you tell Word 97 otherwise, it blindly assumes that you want to use your keystroke shortcuts every time you use Word 97. To tell Word 97 only to save your keystroke shortcuts in the current document, click in the Save changes in list box after Step 8 and click on the name of the current document you're editing. Then proceed with Steps 9 and 10.

Deleting keystroke shortcuts

To get rid of keystroke shortcuts that you never use, you can remove a keystroke shortcut from one command and use it for another one.

To delete a keystroke shortcut, follow these steps:

1. **Choose Tools⇨Customize.**

   The Customize dialog box appears.

2. **Click the Toolbars tab.**

3. **Click the Keyboard button.**

   A Customize Keyboard dialog box appears (refer back to Figure 3-7).

4. **Click in the Categories list box and choose a category such as File or Edit.**

5. **Click in the Commands list box and choose a command that you want to remove a keystroke shortcut from.**

6. **Click on the keystroke shortcut that you want to delete in the Current keys box.**

   Note: Not all commands may have keystroke shortcuts assigned to them.

7. **Click Remove.**

8. **Click Close to make the Customize Keyboard dialog box go away.**

9. **Click Close to make the Customize dialog box disappear.**

Resetting your keystroke shortcuts

Reassigning keystroke shortcuts can be fun and amusing, but it can confuse other people who may want to use your copy of Word 97. In case you need to return your keystroke shortcuts to their original, pristine, unblemished-by-human-hands state of innocence, you can.

To reset your keystroke shortcuts, follow these steps:

1. **Choose Tools⇨Customize.**

   The Customize dialog box appears.

2. **Click the Toolbars tab.**

3. **Click the Keyboard button.**

   A Customize Keyboard dialog box appears (refer to Figure 3-7).

4. **Click Reset All.**

   A dialog box appears, warning you that Word 97 will wipe out all of your custom keystroke shortcuts, as shown in Figure 3-8.

5. **Click Yes (if that's what you really want to do).**

6. **Click Close to make the Customize Keyboard dialog box go away.**

7. **Click Close to make the Customize dialog box disappear.**

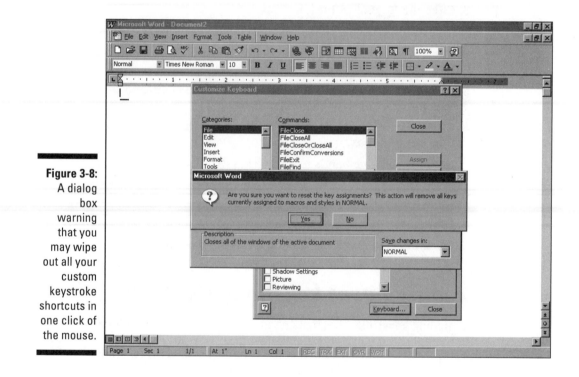

Figure 3-8:
A dialog box warning that you may wipe out all your custom keystroke shortcuts in one click of the mouse.

Chapter 4
Fooling Around with Macros

· ·

In This Chapter
▶ Recording macros as toolbar buttons, menu items, and keystroke combinations
▶ Renaming macros
▶ Deleting macros
▶ Using macros in different documents

· ·

*T*o help you work faster, Word 97 lets you create *macros,* which act like shortcuts. A macro is simply a file that contains one or more instructions. When you want to repeat those instructions rather than type them or click on menu commands to make Word 97 follow them, you just tell Word 97 to follow the instructions that you previously stored in a macro.

Suppose that you have to type a long-winded phrase, such as *Acme's Super Acne Medication Cream,* or choose multiple commands to create a three-column document repeatedly. You can type all those words or choose various commands multiple times and risk making a mistake, or you can use a macro.

If you use a macro, you have to type the words or choose the commands only once. You use Word 97's macro feature to "capture" them (like a bug in amber) and then "replay" them (like a recording) at the touch of a button. In this way, a macro lets you perform complicated tasks without thinking, which is the way most people act when they're working for somebody else anyway.

Recording Your Own Macros

When you record a macro, you can store it in one of three ways:

✔ **As a toolbar button:** If you store a macro on a toolbar, you choose it by simply clicking on its button.

✔ **As a menu command:** If you store a macro on a menu, you choose it by pulling down the menu and then clicking on the macro's name.

✔ **As a unique keystroke combination (such as Ctrl+W):** If you store a macro as a keystroke combination, you can quickly choose the macro by pressing the proper keystrokes. (The only hard part is remembering the macro's particular keystroke combination.)

Which method should you use? It depends on how you like to use Word 97. If you want simple point-and-click access to your macros, store your macros as toolbar buttons. If you don't want macros cluttering your screen as buttons, store them as menu commands. If you want to access your macros faster than you can by clicking on either toolbar buttons or menu commands, store the macros as keystroke combinations. If you don't like macros at all, skip this chapter altogether.

Word 97 gives you the option of saving your macro in a template or in your current document. If you save your macro to a template, then you can use your macro in any document created from that template. If you save your macro in the current document, then you can use your macro only in that particular document.

Macros as toolbar buttons

When you record a macro as a toolbar button, you need to choose two things:

✔ A button to represent the macro

✔ A toolbar (such as the Standard or Formatting toolbar) on which to store the button that represents your macro

To record a macro and store it as a toolbar button, follow these steps:

1. **Choose Tools⇨Macro⇨Record New Macro.**

   A Macro dialog box appears, as shown in Figure 4-1.

2. **Type a descriptive name for your macro (one word only, no spaces allowed) in the Macro name box.**

3. **Click in the Store macro in list box and click on the template or document in which you want to save your macro.**

4. **Type a description for your macro in the Description text box.**

   This step is optional but can be helpful when trying to remember what a particular macro actually does.

5. **Click on the Toolbars button in the Assign Macro To group.**

   The Customize dialog box appears, as shown in Figure 4-2.

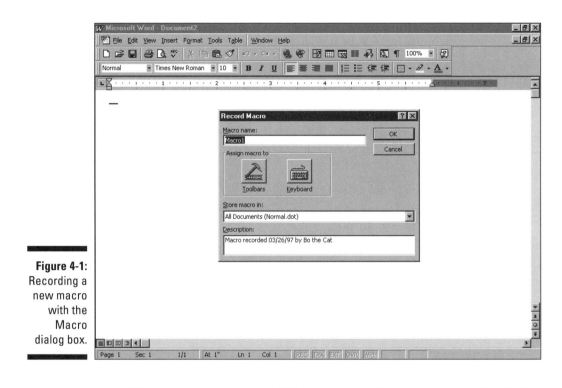

Figure 4-1:
Recording a
new macro
with the
Macro
dialog box.

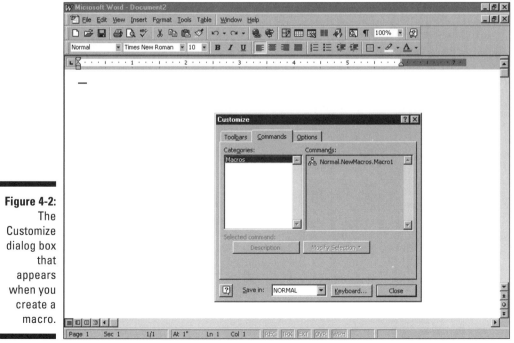

Figure 4-2:
The
Customize
dialog box
that
appears
when you
create a
macro.

6. **Move the mouse pointer over the macro name displayed in the Commands list box, and simultaneously hold down the left mouse button while you drag the mouse to the toolbar on which you want to store your macro.**

   Word 97 displays a dark vertical line on the toolbar to show you where your macro button will appear when you release the left mouse button.

7. **When you're happy with the location of your macro button on a toolbar, release the left mouse button.**

8. **Click on the Modify Selection button.**

   A pop-up menu appears, as shown in Figure 4-3.

9. **Click on Name and type descriptive text that you want to appear on your macro button.**

10. **Click on Change Button Image and click on an image that you want to appear on your macro button.**

11. **Click on Close.**

   The Macro Recording toolbar appears, floating in the middle of the screen, as shown in Figure 4-4. Notice that the mouse pointer displays a cassette tape icon to let you know that Word 97 is recording your macro.

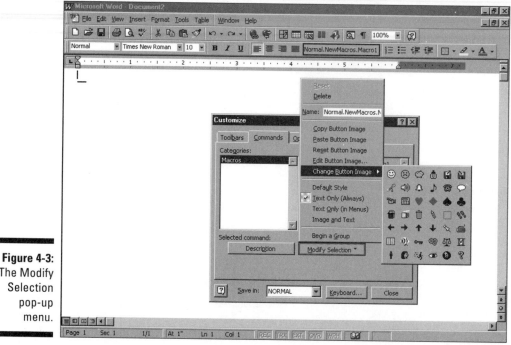

Figure 4-3:
The Modify
Selection
pop-up
menu.

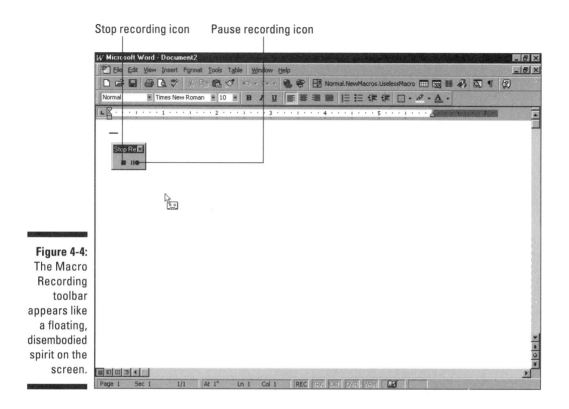

Figure 4-4:
The Macro
Recording
toolbar
appears like
a floating,
disembodied
spirit on the
screen.

12. **Press any keys or choose any command that you want to store in your macro.**

    When you're recording a macro but don't want to record certain keystrokes or commands, you can temporarily "turn off" the macro recorder by clicking on the Pause button (see Figure 4-4). To turn the macro recorder back "on," just click on the Pause Recording button again.

13. **Click on the Stop Recording button on the Macro Recording toolbar when you're done recording your macro.**

Congratulations! You've just recorded a macro. To use this macro at any time, click on its toolbar button.

If you've modified your toolbars so badly that you want to return them to their original, pristine appearance, you can.

The following steps remove *all* changes, including any other macro buttons that you may have added or any modifications that you may have made to the toolbar itself.

To reset a toolbar, follow these steps:

1. **Choose Tools⇨Customize.**

   The Customize dialog box appears.

2. **Click on the Toolbars tab.**

3. **Click on a toolbar that you want to return to its original condition and click on Reset.**

   A Reset Toolbar dialog box appears.

4. **Click on OK.**

5. **Click on Close.**

If you want to remove just one macro button from your toolbar without completely resetting your toolbar, follow these steps:

1. **Choose Tools⇨Customize.**

   The Customize dialog box appears.

2. **Click on the macro button that you want to remove and simultaneously hold down the left mouse button to drag the macro button off the toolbar.**

3. **Release the left mouse button.**

   Word 97 deletes your macro button from the toolbar.

4. **Click on Close.**

When you remove a macro from a toolbar, you just remove the icon; the macro still exists on your hard disk. To delete macros, see the section "Wiping out macros," later in this chapter.

Macros as menu commands

When you record a macro as a menu command, you need to choose two things:

- ✔ A descriptive name for the macro
- ✔ A pull-down menu (such as the Tools or View menu) in which to store the macro

To record a macro and store it as a command on a pull-down menu, follow these steps:

1. **Choose Tools⇨Macro⇨Record New Macro.**

   A Macro dialog box appears (refer back to Figure 4-1).

2. **Type a descriptive name for your macro (one word only, no spaces are allowed) in the Macro name box.**

3. **Click in the Store macro in list box and click on the template or document in which you want to save your macro.**

4. **Type a description for your macro in the Description text box.**

   This step is optional but can be helpful when trying to remember what a particular macro actually does.

5. **Click on the Toolbars button in the Assign Macro To group.**

   The Customize dialog box appears (refer back to Figure 4-2).

6. **Move the mouse pointer over the macro name displayed in the Commands list box, hold down the left mouse button, and drag the mouse to the pull-down menu on which you want to store your macro.**

   Word 97 displays a dark horizontal line on the pull-down menu to show you where your macro button will appear when you release the left mouse button.

7. **When you're happy with the location of your macro button on a pull-down menu, release the left mouse button.**

8. **Click on the Modify Selection button.**

   A pop-up menu appears (refer back to Figure 4-3).

9. **Click on Name and type a descriptive text that you want to appear for your macro.**

10. **Click on Change Button Image and click on an image that you want to appear next to your macro name on the pull-down menu.**

11. **Click on Close.**

    The Macro Recording toolbar appears, floating in the middle of the screen (refer back to Figure 4-4). Notice that the mouse pointer displays a cassette tape icon to let you know that Word 97 is recording your macro.

12. **Press any keys or choose any command that you want to store in your macro.**

    When you're recording a macro but don't want to record certain keystrokes or commands, you can temporarily "turn off" the macro recorder by clicking on the Pause button (refer back to Figure 4-4). To turn the macro recorder back "on," just click on the Pause Recording button again.

13. **Click on the Stop Recording button on the Macro Recording toolbar when you're done recording your macro.**

To use this macro at any time, just display the pull-down menu on which you stored the macro name (in Step 7) and click on the macro name displayed on the menu.

To remove the macro from a pull-down menu, follow these steps:

1. **Choose Tools➪Customize.**

   The Customize dialog box appears.

2. **Click on the pull-down menu containing your macro, point to the macro that you want to remove, hold down the left mouse button, and drag the macro button off the pull-down menu.**

3. **Release the left mouse button.**

   Word 97 deletes your macro button from the pull-down menu.

4. **Click on Close.**

When you remove a macro from a pull-down menu, that macro still exists on your hard disk — it's just hiding. To delete macros, see the section "Wiping out macros," later in this chapter.

Macros as keystroke combinations

When you record a macro as a keystroke combination, you need to choose two things:

- ✔ A descriptive name for your macro.
- ✔ A unique two- or three-keystroke combination to represent your macro.

To record a macro and store it as a keystroke combination, follow these steps:

1. **Choose Tools⇨Macro⇨Record New Macro.**

   A Macro dialog box appears (refer to Figure 4-1).

2. **Type a descriptive name for your macro (one word only, no spaces allowed) in the Macro name box.**

3. **Click in the Store macro in list box and click on the template or document in which you want to save your macro.**

4. **Type a description for your macro in the Description text box.**

   This step is optional but can be helpful when trying to remember what a particular macro actually does.

5. **Click on the Keyboard button in the Assign Macro To group.**

   The Customize Keyboard dialog box appears, as shown in Figure 4-5.

6. **Click in the Press new shortcut key text box and press the keystroke that you want to represent your macro, such as Ctrl+F11.**

7. **Click on Assign.**

   Repeat Steps 6 and 7 for each additional keystroke combination that you want to assign to your macro.

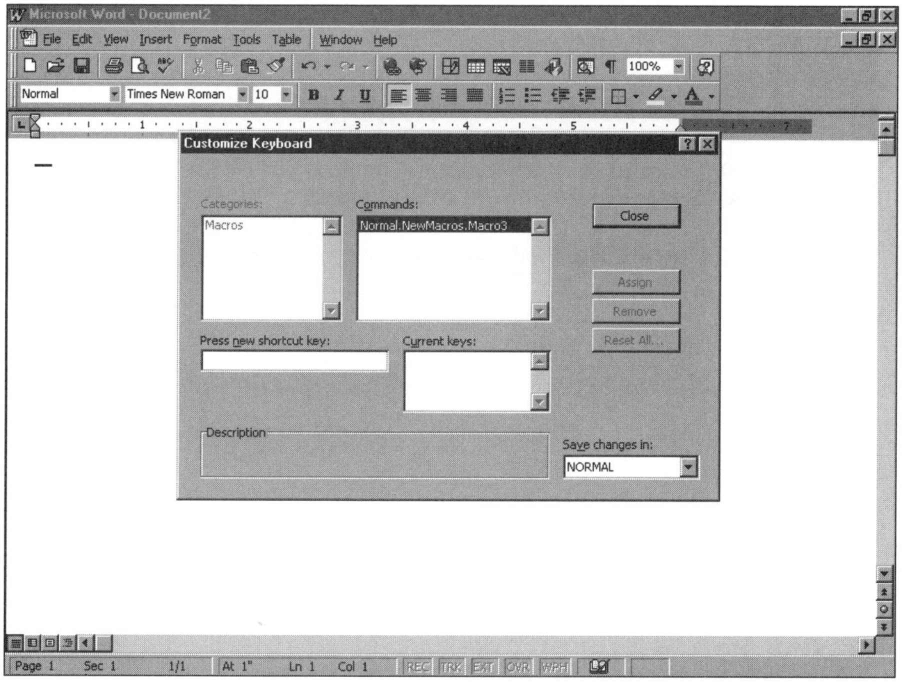

Figure 4-5:
The
Customize
Keyboard
dialog box.

8. **Click on Close.**

The Macro Recording toolbar appears, floating in the middle of the screen (refer to Figure 4-4). Notice that the mouse pointer displays a cassette tape icon to let you know that Word 97 is recording your macro.

9. **Press any keys or choose any command that you want to store in your macro.**

When you're recording a macro but don't want to record certain keystrokes or commands, you can temporarily "turn off" the macro recorder by clicking on the Pause button (refer to Figure 4-4). To turn the macro recorder back "on," just click on the Pause Recording button again.

10. **Click on the Stop Recording button on the Macro Recording toolbar when you're done recording your macro.**

To use this macro at any time, press the keystroke combination that you assigned in Step 6.

Modifying Macros

After you've created a macro, you can rename or delete it at any time by using the steps in the following sections:

Renaming your macros

After you create a macro, you can always create a more descriptive name for your macro. To rename an existing macro, follow these steps:

1. **Choose Tools⇨Macro⇨Macros, or press Alt+F8.**

The Macro dialog box appears.

2. **Click on Organizer.**

The Organizer dialog box appears, as shown in Figure 4-6.

3. **Click on the macro that you want to rename.**

4. **Click on Rename.**

A Rename dialog box appears, as shown in Figure 4-7.

5. **Type a new name for your macro in the New name box and click on OK.**

6. **Click on Close.**

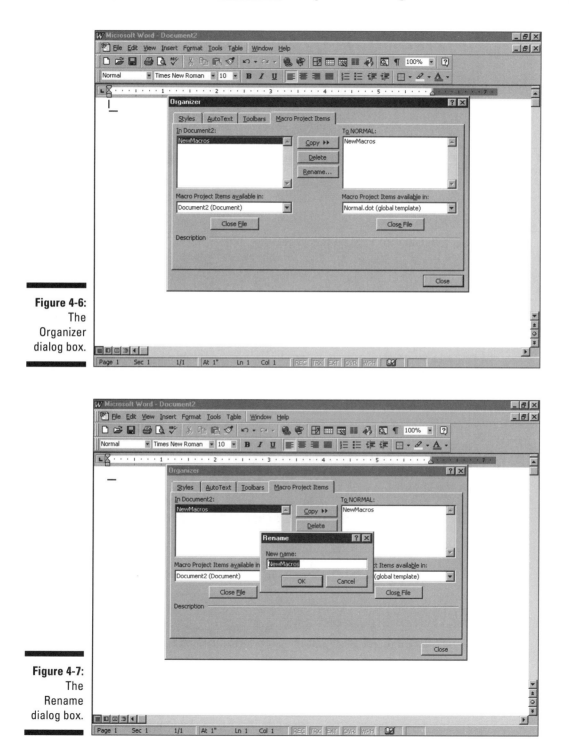

Figure 4-6:
The
Organizer
dialog box.

Figure 4-7:
The
Rename
dialog box.

Wiping out macros

If you decide that you'll never need a certain macro again, you can delete it for good. To delete a macro, follow these steps:

1. **Choose Tools⇨Macro⇨Macros, or press Alt+F8.**

   The Macro dialog box appears.

2. **Click on the macro name that you want to delete and click on Delete.**

   A dialog box appears, asking whether you really want to delete your macro.

3. **Click on Yes.**

   Your macro is gone for good!

4. **Click on Close.**

Sharing Macros between Documents

When you create a macro, Word 97 stores it in the template used to create the document. For example, every time you create a new document, Word 97 uses the NORMAL.DOT template unless you specify a different template to use. (For more information about templates, see Chapter 5.)

After you create several useful macros, you may want to copy them to other templates. That way, you can use your macro no matter which template you use to create another document.

For example, you may store all macros related to faxes in a FAX.DOT template, all macros related to form letters in a FORM.DOT template, and all macros related to business reports in a DULL.DOT template.

To copy your macros to a different template, follow these steps:

1. **Choose Tools⇨Macro⇨Macros, or press Alt+F8.**

   The Macro dialog box appears.

2. **Click on Organizer.**

   The Organizer dialog box appears (refer back to Figure 4-6).

3. **Click on the macro that you want to copy in the list box on the left.**

4. **Click on the Close File button that appears on the right side of the Organizer dialog box.**

   Word 97 renames the Close File button as the Open File button.

Beware of macro viruses

Because Word 97's macro language is basically a miniature programming language, people have been able to use it to create computer viruses. These macro viruses infect your document files and spread to your template files.

Every time you create a new document based on an infected template file, your new document files become infected. And if you share an infected document file with someone else, the macro virus infects that person's document and template files, too.

To protect yourself from macro viruses, get an antivirus program, such as Norton Antivirus or McAfee's VirusScan that checks Word documents for macro viruses. That way, you can safely share your macros with others without worrying about infecting their computer with a macro virus.

As a first line of defense against macro viruses, choose Tools⇨Options, click on the General tab, and make sure that a check mark appears in the Macro virus protection check box. Then, click on OK.

5. Click on the Open File button.

The Open dialog box appears, as shown in Figure 4-8.

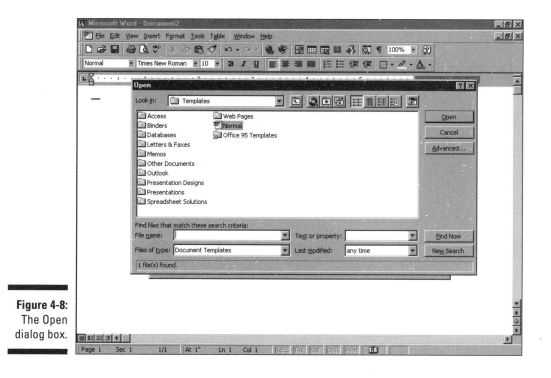

Figure 4-8:
The Open
dialog box.

6. **Click on the template you want to copy your macro to and click on** <u>O</u>**pen.**

   The Organizer dialog box is now visible, and the Open dialog box goes away.

7. **Click on** <u>C</u>**opy in the Organizer dialog box.**

8. **Click on Close.**

Chapter 5

Formatting Text with Styles and Templates

. . . .

In This Chapter

▶ Using styles to format your text

▶ Creating templates to make document formatting easier

▶ Storing your templates somewhere else

. . . .

*T*wo of Word 97's most useful features are styles and templates. A *style* lets you define a specific way to format text. A *template* lets you store multiple styles so that you can use them repeatedly.

If you do a great deal of writing that requires unusual formatting (such as writing screenplays, typing financial reports, or pasting together ransom notes), styles and templates can spare you the headache of manually formatting individual paragraphs all by yourself.

Formatting Text with Styles

To help make your writing look good, Word 97 gives you the option of creating and storing predefined styles. A *style* is simply a specific way to format text, such as the font, font size, alignment, color, boldface, italicizing, underlining, or anything else that keeps your documents from looking as dull as if you typed them on an antique typewriter. (Remember those ancient machines?)

By creating a predefined style, you don't have to keep highlighting text and changing all these formatting options by yourself every time you need a particular style. Instead, you can just click on the text that you want to format and choose a style. Then, Word 97 formats your text for you automatically.

Styles are not the same as macros. A *style* defines the formatting of text but not the text itself. A *macro* can type text for you automatically but does nothing to define the formatting of that text. For more information about macros, see Chapter 4.

Creating a style

Whenever you need to format text in a specific way repeatedly, you should create a style. When you create one, you must define the following items:

- ✔ The style name
- ✔ Whether the style is based on an existing style
- ✔ Whether the style affects an entire paragraph or just a single word
- ✔ The style to use for the paragraph that follows the one you're formatting

The style name lets you identify the specific style that you want to use. Although you can name your styles anything you want (including four-letter words), using memorable style names (such as Hanging Indent, Dialogue, or Eye-Catching Headline) is a good idea.

To save time when you create new styles, you can use an existing style as a starting point. That way, you don't have to waste time creating styles from scratch when you only need to slightly modify an existing style. This technique is similar to copying someone else's term paper and then rewriting it a little instead of writing your own term paper from scratch.

When you create a style, you must decide whether you want to create a character style or a paragraph style. A *character style* changes the formatting for one or more characters. A *paragraph style* changes the format for an entire paragraph. Most of the time, styles affect the format for an entire paragraph because changing the format of a single character (or group of characters) by yourself is usually easy to do without creating a style.

After you create a style, you can define the style for the paragraph that appears after the one you're formatting. That way, if two styles normally appear one after the other, Word can choose the second style for you automatically.

For example, you may create a style, called Character, that centers character names in a screenplay. After using the Character style, Word 97 can immediately choose a style called Dialogue, which formats dialogue on the page. In this way, you can continue typing without having to stop to choose the Dialogue style. Figure 5-1 shows four possible styles within a document.

Slugline style

Headline style

Description style

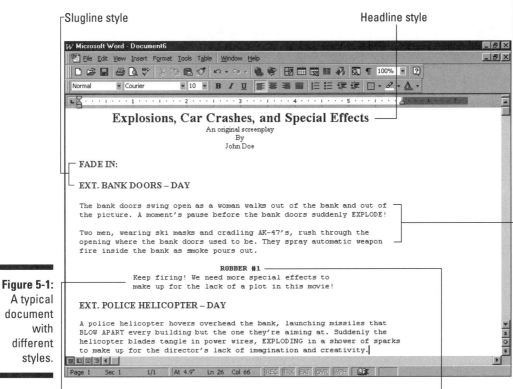

Figure 5-1:
A typical
document
with
different
styles.

Dialog style

Character style

To create your own style, follow these steps:

1. Choose Format⇨Style.

The Style dialog box appears, as shown in Figure 5-2.

2. Click on New.

The New Style dialog box appears, as shown in Figure 5-3.

3. Type a name for your style in the Name box.

4. Click on the arrow in the Style type list box and then choose one of the following:

- Paragraph (format an entire paragraph)
- Character (format a single word)

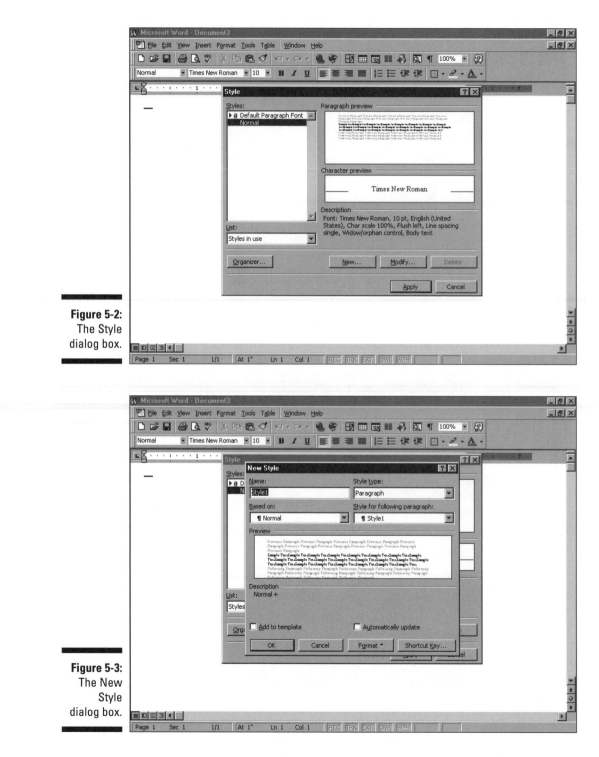

Figure 5-2:
The Style
dialog box.

Figure 5-3:
The New
Style
dialog box.

5. Click on the arrow in the <u>B</u>ased on list box and then choose an existing style if you want to create your new style based on another style.

6. Click on the arrow in the <u>S</u>tyle for Following Paragraph list box and choose a style that you want Word to use in the paragraph immediately after your new style.

7. Click on F<u>o</u>rmat and then choose <u>F</u>ont from the list.

The Font dialog box appears, as shown in Figure 5-4.

8. **Choose the font, font style, and size that you want to use and then click on OK.**

9. Click on F<u>o</u>rmat in the New Style dialog box and then choose <u>P</u>aragraph from the list.

The Paragraph dialog box appears, as shown in Figure 5-5.

10. **Choose the desired <u>L</u>eft or <u>R</u>ight indentation and the Li<u>n</u>e spacing and then click on OK.**

11. Click on F<u>o</u>rmat in the New Style dialog box and choose <u>T</u>abs.

The Tabs dialog box appears, as shown in Figure 5-6.

12. **Choose the <u>T</u>ab stop position, Alignment, and Leader and then click on OK.**

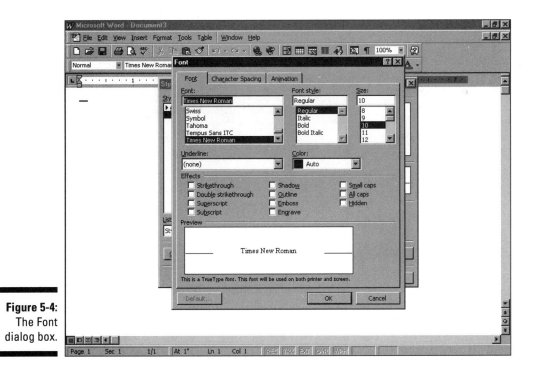

Figure 5-4:
The Font
dialog box.

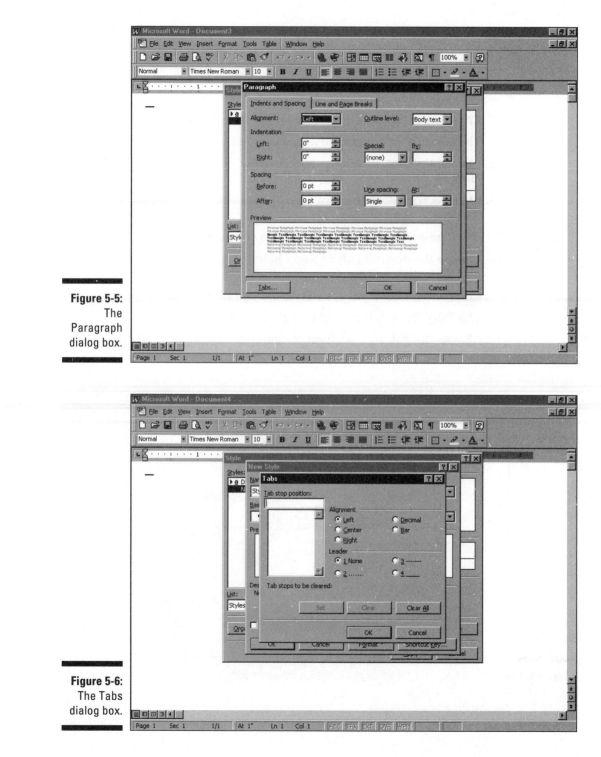

Figure 5-5:
The
Paragraph
dialog box.

Figure 5-6:
The Tabs
dialog box.

13. **Click on F̲ormat in the New Style dialog box; choose B̲order, L̲an-guage, F̲rame, or N̲umbering; and then define any options that you want to save in your style.**

14. **Click on Shortcut K̲ey in the New Style dialog box.**

    The Customize Keyboard dialog box appears, as shown in Figure 5-7.

15. **Click on the Press n̲ew shortcut key box and enter the keystroke combination that you want to assign to your style, such as Ctrl+F9 or something equally unusual.**

16. **Click on A̲ssign and then click on Close.**

17. **Click in the A̲dd to Template check box in the New Style dialog box if you want to save your style in a Word 97 template.**

18. **Click on OK.**

    The Style dialog box appears again.

19. **Click on Close.**

    Your style is now ready to use.

If you click on the Add to Template check box in Step 17, Word 97 saves your style to your document template. Your style is then available for you to use every time you create a new document based on that template.

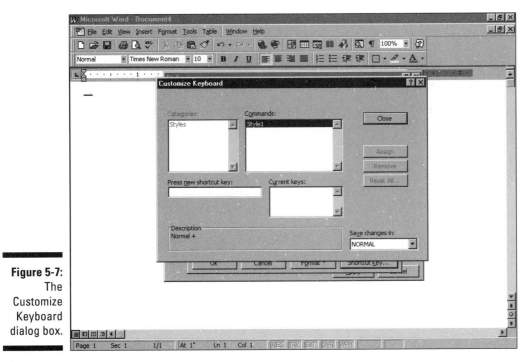

Figure 5-7:
The Customize Keyboard dialog box.

Using a style

After you create a style, you can celebrate if you want. You'll probably want to use your style instead, though. You can use a style in two ways:

- ✔ Choose the style name from the Style list box displayed on the Formatting toolbar.

- ✔ Press the keystroke combination assigned to the style that you want to use (assuming that you assigned a keystroke combination to your style when you created it).

If you have hidden the Formatting toolbar, you won't be able to see the Style list box. To display a hidden Formatting toolbar, choose View➪Toolbars➪Formatting to put a check mark in front of the Formatting toolbar.

To use a style that affects an entire paragraph, follow these steps:

1. **Move the cursor (or click on the mouse) anywhere in the paragraph that you want to format.**

2. **Click on the Style list box and then choose the style name that you want to use.**

   Or, press the keystroke combination assigned to the style that you want to use.

Word 97 magically formats the entire paragraph according to the style.

To use a style that affects a single word, follow these steps:

1. **Highlight the word or words that you want to format.**

2. **Click on the Style list box and then choose the style name that you want to use.**

   Or press the keystroke combination assigned to the style that you want to use.

Word 97 magically formats the entire paragraph according to the style that you choose.

Editing a style

After you create a style, you may decide that it doesn't work quite the way you want. In this case, you can always modify a style.

Be careful when you modify a style. If you've used a specific style to format text and then later change that style, guess what? Word 97 automatically reformats all your text according to the newly modified style. Modify a style only if you're absolutely sure that you want all the text formatted with that style to change as well. Otherwise, create a new style instead.

To edit an existing style, follow these steps:

1. **Choose Format⇨Style.**

   The Style dialog box appears (refer to Figure 5-2).

2. **In the Styles list box, click on the style that you want to edit.**

3. **Click on Modify.**

   The Modify Style dialog box appears, as shown in Figure 5-8.

4. **Click on Format and choose one of these options to modify your style:**

   - Font
   - Paragraph
   - Tabs
   - Border
   - Language
   - Frame
   - Numbering

5. **Click on Shortcut Key if you want to assign a keystroke combination to the style.**

   The Customize Keyboard dialog box appears (refer to Figure 5-7).

6. **Click on the Press new shortcut key box and press the keystroke combination that you want to assign to your style.**

Character styles versus paragraph styles

A character style can format a single character, word, or group of words; a paragraph style can format an entire paragraph. What happens, however, if you use a character style to format words and then later use a paragraph style to format the entire paragraph?

Fortunately, Word 97 isn't as dumb as you may expect. Any characters formatted by using a character style retain their formatting. The paragraph style simply formats all text within a paragraph except for text formatted by character styles. Isn't that comforting?

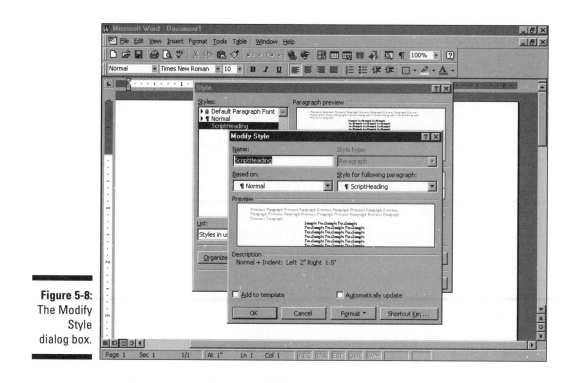

Figure 5-8:
The Modify
Style
dialog box.

7. **Click on Assign and then click on Close.**

8. **Click on the Add to Template check box if you want to save your style for use in other documents.**

9. **Click on OK.**

   The Style dialog box appears again.

10. **Click on Close.**

   Your newly modified style is now ready to use.

True to the form of computer programs, you can accomplish the same task using two or more different methods. For a faster way to edit a style, follow these steps:

1. **Highlight any text formatted by the style that you want to change.**

2. **Make any changes that you want to the style.**

3. **Click on the Styles list box in the Modify Style dialog box and choose the name of the style that you just modified.**

   A Modify Style dialog box appears, as shown in Figure 5-9.

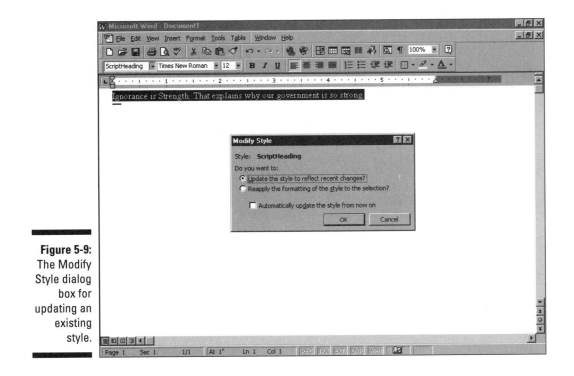

4. Click on OK.

Word 97 reformats all text previously formatted with your newly
modified style.

Wiping out a style

You may occasionally create a style and then later decide that you don't need
it after all. To wipe a style off the face of the earth, follow these steps:

1. Choose Format⇨Style.

The Style dialog box appears (refer to Figure 5-2).

**2. Click on the style that you want to delete, destroy, obliterate, or
otherwise eliminate.**

3. Click on Delete.

A dialog box appears and asks whether you're sure that you want to
delete your chosen style.

4. Click on Yes.

Kiss your style good-bye.

5. Click on Close.

The moment that you delete a style, any text formatted in that style reverts to the Normal style.

If you delete a style, you can immediately retrieve and recover it by pressing Ctrl+Z right away.

Creating Document Templates

If you create documents that require bizarre formatting, tab settings, or paragraph indentations, you may want to create styles or macros to modify those settings at the touch of a button (or the click of a mouse). If you regularly create these types of documents, creating your own, unique document templates instead is much easier.

A document template acts like a cookie cutter for text. Just modify a document once and save all the formatting in the document as a template. Then, the next time that you want a document with all the fancy formatting, spacing, and indentations already designed for you, just create a new document based on your template.

For example, suppose that you need to create a newsletter that has a boldface headline in large print and two columns that divide the page in half. Setting up the column spacing, width, and headline formatting every time that you want to create another newsletter can be a tiresome task, which makes this the perfect job to give to someone who makes less money per hour than you do.

To save time, create your newsletter only once and save it as a template. The next time you create a newsletter, create a new document based on your newsletter template. Then you can just focus on typing the text, because the template will already have set up all the headline formatting and columns for you.

Document templates can contain the following items:

- Text, such as your company name, that must appear in every document based on your template
- Graphics, such as a company logo, that must appear in every document based on your template
- Any formatting or ruler settings
- Any styles that you may create
- Any macros that you may create

Using a template

To show you the power of templates, Word 97 contains several templates that some poor Microsoft employee got paid to create for you. To give you twice as many ways to accomplish the same task and to provide maximum possibility for confusion, Microsoft provides two ways to view and use a Word 97 template:

- ✔ From within a new document
- ✔ From the Windows 95 desktop

If you don't choose a template, Word 97 shrugs its shoulders and assumes that you just want to use a blank template called Normal.

If you open a template that contains macros, Word 97 panics and displays a Warning dialog box, letting you know that if the template is infected by a macro virus, it could infect your Word 97 documents. If you trust the template, click on Enable Macros. If you don't trust the template, click on Disable Macros or Do Not Open.

Choosing a template from within a document

If you've already created and opened a document, you can tell Word 97, "Hey, I want my document to use a different template instead."

To choose a template for your Word document, follow these steps:

1. **Choose Format⇨Style Gallery.**

   The Style Gallery dialog box appears, as shown in Figure 5-10.

2. **Click on a template that you want to view, such as Elegant Fax or Professional Report.**

3. **Click on the Example or Style samples radio button in the Preview group.**

   Click on the Example radio button to see how attractive your document can look if you know what you're doing (see Figure 5-11). Click on the Style Samples radio button to see the type of formatting that the template can create (see Figure 5-12). Either way, Word shows you how the template displays text.

4. **Click on OK when you find a template that you want to use.**

   Your chosen template is ready to use. Just choose a style from the Style list box on the Formatting toolbar to start using a style stored in your template.

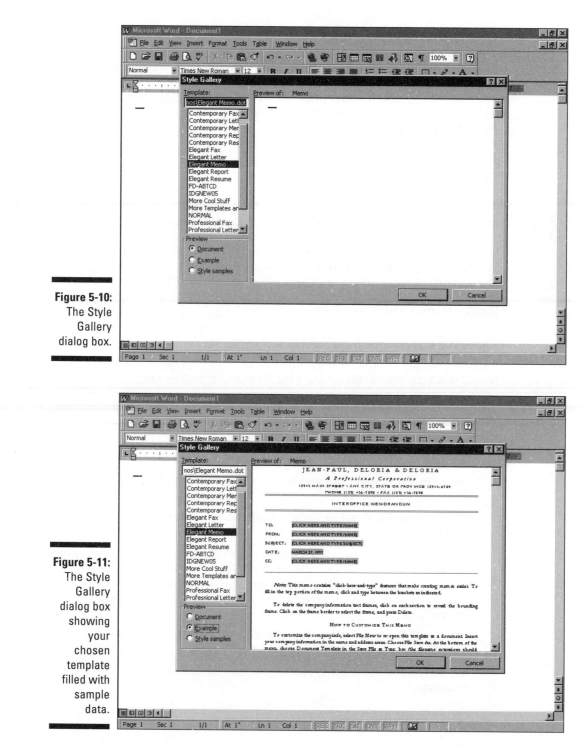

Figure 5-10:
The Style
Gallery
dialog box.

Figure 5-11:
The Style
Gallery
dialog box
showing
your
chosen
template
filled with
sample
data.

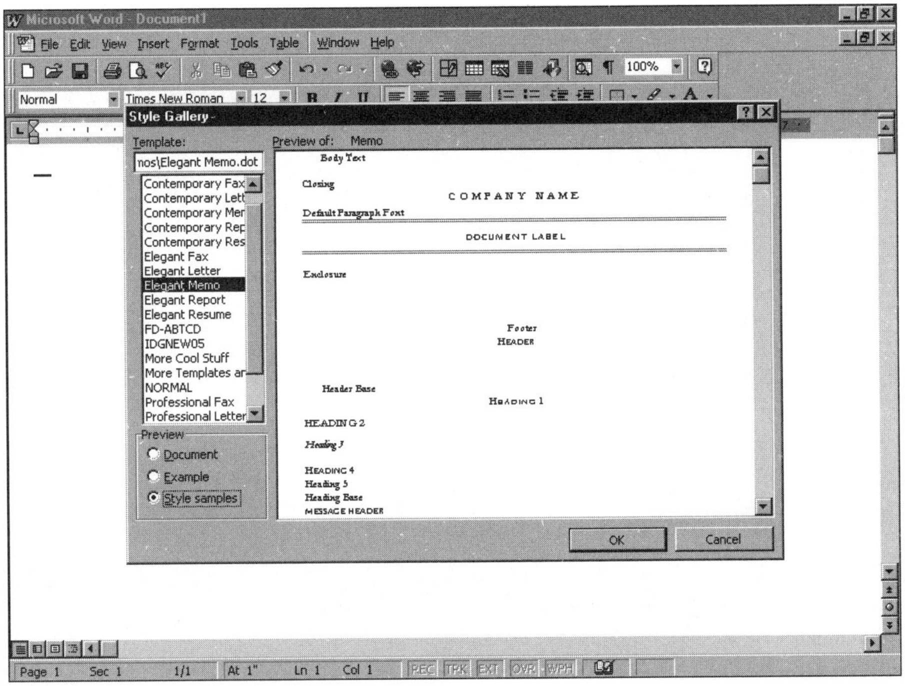

Figure 5-12:
The Style
Gallery
dialog box
showing
your
chosen
template
with the
different
styles used.

Choosing a template from the Windows 95 desktop

If you know that you want to use a template to create a new Word 97 document, choosing a template directly from the Windows 95 desktop is easier than opening a blank document and then changing the template.

To view and choose a template from the Windows 95 desktop, follow these steps:

1. **Click on the Start button on the Windows 95 taskbar and then click on New Office Document.**

   The New Office Document dialog box appears, as shown in Figure 5-13.

2. **Click on one of the following tabs:**
   - Letters & Faxes
   - Memos
   - Other Documents

3. **Click on the template icon that you want to use and then click on OK.**

   Word 97 displays a new document based on your chosen template.

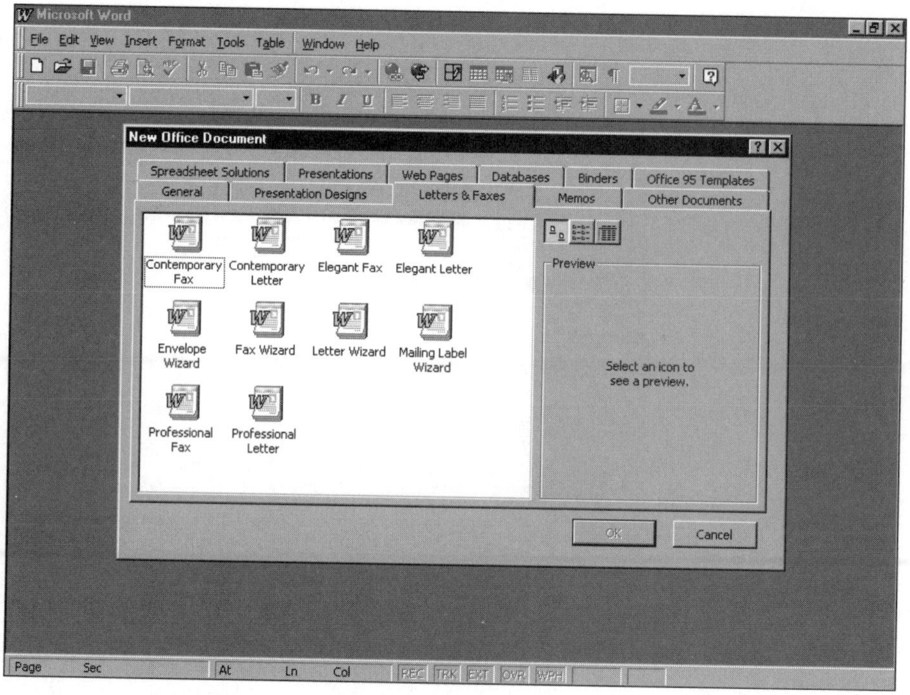

Figure 5-13:
The New
Office
Document
dialog box.

Creating a template by modifying an existing one

As though using a personal computer or Microsoft Office 97 isn't traumatizing enough, you can subject yourself to additional psychological distress by creating your own document templates from scratch.

If someone creates a template for you or if you don't really like the templates that come with Word 97, change them. Modifying an existing template is much easier than creating a new template, just as copying someone else's work is easier than doing the work yourself.

To modify an existing template, follow these steps:

1. Choose File⇨Open.

The Open dialog box appears, as shown in Figure 5-14.

2. Click on the arrow in the Files of type list box and choose Document Templates.

3. Click on the template that you want to modify and then click on Open.

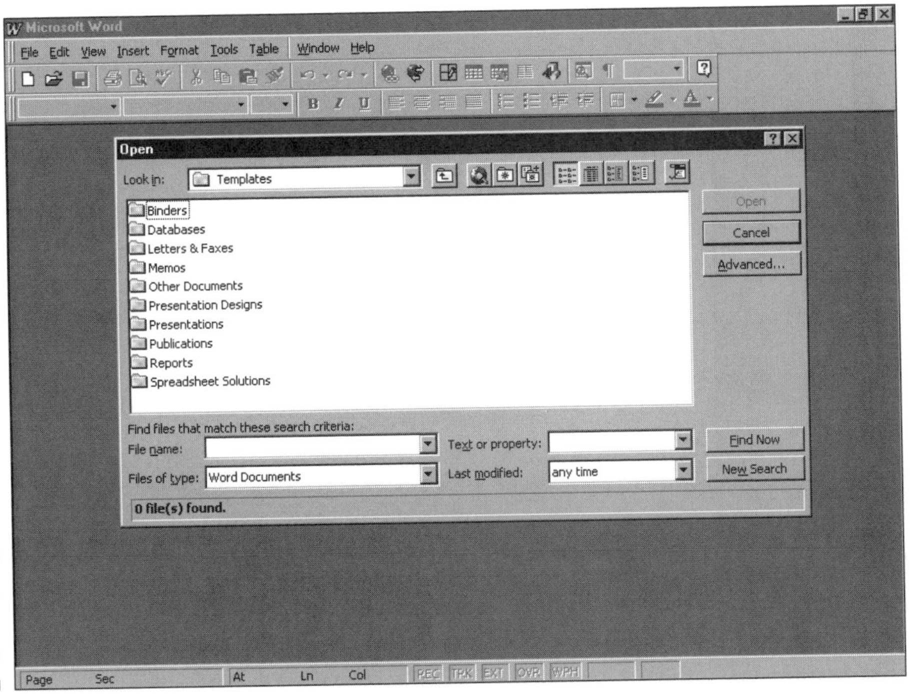

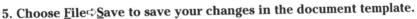

Figure 5-14:
The Open
dialog box.

You may have to search for the templates, which are usually stored in the C:\MSOffice\Templates directory. Word displays your chosen document template, as shown in Figure 5-15.

4. **Click on the style that you want to modify and change any settings, such as paragraph indentation, font, or font size.**

5. **Choose File➪Save to save your changes in the document template.**

If you choose File➪Save As in Step 5, you can create a new template, based on the original one, without changing the original template.

Deleting a template

If you find that you never use a particular document template, you can wipe it out and save a minuscule amount of hard disk space in the process.

To delete a template, load Word 97 as a separate program (not within a binder) and then follow these steps:

1. **Choose File➪Open.**

   The Open dialog box appears (refer to Figure 5-14).

2. **Click on the Files of type list box and choose Document Templates.**

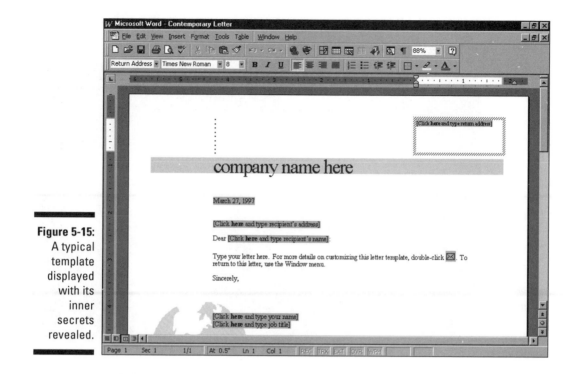

Figure 5-15:
A typical
template
displayed
with its
inner
secrets
revealed.

3. Click on the template that you want to delete and click on the right mouse button.

A pop-up menu appears, as shown in Figure 5-16.

You may have to search for the templates, which are usually stored in the C:\MSOffice\Templates directory.

4. Choose Delete.

A Confirm File Delete dialog box appears.

5. Click on Yes.

6. Click on Cancel to remove the Open dialog box.

You can also use the preceding steps to delete Word 97 documents (or any type of file) from within the Open dialog box as well.

Changing the Location of Your Templates

Microsoft Office normally stores your document templates in a default directory, such as C:\MSOffice\Templates. If this method lives up to your idea of freedom of choice, then dictatorships are probably for you. For those

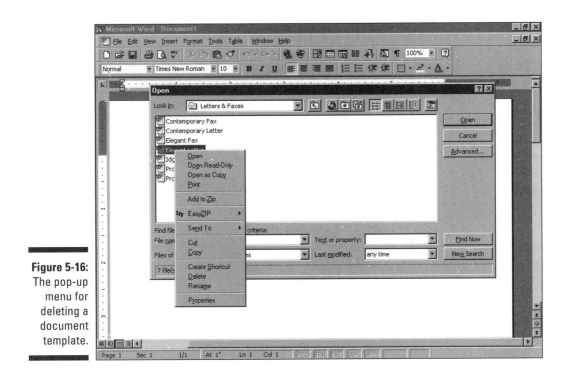

Figure 5-16:
The pop-up
menu for
deleting a
document
template.

other people who may want to make their own decisions about where to
store document templates (in case you share a computer with someone and
want to keep your templates separate), Word 97 lets you choose any drive
or directory that you want.

To change the directory in which Microsoft Office 97 stores your templates,
follow these steps:

1. **Choose Tools➪Options.**

   The Options dialog box appears.

2. **Click on the File Locations tab and highlight User Templates, as
   shown in Figure 5-17.**

3. **Click on Modify.**

   The Modify Location dialog box appears, as shown in Figure 5-18.

4. **Click on the new directory in which you want to store your document
   templates and click on OK.**

5. **Click on OK in the Options dialog box.**

If you change the directory in which you store your Word 97 document
templates, you also change the directory in which Microsoft Office 97 looks
for Excel 97, PowerPoint 97, and Office 97 templates and binders.

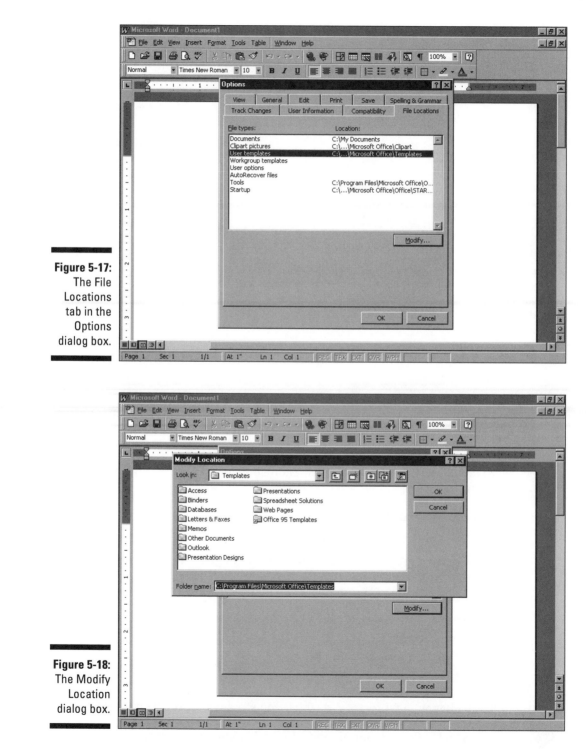

Figure 5-17:
The File Locations tab in the Options dialog box.

Figure 5-18:
The Modify Location dialog box.

Chapter 6

Making Your Own Forms

● ●

In This Chapter

▶ Filling in the blanks with a form template

▶ Making your forms more visually pleasing

▶ Giving users the opportunity to fill out forms online

▶ Distributing your online forms to others

● ●

*I*n addition to creating letters, memos, business reports, and other documents, you can also use Word 97 to create forms. Rather than create a form on your computer, print it, and force someone to use the archaic method of using a pen or pencil to fill it out, Word 97 allows you create a form so that someone can complete it electronically on a computer screen. That way, you don't have to kill a tree just to print your form on paper (that someone will probably just throw out anyway).

Creating a Form Template

Everyone has seen a tax form or an employment application form. A *form* simply provides blank spaces on which you fill in information, such as your name, the date, your telephone number, or who to contact in case you have a terrible accident at work.

You can create two types of forms:

✔ Printed forms
✔ Online forms

Printed forms involve nothing fancier than creating a form in Word 97 and then printing it for someone else to fill out. If all you want to do is create paper forms, you can stop reading this chapter and just use a typewriter and a photocopying machine to make all of your forms instead.

Online forms represent a futuristic fantasy in which we have a truly paperless office (either because society wants to conserve natural resources or because society has already plowed over all the rain forests and has no paper left anyway). With an online form, people sit at a computer and fill out your form by using a keyboard and a mouse.

Because an online form is a special Word 97 document, you may have to create a form template before you can create a form document. After you create a form template, you can create your online forms for people to fill out.

Every time you want someone to fill out your online form, you have to create a new document based on your form template. (That's why you need a form template: If you just created a form and had someone fill it out online, you would have to create a new form all over again for the next person to fill out.)

Whereas a document is a file that contains your text, a *template* is a file that defines the format for any text that appears in your document. To find out more about the wonders of templates, see Chapter 5.

To create a form template, load Word 97 as a separate program and then follow these steps:

1. Choose File⇨New.

The New dialog box appears, as shown in Figure 6-1.

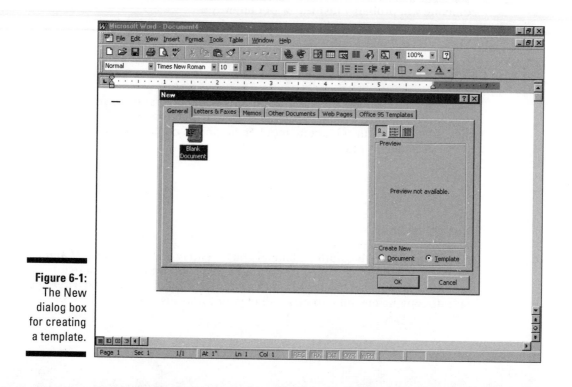

Figure 6-1:
The New dialog box for creating a template.

2. **Click on the Template radio button in the Create New group and then click on OK. Word 97 displays a blank template.**

3. **Choose File⇨Save or press Ctrl+S.**

   The Save As dialog box appears.

4. **Type a name for your form template (such as Tax Form, Invoice, or Job Application) and then click on Save.**

At this point, your form template doesn't do anything until you place text and graphics on the template.

Designing Pretty Forms

After you create a form template, you have to put text or graphics on the form so people can see and admire your form for generations to come. Most forms contain one or more of the following elements:

✔ **Text:** "Name" or "Ship to," for example

✔ **Graphics:** A company logo, for example

✔ **Fields:** Enable someone to fill out your form online

The Forms toolbar contains funny-looking buttons that let you easily design a form. To display the Forms toolbar, follow these steps:

1. **Choose View⇨Toolbars⇨Forms.**

2. **Click on Forms so that a check mark appears in front of it and then click on OK.**

   The Forms toolbar appears, as shown in Figure 6-2.

 Before you create a form in Word 97, draw the form first. That way, you can quickly design your form using paper and pencil. (You'll have to wing it because *Paper-and-Pencil Drawings For Dummies* has yet to be published.) After you know what type of information you want on your form, you can begin struggling with the process of designing your form in Word 97.

Drawing tables on a form

The basic element for designing a form is the table, which enables you to organize text, graphics, and form fields in convenient rows and columns. After you create one or more tables on your form, you can begin inserting text, graphics, and form fields, as shown in Figure 6-3.

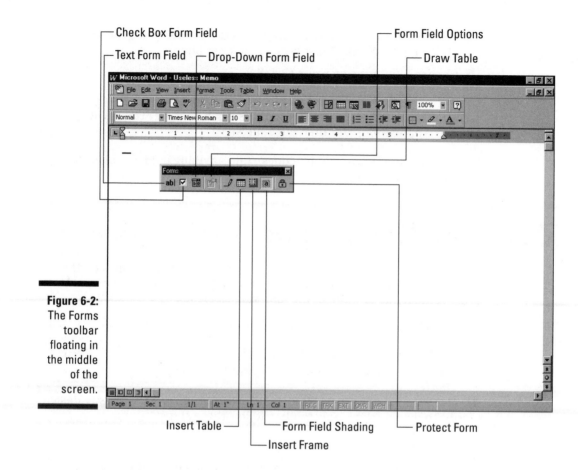

Check Box Form Field

Text Form Field Drop-Down Form Field

Form Field Options

Draw Table

Figure 6-2:
The Forms
toolbar
floating in
the middle
of the
screen.

Insert Table Form Field Shading Protect Form
Insert Frame

To draw a table on your form, follow these steps:

1. **Click on the Insert Table button on the Forms toolbar.**

   A grid appears, as shown in Figure 6-4.

2. **Move the mouse pointer over one of the grid boxes to define the size of your table.**

   For example, if you highlight the grid box in the second row and the third column, you create a table two columns wide and three columns long.

3. **Click on the left mouse button.**

   Word draws your table on the form.

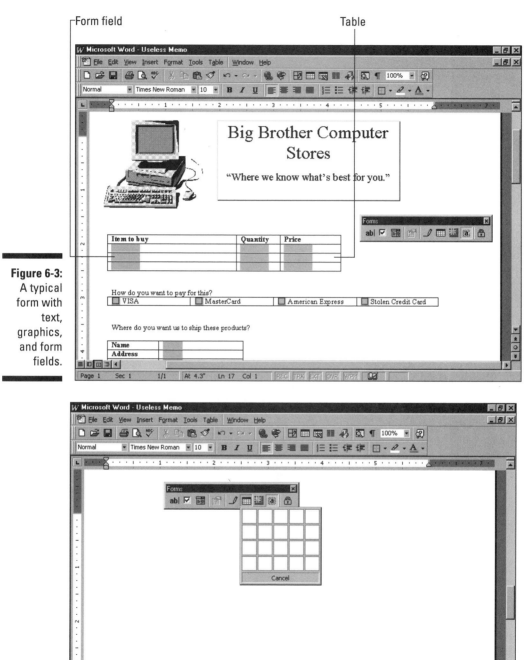

Figure 6-3:
A typical
form with
text,
graphics,
and form
fields.

Figure 6-4:
Creating a
table.

Stretching or shrinking your table

Word 97 has no sense of aesthetics, which means that, after you create a table, it probably won't be the exact size that you want. You then have to stretch or shrink its width and height to your liking.

To change the width of your table columns, follow these steps:

1. **Move the mouse pointer directly over any vertical grid line until the mouse pointer turns into two parallel lines with left- and right-pointing arrows, as shown in Figure 6-5.**

2. **Hold down the left mouse button and drag the mouse right or left.**

3. **Release the mouse button when you're happy with the width of the table column.**

If you want to change the height of a row in your table, follow these steps:

1. **Move the mouse pointer directly over any horizontal grid line until the mouse pointer turns into two parallel lines with up- and down-pointing arrows.**

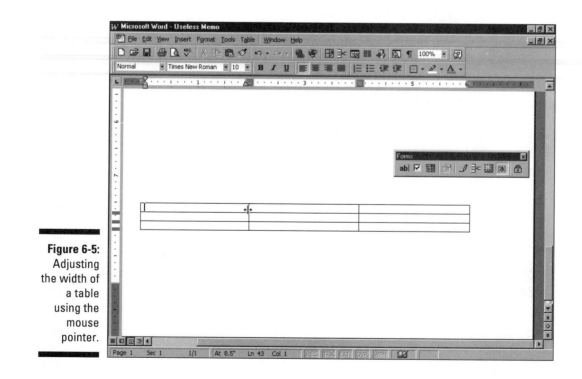

Figure 6-5:
Adjusting
the width of
a table
using the
mouse
pointer.

2. **Hold down the left mouse button and drag the mouse up or down.**

3. **Release the mouse button when you're happy with the height of the table row.**

If the mouse pointer refuses to turn into two parallel lines with up- and down-pointing arrows, you may need to switch to the Page Layout view by choosing View⇨Page Layout.

Adding a row or column

In case you didn't draw your table wide or tall enough, don't worry. Word 97 graciously allows you to add a row or column to your table at any time, even if it's filled with data.

To add a row to a table, follow these steps:

1. **Click in the row that you want to appear below your newly inserted row.**

2. **Choose Table⇨Insert Rows.**

To add a column to a table, follow these steps:

1. **Click in the column that you want to appear to the right of your newly inserted column.**

2. **Choose Table⇨Select Column.**

3. **Choose Table⇨Insert Columns.**

Deleting rows, columns, and entire tables

Like everything else in life, you may make a mistake and have to delete a row or column in your grid. Fortunately, Word 97 lets you selectively delete rows and columns. Or, you can act out your aggressive tendencies and wipe out an entire table.

If you delete a row, column, or table, you also delete any text or graphics within that row, column, or table. If you accidentally delete a row, column, or table, you can undelete it by immediately pressing Ctrl+Z.

To delete a column, follow these steps:

1. **Click in the column that you want to delete.**

2. **Choose Table⇨Select Column.**

Word 97 highlights your chosen column.

3. **Choose Table⇨Delete Columns.**

To delete a row, follow these steps:

1. **Click in the row that you want to delete.**

2. **Choose Table⇨Select Row.**

Word 97 highlights your chosen row.

3. **Choose Table⇨Delete Rows.**

To delete an entire table, follow these steps:

1. **Click anywhere inside the table that you want to delete.**

2. **Choose Table⇨Select Table.**

Word 97 highlights your entire table.

3. **Choose Edit⇨Cut or press Ctrl+X.**

Word 97 obliterates your entire table, right before your eyes.

Putting text on a form

Text typically serves two purposes:

✔ As a label to identify a field, such as "Name," "Marital Status," or "How many years did you repeat the third grade?"

✔ For nonfunctional purposes, such as displaying "We are an equal opportunity employer" at the bottom of your form.

To add text to a form, follow these simple steps (which any moron — even your boss — can understand):

1. **Click in the table row and column in which you want the text to appear.**

If you want to type text outside of a table, just move the cursor where you want the text to appear.

2. **Type your text.**

Text can appear on a form by itself or inside a table. Which method should you use? If you want to align text, putting your text in a specific row and column in a table is easier. If you don't need to align your text in any particular way, just putting it on a form without first creating a table to hold it is easier.

Placing pretty graphics on a form

Graphics usually serve no functional purpose other than to make a form look good. Common uses for graphics include displaying a company logo or decorative picture that makes your form look less like the intimidating corporate piece of paper it really is.

Three of the most common types of graphics that you can add to a Word 97 form are the following:

- ✔ Clip art images
- ✔ Graphic files created by another program
- ✔ WordArt images

Adding clip art to a form

To add a clip art graphic to a form, follow these steps:

1. **Click where you want the picture to appear.**

2. **Choose Insert⇨Picture⇨Clip Art.**

   A dialog box appears, informing you that you can see more clip art images if you have the Office 97 CD in your CD-ROM drive.

3. **Click on OK.**

   The Clip Art dialog box appears, as shown in Figure 6-6.

4. **Click on the picture that you want to add and click on Insert.**

Adding a graphic file to a form

To add graphics stored as a separate file on a floppy, hard, or compact disk, follow these steps:

1. **Click where you want the picture to appear.**

2. **Choose Insert⇨Picture⇨From File.**

   The Insert Picture dialog box appears, as shown in Figure 6-7.

3. **Click on the file that you want to display on your form and click on Insert.**

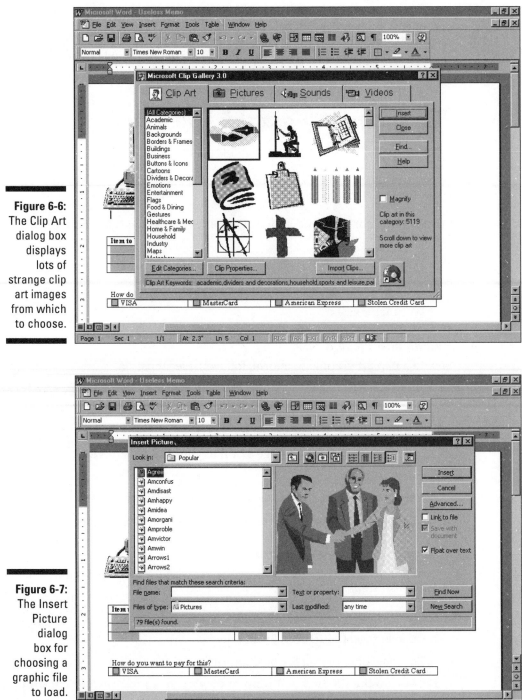

Figure 6-6:
The Clip Art
dialog box
displays
lots of
strange clip
art images
from which
to choose.

Figure 6-7:
The Insert
Picture
dialog
box for
choosing a
graphic file
to load.

Using WordArt on a form

For those creative, artistic types who like the idea of combining text with graphics, Word 97 allows you to use something called WordArt. WordArt simply displays text in a graphic form. Take a look at Figure 6-8 to get a better idea what the heck WordArt really looks like.

To use WordArt, follow these steps:

1. **Click where you want to add WordArt.**

2. **Choose Insert➪Picture➪WordArt.**

   The WordArt Gallery dialog box appears, as shown in Figure 6-8.

3. **Click on the WordArt style that you want to use and click on OK.**

   An Edit WordArt Text dialog box appears, as shown in Figure 6-9.

4. **Type your text and click on OK.**

   You may want to change the Font and Size of your text, too.

5. **Click on OK.**

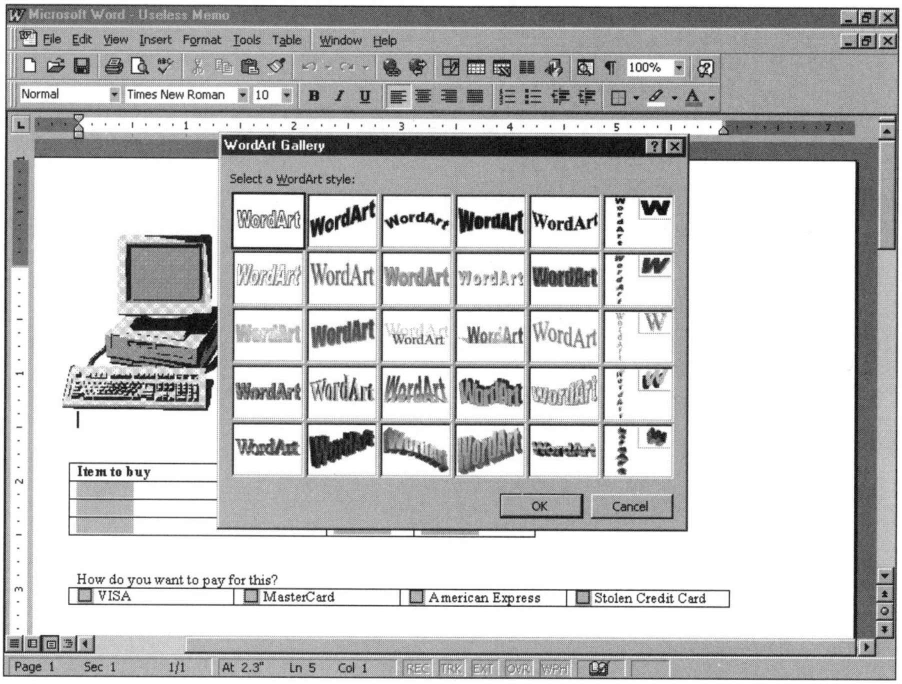

Figure 6-8:
The
WordArt
Gallery
dialog box.

Figure 6-9:
The Edit
WordArt
Text
dialog box.

Creating Online Forms with Form Fields

When you create an online form that someone can fill out by using a computer (as opposed to writing answers on a printed form), you have to use form fields. A *form field* simply displays a fill-in-the-blank space where someone can type an answer or choose from a list of answers (such as Male or Female in response to a blank asking for "Gender"). Form fields provide the only area in which someone can type anything on your online form.

You can add three types of form fields to your form:

  ✔ **Text:** Allows the user to type text such as a name or address

  ✔ **Check box:** Allows the user to choose from one or more options

  ✔ **Drop-down:** Allows the user to pick from a list of displayed options

No matter which type of form field you add, you should also type some descriptive text next to it, just so that people know which type of information the form field expects, such as "Who to contact in case of an emergency," or "Current employer."

Making a text form field

Text form fields can hold text, such as names; numbers, such as ages; dates, such as 05/06/96; or times, such as 12:34. After you know which type of information you want your text form field to display, you can also define these items:

✔ The maximum length of text to display

✔ Any default text that you want to display automatically

✔ How you want your text to appear on the screen

To put a text form field on a form, follow these steps:

1. **Click on the spot where you want the text form field to appear (inside a row and column of a table, for example).**

2. **Click on the Text Form Field icon on the Forms toolbar.**

   Word 97 immediately draws your text form field as a gray rectangle, as shown in Figure 6-10.

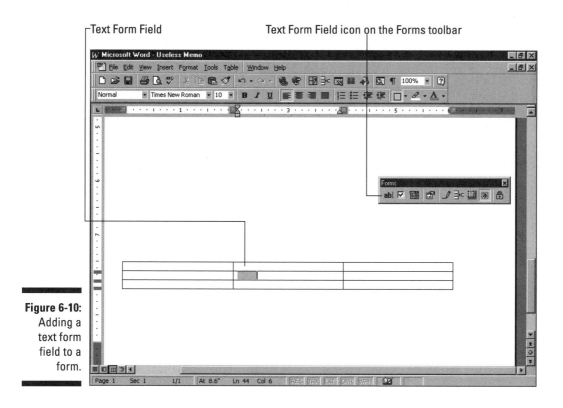

Text Form Field   Text Form Field icon on the Forms toolbar

Figure 6-10:
Adding a text form field to a form.

3. **Click on the Form Field Options button on the Forms toolbar.**

   The Text Form Field Options dialog box appears, as shown in Figure 6-11.

4. **Click on the Type list box and choose the type of text that you want to display:**

   - Regular text
   - Number
   - Date
   - Current date
   - Current time
   - Calculation

5. **Click on the Maximum length box and click on the up or down arrows to choose a maximum length of text to store in your text form field.**

6. **Click on the Default text list box and type the text that you want to appear automatically in the text form field.**

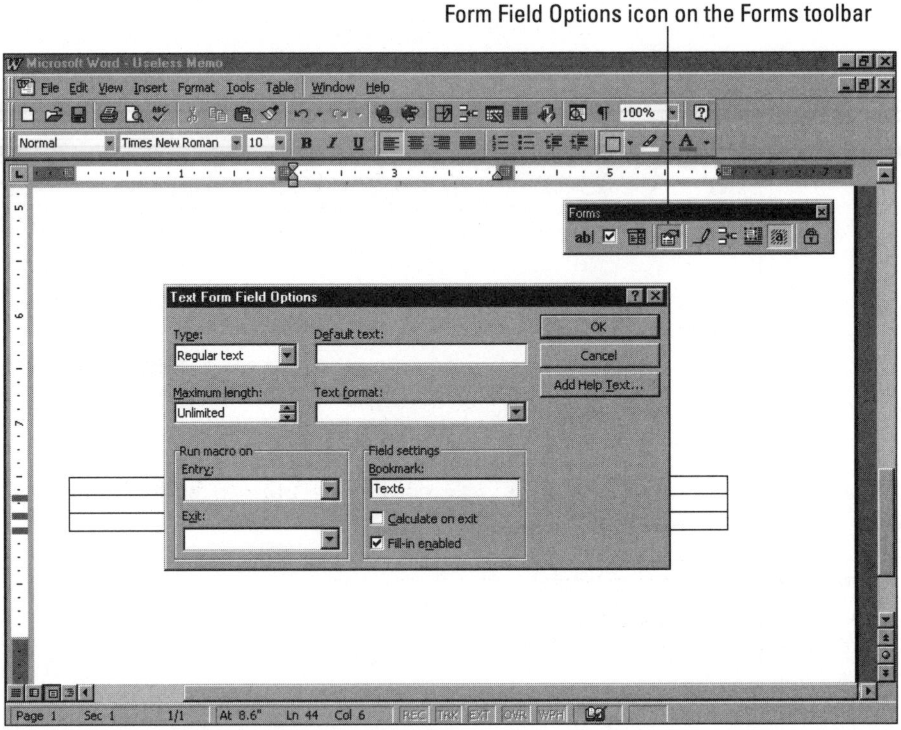

Form Field Options icon on the Forms toolbar

Figure 6-11:
The Text
Form Field
Options
dialog box.

7. **Click on the arrow in the Text format list box and choose a format in which to display your text:**

   - Uppercase

   - Lowercase

   - First capital

   - Title case

8. **Click on OK.**

Using a check box form field

Check box form fields are used for Yes or No responses, such as "Are you available for travel?" or "Do you object to drug testing?" To add a check box form field to your form, follow these steps:

1. **Click where you want the check box form field to appear (inside a row and column in a table, for example).**

2. **Click on the Check Box Form Field button on the Forms toolbar.**

   Word 97 immediately draws your check box form field as a small box, as shown in Figure 6-12.

3. **Type any descriptive next to the check box form field.**

4. **Click on the check box and then the Form Field Options button on the Forms toolbar (refer to Figure 6-11).**

   The Check Box Form Field Options dialog box appears, as shown in Figure 6-13.

5. **Click on one of the following radio buttons in the Check box size group:**

   - Auto: Allows Word 97 to choose the size of your check box

   - Exactly: Allows you to choose a point size if you want to change the size of your check box

6. **Click on one of the following radio buttons in the Default value group:**

   - Not checked

   - Checked

7. **Click on OK.**

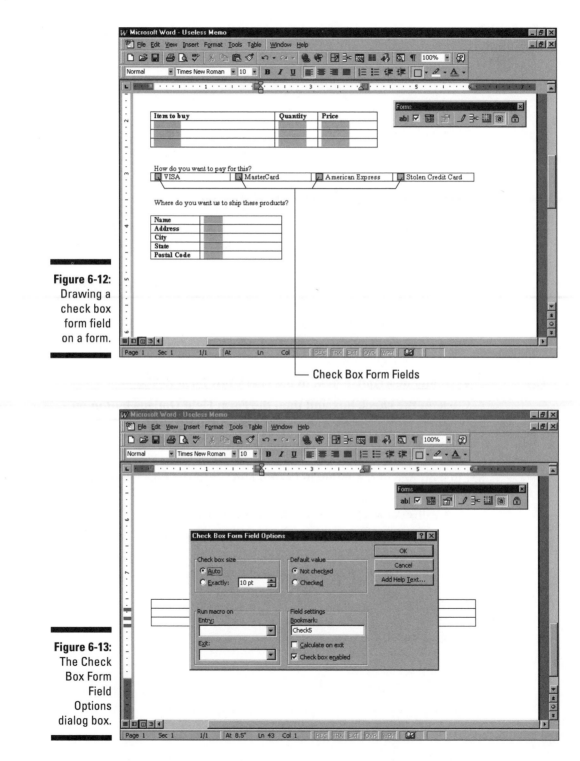

Figure 6-12:
Drawing a
check box
form field
on a form.

Check Box Form Fields

Figure 6-13:
The Check
Box Form
Field
Options
dialog box.

Creating a drop-down form field

Drop-down form fields enable users to choose from a list of acceptable answers. For example, you may have a question that asks for marital status and a drop-down form field that offers several choices, as shown in Figure 6-14.

To create a drop-down form field, follow these steps:

1. **Click where you want the drop-down form field to appear (inside a row and column in a table, for example).**

2. **Click on the Drop-Down Form Field icon on the Forms toolbar.**

   Word 97 immediately draws your drop-down form field as a gray rectangle.

3. **Click on the Form Field Options button on the Forms toolbar.**

   The Drop-Down Form Field Options dialog box appears, as shown in Figure 6-15.

4. **In the Drop-down item text box, type an item that you want to appear in the drop-down form field.**

5. **Click on A̲dd.**

   Word 97 displays your item in the I̲tems in drop-down list box.

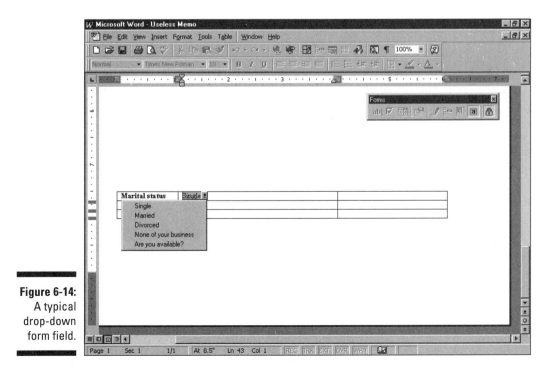

Figure 6-14:
A typical
drop-down
form field.

Drop-Down Form Field ⌐ ⌐ Form Field Options

6. Repeat Steps 4 and 5 until you've typed all the items that you want to appear in your drop-down form field.

In case you add an item that you later want to remove, click on that item and click on <u>R</u>emove.

7. Click on OK.

Adding Online Help

After carefully designing your form and placing your text, check box, or drop-down form fields in the most aesthetically pleasing positions possible, you're almost ready to use your form template to create online forms.

After you design your form, however, you may want to add help prompts to assist any clueless users. For example, if a user has no idea which type of information a particular text form field should contain, pressing F1 can make your online form display an explanation on the status bar at the bottom of the screen or in a dialog box, as shown in Figure 6-16.

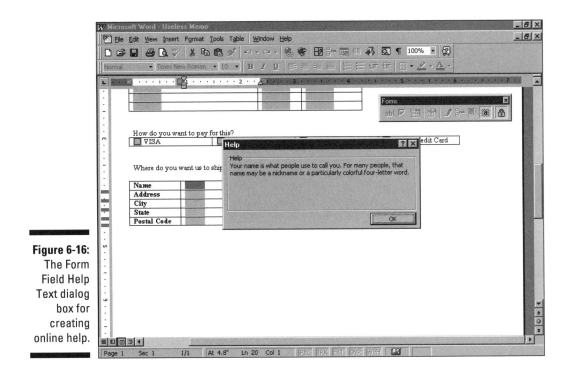

Figure 6-16:
The Form
Field Help
Text dialog
box for
creating
online help.

To create online help for your form fields, follow these steps:

1. **Click on the form field where you want to add online help.**

2. **Click on the Form Field Options icon on the Forms toolbar.**

   The Form Field Options dialog box appears.

3. **Click on Add Help Text.**

   The Form Field Help Text dialog box appears (refer to Figure 6-16).

4. **Click on the Status Bar tab and then click on the Type your own radio button.**

5. **Type any helpful suggestions that you want to appear on the status bar.**

6. **Click on the Help Key (F1) tab and then click on the Type your own radio button.**

7. **Type any helpful suggestions that you want to appear in the help dialog box if the user presses F1.**

   A sample help prompt dialog box appears in Figure 6-17.

8. **Click on OK twice.**

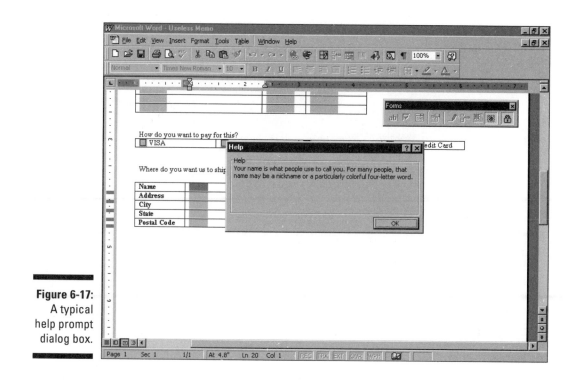

Figure 6-17:
A typical
help prompt
dialog box.

Sharing Your Online Forms

After you've spent countless hours designing your form to perfection, you'll eventually want to distribute it to others so that they can use it, too. When you're absolutely sure that your form template is finished, it's time to save and protect your form template.

Protecting your form template means that when you create a document (online form) based on your form template, the document allows users to type information only in form fields and nowhere else.

When you protect a form, you can test your form to make sure that all the form fields work correctly.

Saving and protecting your precious form templates

To save and protect a form template, follow these steps:

1. **Click on the Protect Form icon on the Forms toolbar.**

2. **Choose File⇨Save, or press Ctrl+S.**

3. **Choose File⇨Close.**

Creating an online form from a form template

After you save and protect a form template, you can create your online forms based on your form template.

Every time that you create a new document based on a form template, you're creating a brand-new form that someone can fill out on the computer. The form template never changes, no matter how many online forms you may create from it. To find out more about templates, see Chapter 5.

To create an online form based on a form template, follow these steps:

1. **Choose File⇨New.**

   The New dialog box appears.

2. **Click on the form template that you want to use and then click on OK.**

   Word 97 displays your form.

Filling out an online form

An online form looks exactly like a form template. The main difference is that you can't type text anywhere except in different form fields. Although you can use a mouse to fill out an online form, you may eventually have to use the keyboard to type certain information, such as a name, address, or naughty word that will get you in trouble if you send it over the Internet.

In case you don't like using your mouse to move the cursor to different form fields, Table 6-1 lists the keystroke commands that you can use to navigate around an online form.

Table 6-1	Keystroke Commands for Navigating Around an Online Form
Keystroke command	**What It Does**
Right arrow or Tab	Moves the cursor to the next form field
Left arrow or Shift+Tab	Moves the cursor to the preceding form field
Spacebar or X	Selects (or deselects) a check box form field
F4 or Alt+down arrow	Displays items in a drop-down form field
F1	Displays a Help dialog box (if you created text for it)

For users to be able to view and fill out an online form, they must use Word 97 to load the online form. If they don't have Word 97, they can't view or fill out your online form — so there!

Chapter 7

Creating an Index and Table of Contents

*B*ecause writing can be a pain in the neck for most people, anything that can make the job easier is welcome. Short of doing all the writing for you, Word 97 does the next best thing: It provides special features to help you create an index and a table of contents (almost) automatically.

After all, which would you rather do: Write a 300-page document and go back, page by page, to create a table of contents and index yourself, or have Word 97 create the table of contents and index as you write?

If you prefer to let Word 97 do the difficult work for you, continue reading. If you prefer to do everything yourself, why did you bother getting a computer?

Making Your Very Own Index

An *index* simply organizes your document's main ideas by page number. That way, people can quickly find what they're looking for without having to read your entire document. Because many people don't like reading anyway, indexes can be a great way to encourage people to at least browse through your text (and maybe even increase our national literacy rate in the process).

To create an index, you must decide:

✔ The words or topics that you want to include in your index

✔ The page numbers on which each word or topic appears

✔ A visually pleasing format to display your index

Indexing a book or document is an art in itself. Although Word 97 can make the task of indexing easier, it can't help you decide which words, topics, or synonyms to add to your index.

Selecting words and individual page numbers

Most indexes list topics and individual page numbers, such as:

Stinger hand-held missile, 49

In this example, "Stinger hand-held missile" is the index entry and "49" is the page number on which it appears.

To mark words for an index, follow these steps:

1. **Highlight the word or words that you want to appear in your index.**

2. **Press Alt+Shift+X.**

   A Mark Index Entry dialog box appears, as shown in Figure 7-1. Your highlighted word or words appear in the Main entry box.

3. **Edit the word or words in the Main ₑntry box so that they look the way you want in your index.**

4. **In the Ṣubentry box, type any index subentries that you want to include.**

   An example of a subentry is as follows:

   > projects, 49
   >
   > avoiding them, 78, 129
   >
   > examples of, 52
   >
   > stopping, 2

   In this case "projects" is the entry and "avoiding them," "examples of," and "stopping" are subentries.

5. **Click on one of the following radio buttons:**

   • **Ċross-reference:** Directs readers to a related index entry

   • **Current Ṗage:** Lists the current page for your index entry

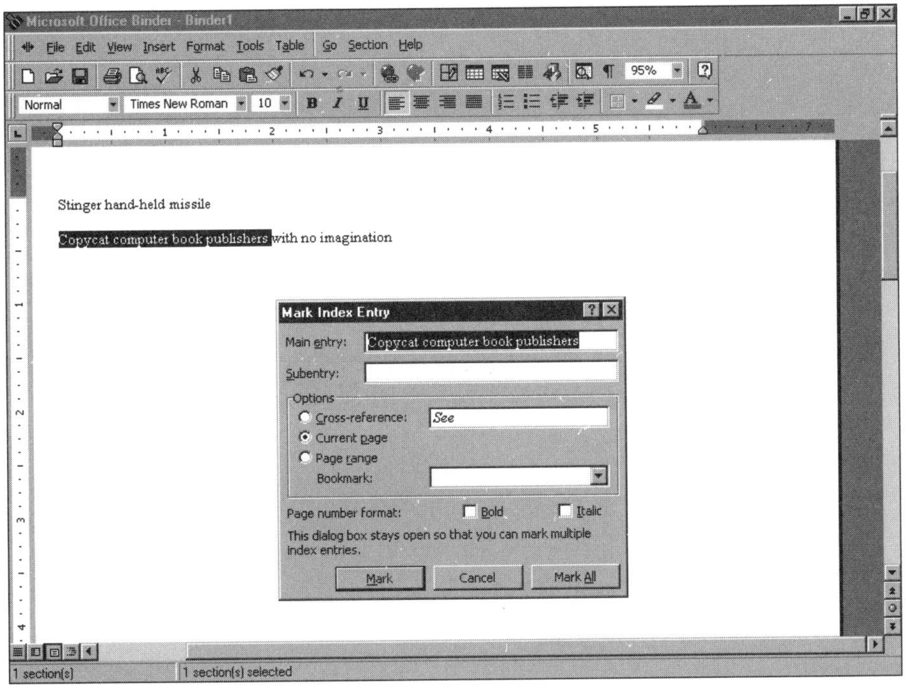

Figure 7-1:
The Mark
Index Entry
dialog box
adding a
word to an
index.

6. **Click on Mark.**

   Word 97 marks your selected word or words by inserting an index entry next to them, as shown in Figure 7-2.

7. **Repeat Steps 1–6 until you've marked all the words that you want to appear in your index.**

8. **Click on Close.**

Marking words and page ranges for your index

Most of the time, the words that you select for your index appear only on a single page. But sometimes an index topic may span two or more pages, as shown in this example:

CIA, selling Stinger missiles illegally, 58–63

In this example, "CIA, selling Stinger missiles illegally" is the index entry, and "58–63" represents the page range in which users can find the index entry.

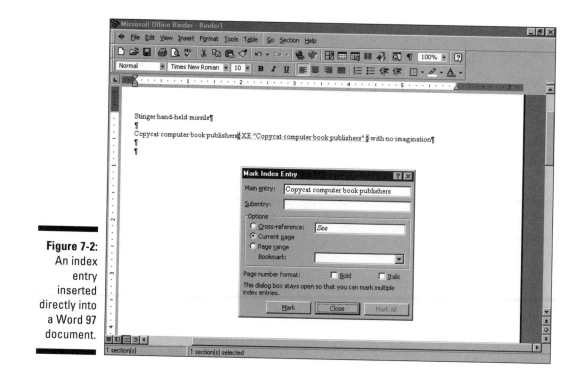

Figure 7-2:
An index
entry
inserted
directly into
a Word 97
document.

When you want to index a page range, you must follow slightly different steps to include your chosen index topic and its page range in your index.

To mark words and page ranges for an index, follow these steps:

1. **Highlight the text (spanning one or more pages) that you want to include in your index.**

2. **Choose Insert⇨Bookmark.**

   A Bookmark dialog box appears, as shown in Figure 7-3.

3. **Type a name for your bookmark in the Bookmark Name box.**

   Your bookmark name must be a single word, so be creative and make it descriptive, too.

4. **Click on Add.**

5. **Highlight the word or words that you want to appear in your index.**

6. **Press Alt+Shift+X.**

   A Mark Index Entry dialog box appears (refer to Figure 7-1). Your highlighted word or words appear in the Main entry box.

7. **Edit the word or words in the Main entry box so that they appear the way you want in your index.**

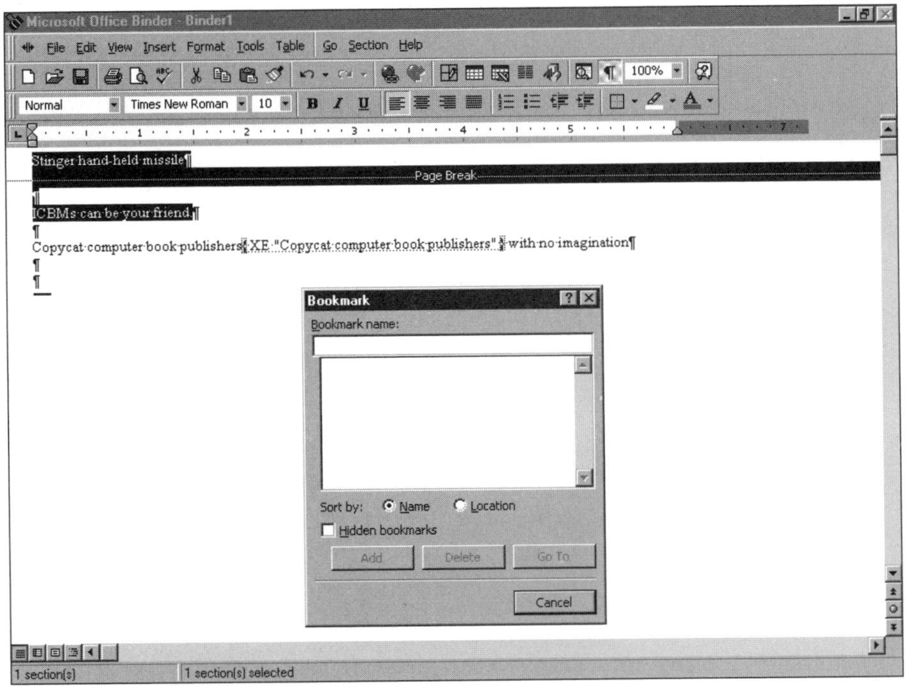

Figure 7-3:
The
Bookmark
dialog box.

8. **In the Subentry box, type any index subentries that you want to include.**

9. **Click on the Page range radio button.**

10. **Click on the Bookmark list box and choose the bookmark name that you created in Step 3.**

11. **Click on Mark.**

    Word 97 marks your selected word or words by inserting an index entry next to them.

12. **Repeat Steps 1–11 until you've marked all the words that you want to appear in your index.**

13. **Click on Close.**

Displaying your index in print

Every time that you mark a word or words to appear in your index, Word 97 stores the words in its tiny electronic brain. When you finish choosing all your index entries, you're ready to display the index in print so that you can take a look at it.

Of course, Word 97 wouldn't seem like a real program if it didn't offer you a billion different options that most people never use. When you create an index, Word 97 bombards you with multiple ways to guarantee that your index looks nice.

Before you can create an index, you have to mark at least one word that you want to include in your index.

This list shows some of the available options that affect the look of your index:

- ✔ **Index format:** Determines the overall look of your index, such as the fonts used for the letter headings

- ✔ **Alignment of page numbers:** Determines how page numbers appear next to an index entry (such as "Dog food, 4" or aligned on the far right side of the page)

- ✔ **Number of columns used:** Determines how many columns used to display your index

To choose the appearance of an index, follow these steps:

1. **Move the cursor to the spot where you want your index to appear.**

2. **Choose Insert⇨Index and Tables.**

   An Index and Tables dialog box appears, as shown in Figure 7-4.

3. **Click on the Index tab.**

4. **In the Formats list box, click on the format that you want (Modern or Bulleted, for example).**

   In the Preview box, Word 97 shows you what your index will look like.

5. **Click on either the Indented or Run-in radio button in the Type group.**

6. **If you want to right-align your index page numbers, click on the Right align page numbers check box.**

7. **Click in the Columns list box and choose the number of columns that you want.**

8. **Click on the Tab leader box and choose a tab leader.**

   Note: The Tab leader box is available only if you clicked in the Right align page numbers check box in Step 6.

9. **Click on OK.**

   Word 97 cheerfully displays your index on the screen for you to admire.

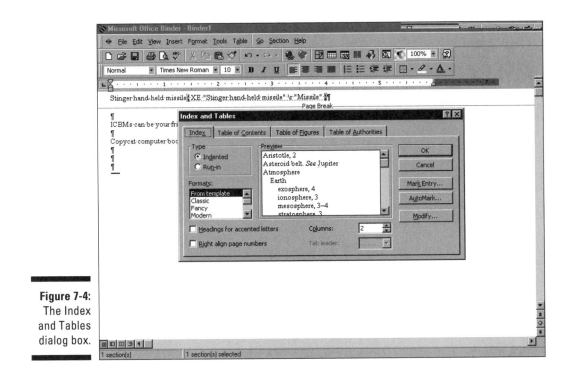

Figure 7-4:
The Index
and Tables
dialog box.

You can create an index only in the same document that contains the word or words that you select to appear in your index. After Word 97 creates your index and you're absolutely sure that none of the index entries will change, you can cut the index and paste it into a new document.

Creating an index (almost) automatically

Because computers are supposed to make our lives easier, you may be happy to know that Word 97 can create an index almost automatically, with just a little help from you. Before Word 97 can perform its automatic indexing magic for you, you must first create a separate document that contains two lists of words.

One list of words must contain the entries that you want to appear in your index. The second list of words must contain the actual words (or phrases) stored in your Word 97 document that you want to mark as an index entry.

You might have these two lists, for example:

CIA   Central Intelligence Agency

DIA   Defense Intelligence Agency

EIEIO	Farmer's Intelligence Agency
annoying people	Telemarketers
Copycat	A well-known rival computer-book publisher

Because the words that you type in both lists are case sensitive, if Word 97 finds the string "Annoying people," it won't store it in the index. Word 97 stores that string in your index only if it finds it typed exactly as "annoying people" (in lowercase letters).

Using the preceding list as a guideline, Word 97 searches through your document for all occurrences of the words that appear in the list on the left. Whenever Word 97 finds the phrase "annoying people," for example, it looks in the list on the right to determine how to store this entry in your index.

Assuming that "CIA" appears on pages 59–65, "DIA" appears on page 90, "EIEIO"appears on page 493, "annoying people" appears on pages 78 and 90, and "Copycat" appears on page 746, Word 97 creates the following index for you:

Central Intelligence Agency, 59–65

Defense Intelligence Agency, 90

Farmer's Intelligence Agency, 493

Telemarketers, 78, 90

A well-known rival computer-book publisher, 746

To create a list of words so that Word 97 knows what to look for in your document and how to store those words in your index, load Word 97 as a separate program and then follow these steps:

1. **Choose File⇨New, or press Ctrl+N.**

   A new blank document appears.

2. **Choose Table⇨Insert Table.**

   An Insert Table dialog box appears. Make sure that the dialog box displays the settings for creating a table composed of two columns. (The number of rows should equal the number of entries that you want to type.)

3. **Click on OK.**

   Word 97 creates a table two columns wide.

4. **In the left column, type the word or words (CIA, for example) that you want Word 97 to search for in your document.**

5. **In the right column in the same row, type the way you want this word or words to appear in your index (Central Intelligence Agency, for example).**

6. **Repeat Steps 4 and 5 until you create a list that contains all the words that you want Word 97 to search for and store in your index.**

   You may need to add rows as necessary by choosing Table⇨Insert Rows.

7. **Choose File⇨Save.**

   A Save As dialog box appears.

8. **Type a name for your document in the File name box and then click on Save.**

9. **Switch to the document that contains the words that you want to index.**

10. **Choose Insert⇨Index and Tables.**

    An Index and Tables dialog box appears (refer to Figure 7-4).

11. **Click on the Index tab.**

12. **Click on AutoMark.**

    An Open Index AutoMark File dialog box appears, as shown in Figure 7-5.

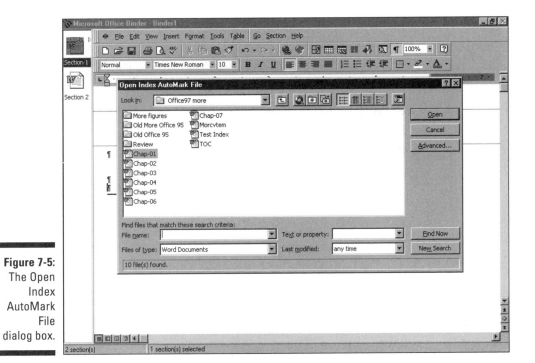

Figure 7-5:
The Open
Index
AutoMark
File
dialog box.

13. **Click on the Word 97 document that contains your two lists of words that you created in Steps 1–6, and then click on Open.**

    Word 97 silently marks all your selected words.

14. **Move the cursor to the spot where you want the index to appear.**

15. **Choose Insert➪Index and Tables.**

    The Index and Tables dialog box appears (refer to Figure 7-4).

16. **Make any changes to the format of your index, and click on OK when you're done.**

    Word 97 magically displays your automatically created index.

Updating your index

Ideally, you should create your index last, after you have already written your entire text. But because human beings don't always like being told what they can do and when they can do it, Word 97 can accommodate those people who insist on changing their text after they've already created an index. Whenever you create an index, you can always update it if you need to add another word or two to your index.

To update an index, follow these steps:

1. **Highlight the word or words that you want to add to your index.**

2. **Press Alt+Shift+X.**

    A Mark Index Entry dialog box appears (refer to Figure 7-1).

3. **Click on Mark.**

4. **Repeat Steps 1–3 for every word that you want to add to your index.**

5. **Click on Close.**

6. **Choose Insert➪Index and Tables.**

    The Index and Tables dialog box appears (refer to Figure 7-4).

7. **Click on the Index tab.**

8. **Click on OK.**

    A dialog box appears and asks whether you want to replace your selected index.

9. **Click on Yes.**

    Word 97 updates your index. Aren't computers wonderful?

Word 97 can create an index based on words stored in only one document. If you want to create an index based on words stored in separate documents, you must create a master document. To learn more about master documents, look in the section "Working with Master Documents" later in this chapter.

Creating a Table of Contents

An index enables readers to quickly find separate topics that may be scattered throughout a large document, such as a book or magazine. A *table of contents,* however, enables your readers to see which topics your book or document discusses. Like an index, a table of contents also lists page numbers so that readers can quickly find what they're looking for without having to read the entire manuscript.

Before you can create a table of contents, you must first create headings within your document (such as the heading for this section, "Creating a Table of Contents") and format them by using Word 97's style feature.

Using Word 97's built-in styles to format headings

To quickly format headings to create a table of contents, use the built-in styles Heading 1, Heading 2, and Heading 3, as shown in Figure 7-6.

To create a table of contents, follow these steps:

1. **Format all the document headings that you want to include in your table of contents by using Heading 1, Heading 2, or Heading 3.**

2. **Move the cursor in the document where you want the table of contents to appear, such as at the beginning of your document.**

3. **Choose Insert⇨Index and Tables.**

4. **Click on the Table of Contents tab, as shown in Figure 7-7.**

5. **In the Formats list box, click on the format that you want, such as Modern or Fancy.**

   Word 97 shows you in the Preview box what your table of contents will look like.

6. **If you want to show page numbers, click on the Show page numbers check box.**

   Because you're working with the table of contents, this option really shouldn't be available, but Word 97 wants to give you a choice anyway. After all, what good is a table of contents without page numbers?

Figure 7-6:
Heading
styles
appear in
the Style
list box.

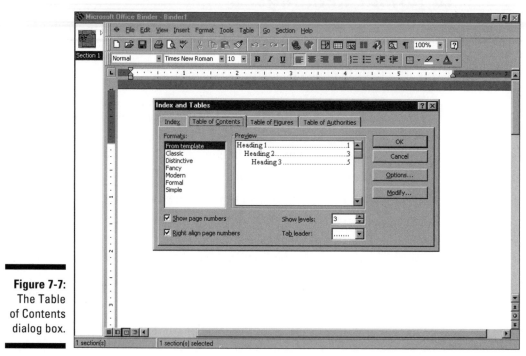

Figure 7-7:
The Table
of Contents
dialog box.

7. **Click on the <u>R</u>ight align page numbers check box if you want your index page numbers to be right-aligned on the page.**

8. **Click on the Show <u>l</u>evels list box and choose how many levels you want to display.**

   Word 97 gives you the option of creating a detailed table of contents or a more general one. For example, you may want to create a detailed table of contents using the Heading 1, Heading 2, and Heading 3 styles. Or you may want a more general table of contents that uses only Heading 1 styles. If you want to include only Heading 1, Heading 2, and Heading 3 styles in your table of contents, choose 3.

9. **Click on the Ta<u>b</u> leader box and then choose a tab leader.**

   A tab leader consists of text or symbols that appear between a table of contents entry and its page number, as in this example:

   Euphemisms for Confusing the Public...............................23

   In this case, the tab leaders are the periods (dots) between the phrase "Euphemisms for Confusing the Public" and the page number 23.

   Note: If you don't choose to right-align page numbers, the Tab leader box appears dimmed.

10. **Click on OK.**

    In the blink of an eye (or longer, depending on the speed of your computer), Word 97 creates your table of contents for you, as shown in Figure 7-8.

Using your own styles to format headings

For stubborn nonconformists (if you're a nonconformist, you probably shouldn't even be using any Microsoft programs in the first place), you can also create a table of contents based on your own styles rather than the Heading 1, Heading 2, and Heading 3 styles all the time. (To learn how to create your own styles, see Chapter 5.)

To create a table of contents based on your own styles, follow these steps:

1. **Format all the document headings by using your own particular styles.**

2. **Place the cursor in the document on the spot where you want the table of contents to be inserted (such as at the beginning of your document).**

3. **Choose <u>I</u>nsert⇨In<u>d</u>ex and Tables.**

4. **Click on the Table of <u>C</u>ontents tab to display the tab (refer to Figure 7-7).**

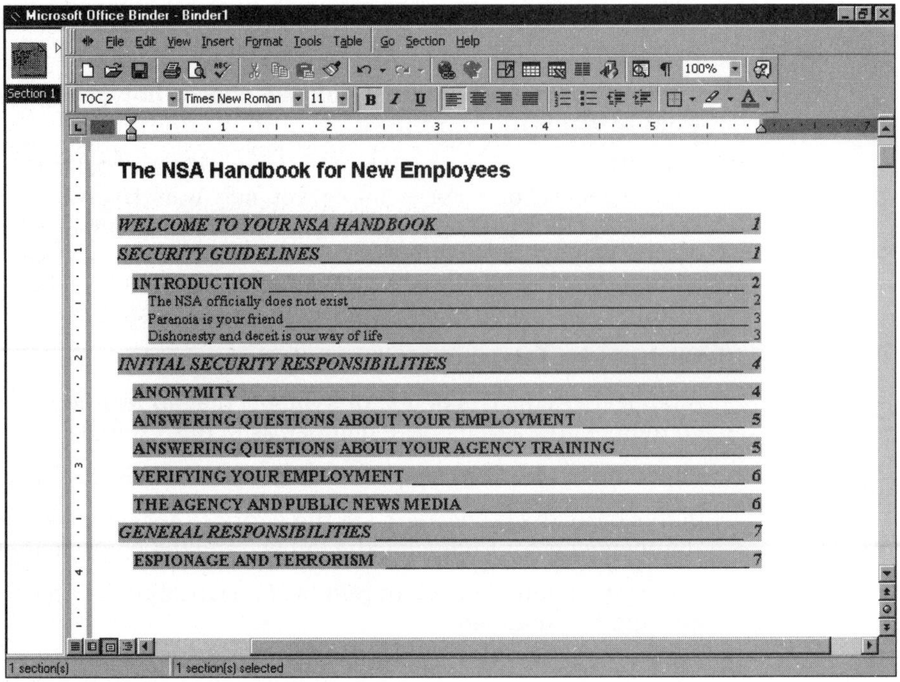

Figure 7-8:
A typical
table of
contents
automatically
created by
Word 97's
minuscule
brain.

5. **In the Formats list box, click on the format that you want, such as Modern or Fancy.**

   Word 97 shows you in the Preview box what your table of contents will look like.

6. **If you want to show page numbers, click on the Show page numbers check box.**

7. **Click on the Right align page numbers check box if you want to right-align the page numbers in your table of contents.**

8. **Click on the Show levels list box and choose how many levels you want to display.**

9. **Click on the Tab leader box and choose a tab leader.**

   Note: If you don't choose to right-align page numbers, the Tab leader box appears dimmed.

10. **Click on Options.**

    A Table of Contents Options dialog box appears, as shown in Figure 7-9.

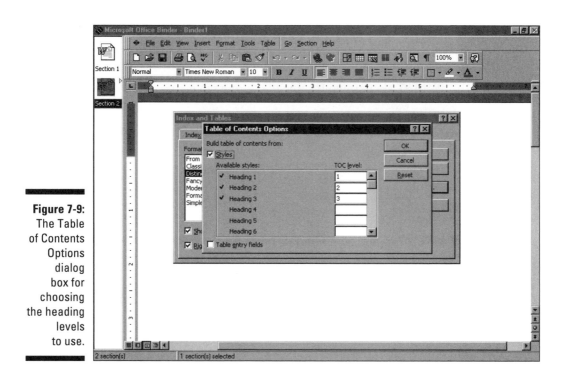

Figure 7-9:
The Table
of Contents
Options
dialog
box for
choosing
the heading
levels
to use.

11. Scroll through the styles displayed in the Available Styles box and type a number in the TOC Level box to the right.

For example, type 1 to make the style appear as a main heading in your table of contents, or type 2 to make the style appear as a subheading.

12. Click on OK.

The Index and Tables dialog box appears again.

13. Click on OK.

Word 97 creates your table of contents for you.

Updating your table of contents

Whenever you add or delete a heading or text that may change the page numbering, you must update your table of contents. To update a table of contents, follow these steps:

1. Make any changes to your document or headings.

2. Move the cursor to anywhere inside the table of contents that you want to update.

Word 97 displays your table of contents in a shade of gray.

3. Press F9.

An Update Table of Contents dialog box appears, as shown in Figure 7-10.

4. Click on one of the following radio buttons:

- Update page numbers only
- Update entire table

5. Click on OK.

Word 97 updates your entire table of contents.

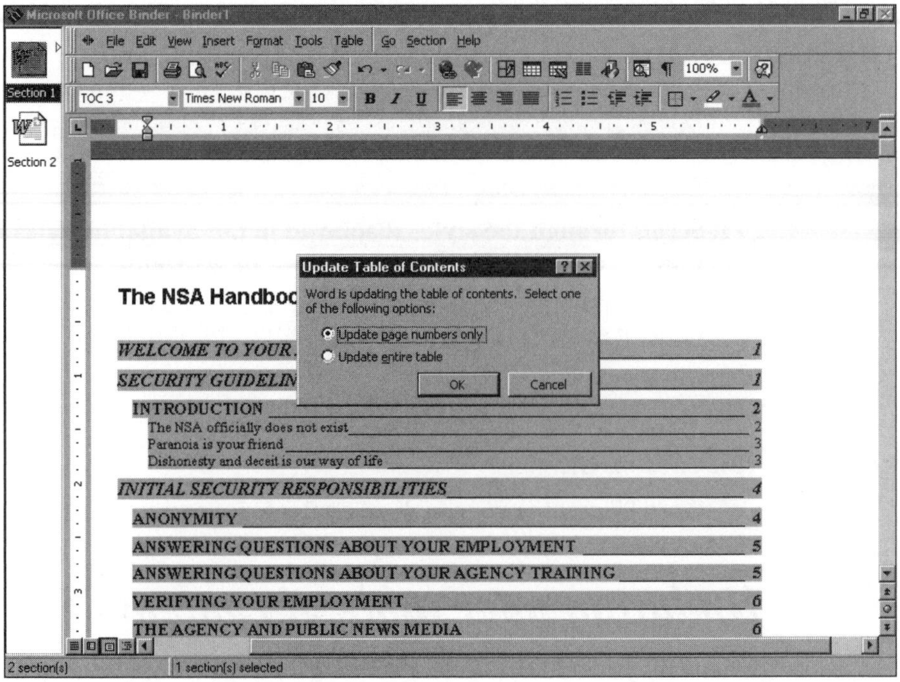

Figure 7-10: The Table of Contents Options dialog box for choosing the heading levels to use.

Working with Master Documents

Most people write with Word 97 in one of three ways:

✔ Cram everything into a single document

✔ Store chapters or logical sections in separate documents

✔ Store chapters or logical sections in separate documents with all documents saved in a single Office 97 binder

If you cram everything into a single document, you might not be able to edit the document easily. If you store chapters in separate documents (as separate files or as separate sections within an Office 97 binder), you can't easily create an index or table of contents. To help deal with this apparent paradox, Word 97 offers the mysterious master document.

A *master document* is an outline stored in a separate file. Every heading in the outline acts as a link to another file, called a *subdocument,* as shown in Figure 7-11.

By using a master document, you can organize, view, and edit individual subdocuments separately or display them in one long, continuous document so that you can create an index or table of contents.

Any changes that you make to a master document appear automatically in the appropriate linked subdocument. Likewise, any changes that you make to a linked subdocument appear automatically in the master document.

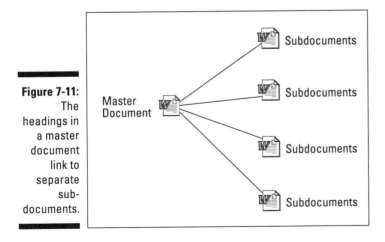

Figure 7-11:
The headings in a master document link to separate sub-documents.

By using a master document, you can create an accurate index and table of contents while keeping text stored in separate files for easy editing and viewing.

Creating a master document from scratch

The best time to create a master document is when you want to write a large document (a novel, a business report, or a legal paper suing someone for no apparent reason other than money, for example) and you want to store parts of it in separate files.

By first creating a master document, you can outline your ideas before you waste time writing aimlessly. After you organize your ideas, you can begin writing.

If you want to create a master document within an Office 97 binder, choose Section⇨Vie<u>w</u> outside first. You cannot store subdocuments within a binder because Office 97 cannot update subdocuments stored inside a binder.

To create a master document, load Word 97 as a separate program and then follow these steps:

1. **Choose <u>V</u>iew⇨<u>M</u>aster Document.**

   Word 97 displays the Outlining and Master Document toolbar, as shown in Figure 7-12.

2. **Type one or more headings using the Heading 1 style (refer to Figure 7-12), where each heading can represent a chapter title.**

3. **Move the cursor to the heading that represents the subdocument you want to create.**

4. **Click on the Create Subdocument icon.**

   Word 97 draws a gray box around your heading and displays a subdocument icon, as shown in Figure 7-13.

5. **Double-click on the subdocument icon that appears in the upper-left corner of the gray box around your chosen heading.**

   Word 97 displays your subdocument all by itself, as shown in Figure 7-14.

6. **Type the text that you want to store in your subdocument.**

7. **Choose <u>F</u>ile⇨<u>C</u>lose when you finish typing your text.**

   Word 97 displays a dialog box, asking you whether you want to save your document.

8. **Click on <u>Y</u>es.**

   A Save As dialog box appears.

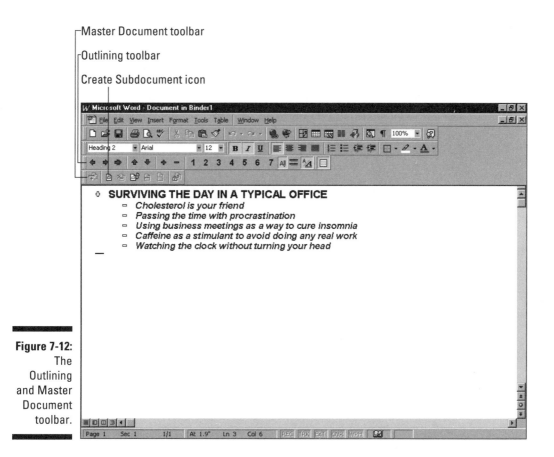

Master Document toolbar

Outlining toolbar

Create Subdocument icon

⬦ **SURVIVING THE DAY IN A TYPICAL OFFICE**
- *Cholesterol is your friend*
- *Passing the time with procrastination*
- *Using business meetings as a way to cure insomnia*
- *Caffeine as a stimulant to avoid doing any real work*
- *Watching the clock without turning your head*

Figure 7-12:
The
Outlining
and Master
Document
toolbar.

9. **Type a name for your subdocument in the File name box and then click on Save.**

   Word 97 displays your subdocument's text in the master document, as shown in Figure 7-15.

10. **Repeat Steps 3–9 for every heading that you want to convert into a subdocument.**

Creating a master document from an existing document

Rather than create a master document from scratch, you can also convert an existing document into a master document. This trick can be handy if you've already created a huge document and suddenly decide that it's getting too bulky to edit and read easily.

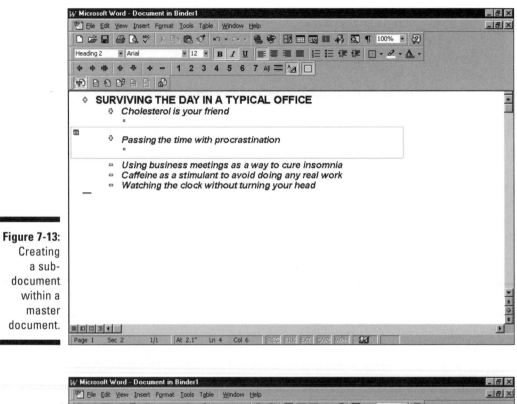

Figure 7-13:
Creating
a sub-
document
within a
master
document.

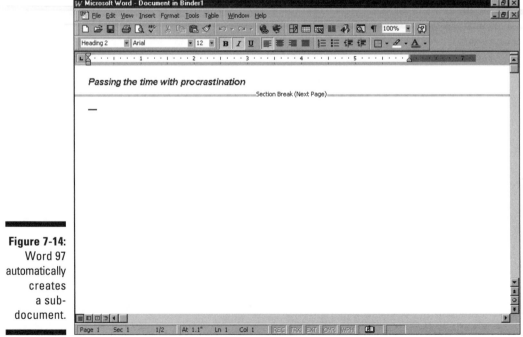

Figure 7-14:
Word 97
automatically
creates
a sub-
document.

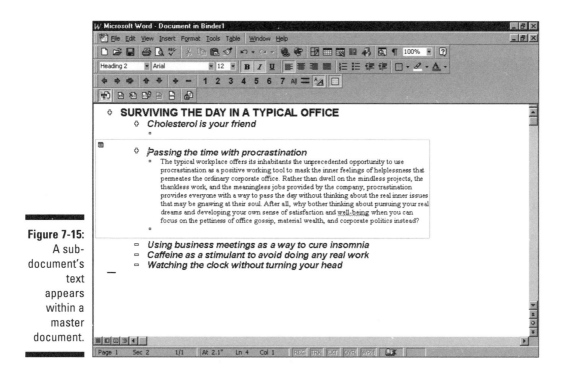

Figure 7-15:
A sub-
document's
text
appears
within a
master
document.

To convert an existing document into a master document, follow these steps:

1. **Open the document that you want to convert into a master document.**

2. **Click on a heading in your document and format it by using the Heading 1, Heading 2, Heading 3, or Heading 4 style.**

3. **Choose View⇨Master Document.**

4. **Highlight the heading and the text that you want to convert into a subdocument.**

5. **Click on the Create Subdocument icon on the Master Document toolbar.**

6. **Double-click on the subdocument icon that appears in the upper-left corner of the gray box around your chosen heading.**

   Word 97 displays the text and heading that you chose in Step 4 as a separate Word 97 document.

7. **Choose File⇨Save.**

   A Save dialog box appears.

8. **Type a name for your master document in the File name box and then click on Save.**

Editing a subdocument

After you create a master document and one or more subdocuments, you may want to edit the text stored in a subdocument. You can edit a subdocument in three ways:

- ✔ Open the subdocument by itself in a separate window.
- ✔ Open the master document and display the subdocument text within the master document.
- ✔ Open the master document and display the text of all the subdocuments in your master document.

No matter which method you choose, any changes that you make to the subdocument appear automatically in the master document.

Editing a subdocument by itself

If you just want to edit the text of a subdocument but don't necessarily care to see the rest of your master document, save yourself some time and edit the subdocument by itself.

To edit a subdocument by itself, follow these steps:

1. **Choose File⇨Open.**

   An Open dialog box appears.

2. **Click on the subdocument that you want to edit and then click on Open.**

3. **Edit your subdocument.**

4. **Choose File⇨Save.**

5. **Choose File⇨Close.**

Editing a subdocument within a master document

Sometimes you may want to view your subdocument within the context of your master document. That way, you can see how the text in your subdocument fits in with the organization of the rest of your master document.

To edit a subdocument from within a master document, follow these steps:

1. **Choose Section⇨View Outside.**

   Skip this step if you're using Word 97 outside of a binder.

2. **Choose File⇨Open.**

   An Open dialog box appears.

3. **Click on the master document containing the subdocument that you want to edit and then click on Open.**

Word 97 displays your subdocument text as a hyperlink, as shown in Figure 7-16.

4. **Click on the hyperlink representing the subdocument that you want to edit. Word 97 displays your subdocument.**

5. **Edit the subdocument text that you want to change.**

6. **Choose File⇨Save.**

7. **Choose File⇨Exit.**

Viewing and editing all your subdocument text at once

When you have multiple subdocuments crammed within a master document, you can also view them all as one continuous string of text, which can be as long as several hundred pages.

To view (and edit) all of your subdocuments within a master document, follow these steps:

1. **Choose Section⇨View Outside.**

   Skip this step if you're using Word 97 outside of a binder.

Expand Subdocuments

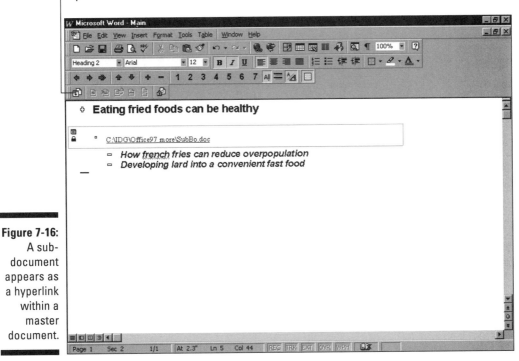

Figure 7-16:
A sub-document appears as a hyperlink within a master document.

2. **Choose File⇨Open.**

   An Open dialog box appears.

3. **Click on the master document containing the subdocument that you want to edit and then click on Open.**

4. **Click on the Expand Subdocuments icon in the Master Document toolbar.**

   Word 97 displays all your hyperlinks as actual text, as shown in Figure 7-17.

5. **Edit any of your subdocument text.**

6. **Choose File⇨Save.**

Collapse Subdocuments icon

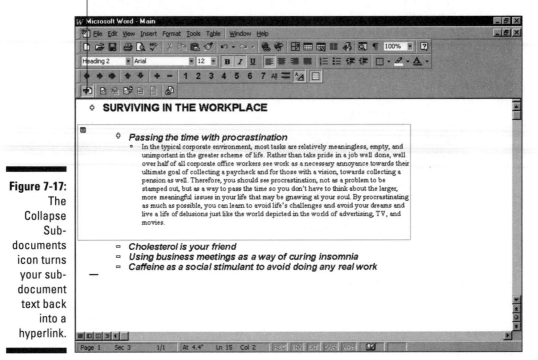

Figure 7-17: The Collapse Subdocuments icon turns your subdocument text back into a hyperlink.

Chapter 8

Sharing Word 97 Documents

• •

• •

*W*riting can be tough, which explains why so many people can make a living working as an editor, script doctor, or co-author. To help you write the best possible text, you may want to share your Word 97 documents with others.

You can print out your entire document so that somebody else can edit it by hand, but this is the computer generation in which printing anything on paper is considered archaic. As a more futuristic alternative, just copy your Word 97 documents on a floppy disk or through a network and allow someone to mark up your Word 97 documents electronically.

By sharing Word 97 files on disk, on a network, or even through the Internet, you can view, edit, and comment on text without wasting paper printing it. When your document looks perfect, you can print it out for the world to see.

Typing Comments

When you print a letter or report, you can pass it around to others and allow them to mark it up with comments about how to improve or alter your text. When you share Word 97 documents on a floppy disk or online over a modem or network, however, you don't have the convenience of scribbling comments in the side margins of a page.

At the simplest level, you could just shove your comments right into the middle of the text with something like, "Hey, this last sentence doesn't make any sense!" Interrupting the flow of text is not only intrusive but also forces you to go through the trouble of deleting all those comments, one by one. Only then can you print a clean copy of your text.

As a simpler solution, Word 97 offers you the chance to type comments directly into a Word 97 document. These comments don't appear in the document itself but in a separate window that you can hide, display, or print at any time.

If you convert (export) a Word 97 document to another file format (WordPerfect, for example), you may lose all your annotations.

Creating a comment

Rather than display your comments intrusively right in the middle of existing text, Word 97 puts a comment mark in the text so that other people can see it. To view the actual comment text itself, you have to display the comment in a separate window at the bottom of your screen, as shown in Figure 8-1.

Comment mark

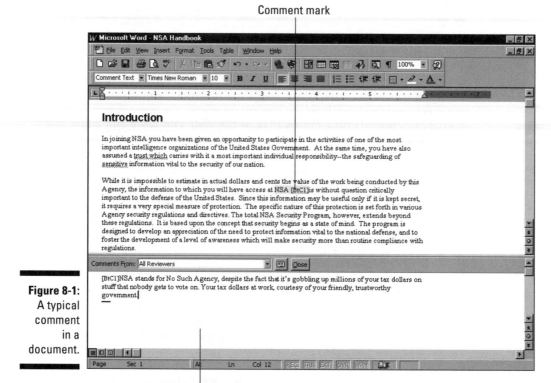

Figure 8-1:
A typical
comment
in a
document.

Comment window

Each comment contains two parts:

- ✔ **The initials of the person who created the annotation.** Word 97 creates the comment abbreviation from the name that you gave it when you installed Microsoft Office 97 on your computer. If you entered your name in Microsoft Office 97 as Bo the Cat, your initials are BtC. To change your initials, choose Tools⇨Options, click on the User Information tab, and type your new initials in the Initials box.

- ✔ **The sequential number of the annotation.** If you entered your name as Bo the Cat in Microsoft Office 97, your first comment would appear as [BtC1], your second comment would appear as [BtC2], and so on.

To create a comment, follow these steps:

1. **Move the cursor to the location in the text where you want to add a comment.**

2. **Choose Insert⇨Comment.**

   At the cursor location in your text, Word places an annotation mark and displays the annotation window at the bottom of your screen (refer to Figure 8-1).

3. **Type your comments in the annotation window.**

4. **Repeat Steps 1–3 for each comment that you want to add.**

5. **Click on the Close button when you finish.**

Believe it or not, if you have a microphone attached to your computer, you can add a sound file as part of your comment. All you have to do is create a sound file (for example, your voice saying, "Bob, you're fired!") and then store it as a comment. If someone reading your comment has a sound card on his or her computer, that person can hear your voice blaring through the speakers. Of course, not many people are likely to add sound comments, but it's nice to know that Microsoft is spending its time creating features that bring us closer to science fiction.

Viewing comments

After you or your fellow co-writers have inserted comments throughout a Word 97 document, you might want to read their comments. That way, you can follow their advice or (more likely) ignore their comments altogether.

To view comments buried within a document, follow these steps:

1. **Choose View⇨Comments.**

   Word 97 displays comment marks in the document and opens the comment window at the bottom of the screen.

2. Click on the comment mark for the comment that you want to view.

Word 97 politely displays the comment in the comment window. If you want to view comments from a certain reviewer, click in the Comment From list box in the comment window and choose that reviewer's initials.

3. Click on the Close button when you finish viewing the comments.

If a document has no comments buried in its text, the Comments command in the View menu appears dimmed.

Deleting a comment

Comments are meant to be temporary. After all, you don't have to store a comment in a document after you respond to the comment.

To delete a comment, follow these steps:

1. Choose View⇨Comments.

Word 97 displays any comment marks littered throughout the document and opens the comment window at the bottom of the screen.

2. Highlight the comment mark that corresponds to the comment that you want to wipe out.

3. Press Delete or Backspace.

This action deletes the comment mark along with the comment in the comment window.

4. Click on Close.

Printing a document with comments

Occasionally, you may want to print your document with comments so that you can see all of the comments at one time. To print all of the comments buried within a document, follow these steps:

1. Choose Tools⇨Options.

The Options dialog box appears.

2. Click on the Print tab.

3. Click on the Comments check box in the Include with document group.

4. Click on OK.

The next time that you print your document, Word 97 will also print your comments along with the rest of the document text.

Tracking Changes in Your Text

Comments are great for jotting down ideas or suggestions, but what if you want to get right into the text and modify it yourself? With paper copies of text, you can *mark up* the text (make revision marks) with a red pen, indicating where to delete, add, or rearrange words. With Word 97, you can also indicate where you delete, add, or rearrange words in your text file.

On a paper copy of your marked-up text, you can easily see your revision marks. Word 97, however, normally doesn't let you see the original text that you cross out and modify. If you want to modify text and still be able to view the original text *and* your revisions, Word 97 enables you to track any changes made to a document.

If you convert (export) a Word 97 document to another file format (WordPerfect, for example), Word 97 can't track any changes in the text.

Tracking your document changes

When you track changes in a document, the original text appears in one color and any modifications (deletions or additions) appear in a different color. That way, you can see what someone may have added and what he or she may have deleted.

To tell Word 97 to track changes, follow these steps:

1. **Choose Tools⇨Track Changes⇨Highlight Changes.**

   The Highlight Changes dialog box appears, as shown in Figure 8-2.

2. **Click in the Track changes while editing check box so that a check mark appears.**

3. **Click on Options.**

   The Options dialog box appears, shown in Figure 8-3, with these options available for customizing the appearance of your revised text:

   - **Inserted text:** Choose the color and appearance of any new text that you add.

   - **Deleted text:** Choose the color and appearance of any text that you delete.

   - **Changed formatting:** Choose the color and appearance of any text that you reformat.

   - **Changed lines:** Choose the color and appearance of the revision marks that appear in the margins of your document. Revision lines help you easily locate revised text.

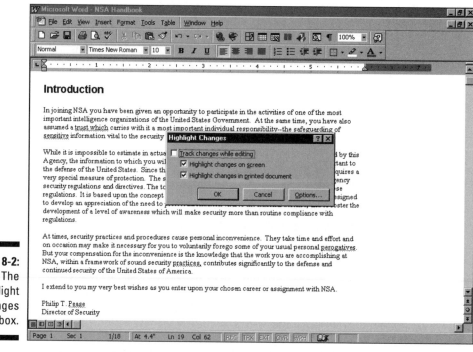

Figure 8-2:
The Highlight Changes dialog box.

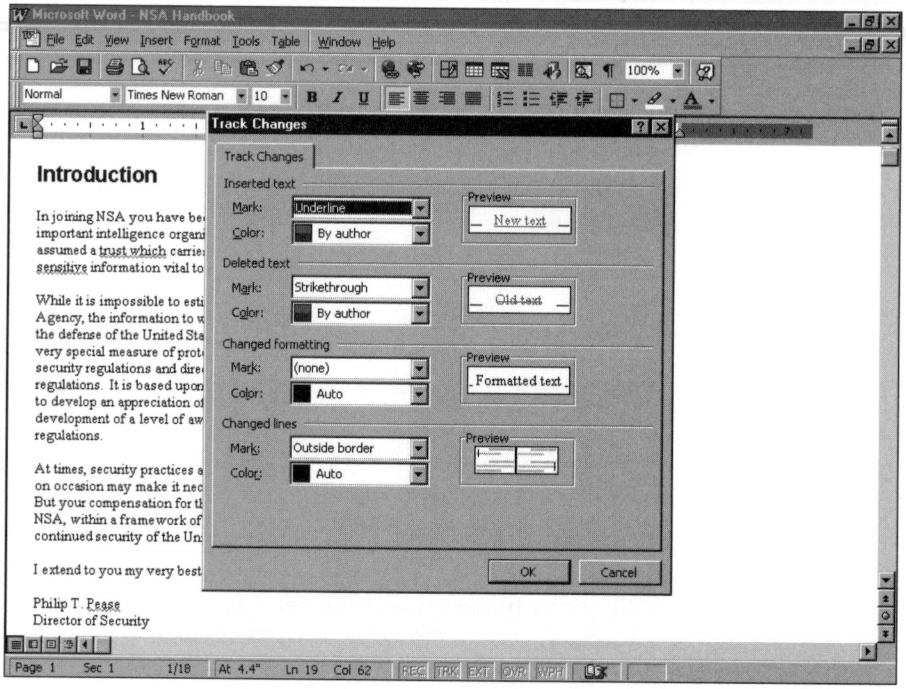

Figure 8-3:
The Track Changes dialog box.

4. **Customize the way that Word 97 displays the color and appearance of inserted text, deleted text, and changed lines.**

   For example, you can make inserted text appear red with an underline or make deleted text appear yellow with strikethrough.

5. **Click on OK twice.**

   From now on, every time you add, delete, copy, or move text, Word 97 displays the original text and the new text in the colors and appearance that you chose in Step 4. Figure 8-4 shows what a document with multiple revision marks looks like.

Reviewing your changes

After an editor, co-worker, or critic has littered your document with changes, you can review the document and selectively accept or reject each change. To review changes made to your document one by one, follow these steps:

1. **Press Ctrl+Home to move the cursor to the top of your document.**

2. **Choose Tools➪Track Changes➪Accept or Reject Changes.**

   The Accept or Reject Changes dialog box appears, as shown in Figure 8-5.

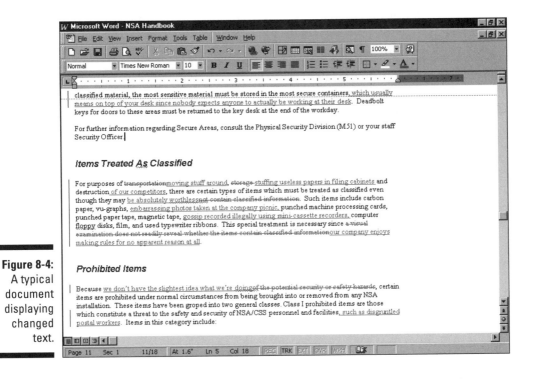

Figure 8-4:
A typical document displaying changed text.

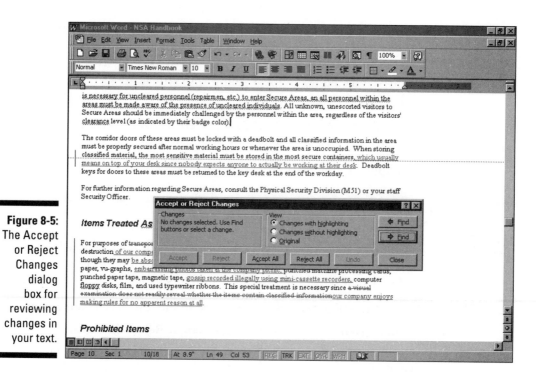

Figure 8-5:
The Accept
or Reject
Changes
dialog
box for
reviewing
changes in
your text.

3. **Click on the Find button (that's the Find button with the arrow pointing to the right).**

   Word 97 highlights the first change that it finds.

4. **Click on Accept or Reject.**

   If you click on Accept, Word 97 displays any added text as part of your document without color or underlining. If you click on Reject, the changed text disappears as if someone had never typed it.

5. **Repeat Steps 3–4 for each change that you want to review.**

6. **Click on Close.**

Accepting (or rejecting) changed text all at once

In case you're feeling lazy or you have complete confidence (or no confidence) in the person who added or modified text within your document, you can accept (or reject) all changes at one time.

To accept or reject all changed text in a document without first reviewing them, follow these steps:

1. **Choose Tools➪Track Changes➪Accept or Reject Changes.**

   The Accept or Reject Changes dialog box appears (refer to Figure 8-5).

2. **Click on Accept All or Reject All.**

   A dialog box appears asking whether you're sure that you know what you're doing.

3. **Click on Yes.**

4. **Click on Close.**

If you accept or reject all your revision marks and suddenly change your mind, press Ctrl+Z to immediately cancel the preceding four steps.

Comparing Documents

In an ideal world, people would share a single Word 97 document and type any comments or changes in the text. In the real world, though, people often make two or more copies of the same document and then wind up with separate comments and modified text separated throughout multiple copies of the same document.

If this has happened to you, use Word 97's fancy new feature to compare two documents and see what differences might exist. Then, combine your two separate documents into a single document.

To compare two documents, follow these steps:

1. **Load the first document that you want to compare.**

2. **Choose Tools➪Track Changes➪Compare Documents.**

   A Select File to Compare With Current Document dialog box appears.

3. **Click on the document that you want to compare with the currently displayed document and click on Open.**

   Word 97 displays the changes between the two documents, as shown in Figure 8-6.

4. **Choose Tools➪Track Changes➪Accept or Reject Changes.**

   The Accept or Reject Changes dialog box appears (refer to Figure 8-5).

5. **Click on the Find button (that's the Find button with the arrow pointing to the right).**

   Word 97 highlights the first change that it finds.

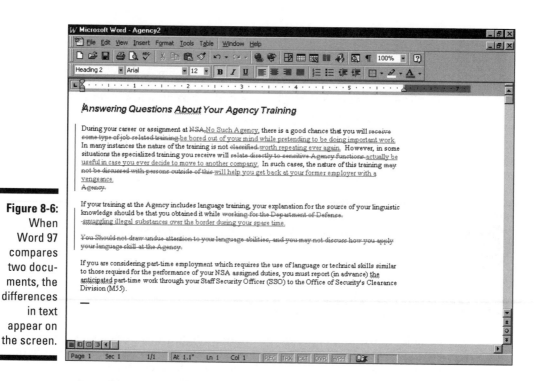

Figure 8-6:
When
Word 97
compares
two docu-
ments, the
differences
in text
appear on
the screen.

6. Click on Accept or Reject.

If you click on Accept, Word 97 displays any added text as part of your document without color or underlining. If you click on Reject, the changed text disappears as if no one had ever typed it.

7. Repeat Steps 5–6 for each change that you want to review.

8. Click on Close.

After you consolidate any changes in a single document, you may want to delete all copies of that document to avoid the scenario of someone making changes to an older version of your document by mistake.

Part III
Number Crunching with Microsoft Excel 97

In this part . . .

Everyone loves money, yet most people hate math (which may explain why most people don't have much money). To turn your computer into a calculating machine, Excel 97 enables you to use one of its many built-in functions to solve complicated calculations.

Functions are simply formulas that someone already has written for you (and verified to make sure that they work correctly). By using built-in functions you can save yourself the time and trouble of creating worksheets by yourself.

Because neither computers nor people are perfect, Excel 97 provides auditing features to help you verify that your worksheets actually calculate numbers correctly. This part of the book shows you how to verify the accuracy of your worksheets, as well as how to create maps out of your data so that you can impress your boss (even if you don't have the slightest idea of what you're doing otherwise).

Chapter 9

Changing the Appearance of Your Worksheets

. . . .

In This Chapter

▶ Changing the way Excel 97 works

▶ Hiding rows and columns

▶ Freezing rows and columns

. . . .

*N*obody likes being told what to do, which explains why many people don't like school. In the same manner, many software programs provide little flexibility on how the application looks, works, or acts.

If you don't like the way your new program works, you may find out the hard way that you just blew several hundred dollars, an hour or two trying to learn the program, and several megabytes of your precious hard disk space.

Fortunately, Excel 97 doesn't rely on this fixed-in-stone approach to software usage. Instead, Excel 97 lets you mold program features just as if they were putty in your hands. By customizing program features, you can personalize your copy of Excel 97, which has the added advantage of confusing the living daylights out of someone who tries to use your computer without your permission.

Excel was originally written as a Macintosh spreadsheet program and quickly overtook the spreadsheet competition. Microsoft then wrote a version of Excel for Windows, which soon became even more popular than the mighty Lotus 1-2-3 spreadsheet application. This history lesson has nothing to do with customizing Excel 97, but it's kind of neat to know this stuff anyway.

Changing the Way Excel 97 Works and Looks

Because the way Excel 97 works and looks can affect the way that you use the program, take a little time to customize some of the more obscure features in Excel 97. That way, you can make your copy of Excel 97 more comfortable to use.

Saving files automatically

To make saving your files easier, Excel 97 can periodically save your files without you even thinking about it. If you forget to save your file, Excel 97 shrugs its shoulders, rolls its eyes, and saves the file for you, all on its own.

You can save your files automatically if you use Excel 97 as a separate program. If you use Excel 97 within a binder, you won't be able to turn on this automatic file-saving feature.

To make Excel 97 save your files automatically, follow these steps:

1. **Choose Tools⇨Add-Ins.**

   The Add-Ins dialog box appears, as shown in Figure 9-1.

2. **Click in the AutoSave check box so that a check mark appears, and click on OK.**

3. **Choose Tools⇨AutoSave.**

   An AutoSave dialog box appears, as shown in Figure 9-2.

4. **Click in the Automatic Save Every check box so that a check mark appears.**

5. **In the Minutes text box, type the time interval for Excel 97 to automatically save your file (such as every 6 minutes).**

6. **Click on OK.**

   If you want Excel 97 to save all open workbooks, click on the Save All Open Workbooks radio button. If you just want to save the workbook that you're using at the time, click on the Save Active Workbook Only radio button.

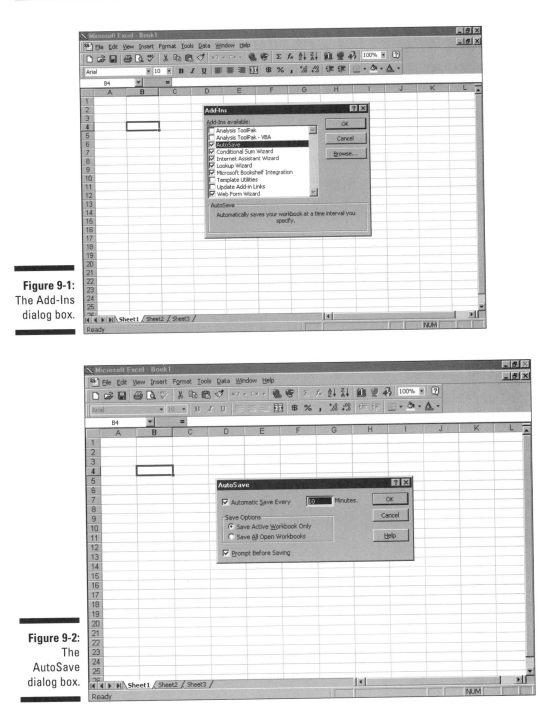

Figure 9-1:
The Add-Ins
dialog box.

Figure 9-2:
The
AutoSave
dialog box.

Where did I put that file?

Office 97 normally saves your files in the `C:\Mydocuments` directory. So, the next time you forget where you stored your file, look in that directory first. You may want to store your files in a different directory, however.

To tell Excel 97 to store your files in a different directory, follow these steps:

1. **Choose Tools⇨Options.**

2. **Click on the General tab, as shown in Figure 9-3.**

3. **Click on the Default file location box and type the name of the directory where you want Excel 97 to store your files.**

   For example, type **c:\secret stuff** in the Default file location box.

4. **Click on OK.**

   From now on, Excel 97 will use the new default file location that you specified in Step 3.

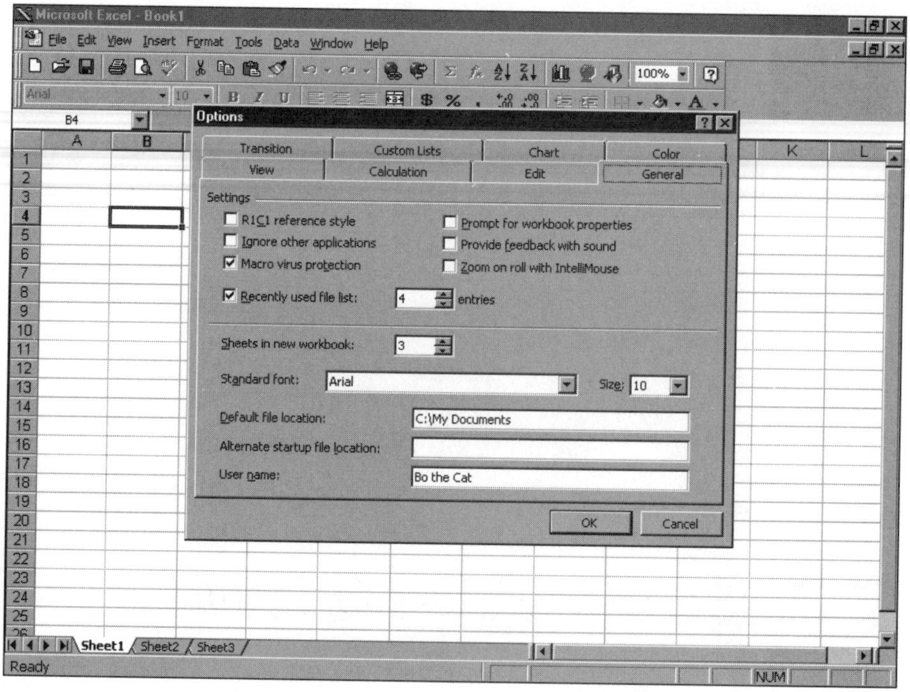

Figure 9-3:
The General tab in the Options dialog box.

Messing Around with the Appearance of Excel 97

To help you adapt to Excel 97 (and to encourage users of rival spreadsheets to defect to Excel 97), Microsoft makes customizing the look of Excel 97 easy. You can modify the font and text size to make your screens easier to read, and you can customize the way that Excel labels its columns.

Playing with fonts

Unless you specify otherwise, Excel 97 displays text in the Arial font at 10-point size. Although this font is fine for most people, you may want to choose a different font (for aesthetic reasons) or a different point size (to make your numbers easier to see, in case the tiny 10-point size is too small for you).

To change the font and point size of text displayed in Excel 97, follow these steps:

1. **Choose Tools▷Options.**

2. **Click on the General tab (refer to Figure 9-3).**

3. **Click on the Standard font list box and select the font that you want to use.**

   For example, choose Courier in the Standard font list box.

4. **Click on the Size list box and select the point size that you want to use.**

   For example, choose 15 in the Size list box.

5. **Click on OK.**

You may have to experiment to find the font and point size that looks best to you; Excel 97 won't actually display your new font and point size until you click on OK and exit the Options dialog box. Aren't computers doing a wonderful job of making your life easier?

Labeling columns by number

Excel 97 labels its columns with letters and its rows with numbers. For example, cell A3 is located in the first column (A) and the third row (3). Some other spreadsheets (with which you may be more familiar) may label both columns *and* rows with numbers, however. If you prefer to label your columns with numbers, simply customize the label.

To label columns with numbers instead of letters, follow these steps:

1. **Choose Tools⇨Options.**

2. **Click on the General Tab (refer to Figure 9-3).**

3. **Click on the R1C1 radio button in the Reference Style group.**

   The R1C1 radio button tells Excel 97, "I want all my columns to be labeled with numbers from now on."

4. **Click on OK.**

   Excel 97 immediately labels all your columns with numbers rather than letters.

Changing Your Point of View

How you view something can affect how well you learn from it. You can stare at a wall-sized listing of financial numbers that are scattered all over the place and not learn anything at all. But if you look at only a small portion of that same listing of numbers, you may be able to get a better idea of your company's financial picture.

Fortunately, Excel 97 gives you the option to view your worksheets in different ways. At the simplest level, this option enables you to read your worksheets more easily. On a more advanced level, flexibility in viewing your worksheets can help you evaluate what your numbers really mean.

Hiding rows and columns on a worksheet

Unless you create simple worksheets that can fit onto a single computer screen, you normally won't be able to see an entire worksheet at one time. Rather than force you to tediously scroll up, down, right, or left (and risk missing some important connections among your numbers), Excel 97 can selectively hide and display rows and columns. Figure 9-4 and Figure 9-5 show how hiding rows can help you evaluate the data on your worksheet more easily.

The whole purpose of hiding rows or columns is to display only those numbers that are most important at the moment. For example, you don't want to wade through endless rows of numbers when you just need to look at the bottom line to find out whether your company is making a profit.

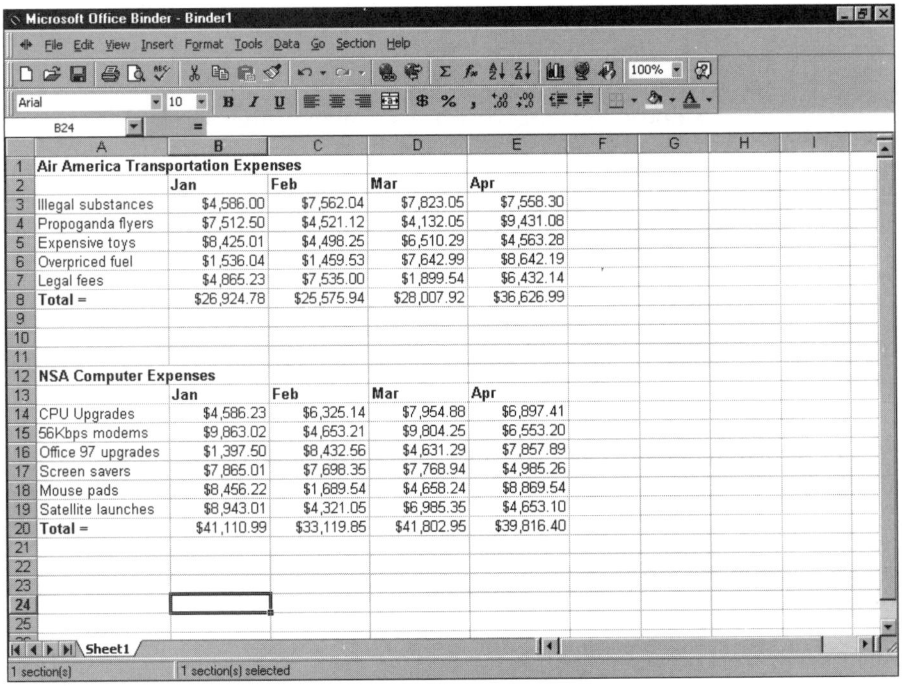

Figure 9-4:
A hideous
worksheet
with lots of
irrelevant
numbers.

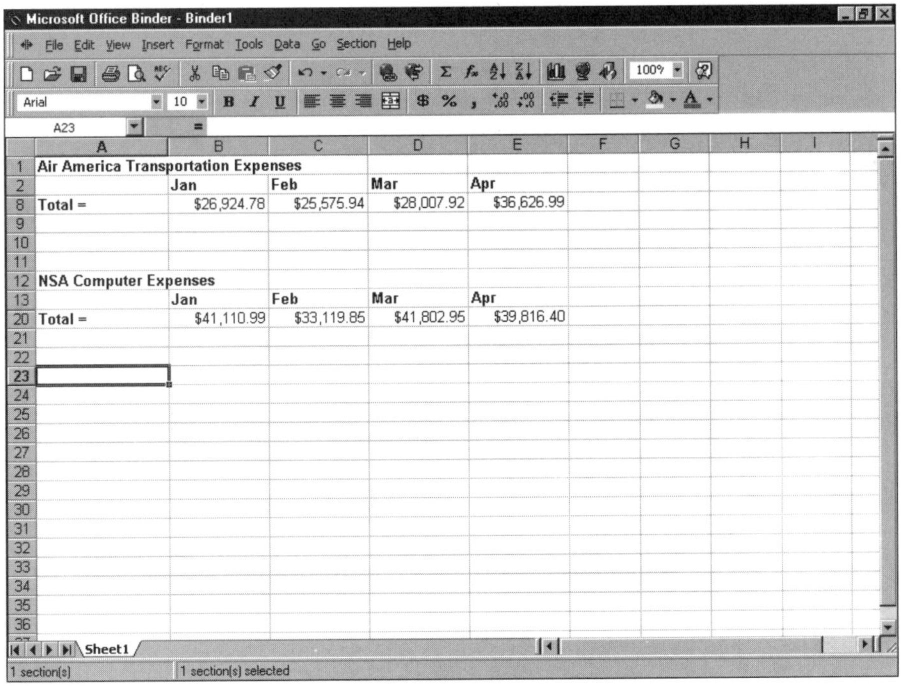

Figure 9-5:
The same
worksheet
with
unneeded
rows
hidden.

To hide a row or a column on a worksheet, follow these steps:

1. **Highlight the rows or columns that you want to hide.**

2. **Choose Format⇨Row (or Format⇨Column)⇨Hide.**

   Excel 97 hides the selected rows or columns.

Hiding a row or column does not delete it. Hiding a row or column simply tucks it conveniently out of sight.

You may wonder, "How can I find a hidden row or column after if it's hidden?" Fortunately, when Excel 97 hides rows or columns, it marks them by skipping the numbering in the row or column labels to show how many rows or columns are hidden.

To unhide a row or column on a worksheet, follow these steps:

1. **Highlight the range of cells containing the hidden rows or columns that you want to unhide.**

   For example, if you want to unhide Rows 3–6, you select Rows 2–7.

2. **Choose Format⇨Row (or Format⇨Column)⇨Unhide.**

   Excel 97 displays your previously hidden rows or columns.

To unhide all hidden rows or columns on a worksheet, click on the Select All button (refer to Figure 9-5) and then choose Format⇨Row (or Format⇨ Column)⇨Unhide.

Freezing labels on a worksheet

If you clutter up a worksheet with endless rows and columns filled with numbers, the worksheet may not make sense to anyone. To help identify what certain numbers mean, write descriptive labels next to your rows or columns of numbers so that anyone can see what those numbers represent. Some examples of descriptive labels are *Total amount, January sales,* or *Profits lost due to our incompetence.*

Unfortunately, if you scroll too far up/down or right/left, your descriptive labels also scroll up/down or right/left, which means they disappear out of sight altogether. Before you know it, you are staring at unlabeled rows and columns of numbers that don't make any sense.

For example, Figure 9-6 shows a worksheet with labels that identify your numbers. The moment that you start scrolling, however, the labels scroll out of sight, as shown in Figure 9-7.

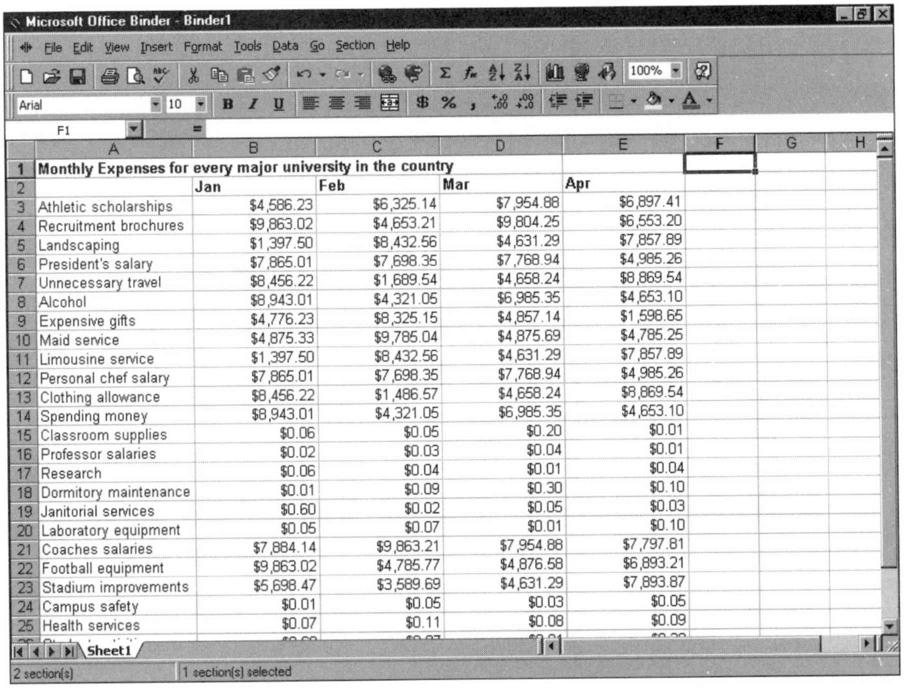

Figure 9-6:
A worksheet with easy-to-see labels.

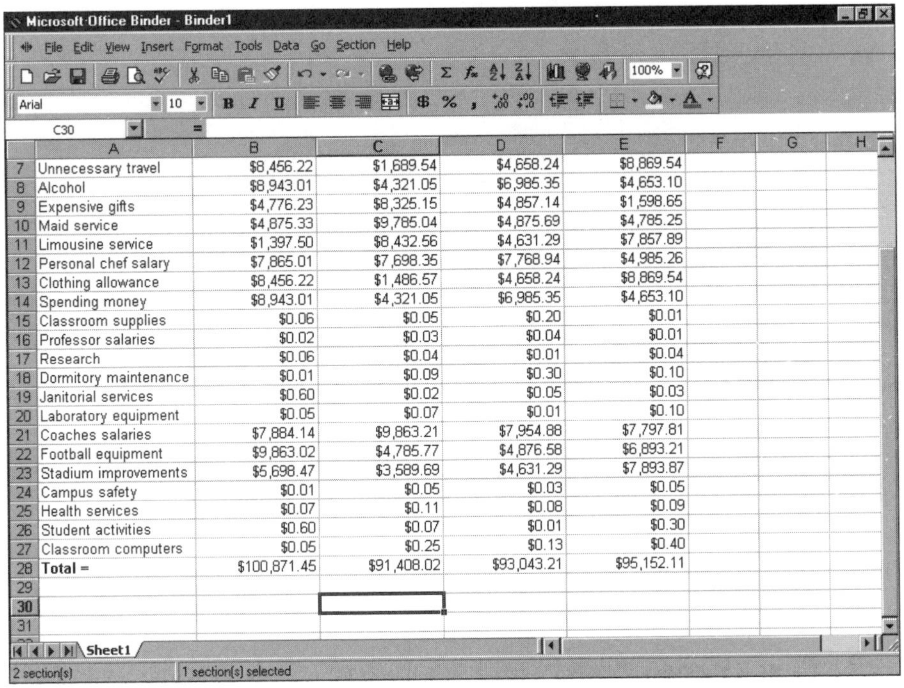

	A	B	C	D	E	F	G	H
1	Monthly Expenses for every major university in the country							
2		Jan	Feb	Mar	Apr			
3	Athletic scholarships	$4,586.23	$6,325.14	$7,954.88	$6,897.41			
4	Recruitment brochures	$9,863.02	$4,653.21	$9,804.25	$6,553.20			
5	Landscaping	$1,397.50	$8,432.56	$4,631.29	$7,857.89			
6	President's salary	$7,865.01	$7,698.35	$7,768.94	$4,985.26			
7	Unnecessary travel	$8,456.22	$1,689.54	$4,658.24	$8,869.54			
8	Alcohol	$8,943.01	$4,321.05	$6,985.35	$4,653.10			
9	Expensive gifts	$4,776.23	$8,325.15	$4,857.14	$1,598.65			
10	Maid service	$4,875.33	$9,785.04	$4,875.69	$4,785.25			
11	Limousine service	$1,397.50	$8,432.56	$4,631.29	$7,857.89			
12	Personal chef salary	$7,865.01	$7,698.35	$7,768.94	$4,985.26			
13	Clothing allowance	$8,456.22	$1,486.57	$4,658.24	$8,869.54			
14	Spending money	$8,943.01	$4,321.05	$6,985.35	$4,653.10			
15	Classroom supplies	$0.06	$0.05	$0.20	$0.01			
16	Professor salaries	$0.02	$0.03	$0.04	$0.01			
17	Research	$0.06	$0.04	$0.01	$0.04			
18	Dormitory maintenance	$0.01	$0.09	$0.30	$0.10			
19	Janitorial services	$0.60	$0.02	$0.05	$0.03			
20	Laboratory equipment	$0.05	$0.07	$0.01	$0.10			
21	Coaches salaries	$7,884.14	$9,863.21	$7,954.88	$7,797.81			
22	Football equipment	$9,863.02	$4,785.77	$4,876.58	$6,893.21			
23	Stadium improvements	$5,698.47	$3,589.69	$4,631.29	$7,893.87			
24	Campus safety	$0.01	$0.05	$0.03	$0.05			
25	Health services	$0.07	$0.11	$0.08	$0.09			

Figure 9-7:
The same worksheet after the descriptive labels have scrolled out of sight.

	A	B	C	D	E	F	G	H
7	Unnecessary travel	$8,456.22	$1,689.54	$4,658.24	$8,869.54			
8	Alcohol	$8,943.01	$4,321.05	$6,985.35	$4,653.10			
9	Expensive gifts	$4,776.23	$8,325.15	$4,857.14	$1,598.65			
10	Maid service	$4,875.33	$9,785.04	$4,875.69	$4,785.25			
11	Limousine service	$1,397.50	$8,432.56	$4,631.29	$7,857.89			
12	Personal chef salary	$7,865.01	$7,698.35	$7,768.94	$4,985.26			
13	Clothing allowance	$8,456.22	$1,486.57	$4,658.24	$8,869.54			
14	Spending money	$8,943.01	$4,321.05	$6,985.35	$4,653.10			
15	Classroom supplies	$0.06	$0.05	$0.20	$0.01			
16	Professor salaries	$0.02	$0.03	$0.04	$0.01			
17	Research	$0.06	$0.04	$0.01	$0.04			
18	Dormitory maintenance	$0.01	$0.09	$0.30	$0.10			
19	Janitorial services	$0.60	$0.02	$0.05	$0.03			
20	Laboratory equipment	$0.05	$0.07	$0.01	$0.10			
21	Coaches salaries	$7,884.14	$9,863.21	$7,954.88	$7,797.81			
22	Football equipment	$9,863.02	$4,785.77	$4,876.58	$6,893.21			
23	Stadium improvements	$5,698.47	$3,589.69	$4,631.29	$7,893.87			
24	Campus safety	$0.01	$0.05	$0.03	$0.05			
25	Health services	$0.07	$0.11	$0.08	$0.09			
26	Student activities	$0.60	$0.07	$0.01	$0.30			
27	Classroom computers	$0.05	$0.25	$0.13	$0.40			
28	Total =	$100,871.45	$91,408.02	$93,043.21	$95,152.11			
29								
30								
31								

To offset the problem of losing descriptive labels as you scroll through a large worksheet, Excel lets you *freeze,* or anchor, labels in specific rows or columns. When you freeze a row or column containing a label, that particular row or column never moves no matter how much you scroll through your worksheet (see Figure 9-8).

To freeze a row or column, follow these steps:

1. **If you are using Excel 97 in a binder, choose Section⇨View Outside.**

   Skip this step if you're using Excel 97 outside a binder.

2. **Click on the row number directly below the row that you want to freeze.**

   Or click on the column letter to the right of the column that you want to freeze.

   If you want to freeze Row 2, for example, click on the Row 3 label to select the entire row. Or if you want to freeze Column C, click on the Column D label to select the entire column.

3. **Choose Windows⇨Freeze Panes.**

   Excel displays a dark gray line to show where you froze your row or column (refer to Figure 9-8).

Figure 9-8: The same worksheet with descriptive labels frozen in place.

	A	B	C	D	E	F	G	H
1	Monthly Expenses for every major university in the country							
2		Jan	Feb	Mar	Apr			
15	Classroom supplies	$0.06	$0.05	$0.20	$0.01			
16	Professor salaries	$0.02	$0.03	$0.04	$0.01			
17	Research	$0.06	$0.04	$0.01	$0.04			
18	Dormitory maintenance	$0.01	$0.09	$0.30	$0.10			
19	Janitorial services	$0.60	$0.02	$0.05	$0.03			
20	Laboratory equipment	$0.05	$0.07	$0.01	$0.10			
21	Coaches salaries	$7,884.14	$9,863.21	$7,954.88	$7,797.81			
22	Football equipment	$9,863.02	$4,785.77	$4,876.58	$6,893.21			
23	Stadium improvements	$5,698.47	$3,589.69	$4,631.29	$7,893.87			
24	Campus safety	$0.01	$0.05	$0.03	$0.05			
25	Health services	$0.07	$0.11	$0.08	$0.09			
26	Student activities	$0.60	$0.07	$0.01	$0.30			
27	Classroom computers	$0.05	$0.25	$0.13	$0.40			
28	Total =	$100,871.45	$91,408.02	$93,043.21	$95,152.11			

To freeze both a row and a column at the same time, follow these steps:

1. **If you're using Excel 97 in a binder, choose Section⇨View Outside.**

   Skip this step if you're using Excel 97 outside a binder.

2. **Click on the cell directly to the right of the column and below the row that you want to freeze.**

   If you want to freeze Column A and Row 2, for example, click on the cell in Column B and Row 3.

3. **Choose Window⇨Freeze Panes.**

   Excel 97 displays a dark gray line to show where you froze your row and column.

To unfreeze any rows and columns that you have frozen, follow these steps:

1. **If you're using Excel 97 in a binder, choose Section⇨View Outside.**

   Skip this step if you're using Excel 97 outside a binder.

2. **Choose Window⇨Unfreeze Panes.**

Splitting screens on a worksheet

If you want to see two or more parts of your worksheet at one time, you can split your screen into miniature views of your worksheet, known as *panes*. Each pane acts as an independent window that you can scroll separately from the rest of your worksheet. To show you where one pane begins and another pane ends, Excel displays thick pane lines, as shown in Figure 9-9.

To split a screen in half horizontally, follow these steps:

1. **If you're using Excel 97 in a binder, choose Section⇨View Outside.**

   Skip this step if you're using Excel 97 outside a binder.

2. **Select the row directly below the row where you want to split your worksheet.**

   For example, if you want to split your worksheet between Rows 8 and 9, click on the Row 9 label.

3. **Choose Windows⇨Split.**

   Excel displays a horizontal pane line to show you where you split your worksheet (see Figure 9-9).

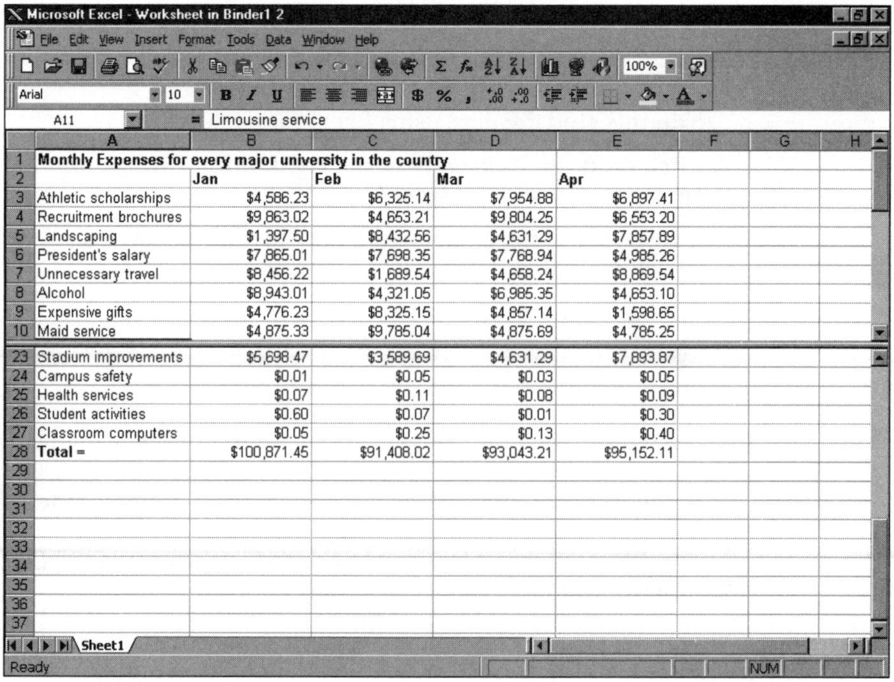

Figure 9-9:
Splitting a
worksheet
into two
separate
panes.

To split a screen in half vertically, follow these steps:

1. **If you're using Excel 97 in a binder, choose Section⇨View Outside.**

   Skip this step if you're using Excel 97 outside a binder.

2. **Select the column directly to the right of where you want to split your worksheet.**

   For example, if you want to split your worksheet between Columns B and C, click on the Column C label.

3. **Choose Windows⇨Split.**

   Excel displays a vertical pane line to show you where you split your columns.

You can also split your worksheet into four different panes to give you yet another view of your numbers.

To split your worksheet into four panes, follow these steps:

1. **If you're using Excel 97 in a binder, choose Section⇨View Outside.**

   Skip this step if you're using Excel 97 outside a binder.

2. **Click on the cell directly to the right of the column and below the row where you want to split.**

   For example, if you want to split your worksheet between Columns B and C and between Rows 9 and 10, click on the cell in Column C and Row 10.

3. **Choose Windows⇨Split.**

   Excel splits your worksheet into four panes (see Figure 9-10).

To remove your splits, follow these steps:

1. **If you're using Excel 97 in a binder, choose Section⇨View Outside.**

   Skip this step if you're using Excel 97 outside a binder.

2. **Choose Windows⇨Remove Split.**

   The worksheet window returns to its normal appearance.

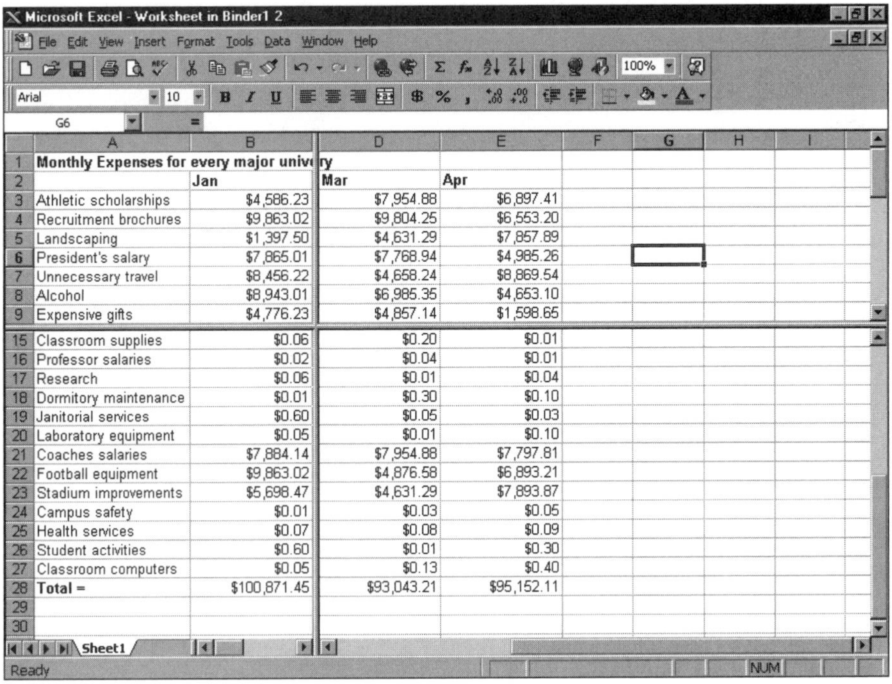

	A	B	D	E	F	G	H	I
1	Monthly Expenses for every major univ	ry						
2		Jan	Mar	Apr				
3	Athletic scholarships	$4,586.23	$7,954.88	$6,897.41				
4	Recruitment brochures	$9,863.02	$9,804.25	$6,553.20				
5	Landscaping	$1,397.50	$4,631.29	$7,857.89				
6	President's salary	$7,865.01	$7,768.94	$4,985.26				
7	Unnecessary travel	$8,456.22	$4,658.24	$8,869.54				
8	Alcohol	$8,943.01	$6,985.35	$4,653.10				
9	Expensive gifts	$4,776.23	$4,857.14	$1,598.65				
15	Classroom supplies	$0.06	$0.20	$0.01				
16	Professor salaries	$0.02	$0.04	$0.01				
17	Research	$0.06	$0.01	$0.04				
18	Dormitory maintenance	$0.01	$0.30	$0.10				
19	Janitorial services	$0.60	$0.05	$0.03				
20	Laboratory equipment	$0.05	$0.01	$0.10				
21	Coaches salaries	$7,884.14	$7,954.88	$7,797.81				
22	Football equipment	$9,863.02	$4,876.58	$6,893.21				
23	Stadium improvements	$5,698.47	$4,631.29	$7,893.87				
24	Campus safety	$0.01	$0.03	$0.05				
25	Health services	$0.07	$0.08	$0.09				
26	Student activities	$0.60	$0.01	$0.30				
27	Classroom computers	$0.05	$0.13	$0.40				
28	Total =	$100,871.45	$93,043.21	$95,152.11				
29								
30								

Figure 9-10: A worksheet split into four separate panes.

Zooming in for a closer look

In case your eyesight is poor or you like looking at your entire worksheet at one time, you can make the numbers on your worksheet appear larger (called *zooming in*) or smaller (called *zooming out*). Normally, Excel 97 displays your worksheet on-screen exactly as it appears when you print it.

To make your worksheet numbers appear bigger, select a higher magnification, such as 200%. To make your worksheet numbers appear smaller, select a lower magnification, such as 50%. To make your worksheet appear normal size again, select 100%.

To change the zoom magnification on your worksheet, follow these steps:

1. Choose <u>V</u>iew⇨<u>Z</u>oom.

A Zoom dialog box appears, as shown in Figure 9-11.

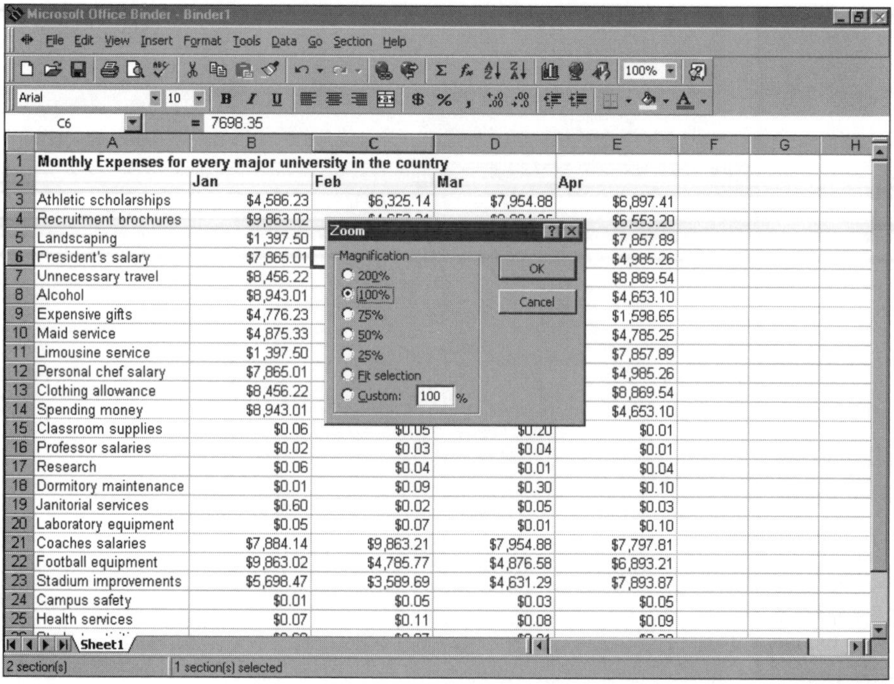

Figure 9-11:
The Zoom dialog box.

2. Click on a magnification (such as 100%) and click on OK.

Excel displays your worksheet in your chosen magnification. You also can enter a specific magnification, such as 214%, in the Custom text box. Excel displays your worksheet using the magnification that you entered, as shown in Figure 9-12. (In the case of Figure 9-11, I stuck to a 100% setting.)

TIP

Excel 97 provides two other ways to change the magnification of a worksheet:

- Clicking in the Zoom list box on the Standard toolbar
- Holding down the Ctrl key and spinning the gray wheel on your IntelliMouse (This assumes that you're using Microsoft's IntelliMouse, which has a gray wheel in the middle of its two buttons.)

Microsoft Office Binder - Binder1
File Edit View Insert Format Tools Data Go Section Help
214%
Arial
10
A2
A
B
C
1 Monthly Expenses for every major university in the
2 Jan Feb
3 Athletic scholarships $4,586.23 $6,325
4 Recruitment brochures $9,863.02 $4,653
5 Landscaping $1,397.50 $8,432
6 President's salary $7,865.01 $7,698
7 Unnecessary travel $8,456.22 $1,689
8 Alcohol $8,943.01 $4,321
9 Expensive gifts $4,776.23 $8,325
10 Maid service $4,875.33 $9,785
11 Limousine service $1,397.50 $8,432
Sheet1
2 section(s)
1 section(s) selected

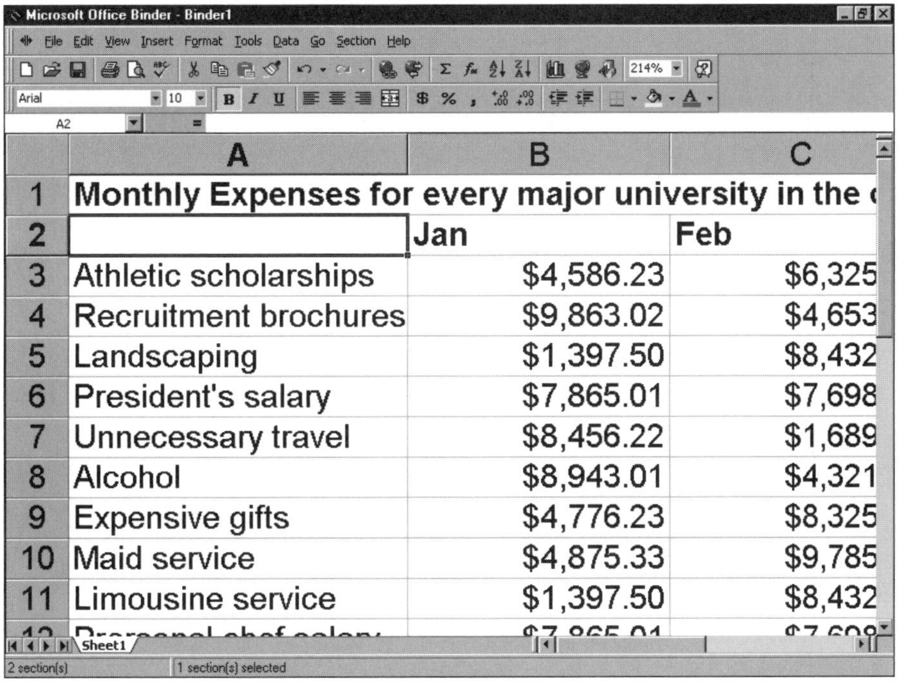

Figure 9-12: Displaying your worksheet at a higher magnification.

Chapter 10

Goal Seeking and Pivot Tables

*E*xcel 97 is more than a simple spreadsheet. By digging into Excel 97's more obscure features, you can learn how to use Excel 97 to do all sorts of weird calculations, such as goal-seeking and storing data in pivot tables.

Seeking Your Goals

The typical worksheet works something like this: enter data, create a formula, and get an answer. Then you can change any of your data and Excel 97 uses your formula to calculate a new result automatically.

Excel 97 offers a unique feature called goal-seeking, which allows you to specify the answer you want so that Excel 97 can figure out what data it needs to calculate your chosen answer.

For example, suppose that you've created a worksheet to measure the sales results for each of your company's products, as shown in Figure 10-1. Looking at the February sales totals tells you that sales went down.

Pop quiz! If you wanted your February sales results to equal $40,000, how much extra would sales of "Visual Ada for OS/2" have to increase to meet that goal? Instead of trying to figure this out yourself, just tell Excel 97 what result you want and which cell values to change to get that result.

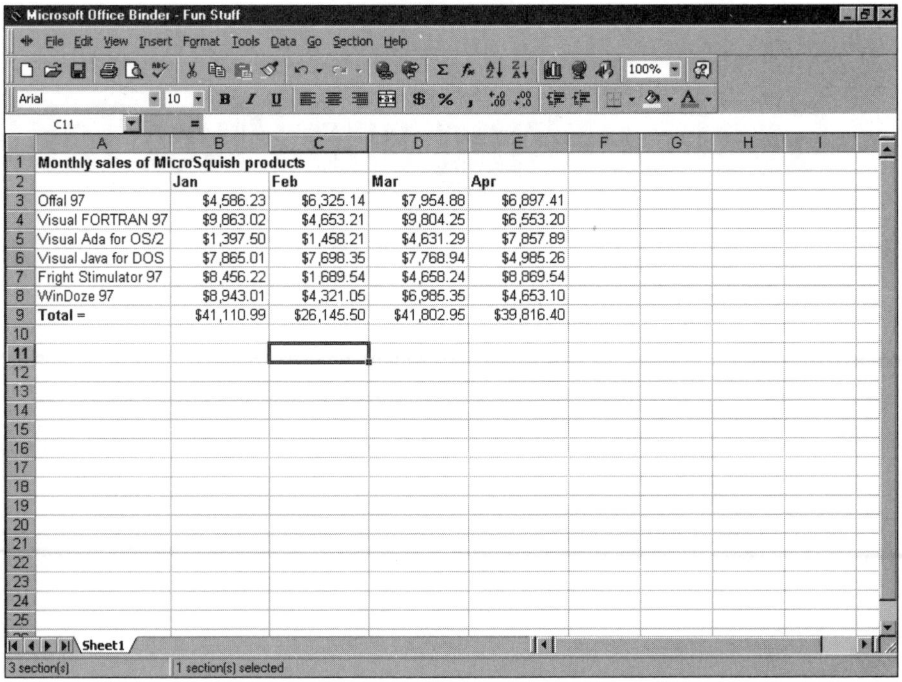

	A	B	C	D	E
1	Monthly sales of MicroSquish products				
2		Jan	Feb	Mar	Apr
3	Offal 97	$4,586.23	$6,325.14	$7,954.88	$6,897.41
4	Visual FORTRAN 97	$9,863.02	$4,653.21	$9,804.25	$6,553.20
5	Visual Ada for OS/2	$1,397.50	$1,458.21	$4,631.29	$7,857.89
6	Visual Java for DOS	$7,865.01	$7,698.35	$7,768.94	$4,985.26
7	Fright Stimulator 97	$8,456.22	$1,689.54	$4,658.24	$8,869.54
8	WinDoze 97	$8,943.01	$4,321.05	$6,985.35	$4,653.10
9	Total =	$41,110.99	$26,145.50	$41,802.95	$39,816.40

Figure 10-1: Using goal-seeking in a real-life example.

To use goal-seeking to find an answer that you've been seeking, follow these steps:

1. **Click on the cell in which you want the new answer to appear.**

   This cell must contain a formula.

2. **Click on Tools⇨Goal Seek.**

   The Goal Seek dialog box appears with the address of the selected cell in the Set cell text box, as shown in Figure 10-2.

3. **Click in the To value text box and type the answer that you want.**

   For example, you may want to find out the how to create a February sales total of $40,000. Type **40000** in the To value text box.

4. **Click in the By changing cell text box.**

   This box is where you tell Excel 97 which value to change to reach your goal.

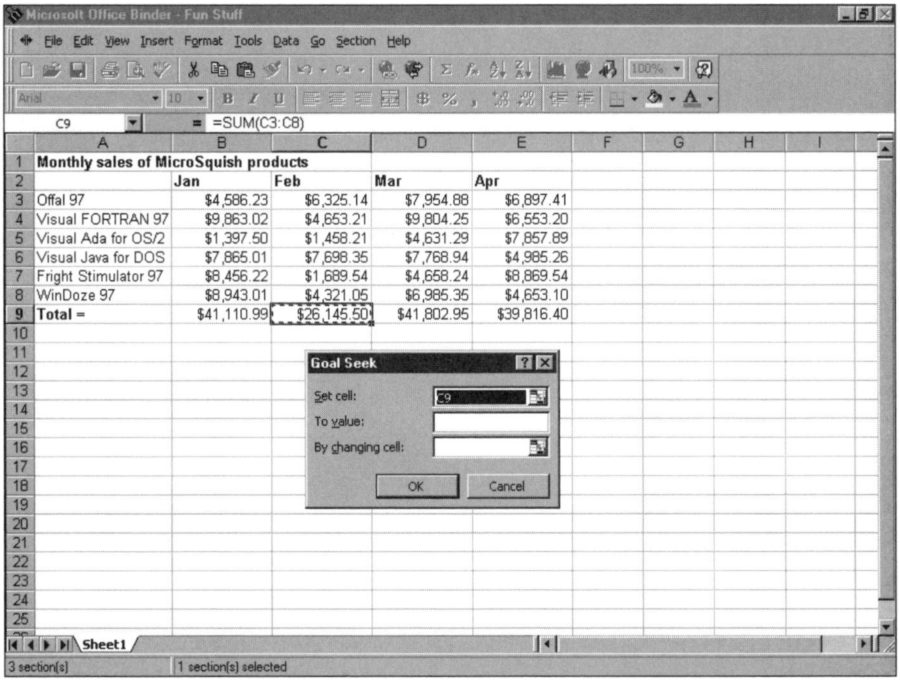

Figure 10-2:
The Goal
Seek
dialog box.

5. **Click in the cell containing the value that you want Excel to change to get to your answer.**

   The cell to be changed must contain a value (a number), not a formula. Excel 97 automatically types the cell address in the By changing cell box.

6. **Click on OK.**

   Excel automatically changes your chosen cell to provide the result that you requested. The Goal Seek Status dialog box shows the target value and the current value, which should be the same as that shown in Figure 10-3.

7. **Click on OK to accept the changes or click on Cancel to have the numbers revert to their original state.**

   - Goal-seeking can change only the values in a single cell.

   - If you click on the OK button in the Goal Seek Status dialog box by mistake and want the numbers back the way they were, press Ctrl+Z before you do anything else.

File Edit View Insert Format Tools Data Go Section Help

	A	B	C	D	E	F	G	H	I
1	Monthly sales of MicroSquish products								
2		Jan	Feb	Mar	Apr				
3	Offal 97	$4,586.23	$6,325.14	$7,954.88	$6,897.41				
4	Visual FORTRAN 97	$9,863.02	$4,653.21	$9,804.25	$6,553.20				
5	Visual Ada for OS/2	$1,397.50	$15,312.71	$4,631.29	$7,857.89				
6	Visual Java for DOS	$7,865.01	$7,698.35	$7,768.94	$4,985.26				
7	Fright Stimulator 97	$8,456.22	$1,689.54	$4,658.24	$8,869.54				
8	WinDoze 97	$8,943.01	$4,321.05	$6,985.35	$4,653.10				
9	Total =	$41,110.99	$40,000.00	$41,802.95	$39,816.40				

C9 =SUM(C3:C8)

Goal Seek Status

Goal Seeking with Cell C9
found a solution.

Target value: 40000
Current value: $40,000.00

OK   Cancel   Step   Pause

Figure 10-3:
The Goal
Seek Status
dialog box
letting you
know that it
has found a
solution.

Sheet1

3 section(s)   1 section(s) selected

Storing Stuff in Tables

Although Excel 97 is a spreadsheet, many people have tortured it into a simple database rather than learning how to use a separate database program such as Access 97. To Excel 97, a database is nothing more than a bunch of information in rows and columns (called a *table*) that you can store and manipulate.

To create an Excel 97 database table, start by typing headings in one row to label the columns of information that you want to include. For a customer list, you might have items such as FIRST NAME, LAST NAME, or MONEY THEY OWE US.

In database terms, each item in a column is called a *field*. All the items in a single row of the table is called a *record*. So, the database is nothing more than a bunch of records that consist of a bunch of fields.

Type the data for each record just as you enter data in a normal worksheet, directly below the field-name labels, as shown in Figure 10-4.

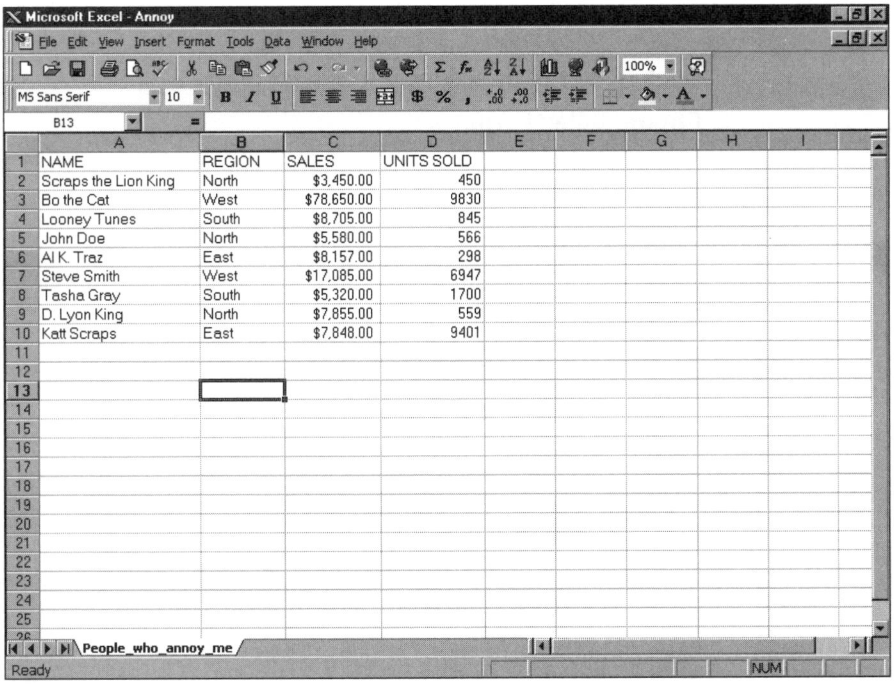

	A	B	C	D
1	NAME	REGION	SALES	UNITS SOLD
2	Scraps the Lion King	North	$3,450.00	450
3	Bo the Cat	West	$78,650.00	9830
4	Looney Tunes	South	$8,705.00	845
5	John Doe	North	$5,580.00	566
6	Al K. Traz	East	$8,157.00	298
7	Steve Smith	West	$17,085.00	6947
8	Tasha Gray	South	$5,320.00	1700
9	D. Lyon King	North	$7,855.00	559
10	Katt Scraps	East	$7,848.00	9401

Figure 10-4: The typical appearance of a database table in Excel 97.

Type the field names (column headings) in UPPERCASE and type the actual data in lowercase. This will make it easier to see your column headings from your data.

Typing data in a table

Typing data directly into a database table is easy enough, but it does have some drawbacks. If you have lots of fields, you'll be scrolling left and right an awful lot, which means that you might not be able to see the first fields in the record as you enter the last field.

To make typing data easier, Excel 97 allows you to use something called a data form, which lets you type data in a dialog box. After typing your data in the dialog box, Excel 97 takes the time to put the data in your actual worksheet cells.

You can use the data form to type all sorts of data into an Excel 97 worksheet, not just database information.

To use a data form, follow these steps:

1. Click in one of the cells in your data table.

2. Choose Data⇨Form.

A dialog box appears, asking whether you want to use the top row as the header row.

3. Click on OK.

The data form dialog box, with the name of the current worksheet in the title bar, appears, as shown in Figure 10-5, displaying the first record.

4. Click on New.

All the fields in the dialog box are cleared so that you can start entering a new record.

5. Type the data for the first field and then press the Tab key to move to the next field.

6. Continue entering data until all the fields for the record are entered; then, click on New again (or just press Enter).

Each time that you click on New, the new record is placed at the bottom of the table, the text boxes are cleared, and you can start entering the next record.

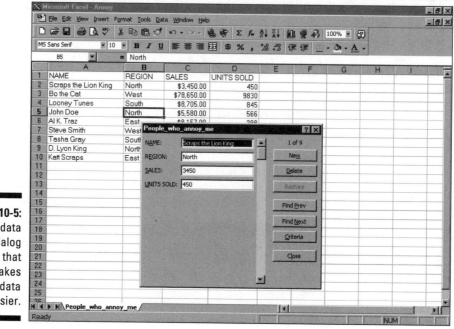

Figure 10-5:
The data form dialog box that makes typing data easier.

7. After entering all the records for this session using the data form, click on Close.

See how easy entering data in records is? And you didn't have to use the scroll bar even once.

✔ Before using the data form, format the cells in your database table first. That way, Excel 97 automatically formats your data as you type it.

✔ If you're typing in numbers that should be treated as text (such as zip codes), be sure to type an apostrophe (') before typing the rest of the number.

Sorting your tables

Sorting databases is something that you'll do frequently. You may want to sort the list by last name to make finding a particular person in the list easier, or you may want to sort by zip code (if you're creating mailing labels, for example).

To sort a table, follow these steps:

1. Click in any cell in the column by which you want to sort the table.

For example, if you want to sort the table by name, click in any cell in the column that contains the names (refer to Figure 10-4).

2. Choose Data⇨Sort.

A Sort dialog box appears as shown in Figure 10-6.

3. Click in the Sort by list box and choose a field to sort by.

4. Click in the first Then by list box and choose a second field to sort by (optional).

5. Click in the second Then by list box and choose a third field to sort by (optional).

6. Click on the Ascending (or Descending) radio buttons for each Sort by list box and click on OK.

If you need to sort only one field, just click on the Sort Ascending or Sort Descending icon on the Standard toolbar.

Sorting doesn't physically change your data; it just changes the way that data looks on-screen. To undo a sort, press Ctrl+Z right away.

Sort Ascending Icon ⎯⎯ ⎯⎯ Sort Descending Icon

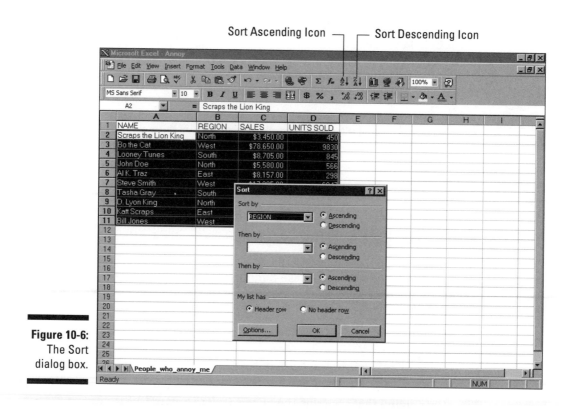

Figure 10-6:
The Sort
dialog box.

Analyzing Data with PivotTables

Staring at lists of information in a database table can seem meaningless at
first glance (or even after an extended period of time), as shown in Figure
10-7. So, to help you make sense of your database table, Excel 97 offers a
unique feature called a PivotTable, which essentially converts a dull list into
a normal-looking worksheet.

A PivotTable can rearrange data stored in an Excel 97 worksheet or imported from an external database.

A PivotTable consists of four parts, as shown in Figure 10-8:

  ✔ **Page field:** Filters the type of data displayed in the PivotTable, as
     shown in Figure 10-9

  ✔ **Row field:** Displays data in rows (such as a list of products)

  ✔ **Column field:** Displays data in columns (such as headings by months)

  ✔ **Data area:** Used to calculate totals for the PivotTable

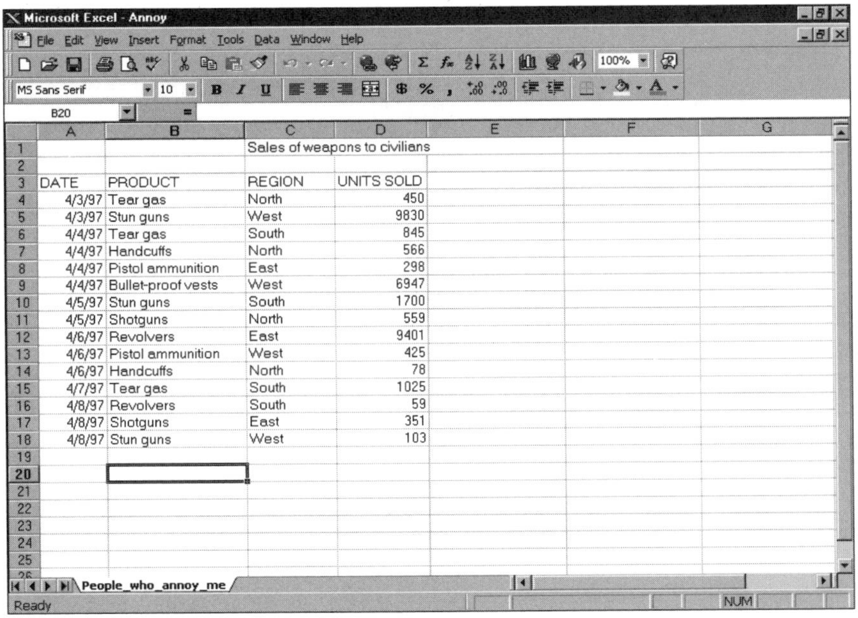

Figure 10-7:
A typical
confusing
list of
meaningless
information
in a
database
table.

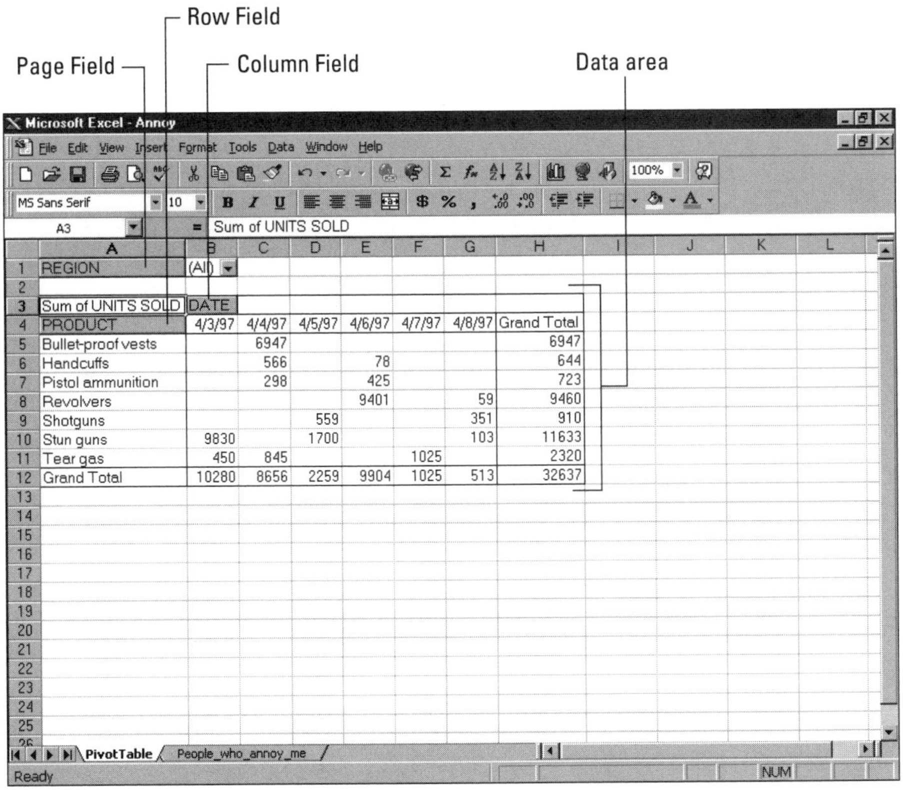

Row Field

Page Field

Column Field

Data area

Figure 10-8:
A
PivotTable
converts a
list of
information
into a
worksheet.

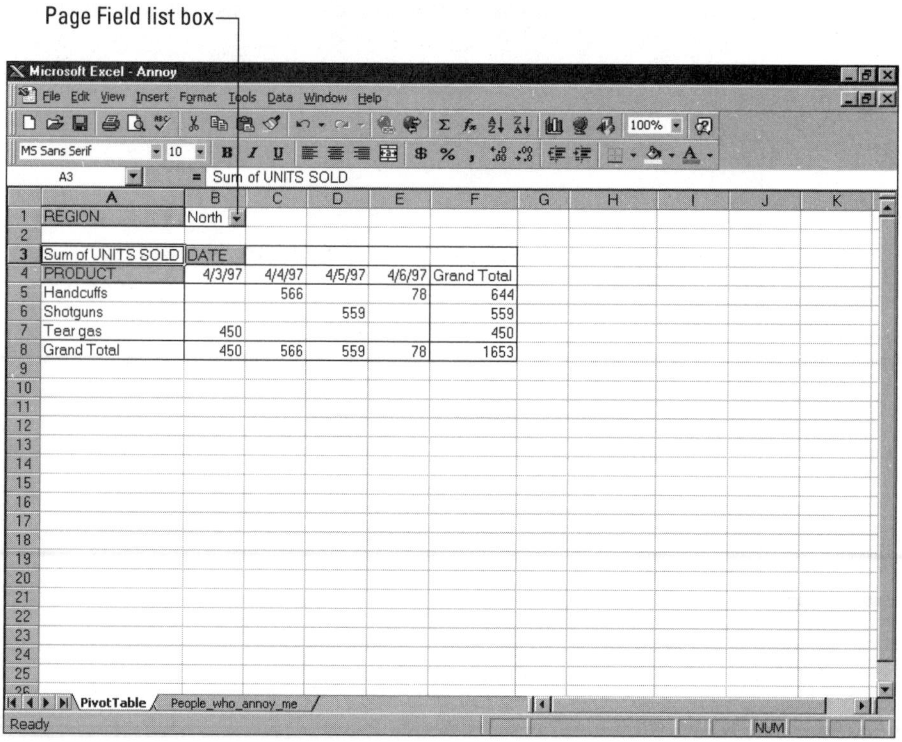

Page Field list box

Figure 10-9:
The same
PivotTable,
shown in
Figure 10-8,
"filtered"
using the
Page field
to display
data only
from the
North
region.

Creating a PivotTable

To create a PivotTable with the PivotTable Wizard, follow these steps:

1. **Choose Data➪PivotTable Report.**

   The first PivotTable Wizard dialog box appears, as shown in Figure 10-10.

2. **Click in the Microsoft Excel list or database radio button and click on Next.**

   The second PivotTable Wizard dialog box appears, as shown in Figure 10-11.

3. **Highlight your database table so that the Range box contains the headings and the data in your database table. Then, click on Next.**

   The third PivotTable Wizard dialog box appears, as shown in Figure 10-12. This dialog box is where you specify which fields to use in the PivotTable. The field names appear as buttons on the right side of the dialog box.

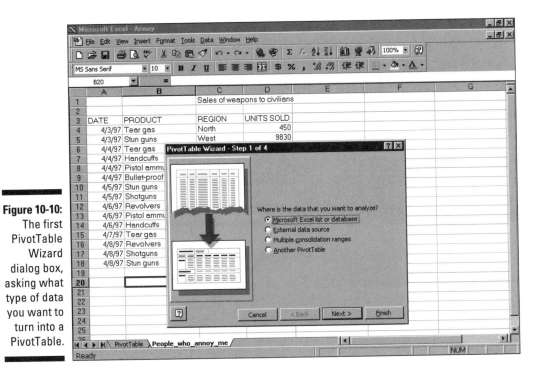

Figure 10-10:
The first
PivotTable
Wizard
dialog box,
asking what
type of data
you want to
turn into a
PivotTable.

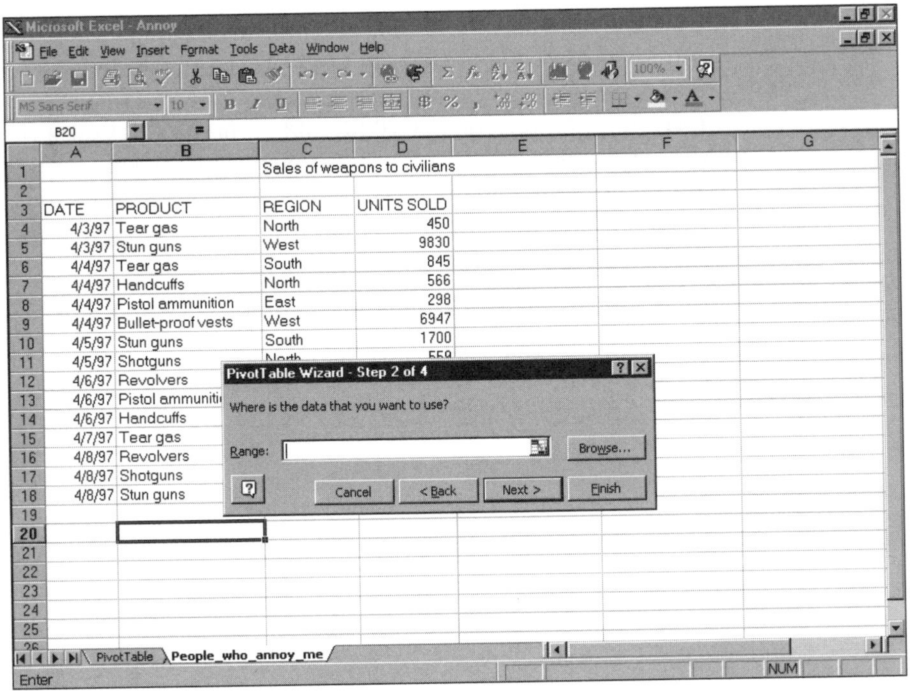

Figure 10-11:
The second
PivotTable
Wizard
dialog box,
which is for
choosing
data stored
in an Excel
database
table.

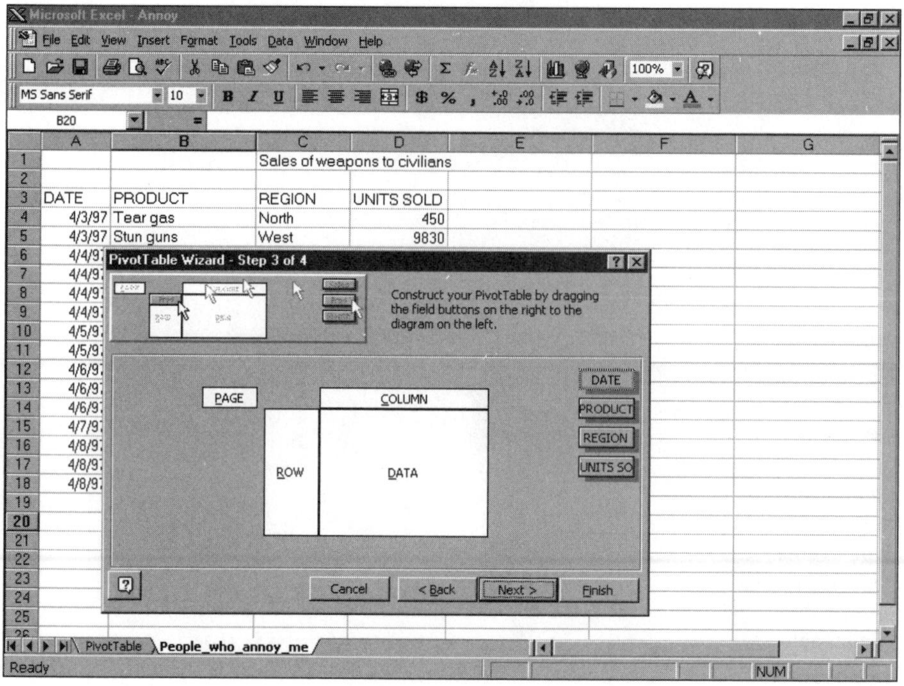

Figure 10-12:
The third PivotTable Wizard dialog box for constructing your PivotTable.

4. **Drag the appropriate field-name buttons (such as DATE or PRODUCT) into the PAGE, ROW, COLUMN, and DATA portions of the dialog box.**

   For example, drag the PRODUCT button onto the ROW field, drag the DATE button onto the COLUMN field, drag the UNITS SOLD button onto the DATA field, and drag the REGION button onto the PAGE field, as shown in Figure 10-13.

5. **Click on Next to display the final PivotTable Wizard dialog box, as shown in Figure 10-14.**

6. **Click in the New worksheet or Existing worksheet radio button.**

   If you click on the Existing worksheet radio button, you also need to click in a cell where you want the PivotTable to appear.

7. **Click on Finish to finish creating the PivotTable.**

   Your finished PivotTable appears.

To use the Page field to "filter" out the data displayed, click in the Page field list box (refer to Figure 10-9) and choose a new page (such as North or East).

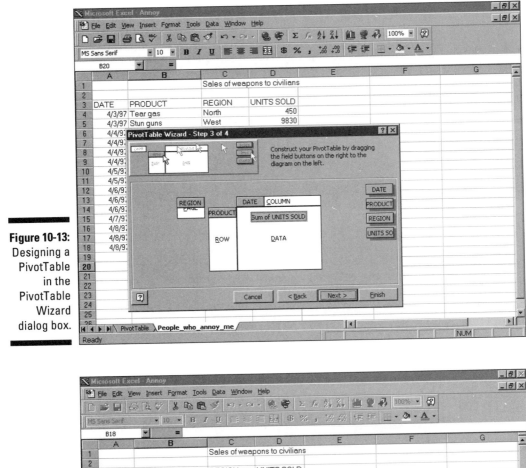

Figure 10-13:
Designing a
PivotTable
in the
PivotTable
Wizard
dialog box.

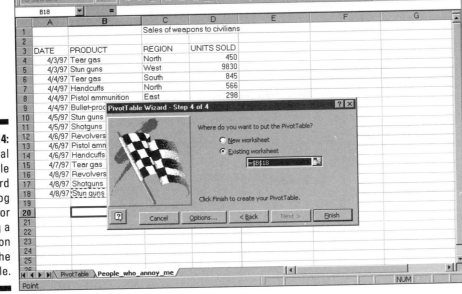

Figure 10-14:
The final
PivotTable
Wizard
dialog
box for
choosing a
location
for the
PivotTable.

Formatting a PivotTable

If you don't like the way PivotTable Wizard formats your data, you can choose a different formatting style at any time. Just follow these steps:

1. **Click in any cell inside your PivotTable.**

2. **Choose Format⇨AutoFormat.**

   An AutoFormat dialog box appears, as shown in Figure 10-15.

3. **Click on a format in the Table format list and click on OK.**

Deleting a PivotTable

If you decide that you don't need your PivotTable anymore, you can wipe it off your worksheet completely by following these steps:

1. **Click in the cell that appears directly above the ROW field and to the left of the COLUMN field of your PivotTable.**

   Excel 97 highlights your entire PivotTable.

2. **Choose Edit⇨Delete.**

   A Delete dialog box appears.

3. **Click on OK.**

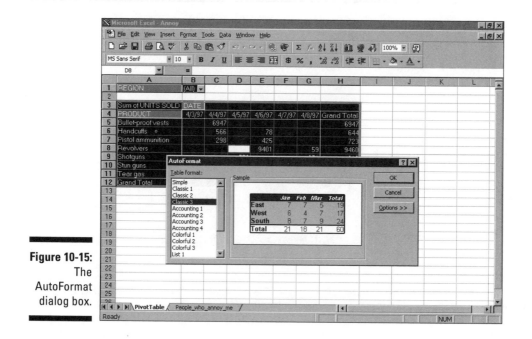

Figure 10-15:
The AutoFormat dialog box.

Chapter 11

Verifying that Your Worksheets Really Work

. . . .

In This Chapter

▶ Tracing your formulas for problems

▶ Dealing with error messages

▶ Examining your cells in detail

▶ Looking for an oddball formula

▶ Correcting spelling errors

. . . .

*A*fter you type labels, numbers, and formulas into a worksheet, your job still isn't over. Now you must make sure that your formulas calculate the correct answer. After all, you can create the best-looking spreadsheet in the world with fancy fonts, but if it consistently calculates wrong answers, no one can use it (except for the United States government's budget accountants).

To make sure that your spreadsheet calculates its formulas correctly, you may need to spend time examining each formula. Naturally, doing so can be a pain in the neck, but spending time checking your formulas is much easier than making a big mistake and going bankrupt later because of your spreadsheet's faulty calculations.

How Excel 97 Helps Verify Your Formulas

To help you verify that your formulas are working correctly, Excel 97 comes with a special auditing feature that can identify:

✔ Where a formula gets its data (so that you can see whether a formula is getting all the data it needs)

✔ How one formula may depend on the (possibly incorrect) calculation from another formula

If a formula isn't getting all the right data, it obviously can't calculate the correct results. Likewise, calculations from one formula can be used as data by another formula; if one formula calculates wrong answers, any formulas that depend on that first formula are messed up as well.

Most of Excel 97's auditing features are hidden on the Auditing toolbar, as shown in Figure 11-1. To display the Auditing toolbar, choose Tools⇨ Auditing⇨Show Auditing Toolbar.

Tracing Your Formulas

The whole purpose of the Auditing toolbar is to help you trace your formulas. To use auditing, you need to understand Excel 97's weird terminology. A *precedent* is a cell that contains data used by a formula, and a *dependent* is a cell that contains a formula.

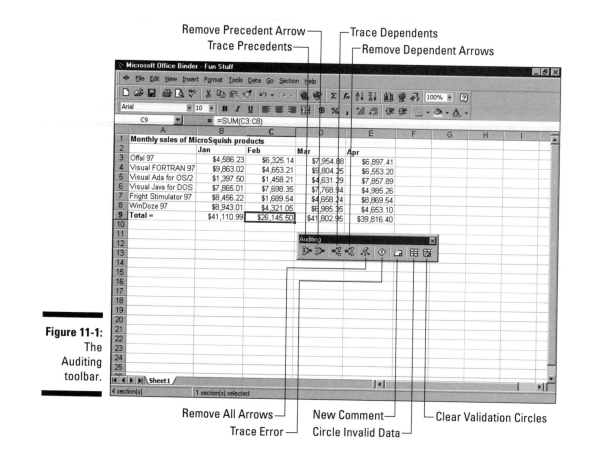

Figure 11-1: The Auditing toolbar.

For example, suppose that a formula appears in the cell B7 like this:

```
=B5+B6
```

In this example, the cells B5 and B6 are called the precedents, and the cell B7 is the dependent. As long as you remember these definitions, you won't get confused between the Trace Precedents and the Trace Dependents icons on the Auditing toolbar.

Understanding where a formula gets its data

A formula is only as good as the data that it receives. Feed a formula the wrong data and you always get the wrong answer. (This law of nature explains why governments are perpetually clueless: As long as they keep asking the wrong questions, they never come up with the correct answers.)

If you want to know where your formula is getting its data, follow these steps:

1. Click in the cell containing the formula that you want to examine.

2. Click on the Trace Precedents icon on the Auditing toolbar.

Excel 97 draws one or more arrows to show all the cells from which your formula, chosen in Step 1, is getting its data (see Figure 11-2).

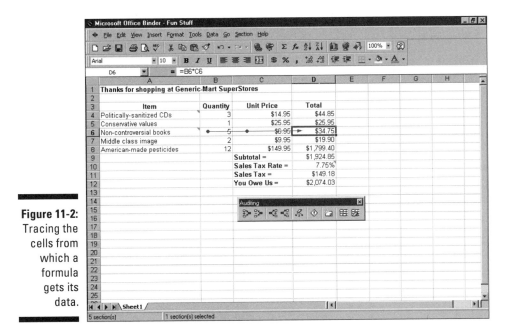

Figure 11-2: Tracing the cells from which a formula gets its data.

If a formula uses data stored in an individual cell, that cell is marked by a dot. If a formula doesn't use data in a cell, no dot appears, even if the arrow is drawn over it.

Knowing which formulas a cell affects

The beauty of spreadsheets is that you can change one number in a cell and watch that change ripple throughout the rest of your spreadsheet as it recalculates formulas from top to bottom. In case you want to know how the data stored in one cell may affect any formulas stored in other cells, you can use Excel 97's auditing features to show you all the formulas that depend on a particular cell.

To identify which formulas a cell affects, follow these steps:

1. **Click in the cell that you want to examine.**

2. **Click on the Trace Dependents icon on the Auditing toolbar.**

   Excel draws one or more arrows that show which formulas your cell will change, as shown in Figure 11-3.

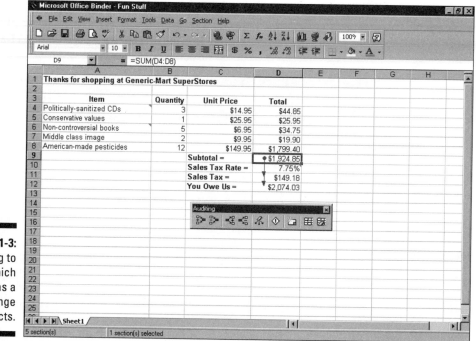

Figure 11-3: Tracing to see which formulas a change affects.

Getting rid of those precedent and dependent arrows

After you trace your cells and formulas so that you know how they affect one another, you'll probably want to remove those silly arrows so that you can see what you're doing. Excel provides three ways to remove these arrows:

- ✔ Click on the cell that contains an arrowhead (the cell containing a formula) and click on the Remove Precedent Arrows icon.
- ✔ Click on the cell that contains a dot and click on the Remove Dependent Arrows icon. (You have to complete this step for each cell that contains a dot in the same arrow.)
- ✔ Click on the Remove All Arrows icon.

Knowing What to Do when a Formula Displays an Error Message

Sometimes you may create a formula and, rather than display a result, the cell displays an error message (#VALUE!, for example). Table 11-1 shows some of the most common error messages and a description of how you confused Excel 97.

Table 11-1	Common Error Messages in Excel 97 Formulas
#DIV/0!	Your formula is trying to divide by zero.
#VALUE!	Your formula isn't receiving the type of data that it expects. For example, a formula might get a text string when it expects an integer.
#####	The cell width is too small to display the entire number. (To fix this problem, simply increase the width of your cell.)

Whenever your formula displays an error message rather than an actual result, you can hunt down and correct the mistake right away by following these steps:

1. **Click in the cell that contains the error message.**

2. **Click on the Trace Error icon on the Auditing toolbar.**

Excel 97 draws a line showing you all the cells that feed data to your formula (see Figure 11-4). In this example, Excel 97 is telling you that you're trying to multiply the text string stored in the cell C9 by the text string stored in C10. Because you can't multiply strings, Excel 97 displays an error message in the cell D11.

Validating Your Data

When you're creating a formula, you usually have a good idea of what type of data is not acceptable. For example, if you're calculating weekly paychecks by multiplying hourly wage by the number of hours worked, you know that nobody can work a negative number of hours (although many people may try).

To catch such data entry errors, you can specify certain restrictions on the type of data that a cell should contain, such as a minimum and maximum value. The moment that someone tries to type data that doesn't meet your specified restrictions, Excel 97 pops up an error message.

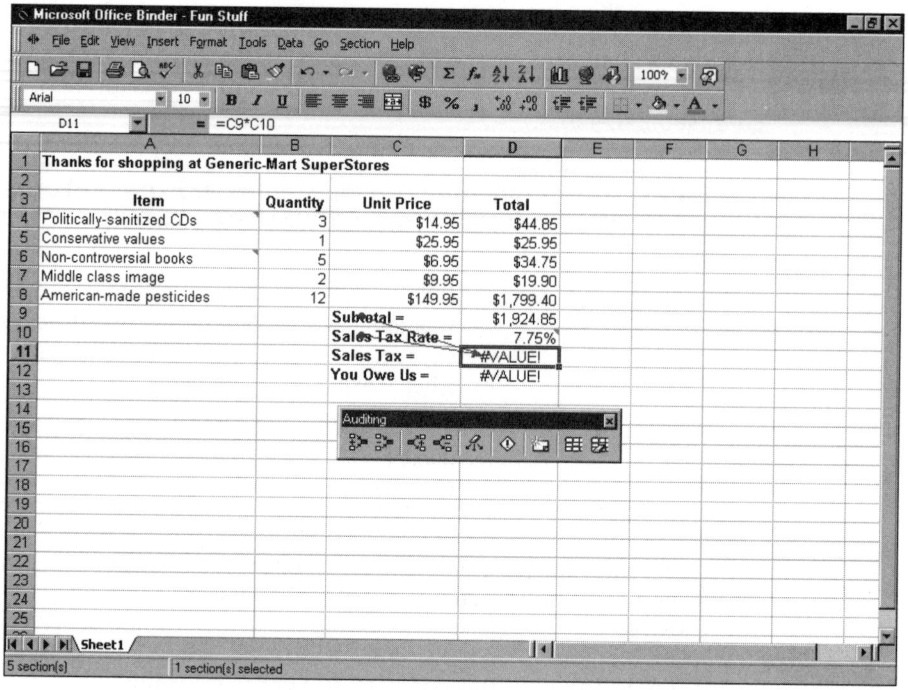

Figure 11-4:
Tracing an error message to see which cells may be to blame.

Defining validation criteria for a cell

To define the type of data that a cell is allowed to contain, follow these steps:

1. **Click in the cell for which you want to specify the type of data that it can contain.**

2. **Choose Data⇨Validation.**

   A Data Validation dialog box appears, as shown in Figure 11-5.

3. **Click in the Allow list box and choose the type of data allowed in the cell, such as Whole numbers, Decimals, or Text.**

4. **Click in the Data list box and choose a criteria, such as between, equal to, or greater than.**

5. **Click in the Minimum and Maximum list boxes and type the minimum and maximum values allowed in your chosen cell.**

6. **Click on OK.**

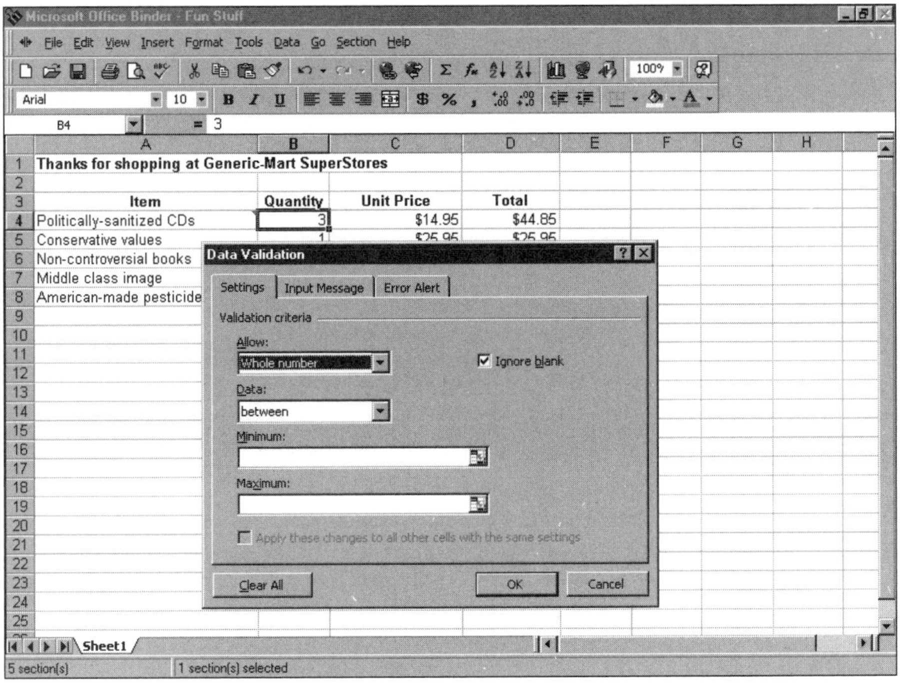

Figure 11-5:
The Data Validation dialog box allows you to specify a range of valid data for a cell.

Creating an input message

When you define a range of valid data for a cell, you might want to inform the user of the range of available data that the cell should contain. Although not necessary, such an input message can guide the user into typing valid data in a particular cell.

To create an input message for a cell, follow these steps:

1. **Click in the cell for which you have already defined a range of valid data.**

2. **Choose Data⇨Validation.**

   A Data Validation dialog box appears.

3. **Click on the Input Message tab, as shown in Figure 11-6.**

4. **Type a title for your input message dialog box in the Title text box.**

5. **Type the message for your input message dialog box in the Input message text box.**

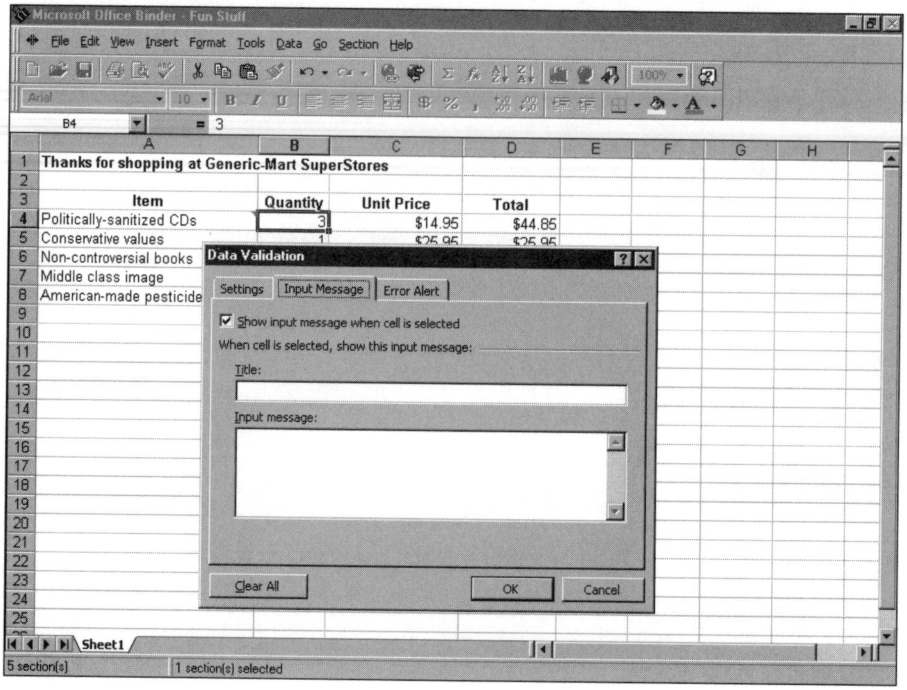

Figure 11-6: The Input Message tab in the Data Validation dialog box.

6. **Click on OK.**

From this point on, whenever the user highlights the cell chosen in Step 1, Excel 97 displays a short input message dialog box (see Figure 11-7).

Creating an error message

If someone tries to type invalid data in a cell, Excel 97 can display an error message dialog box informing the user of the mistake.

To create an error message for a cell, follow these steps:

1. **Click in the cell for which you have already defined a range of valid data.**

2. **Choose Data⇨Validation.**

   A Data Validation dialog box appears.

3. **Click on the Error Alert tab, as shown in Figure 11-8.**

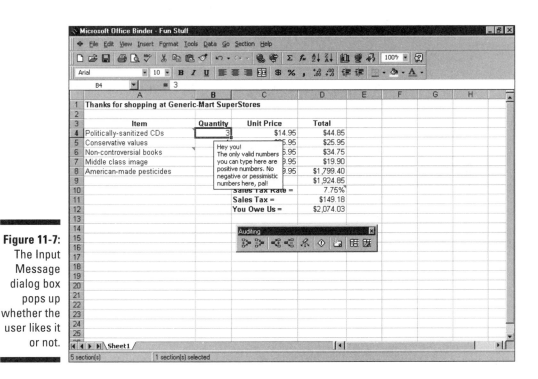

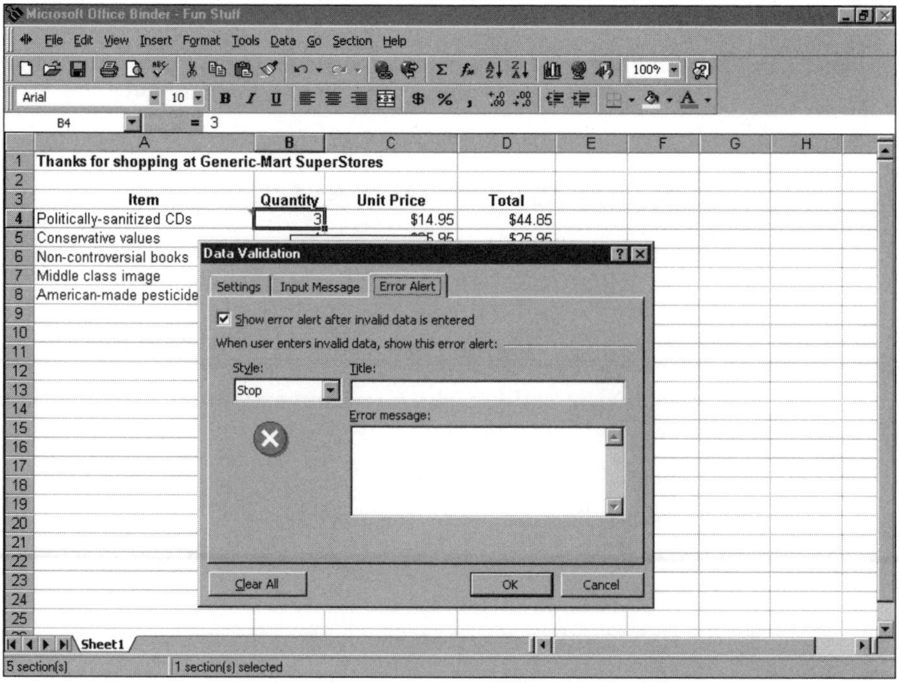

Figure 11-8:
The Error
Alert tab in
the Data
Validation
dialog box.

4. **Click in the Style list box and choose the type of icon that you want to display, such as Warning, Information, or Stop.**

5. **Type a title for your error message dialog box in the Title text box.**

6. **Type the message for your error message dialog box in the Error message text box.**

7. **Click on OK.**

From this point on, Excel 97 will display an error message dialog box if the user types invalid data, as shown in Figure 11-9.

Identifying invalid data in formulas

By using data validation, you can keep users from typing in nonsensical data, such as a negative number for an age. But what if you want to validate data for your cells that contain formulas as well?

It's perfectly possible for your users to type valid data in cells that feed information to a formula. Unfortunately, the data that the formula calculates might not make sense. For example, suppose that you have a formula that

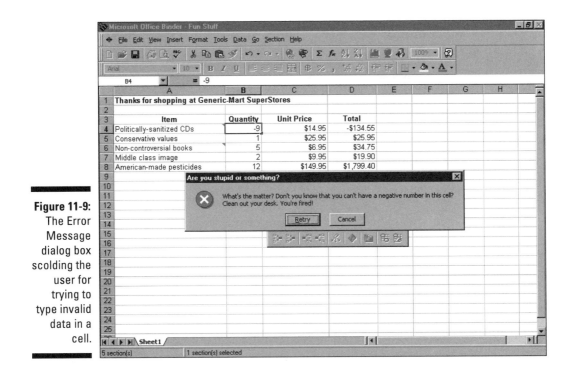

Figure 11-9:
The Error
Message
dialog box
scolding the
user for
trying to
type invalid
data in a
cell.

calculates a subtotal. Normally, the subtotal should add up to a positive
number, but what if the subtotal adds up to zero? That should be a clear
signal that:

✔ Someone didn't type any data into the proper cells.

✔ Someone typed data in the proper cells but your validation rules for
those cells aren't correct.

To identify invalid data in a formula, follow these steps:

1. **Click on the cell containing the formula to which you want to apply
   data validation.**

2. **Follow Steps 2–6 in the "Defining validation criteria for a cell"
   section, earlier in this chapter.**

3. **Click on the Circle Invalid Data icon on the Auditing toolbar.**

   If Excel 97 finds any data that doesn't match your data validation
   criteria for a formula, Excel 97 circles the offending formula in red (but
   because the publisher can't afford color, the circles appear as black and
   white), as shown in Figure 11-10.

Microsoft Office Binder - Fun Stuff

File Edit View Insert Format Tools Data Go Section Help

	A	B	C	D	E	F	G	H
1	Thanks for shopping at Generic-Mart SuperStores							
2								
3	Item	Quantity	Unit Price	Total				
4	Politically-sanitized CDs	0	$14.95	$0.00				
5	Conservative values	0	$25.95	$0.00				
6	Non-controversial books	0	$6.95	$0.00				
7	Middle class image	0	$9.95	$0.00				
8	American-made pesticides	0	$149.95	$0.00				
9			Subtotal =	$0.00				
10			Sales Tax Rate =	7.75%				
11			Sales Tax =	$0.00				
12			You Owe Us =	$0.00				

Auditing

Figure 11-10:
Excel 97 circles invalid data in a formula.

Sheet1

5 section(s)   1 section(s) selected

To remove any red circles around invalid formula data, click on the Clear Validation Circles icon on the Auditing toolbar.

Finding the Oddball Formula

Often, you need a row or column of nearly identical formulas, such as Row 7, as shown in Figure 11-11. In this example, all the cells in Row 9 should add the contents of the cells in Rows 3, 4, 5, 6, 7, and 8.

But here's the dilemma. How do you know that one formula in that row isn't adding up all the rows as it's supposed to? In case you don't relish the idea of examining each formula one by one, Excel 97 has an easier method that enables you to quickly find in a row or column a formula that doesn't fit the other formulas in the same row or column.

To find an oddball formula in a row or column, follow these steps:

1. **Highlight the row or column containing the formulas that you want to check.**

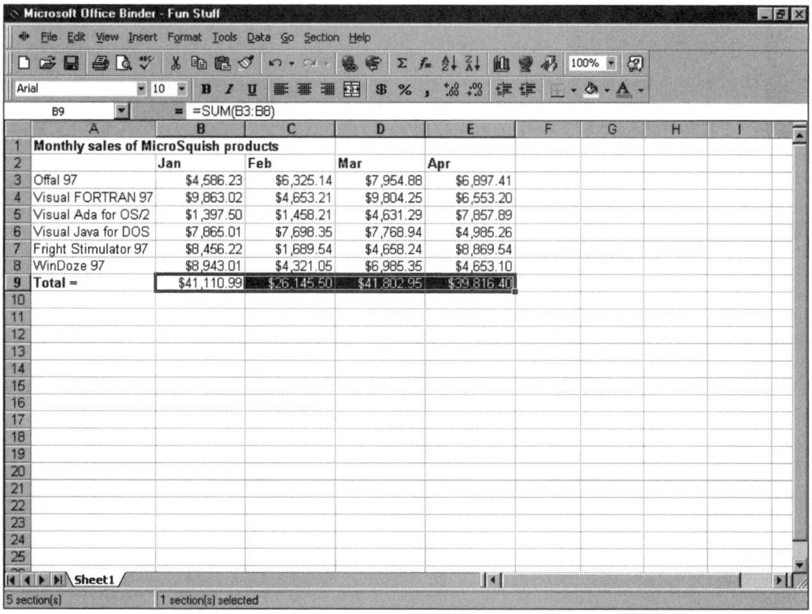

Figure 11-11:
A row of
nearly
identical
formulas.

2. Choose <u>E</u>dit⇨<u>G</u>o To or press Ctrl+G.

The Go To dialog box appears, as shown in Figure 11-12.

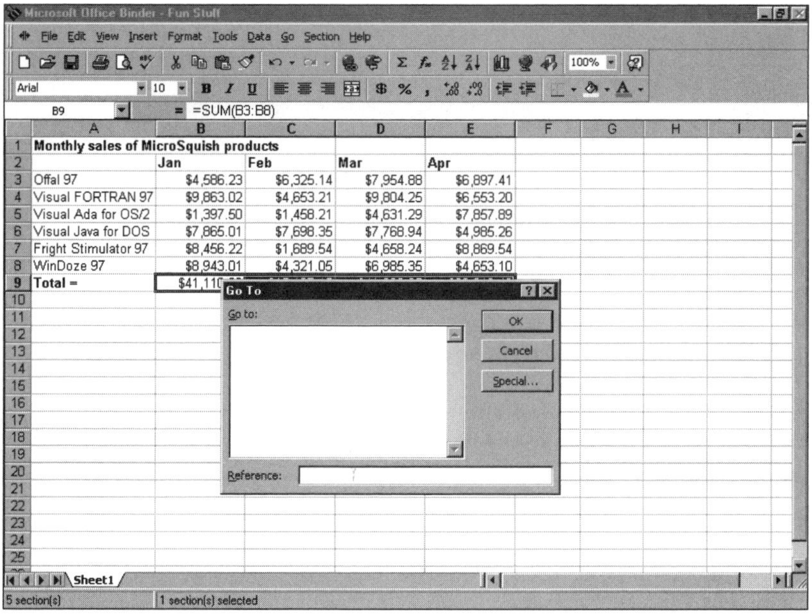

Figure 11-12:
The Go To
dialog box.

3. Click on Special.

The Go To Special dialog box appears, as shown in Figure 11-13.

4. Click on either the Row differences or Column differences radio button; then click on OK.

Excel 97 highlights the cell or cells containing formulas that are not similar to their neighboring cells.

Checking Your Spelling

Just because you don't know how to spell doesn't mean that you're stupid. Unfortunately, misspellings and typos can make you look stupid even if your data is 100 percent accurate and up-to-date. Unless you want to prevent your boss from giving you a raise just because you titled your spreadsheet "Our 1997 Anual Budgett Report," rest assured that Excel 97 can check your spelling before you print your spreadsheet for other people to see.

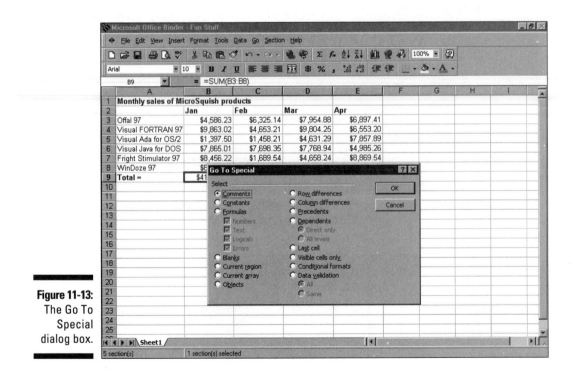

Figure 11-13:
The Go To
Special
dialog box.

To check your spelling, follow these steps:

1. **Press F7, choose Tools⇨Spelling, or click on the Spelling icon on the Standard toolbar.**

   The Spelling dialog box appears and highlights the first word that Excel 97 suspects is misspelled, as shown in Figure 11-14.

2. **Choose one of the following:**

   - **Ignore:** If you know that the word is spelled correctly

   - **Ignore All:** If you want Excel 97 to ignore all additional occurrences of the word

   - **Change:** If you want Excel 97 to correct your spelling with the word displayed in the Change To box

   - **Change All:** If you want Excel 97 to correct all additional occurrences of the word

   - **Add:** To add the word to Excel 97's dictionary

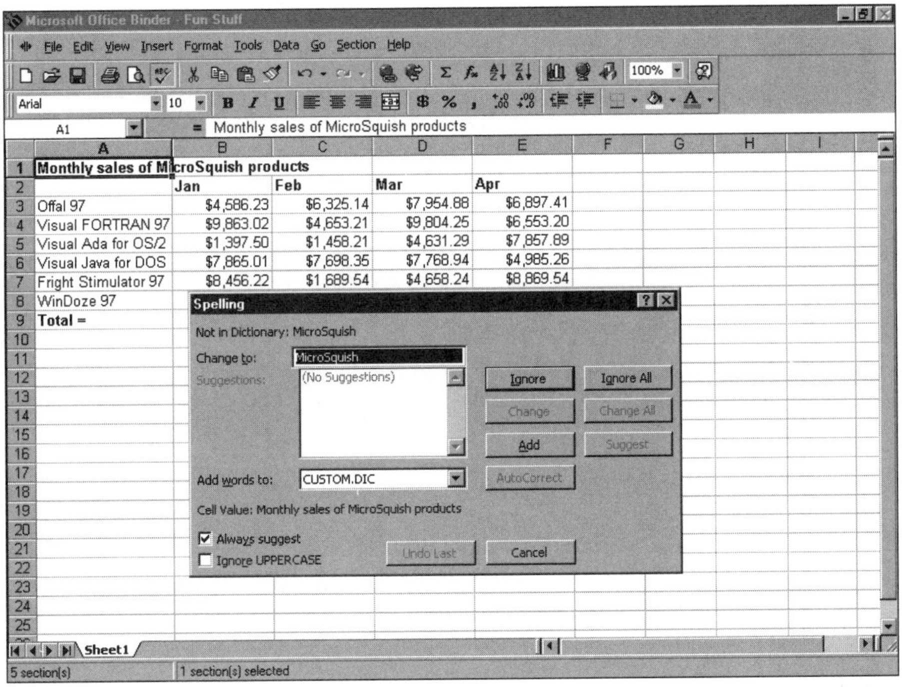

Figure 11-14: The Spelling dialog box, which enables you to correct misspelled words.

3. Repeat Step 2 for each word that Excel 97 highlights as being misspelled.

Click on Cancel if you want to stop checking before the spell checker is finished. Otherwise, Excel 97 displays a dialog box to let you know when the spelling in your entire worksheet has been checked.

Chapter 12

Printing Pretty Pages

• •

In This Chapter

▶ Making cells look nice

▶ Fitting your work on a single page

▶ Messing with margins

▶ Placing headers and footers on a page

▶ Choosing paper size and changing its orientation

▶ Deciding whether to print gridlines, headings, and page orders

• •

*A*fter you have typed all your text and numbers, made sure that your formulas work properly, and formatted it all to look nice, your next headache (if you choose to accept the assignment) is to make your pages look presentable when you print them.

You could waste your time and paper, of course, by adjusting the format of your worksheet, printing it, readjusting your worksheet, and printing it again until you finally get it right. If everyone who uses Excel 97 did that, global deforestation would occur at a much faster rate. In the interest of ecology and your own patience, you should adjust the appearance of your worksheet and print it only when it's absolutely ready.

Prettying Up Individual Cells

Normally, the cells in a worksheet look plain, dull, and ordinary. Rather than force you to endure plain cells displaying only black and white, Excel 97 gives you the chance to spice up individual cells with color, borders, and text manipulation.

Splashing cells with color

For your first steps in beautifying your worksheet cells, throw some color in them. Color can serve purely aesthetic purposes or it can highlight certain features of your worksheet.

To add color to a cell, follow these steps:

1. **Click in the cell to which you want to add color.**

2. **Choose Format➪Cells or press Ctrl+1.**

   The Format Cells dialog box appears.

3. **Click on the Patterns tab, as shown in Figure 12-1.**

4. **Click on a color.**

   Your chosen color appears in the Sample box so that you can get a better idea of what the color actually looks like.

5. **Click on OK.**

Putting a border around a cell

Besides using color to emphasize a cell, you can also put borders around a cell. To add a border around a cell, follow these steps:

1. **Click in the cell to which you want to add a border.**

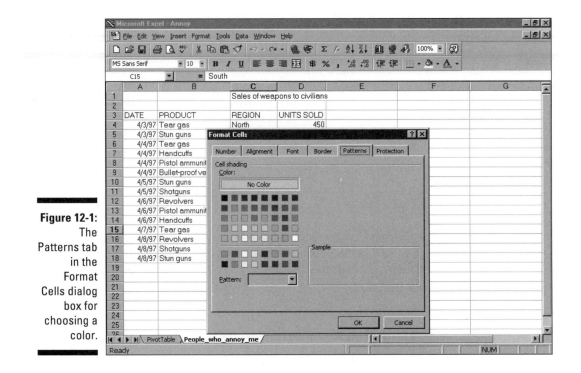

Figure 12-1:
The Patterns tab in the Format Cells dialog box for choosing a color.

2. **Choose Format➪Cells or press Ctrl+1.**

    The Format Cells dialog box appears.

3. **Click on the Border tab, as shown in Figure 12-2.**

4. **Click on a line style in the Style box to choose a thick, thin, or dotted line for your border.**

5. **Click on the border buttons in the Border group to choose a top, bottom, left, or right border for your chosen cell.**

6. **Click in the Color list box and choose a color for your border.**

7. **Click on OK.**

Cramming text in a cell

You can type a bunch of text in a cell, but if the cell isn't wide enough, Excel 97 mindlessly allows the text to spill across to any neighboring cells. At this point, you can increase the width of the cell that contains the text (so that the entire text fits inside the wider cell).

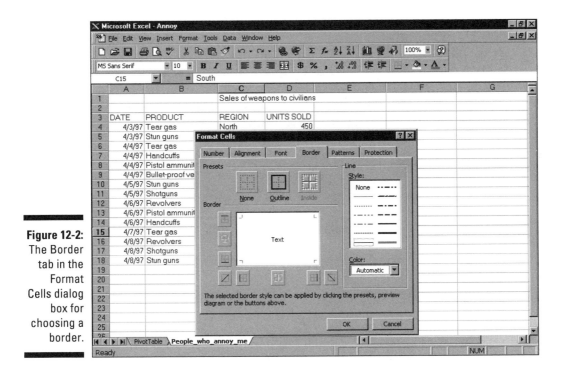

Figure 12-2:
The Border tab in the Format Cells dialog box for choosing a border.

Unfortunately, widening one cell automatically widens the entire column of cells simultaneously. If you want text to appear in one cell without having to widen the cell too much, you can tell Excel 97 to wrap text inside a cell.

Text-wrapping simply makes the cell taller (increases the row height) without adjusting the column width one bit.

Text-wrapping increases the height of all the cells in the same row.

To apply text-wrapping to a cell, follow these steps:

1. **Click in the cell to which you want to apply text-wrapping.**

2. **Choose Format⇨Cells or press Ctrl+1.**

   The Format Cells dialog box appears.

3. **Click on the Alignment tab, as shown in Figure 12-3.**

4. **Click in the Wrap text check box so that a check mark appears.**

5. **Click on OK.**

   Excel 97 crams your text inside your chosen cell, as shown in Figure 12-4.

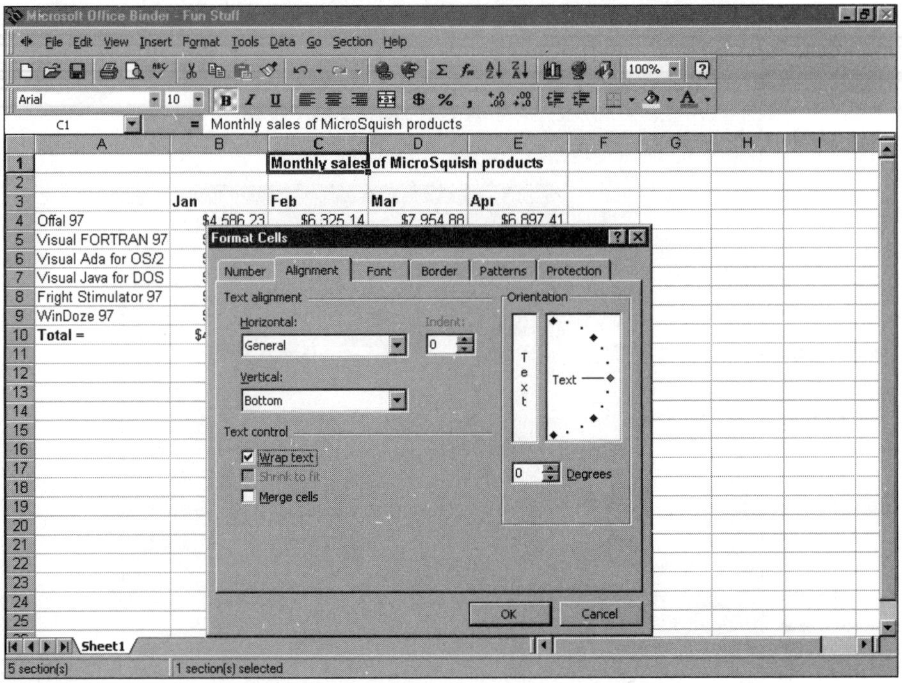

Figure 12-3: The Alignment tab in the Format Cells dialog box for shoving text inside a cell.

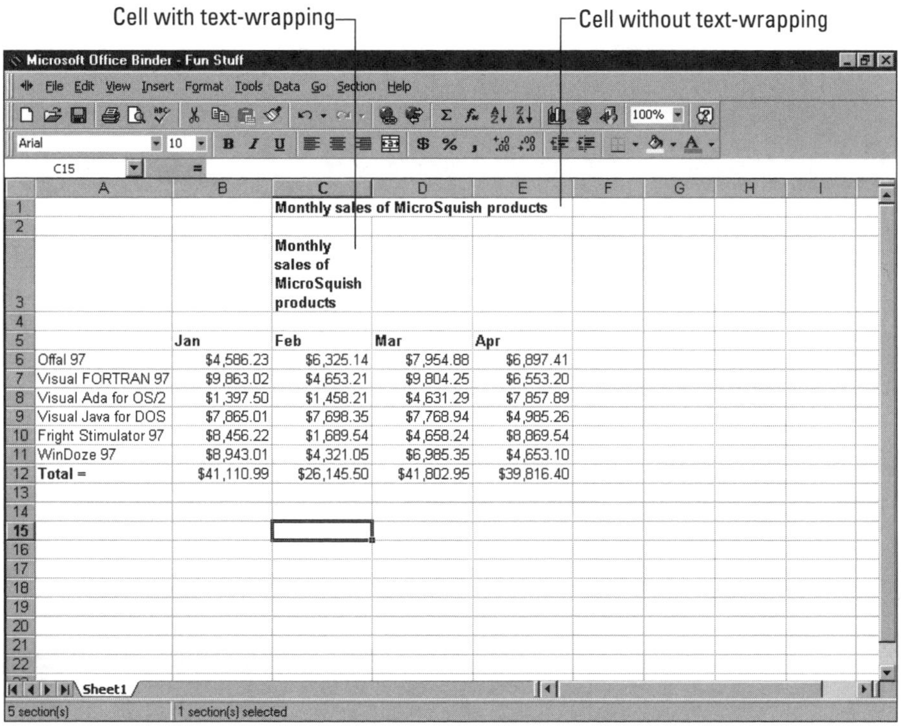

Cell with text-wrapping

Cell without text-wrapping

Figure 12-4:
Text-
wrapping in
a cell.

Merging text in multiple cells

Often, you may find that two or more cells have identical information in them, such as the same person's name. Instead of cluttering up your worksheet with redundant labels, Excel 97 lets you merge cells with identical contents into one big cell. That way, your worksheet can be easier to study and understand (you hope).

To merge text in multiple cells, follow these steps:

1. **Highlight the cells that contain identical text.**

2. **Choose Format⇨Cells or press Ctrl+1.**

   The Format Cells dialog box appears.

3. **Click on the Alignment tab (refer to Figure 12-3).**

4. **Click in the Vertical list box and choose Center (or Top, Bottom, or Justify).**

5. **Click in the Merge cells check box so that a check mark appears.**

   A dialog box appears, letting you know that Excel 97 is about to merge all the text into one big cell.

6. Click on OK.

Excel 97 merges your cells together, as shown in Figure 12-5.

Squeezing (Or Blowing Up) Your Work

Nothing is more frustrating than creating a spreadsheet in which everything fits on one page except for one line that prints on a second page (see Figure 12-6). Instead of printing your spreadsheet on two pages and leaving the second page mostly blank, you can tell Excel 97 to squeeze all your work on a single page.

To shrink or expand your spreadsheet, follow these steps:

1. **Choose File⇨Print Preview (or Section⇨Print Preview if you're using Excel 97 within a binder).**

   Excel displays your worksheet exactly as it will look when you print it, as shown in Figure 12-7.

Figure 12-5:
Merging
multiple
cells
together.

	A	B	C	D	E	F	G	H	I
1				Monthly sales of MicroSquish products					
2									
3	Sales Region	Product	Jan	Feb	Mar	Apr			
4	West	Visual Ada for OS/2	$4,586.23	$6,325.14	$7,954.88	$6,897.41			
5	North	Visual Ada for OS/2	$9,863.02	$4,653.21	$9,804.25	$6,553.20			
6	East	Visual Ada for OS/2	$1,397.50	$1,458.21	$4,631.29	$7,857.89			
7	South	Visual Ada for OS/2	$7,865.01	$7,698.35	$7,768.94	$4,985.26			
8	West	WinDoze 97	$8,456.22	$1,689.54	$4,658.24	$8,869.54			
9	North	WinDoze 97	$8,943.01	$4,321.05	$6,985.35	$4,653.10			
10	East	FORTRAN for DOS	$5,463.25	$1,474.01	$1,223.30	$8,645.10			
11	South	FORTRAN for DOS	$4,468.77	$4,563.29	$9,814.20	$12,245.21			
12		Total =	$51,043.01	$32,182.80	$52,840.45	$60,706.71			
13									
14									
15	Sales Region	Product	Jan	Feb	Mar	Apr			
16	West		$4,586.23	$6,325.14	$7,954.88	$6,897.41			
17	North	Visual Ada for OS/2	$9,863.02	$4,653.21	$9,804.25	$6,553.20			
18	East		$1,397.50	$1,458.21	$4,631.29	$7,857.89			
19	South		$7,865.01	$7,698.35	$7,768.94	$4,985.26			
20	West	WinDoze 97	$8,456.22	$1,689.54	$4,658.24	$8,869.54			
21	North		$8,943.01	$4,321.05	$6,985.35	$4,653.10			
22	East	FORTRAN for DOS	$5,463.25	$1,474.01	$1,223.30	$8,645.10			
23	South		$4,468.77	$4,563.29	$9,814.20	$12,245.21			
24		Total =	$51,043.01	$32,182.80	$52,840.45	$60,706.71			
25									

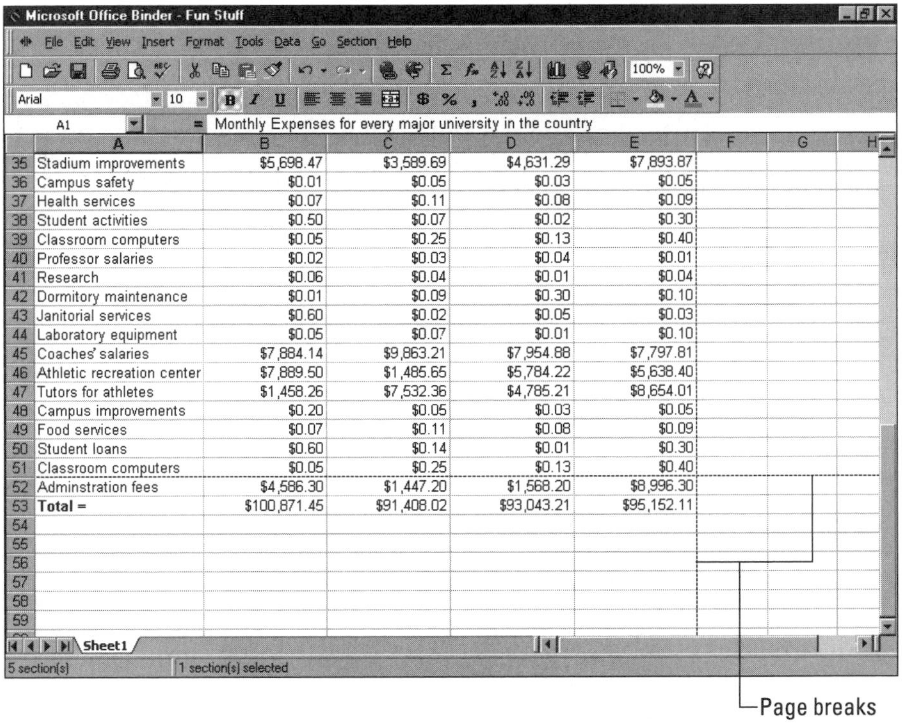

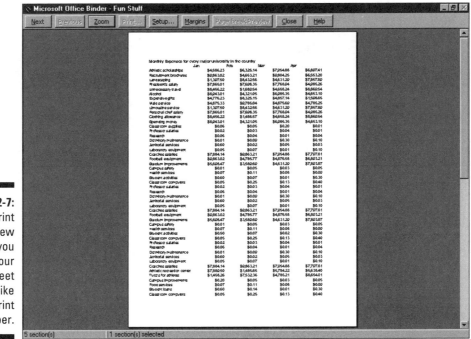

Figure 12-6:
A typical worksheet inconveniently divided by a page break.

Page breaks

Figure 12-7:
Print Preview shows you what your worksheet will look like if you print it on paper.

2. **Click on Setup.**

    The Page Setup dialog box appears, as shown in Figure 12-8.

3. **Click on the Fit to option button and then click on the Page(s) wide by list box and the Tall list box to specify how you want Excel to squeeze your spreadsheet on your pages.**

    For example, if you want to squeeze everything on one page, both the Page(s) wide by and the Tall list boxes should have 1 in it.

4. **Click on OK.**

    Excel 97 displays your newly scaled worksheet.

5. **Click on Close when you're happy with the way your worksheet will look when it's printed.**

As an alternative to clicking on the Fit to option button in Step 3, you can click on the Adjust to option button and then click on the % normal size list box to change the scaling of your worksheet.

This option lets you specify an exact percentage to shrink or expand your worksheet. To shrink your worksheet, choose a percentage less than 100 (90, for example). To expand your worksheet, choose a percentage larger than 100 (120, for example).

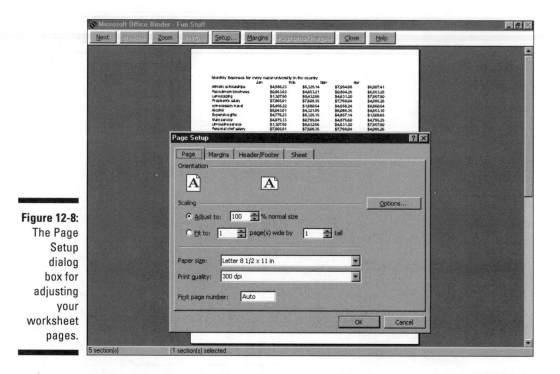

Figure 12-8:
The Page
Setup
dialog
box for
adjusting
your
worksheet
pages.

Shrinking or expanding your worksheet lets you change the way page breaks separate your worksheet. If you already know where you want to put a page break, you can easily tell Excel 97, "See that row? Put a page break right there."

To place a page break, follow these steps:

1. **Click in the row label that you want to appear directly below the page break.**

   If you want to put a page break between Rows 6 and 7, click on the row label 7.

2. **Choose Insert⇨Page Break.**

To remove a page break, follow these steps:

1. **Click in any cell in the row directly beneath the page break.**

2. **Choose Insert⇨Remove Page Break.**

Setting Page Margins

Another problem you might face when you print your entire worksheet is when you bind it together and then suddenly realize that narrow margins are forcing you to pry apart the binding just to see the left column of your worksheet. To prevent this problem and to give you another way to make your worksheets look aesthetically pleasing, Excel 97 lets you adjust its top, bottom, right, and left margins.

Adjusting page margins the fast way

If you're in a hurry and want to adjust your page margins quickly, using your mouse is the easiest route. Although using the mouse isn't precise, it's fast and easy, which is a rare commodity in anything involving personal computers.

To adjust your page margins quickly, follow these steps:

1. **Choose File⇨Print Preview (or Section⇨Print Preview if you're using Excel 97 within a binder).**

   Excel displays your worksheet exactly as it will look when you print it (refer to Figure 12-7).

2. Click on <u>M</u>argins.

Excel 97 displays your worksheet's margins, as shown in Figure 12-9.

3. Move the mouse pointer over any of the page margins so that the pointer turns into a double-pointing arrow (refer to Figure 12-9).

4. Hold down the left mouse button and drag the mouse to where you want the new margin to appear.

The original page margin line remains visible and a new dotted line appears under the mouse pointer so that you know where the new page margin will appear.

5. When you're happy with the page margin position, release the left mouse button.

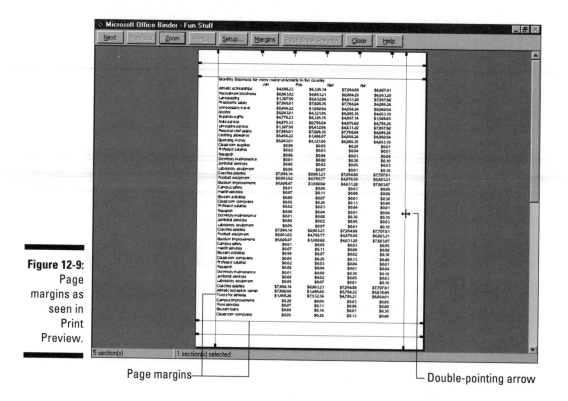

Figure 12-9:
Page margins as seen in Print Preview.

Page margins

Double-pointing arrow

Adjusting page margins the slower, more precise way

In case you absolutely must have page margins narrowed to two decimal places, you can specify exact values rather than just move the page margins around and guess where they should appear.

To adjust your page margins by typing values, follow these steps:

1. **Choose File⇨Page Setup (or choose Section⇨Page Setup if you're using Excel 97 within a binder).**

   The Page Setup dialog box appears (refer to Figure 12-8).

2. **Click on the Margins tab, as shown in Figure 12-10.**

3. **Click on the Top, Bottom, Left, or Right list boxes and choose a value for your page margins.**

4. **Click on the Horizontally and Vertically check boxes in the Center on Page group if you want your worksheet neatly centered on the page.**

5. **Click on OK.**

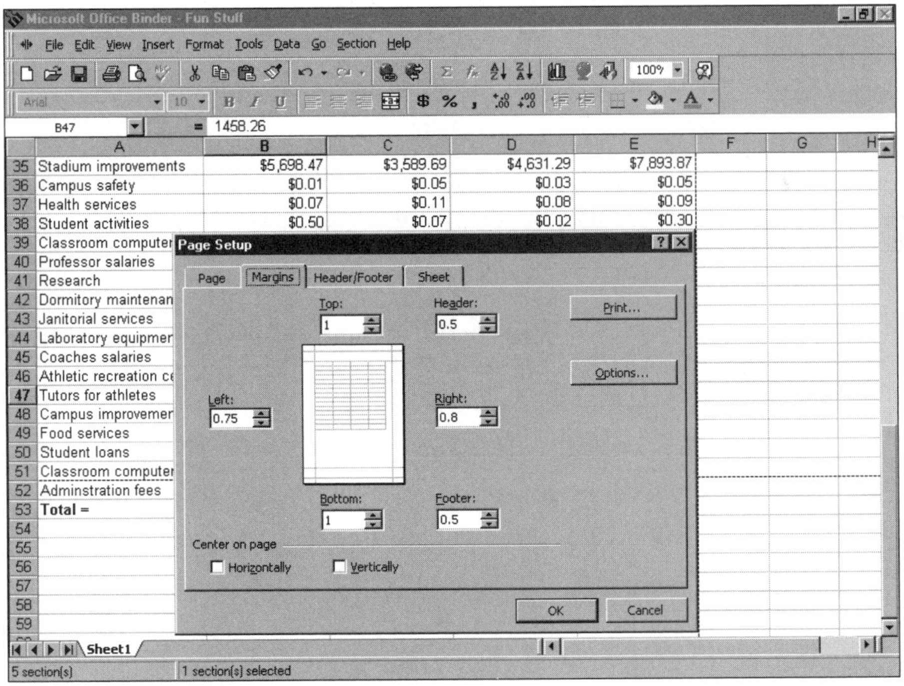

Figure 12-10: Defining precise values for your page margins.

Playing with Headers and Footers

A *header* consists of text that appears at the top of every page in your worksheet, but only when you print it. Here are some typical examples of headers:

- 1996 Annual Report
- Prepared by John Doe (who deserves a fat raise)
- Top Secret: Destroy after reading

A *footer* consists of text that appears at the bottom of every page in your worksheet, but only when you print it. Here are some typical examples of footers:

- Page 5
- Copyright ©1997
- Warning: Profit margins seem larger than they really are

To help make the process of choosing a header or footer as mindless as possible, Excel 97 provides a list box that contains some common types of headers and footers. You can also create your own headers and footers, and be as bad (creative) as you wanna be.

Choosing a header and footer

If you don't want to think for yourself, the simplest solution is to choose a header or footer that Excel 97 has already created for you.

To choose one of the default headers or footers, follow these steps:

1. **Choose File⇨Page Setup (or choose Section⇨Page Setup if you're using Excel 97 within a binder).**

   The Page Setup dialog box appears (refer to Figure 12-8).

2. **Click on the Header/Footer tab.**

3. **Click on the Header list box and then choose a header.**

4. **Click on the Footer list box and then choose a footer.**

5. **Click on OK.**

Making your own headers and footers

Unfortunately, being forced to choose from one of Excel 97's default headers or footers can seem as limiting as choosing between two equally obnoxious and unappealing politicians. To give you even greater freedom, Excel 97 also lets you create your own custom headers and footers.

To create a custom header or footer, follow these steps:

1. **Choose File⇨Page Setup (or choose Section⇨Page Setup if you're using Excel 97 within a binder).**

   The Page Setup dialog box appears (refer to Figure 12-8).

2. **Click on the Header/Footer tab.**

3. **Click on Custom Header.**

   The Header dialog box appears, as shown in Figure 12-11.

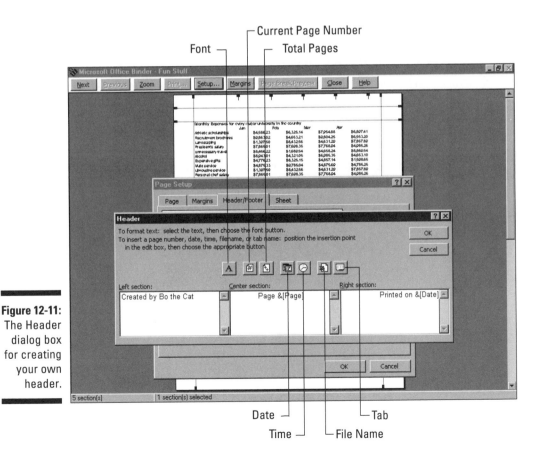

Figure 12-11: The Header dialog box for creating your own header.

4. **Click in the text box displayed in the Left Section box.**

5. **Type the text that you want to display as your header.**

   If you want Excel 97 to insert or format text for you, click on one of the following buttons:

   - **Font:** Enables you to change your header/footer's font and font size
   - **Current Page Number:** Displays the current page number
   - **Total Pages:** Displays the total number of pages in your worksheet
   - **Date:** Inserts the date on which you print the worksheet
   - **Time:** Inserts the time at which you print the worksheet
   - **File Name:** Inserts the filename of your worksheet
   - **Tab:** Inserts the worksheet name

6. **Click in the Center Section box, type more text, and then click in the Right Section box to type even more text if you want.**

7. **Click on OK.**

   The Page Setup dialog box appears again.

8. **Click on Custom Footer.**

   The Footer dialog box that appears looks suspiciously similar to the Header dialog box (refer to Figure 12-11).

9. **Repeat Steps 5–7 and fill in the information for your footer.**

10. **Click on OK.**

    The Page Setup dialog box appears again.

11. **Click on OK.**

Changing the Paper Size and Orientation

Sometimes a worksheet won't fit within the confines of a typical piece of paper. When this situation occurs, you can tell Excel 97 to print your worksheets sideways or on legal-sized paper so that everything fits on a single page.

Changing the page orientation

The two types of page orientation are portrait and landscape. In _portrait orientation,_ a page is taller than it is wide. Think about how you would orient a canvas to paint someone's portrait. Because most people are taller than they are wide, height is more important.

In _landscape orientation,_ a page is wider than it is tall. If you paint a landscape, width is more important than height, so you should use landscape orientation when you want to print your worksheets sideways on a sheet of paper.

To change the page orientation of your worksheet, follow these steps:

1. **Choose File⇨Page Setup (or choose Section⇨Page Setup if you're using Excel 97 within a binder).**

   The Page Setup dialog box appears (refer to Figure 12-8).

2. **Click on the Page tab.**

3. **Click on either the Portrait or the Landscape radio button.**

4. **Click on OK.**

Choosing the size of your paper

Many people use paper that measures $8^1/_2$ x 11 inches. If you want to cram more of your worksheet on a single page, you can just stuff your printer with different sizes of paper. Immediately after you load your printer with a different size of paper, you also have to tell Excel 97 the size of the new paper so that it prints your worksheets on the paper correctly.

To tell Excel 97 the size of the paper on which to print, follow these steps:

1. **Choose File⇨Page Setup (or choose Section⇨Page Setup if you're using Excel 97 within a binder).**

   The Page Setup dialog box appears (refer to Figure 12-8).

2. **Click on the Page tab.**

3. **Click on the Paper size list box and then choose a paper size.**

4. **Click on OK.**

Printing Gridlines, Headings, and Page Orders

The entire purpose of displaying gridlines and headings is to help you place your labels, numbers, and formulas. Normally, when you print a worksheet, you don't want your gridlines and row or column headings to appear, because they can be as distracting as the wires holding up a marionette during a puppet show.

Because Excel 97 gives you options for practically everything imaginable, you can also choose to print your gridlines and headings. Then you can see exactly which cells contain labels, numbers, and formulas.

 One good time to print gridlines and headings is when you're printing a worksheet with all its formulas revealed (you can reveal your formulas by pressing Ctrl+`; the ` character usually shares the same key as the ~ symbol). Then you can see exactly which cells contain the data a formula uses.

If you have a particularly large worksheet (three pages or more), you can even tell Excel 97 in which order you want to print everything. Then you don't have to re-sort your worksheets by hand after printing them. The two choices for printing your worksheets are as follows:

- ✔ Down, then over
- ✔ Over, then down

Which method you choose depends on your personal preferences and how you organized your data in a worksheet. For example, you may want to print Over, then down if your data were to be organized as follows:

1st Quarter sales				*2nd Quarter sales*			
	Jan.	Feb.	Mar.		Apr.	May	Jun.
Cat food				Cat food			
Dog food				Dog food			
Fish food				Fish food			

3rd Quarter sales

	Jul.	Aug.	Sep.
Cat food			
Dog food			
Fish food			

4th Quarter sales

	Oct.	Nov.	Dec.
Cat food			
Dog food			
Fish food			

Suppose that your worksheets were organized in this way:

1st Quarter sales

	Jan.	Feb.	Mar.
Cat food			
Dog food			
Fish food			

3rd Quarter sales

	Jul.	Aug.	Sep.
Cat food			
Dog food			
Fish food			

2nd Quarter sales

	Apr.	May	Jun.
Cat food			
Dog food			
Fish food			

4th Quarter sales

	Oct.	Nov.	Dec.
Cat food			
Dog food			
Fish food			

In this case, you would probably want to print Down, then over to make sure that your data appeared in the right order.

To change the print order of your worksheet or to make Excel 97 print gridlines and headings, follow these steps:

1. **Choose File⇨Page Setup (or choose Section⇨Page Setup if you're using Excel 97 within a binder).**

   The Page Setup dialog box appears (refer to Figure 12-8).

2. **Click on the Sheet tab, as shown in Figure 12-12.**

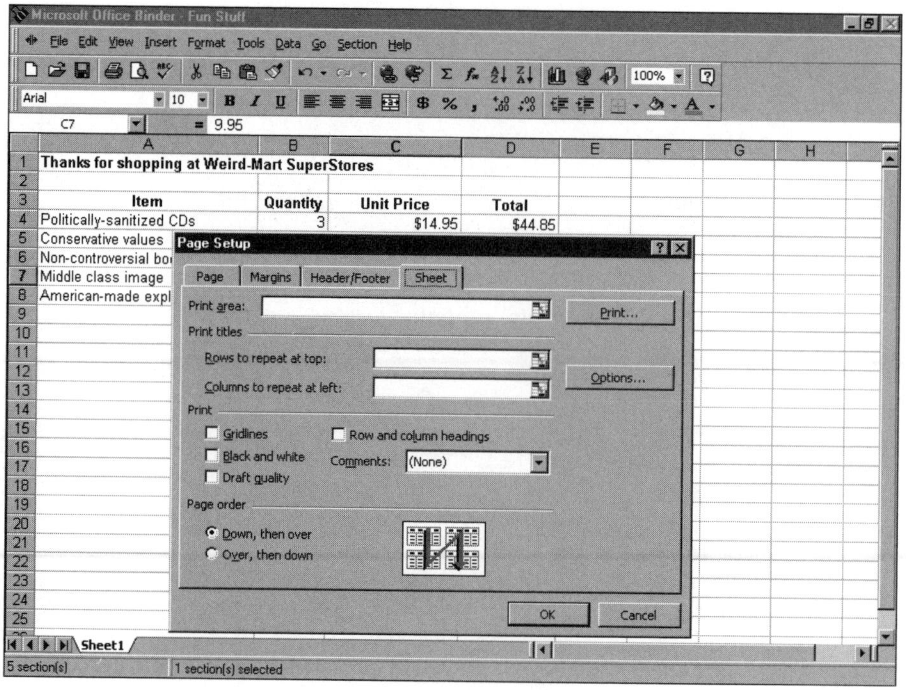

Figure 12-12:
The Sheet tab in the Page Setup dialog box.

3. Click in the <u>G</u>ridlines check box so that a check mark appears if you want to print gridlines.

4. Click in the Row and Co<u>l</u>umn Headings check box so that a check mark appears if you want to print row and column headings.

5. Click on either the <u>D</u>own, then over radio button or the O<u>v</u>er, then down radio button in the Page order group.

6. Click on OK.

Chapter 13

Making Maps Out of Your Data

*I*f you have a worksheet filled with rows and columns of numbers and text, chances are good that nobody (maybe not even you) completely understands what those numbers are telling you. Are profits up? Are sales down? Did somebody just type a lot of meaningless numbers in the worksheet to make him- or herself look more important?

To help you better understand numbers, you should use Excel 97's Chart Wizard to help you create a bar, pie, or line chart. If you've organized your data according to geographical regions such as countries, states, or provinces, however, displaying your data on a map can make your data easier to understand.

By using a map, you can pinpoint the countries where sales are up (or down), identify new markets to tackle, or just make more meaningful charts than bar, column, line, or pie charts. Figure 13-1 shows a boring column chart, whereas Figure 13-2 shows the same data displayed as a map. Can you guess which one makes more sense at first glance?

Installing Microsoft Map

To help you create maps, Microsoft Office 97 comes with a special program called (what else?) Microsoft Map. Microsoft Map may not have installed on your computer when you first installed Microsoft Office 97, so you may need to install Microsoft Map separately.

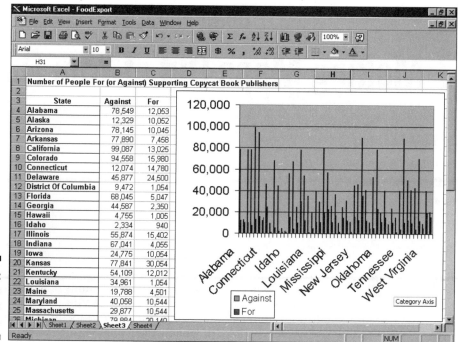

Figure 13-1:
A generic column chart.

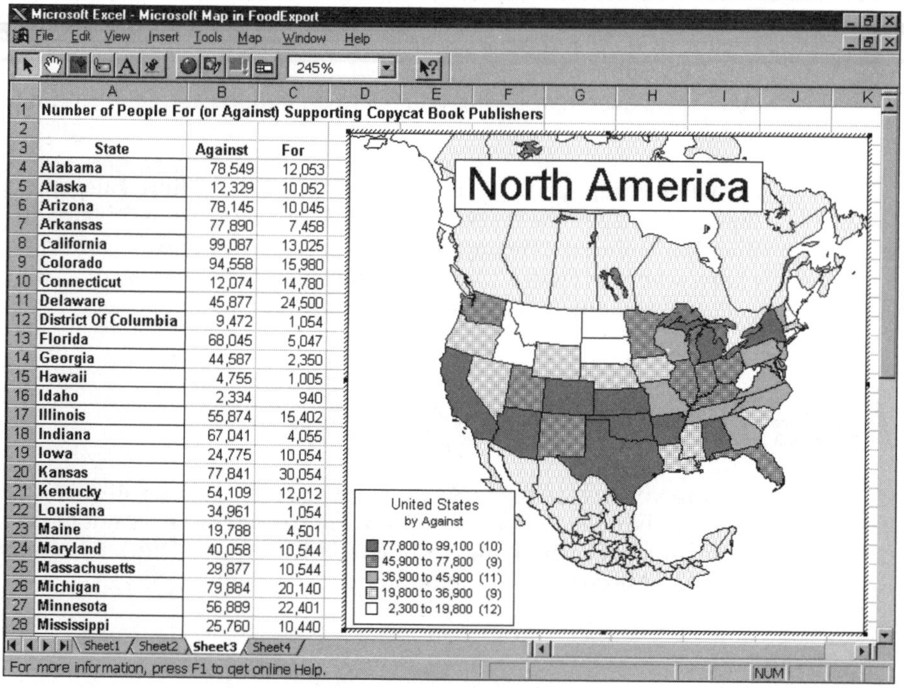

Figure 13-2:
The same data plotted on a map.

To install Microsoft Map, follow these steps:

1. **Insert the Microsoft Office 97 CD in your computer's CD-ROM drive.**

   A Microsoft Office 97 window appears automatically, as shown in Figure 13-3.

2. **Double-click on the Setup icon.**

   The Microsoft Office 97 Setup window appears.

3. **Click on Add/Remove.**

   A Microsoft Office 97 – Maintenance dialog box appears, as shown in Figure 13-4.

4. **Click on Microsoft Excel and click on Change Option.**

   The Microsoft Office 97 – Microsoft Excel window appears. (See Figure 13-5.)

5. **If no check mark appears in the Microsoft Map check box, click in the Microsoft Map check box and then click on OK.**

   The Microsoft Office 97 – Maintenance window appears again.

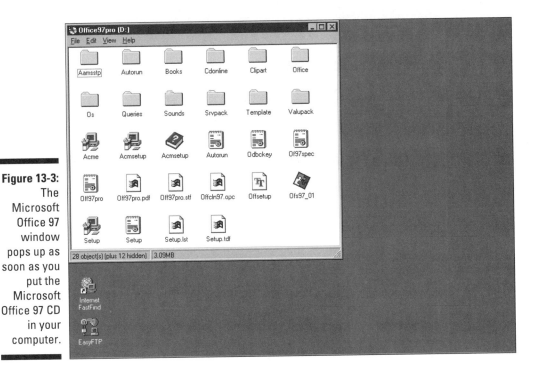

Figure 13-3: The Microsoft Office 97 window pops up as soon as you put the Microsoft Office 97 CD in your computer.

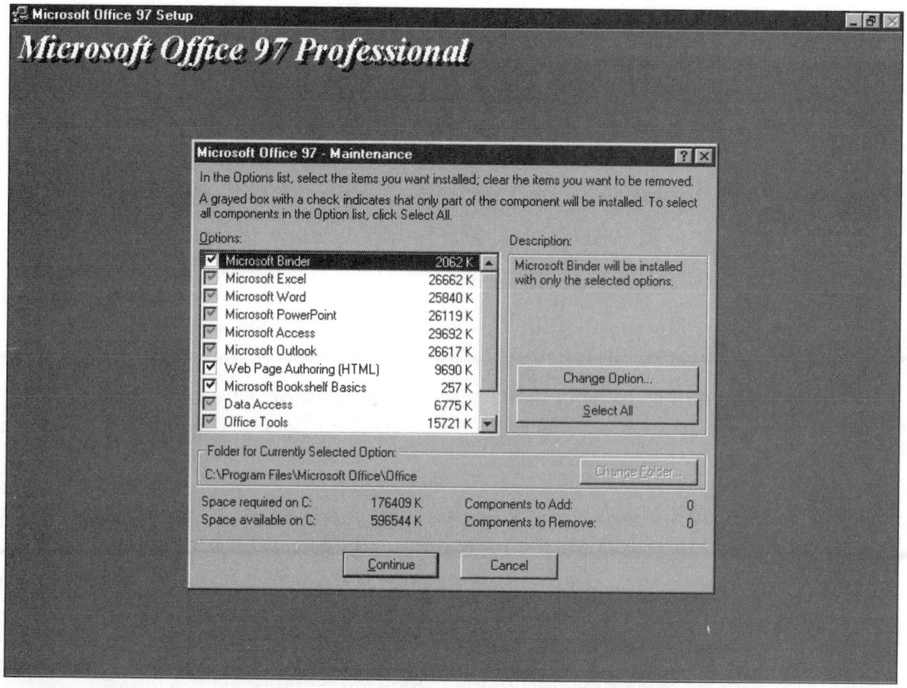

Figure 13-4:
The Microsoft Office 97 – Maintenance window.

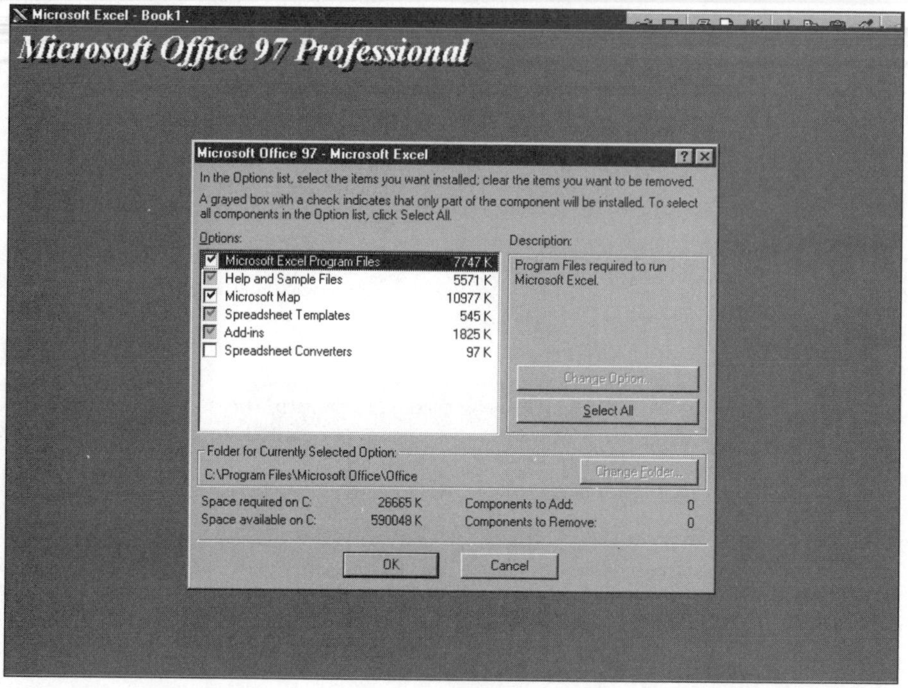

Figure 13-5:
The Microsoft Office 97 – Microsoft Excel window.

6. **Click on <u>C</u>ontinue and follow any additional instructions that may appear on the screen.**

Microsoft Map is now ready for use within Microsoft Excel 97.

Mapping Your Data

Microsoft Map gives you two ways to create a map:

✔ Type numerical data, organize it by regions, and then create a map from your data

✔ Draw your map first and then add meaningful labels

Which method should you choose? If you want your map to represent any numerical data, choose the first method. That way, your maps can display facts such as the number of products sold in each state or province.

If you don't have any numerical data, choose the second method. For example, you might want to create a map so that you can label which states your company is currently doing business in and which states your company hasn't sold a single product in.

Turning numerical data into a map

To create a map from numerical data, you need a worksheet that contains two items:

✔ The names of geographical regions such as states, provinces, or countries

✔ Numerical data related to each geographical region, such as population, imports and exports, or ozone depletion levels

To get Microsoft Map to recognize geographical regions typed into your worksheet, you must spell the region (country, state, or province) correctly. In case you don't know the correct spelling for Afghanistan (even though it's right here in front of your eyes), you can find out by following these steps:

1. **Load Excel 97.**

2. **Choose <u>F</u>ile⇨<u>O</u>pen (or <u>S</u>ection⇨Add from <u>F</u>ile if you're using Excel 97 within a binder).**

3. Load the Mapstats.XLS file.

This file contains all the names and abbreviations that Microsoft Map can recognize in any worksheet you create. If you misspell a geographical region (such as ARKANSAW for Arkansas), Microsoft Map won't know how to map that particular data.

So, where can you find the Mapstats.XLS file? To find out, follow these steps:

1. Load the Windows Explorer.

2. Choose Tools⇨Find⇨Files or Folders.

A Find: All Files dialog box appears.

3. Type MAPSTATS.XLS in the Named text box.

4. Click in the Look in list box and choose C: (or whatever drive letter you think the Mapstats.XLS file might be located on).

5. Click on Find Now.

The bottom of the Find: All Files dialog box displays the location of the Mapstats.XLS file (if it really is on your hard disk).

To create a map from numerical data, follow these steps:

1. Fill one entire column with geographical region names and at least one other column with numerical data, such as Units Sold, Population, or Average Income. Figure 13-6 shows data arranged in columns.

2. Highlight the column headings and the columns of data that you want to map.

At the very least, you need to highlight the column containing the geographical regions plus another column of numerical data.

3. Choose Insert⇨Map or click on the Map icon on the Standard toolbar.

The mouse pointer turns into a crosshair.

4. Move the mouse pointer where you want to draw the map, hold down the left mouse button, drag the mouse, and release the left mouse button.

If multiple maps are available, a Multiple Maps Available dialog box appears, as shown in Figure 13-7.

5. Click on the map that you want to use and click on OK.

Excel 97 draws a map and displays the Microsoft Map Control dialog box appears, as shown in Figure 13-8. Notice that each of your column headings appears as a button at the top of the dialog box.

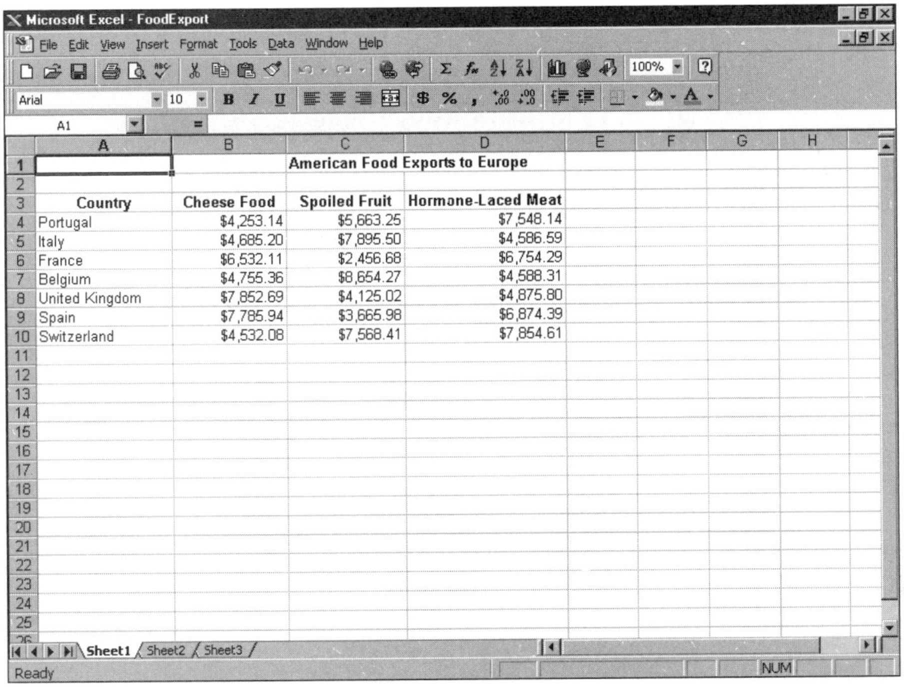

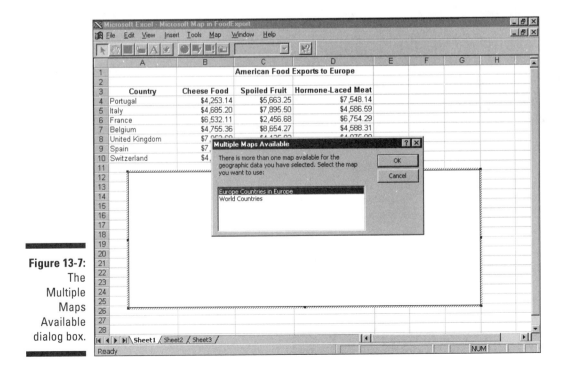

Figure 13-6:
The ideal format for a worksheet about to be converted into a map.

Figure 13-7:
The Multiple Maps Available dialog box.

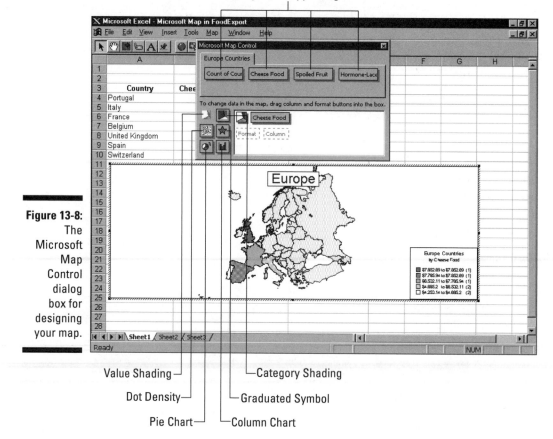

Column heading labels appearing as buttons

Figure 13-8:
The
Microsoft
Map
Control
dialog
box for
designing
your map.

Value Shading ⎯

Dot Density ⎯

Pie Chart ⎯ ⎯ Column Chart

⎯ Category Shading

⎯ Graduated Symbol

6. Click on a format button and drag it over the dotted line box labeled Format.

Microsoft Map gives you six different format buttons from which to choose:

- **Value Shading:** (Chosen by default) Displays data as ranges of gray shading

- **Category Shading:** Displays data in distinct colors (not recommended when data consists of individual numbers, because each number gets its own color)

- **Dot Density:** Displays data as a dot on the map

- **Graduated Symbol:** Displays data as circles of varying sizes

- **Pie Chart:** Displays two or more sets of data as a pie chart

- **Column Chart:** Displays two or more sets of data as a column chart

7. **Move the mouse pointer over a column heading button, hold down the left mouse button, and drag the mouse over the dotted line boxes labeled Format and Column. Then release the left mouse button.**

8. **Repeat for each column heading that you want to display on your map.**

9. **Click in the close box of the Microsoft Map Control dialog box to make it go away.**

   Your map may not be perfect just yet, but you'll learn how to edit it in the following "Editing Your Map" section.

Creating a map from scratch

Sometimes you may just want to draw a map so that you can label it yourself. For example, you might want to create a map and label certain regions to represent potential markets that your company should pursue.

To create a map from scratch, follow these steps:

1. **Choose Insert⇨Map or click on the Map icon on the Standard toolbar.**

   The mouse pointer turns into a crosshair. An Unable to Create Map dialog box pops up, as shown in Figure 13-9.

2. **Click on the map name that you want to draw and click on OK.**

   Excel 97 draws your chosen map.

Moving a map

Don't worry about the exact location where you draw your map; you can always move it later. To move your map to a different location, follow these steps:

1. **Click anywhere on the worksheet outside of the map.**

2. **Move the mouse pointer directly over the map and click on the left mouse button once.**

   White handles appear around the edges of the map.

3. **Hold down the left mouse button and drag the mouse to move the map.**

   Release the left mouse button when you're happy with the new location of the map on your worksheet.

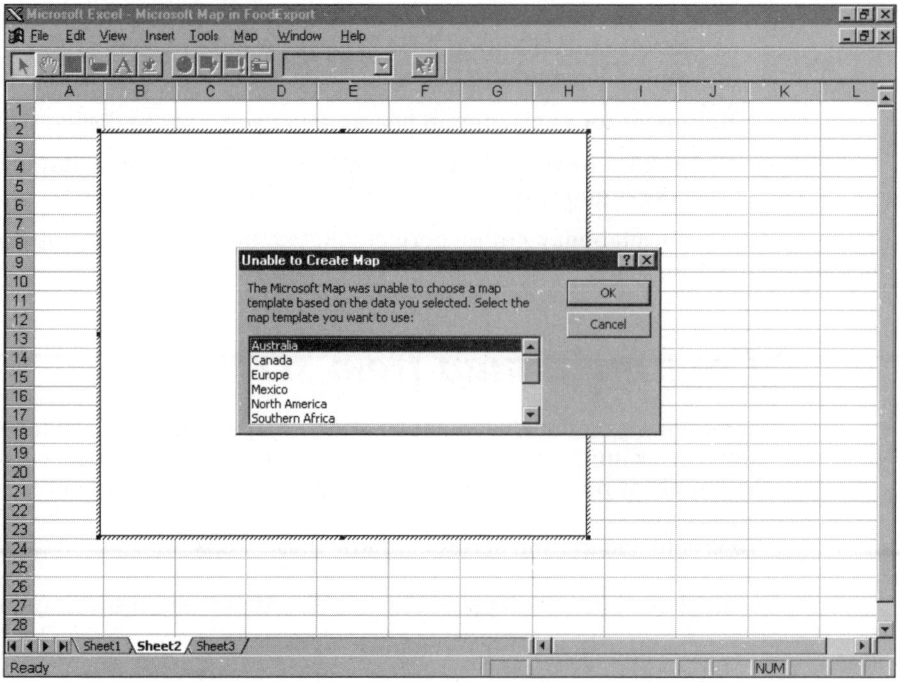

Figure 13-9:
The Unable
to Create
Map dialog
box.

Editing Your Map

To edit your map, you need to display the Microsoft Map pull-down menus and toolbar, which you can display by following these steps:

1. **Move the mouse pointer over the map that you want to edit.**

   The mouse pointer turns into a weird combination of a pointing arrow and a crosshair with arrowheads.

2. **Double-click with the left mouse button.**

   The Microsoft Map pull-down menus and toolbar appear, as shown in Figure 13-10.

Changing how your map represents data

When you first create your map, the Microsoft Map Control dialog box (refer to Figure 13-8) pops up so that you can define a format and data for your map, such as shading or column charts. In case you want to change the way your map represents data, you just need to display the Microsoft Map Control dialog box again.

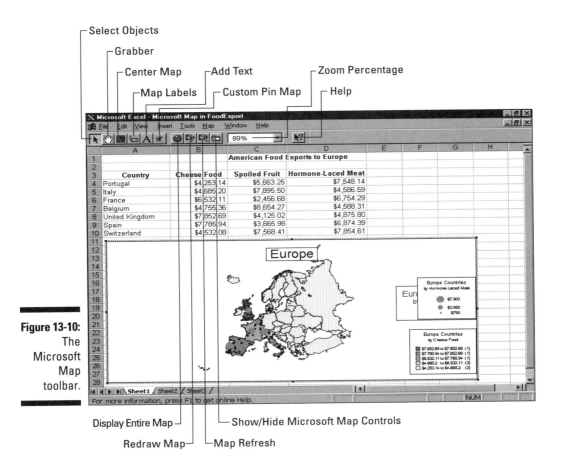

Select Objects

Grabber

Center Map ——Add Text ——Zoom Percentage

Map Labels ——Custom Pin Map ——Help

Figure 13-10:
The
Microsoft
Map
toolbar.

Display Entire Map ┘ └——Show/Hide Microsoft Map Controls

Redraw Map ┘ └—Map Refresh

To change the format for the data displayed on your map, follow these steps:

1. **Click on the Show/Hide Microsoft Map Controls button.**

   The Microsoft Map Controls dialog box appears.

2. **Move the mouse pointer over the format button that you want to use (such as Dot Density), hold down the left mouse button, and drag the mouse over the current format button that your map is using.**

3. **Release the left mouse button.**

4. **Click on the close box of the Microsoft Map Controls dialog box.**

Moving your map within its box

After you have your map drawn, you may not be happy with the exact position of the map. To move just the map itself (not any accompanying labels), you have two choices:

> ✔ Move the map using the Grabber icon
>
> ✔ Center the map using the Center Map icon

If you want to move the map yourself, use the Grabber icon. If you absolutely must have one portion of the map appear in the center of the map box, use the Center Map icon.

To use the Grabber icon to adjust the position of the map yourself, follow these steps:

1. Click on the Grabber icon on the Microsoft Map toolbar.

2. Move the mouse pointer over the map.

   The mouse pointer appears as a hand when it is directly over the map.

3. Hold down the left mouse button and drag the mouse to move the map within the confines of the map box.

4. Release the left mouse button when you're happy with the location of the map.

If you want a specific portion of your map to appear in the center of the map box, use the Center Map icon by following these steps:

1. Click on the Center Map icon on the Microsoft Map toolbar.

2. Move the mouse pointer over the part of the map that you want to appear in the center of the map box.

   The mouse pointer turns into a weird-looking crosshair.

3. Click with the left mouse button.

   Your chosen part of the map immediately moves to become the center of the map box.

If you want to see all of your map within the confines of the map box, click on the Display Entire icon on the Microsoft Map toolbar.

Resizing and moving map labels

Map labels are supposed to clarify the data on your map, but they may not offer enough explanation or they may cover crucial parts of the map. To solve these problems, move your labels around or edit them.

To move a label, follow these steps:

1. Move the mouse pointer over the label that you want to move.

2. **Hold down the left mouse button and drag the mouse to where you want to move the label.**

3. **Release the left mouse button when you're happy with the new location of your label.**

To resize a label, follow these steps:

1. **Move the mouse pointer over the label that you want to resize and click with the left mouse button.**

2. **Move the mouse pointer over one corner of the label until the mouse pointer turns into a double arrow.**

3. **Hold down the left mouse button and drag the mouse.**

4. **Release the left mouse button when you're happy with the new size of your label.**

Adding text to a map

A picture might be worth a thousand words, but sometimes you may need to type a few words of your own to clarify or explain what the map data really means. Microsoft Map lets you type text directly on a map.

To type text on a map, follow these steps:

1. **Click on the Add Text icon on the Microsoft Map toolbar.**

2. **Click anywhere on the map where you want to type text.**

   A vertical line appears.

3. **Start typing.**

4. **Press Enter when you're done.**

Sticking pins in your map

Rather than type plain text on a map, you might want to use the electronic equivalent of a push pin on your map instead. This feature lets you draw a push pin on your map along with accompanying text, as shown in Figure 13-11.

To stick a push pin in your map, follow these steps:

1. **Click on the Custom Pin Map icon on the Microsoft Map toolbar.**

   The mouse pointer turns into a push pin icon whenever it appears over your map.

Push pins

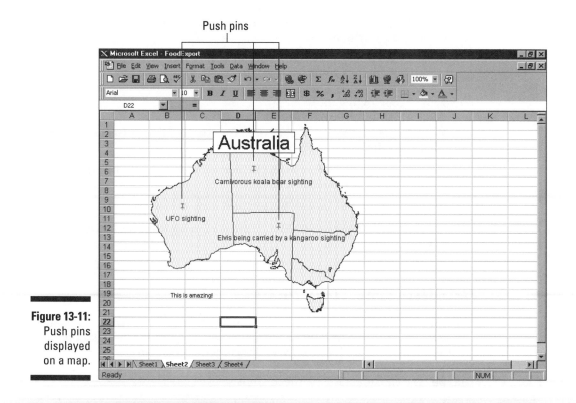

Figure 13-11:
Push pins
displayed
on a map.

2. Click with the left mouse button where you want to put the push pin.

A gray vertical line appears next to the push pin icon.

3. Type the text that you want to add and press Enter when you're done.

Modifying your push pin icon

The push pin icon may appear too small (or large), so take some time to modify its appearance by following these steps:

1. Click on the Select Objects icon on the Microsoft Map toolbar.

2. Double-click on the push pin icon.

A Symbol dialog box appears.

3. Click on the new symbol that you want to represent your push pin.

4. Click on Font.

A Font dialog box appears.

5. Choose a different size for your push pin, such as 18 or 26, and click on OK.

6. **Click on OK again.**

Your new push pin symbol appears on the map.

Moving your push pin label

When you create a push pin label, it appears to the right of the push pin icon. This isn't always the best place for the label, so you can move it around by following these steps:

1. **Click on the Select Objects icon on the Microsoft Map toolbar.**

2. **Click on the push pin icon.**

   Dark gray borders appear around the push pin and the label, as shown in Figure 13-12.

3. **Move the mouse pointer over the label until it turns into a crosshair.**

4. **Hold down the left mouse button and drag the mouse to move the label to a new location.**

   Release the left mouse button when you're happy with the new location of the label.

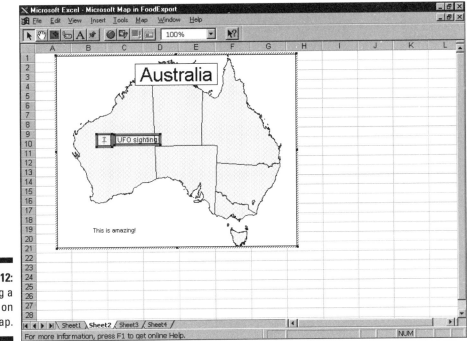

Figure 13-12:
Selecting a push pin on a map.

Chapter 14

Sharing Your Excel 97 Files

• •

• •

The three dominant spreadsheets on the market are Microsoft Excel (available for both Windows and the Macintosh); Lotus 1-2-3 (available on both Windows and OS/2 — the Macintosh version got dumped years ago); and Quattro Pro, which is a clone of 1-2-3.

Quattro Pro (and many lesser-known spreadsheets) can use 1-2-3 files, so if you ever want to convert an Excel 97 file for someone else's use, you probably can (it works nine times out of ten). Just convert your file to a 1-2-3 file.

The process of converting Excel 97 files into 1-2-3 files isn't difficult. If you're fortunate enough to share your Excel 97 files with someone else who also uses Excel 97, you can use all sorts of neat features to add comments without printing a copy on paper and marking it up by hand. When your worksheets look perfect, you can print them for the world to see. In fact, you can even post them as Web pages on the World Wide Web.

Converting Files from or for Other Spreadsheets

When you convert an Excel 97 file into another file format, you *export* the file. When you export a file, you make a copy of your original Excel 97 file and save the second copy in a different file format, such as 1-2-3.

Sharing Excel 97 files with the Excel Viewer

Excel 97 is the Number One spreadsheet in the universe, but not everyone has a copy of the program buried on his or her hard disk. Because many people refuse to buy Microsoft programs, the easiest way to share your Excel 97 files with others is to hand them to people along with a copy of a special program called the Excel Viewer.

The Excel Viewer is a free program that allows you only to view and print Excel 97 files,

but not edit them. (Hey, what do you want for nothing?)

By giving all the people you know a copy of Excel Viewer, you can freely share your files with them without converting your Excel 97 files to a strange file format, such as Lotus 1-2-3. To get a free copy of Excel Viewer, download it from CompuServe or America Online or from Microsoft's Web site at http://www.microsoft.com.

Here are two reasons that you may have to convert a file:

✔ You used Excel 97 to create a file, but you want to give that file to someone who uses a different spreadsheet program.

✔ Someone gave you a file created by another spreadsheet program and you want to view and edit that spreadsheet in Excel 97.

When someone gives you a file created by a different spreadsheet and you want to edit it in Excel, you import the file. When you *import* a file, Excel 97 loads the file and allows you to save a copy of it as an Excel 97 worksheet.

When you convert a file from Excel 97 to another file format, you may lose cell formatting, formulas, and features available only in Excel 97. In other words, if you convert an Excel 97 file to a 1-2-3 file, be careful: The conversion may not be 100 percent accurate (but you're probably used to nothing working the way it should if you've been using personal computers long enough).

Exporting an Excel 97 file

Excel 97 knows how to save files for older versions of Excel as well as various versions of Lotus 1-2-3. In case you want to save a file for an obscure spreadsheet that should have been yanked off the market decades ago, you can also save your Excel 97 files as text, dBASE, or another oddball format, which virtually guarantees that anyone in the universe with a computer can use your Excel 97 files.

Just to numb your mind with all the possibilities, Excel can save a file in any of these formats:

- **Excel version 97 & 5.0/95:** Saves an Excel 97 file into a special file format that allows both Excel 97 and Excel 95 to edit, view, and save the file. If you need to share your Excel 97 files constantly with someone who still uses Excel 95, use this file format.

- **Excel version 5.0/95:** Exports an Excel 97 file for Excel 95.

- **Excel versions 2.1, 3.0, and 4.0:** Exports an Excel 97 file into an older version of Excel. Because many programs can import older versions of Excel files, this method may be the simplest and most reliable way to transfer Excel files to another program.

- **Lotus 1-2-3 versions 1.0 to 4.0:** Exports an Excel 97 file into an older version of Lotus 1-2-3. Because most programs can import either Excel or 1-2-3 files, this format and the Excel format may be the only formats that you may ever have to use.

- **dBASE II, III, and IV:** Exports an Excel 97 file into a dBASE data file. This format is especially handy if you want to transfer an Excel file to a database program (Alpha Five, dBASE, FoxPro, or Paradox, for example).

- **DIF (Data Interchange Format) and SYLK (Symbolic Link format):** Exports an Excel 97 file into a DIF or SYLK file, two older formats once touted as "standards" that almost everyone ignored anyway. Still, if you want to transfer an Excel 97 file to an older spreadsheet, such as SuperCalc, choose this option.

- **WQ1 (QuattroPro/DOS):** Exports an Excel 97 file into an ancient WQ1 file format originally used by Quattro Pro Version 1.0 for DOS. If you need to transfer your Excel 97 files to someone using any version of Quattro Pro, save your files in this format.

- **CSV (Comma Separated Values format):** Exports an Excel 97 file into a special text file that's most useful for exporting an Excel 97 file to a Macintosh, OS/2, or nonspreadsheet Windows program.

- **Text:** Exports an Excel 97 file into a text file that any program can use, even programs running on obscure computers such as the Amiga or Atari.

Practically every program in the world knows how to use an Excel, Lotus 1-2-3, or dBASE file. To retain all your formatting, try saving your file as an older version of an Excel file first. If that doesn't work, try 1-2-3. Ninety-nine percent of the time, these two file formats are the only ones you ever need, so you can ignore all the weird formats such as DIF, SYLK, or CSV.

To export an Excel 97 file and save it in a different file format, follow these steps:

1. **Choose File⇨Save As. (Or choose Section⇨Save as File.)**

   The Save As dialog box appears.

2. **Click on the Save as type list box and then choose a file format.**

3. **Type a name for your file in the File name box.**

   To avoid any confusion between your original Excel 97 file and the exported file, save your exported file under a different name.

4. **Click on Save.**

Importing a file into Excel 97

Excel 97 knows how to import files created by a variety of programs, including Works, Quattro Pro, Lotus 1-2-3, dBASE, and older versions of Excel.

To import a file into Excel 97, follow these steps:

1. **Load Excel 97 as a separate program (not within an Office binder).**

2. **Choose File⇨Open.**

   The Open dialog box appears.

3. **Click on the Files of type list box and choose the file format that you want to import (such as 1-2-3 Files, Excel Files, or dBASE Files).**

4. **Click on the file that you want to import and then click on Open.**

   If all goes well, Excel 97 displays the data exactly as it appears in its original file format. Most likely, though, you may have to go through your imported file and edit it slightly.

If you have a foreign file format that you want to add to an Office 97 binder, you must first convert that foreign file into an Excel 97 file. After you convert it into an Excel 97 file, you can add it to your Office 97 binder.

To import a file into an Office 97 binder, follow these steps:

1. **Repeat Steps 1 – 4 in the preceding steps for importing a file.**

2. **Choose File⇨Save to save your newly imported file as a genuine, 100-percent-authentic Excel 97 file.**

3. **Open the Office 97 binder to which you want to add your newly converted file.**

4. **Choose Section⇨Add from File.**

The Add from File dialog box appears.

5. **Click on the Excel 97 file that you saved in Step 2 and then click on Add.**

Adding Comments to Cells

When you share your Excel 97 files with other people, you may want to add comments to your worksheets to ask for more help, question certain formula assumptions, or tell your co-worker what a jerk your boss was last Friday afternoon. You can print your worksheets on paper and attach comments to them with a paper clip, but Excel 97 has a neat feature that enables you to attach comments directly to your individual worksheet cells instead.

Attaching a comment

Notes can come in handy when you want to remind yourself about the contents of a certain cell ("January sales were down because Bob messed up") or if you're sharing Excel 97 worksheets with others ("Jane, verify that this figure is accurate; if it's not, you'll be suspected of embezzlement").

To attach a comment to a cell, follow these steps:

1. **Click on the cell to which you want to attach your comment.**

2. **Choose Insert⇨Comment.**

The Comment window appears, as shown in Figure 14-1.

3. **Type your comment and click anywhere on the worksheet when you're done.**

Excel 97 draws a little red dot in the upper-right corner of the cell to let you know that the cell contains a comment, as shown in Figure 14-2.

The comment window automatically includes the name that you gave Office 97 when you first installed the program. If you want to change the name that appears in the comment window, choose Tools⇨Options, click on the General tab, type a new name in the User name box, and click on OK.

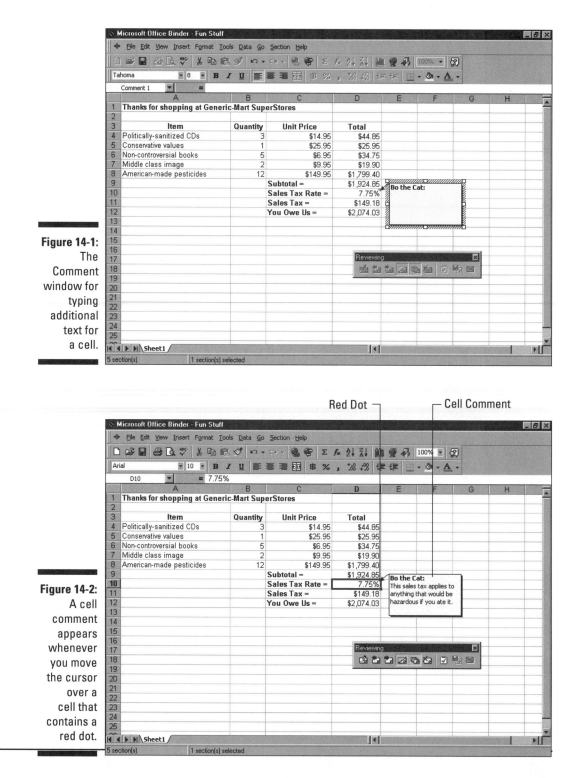

Figure 14-1:
The Comment window for typing additional text for a cell.

Figure 14-2:
A cell comment appears whenever you move the cursor over a cell that contains a red dot.

Finding all comments in a worksheet

After you or someone else has scattered various comments in different cells, the hard part may be finding them so that you can read them. If you want, you can look for every red dot that appears in a cell, but if you have that much time on your hands, you probably need a hobby to soak up your free time. For an easier method, just have Excel 97 show you all the cell comments in a worksheet.

To find all the cell comments buried throughout a worksheet, follow these steps:

1. **Choose <u>V</u>iew⇨<u>C</u>omments.**

   All the comment windows appear along with the Reviewing toolbar, as shown in Figure 14-3.

2. **Click on the Hide All Comments icon on the Reviewing toolbar to make your comment windows disappear again.**

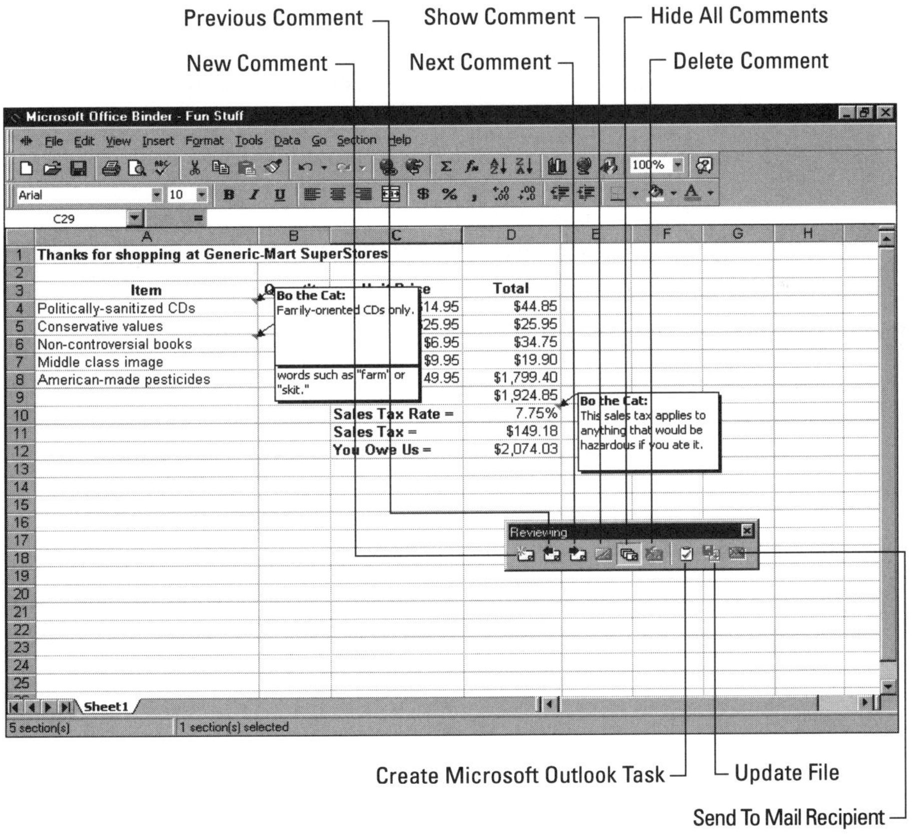

Figure 14-3: Viewing all your comments.

Editing a comment

Whenever you want, you can edit a comment in case you need to add more information or just feel like typing a dirty joke in place of a useful comment. To edit a comment, follow these steps:

1. **Click on the cell containing the comment that you want to edit.**

2. **Choose Insert⇨Edit Comment.**

   The comment window pops up.

3. **Click anywhere inside the comment window and use the arrow, Backspace, and Delete keys to edit your comment.**

4. **Click anywhere outside of the comment window when you're done.**

Printing comments

When you print your worksheets, Excel 97 normally refuses to print any cell comments. In case you want (or need) to print your comments along with your worksheets, you can do so by following these steps:

1. **Choose File⇨Page Setup (or choose Section⇨Page Setup if you're using Excel 97 within a binder).**

   The Page Setup dialog box appears.

2. **Click on the Sheet tab.**

3. **Click in the Comments list box and choose one of the following:**

   - (None)

   - At end of sheet

   - As displayed on sheet: Make sure that you choose View⇨Comments before printing your worksheet

4. **Click on OK.**

Deleting comments

After littering a worksheet with comments, you'll eventually want to get rid of them so that they don't keep sprouting messages whenever you move the mouse pointer over them.

To delete a comment, follow these steps:

1. **Click in the cell containing the comment that you want to delete.**

2. **Choose Insert⇨Edit Comment.**

   The comment window pops up.

3. **Move the mouse pointer over the comment window border and click on the left mouse button.**

4. **Press Del or choose Edit⇨Clear⇨Comments.**

If you delete a comment by mistake, press Ctrl+Z to recover it.

Playing with Scenarios

Creating a worksheet and plugging in numbers can give you an accurate calculation, but what if you aren't sure which values you should use? Suppose that you're creating a report that lists how much money your company has lost in the past year, and not all the sales results for the fourth quarter are available yet.

Rather than just give up and go home (which is probably the more appealing option), you can create your worksheet anyway and then create separate scenarios. A *scenario* is just an identical copy of your worksheet with slightly different numbers plugged into it.

One scenario may contain numbers that show a highly optimistic possibility, whereas another scenario may contain numbers that show a more pessimistic result. By letting you plug in different numbers to the same worksheet and store separate copies of them, you can forecast the range of possible outcomes. If fourth-quarter sales are high, for example, you can pay off your bills; if fourth-quarter sales are lower than expected, you can start looking for another job tomorrow.

Creating a scenario

Before you create a scenario, you must create your worksheet. Then you must specify which cells will contain different numbers between your scenarios. The cells that you choose are called *changing cells* because the contents of these cells will — obviously — vary among your multiple scenarios.

To create a scenario, follow these steps:

1. **Choose Tools⇨Scenarios.**

   The Scenario Manager dialog box appears, as shown in Figure 14-4.

2. **Click on Add.**

   The Add Scenario dialog box appears, as shown in Figure 14-5.

3. **In the Scenario name box, type a descriptive name for your scenario (Best-Case Scenario if Bob Doesn't Ruin Our Latest Deal, for example).**

4. **Click in the Changing cells box.**

5. **Highlight all the cells that will contain varying data.**

   You may have to move the Add Scenario dialog box out of the way in order to see your worksheet. (You must do this step only the first time that you create a scenario.)

6. **Click on OK.**

   The Scenario Values dialog box appears, as shown in Figure 14-6.

7. **Type a value for each of your changing cells and then click on OK.**

8. **Repeat Steps 2 – 7 for each scenario that you want to create.**

9. **Click on Close.**

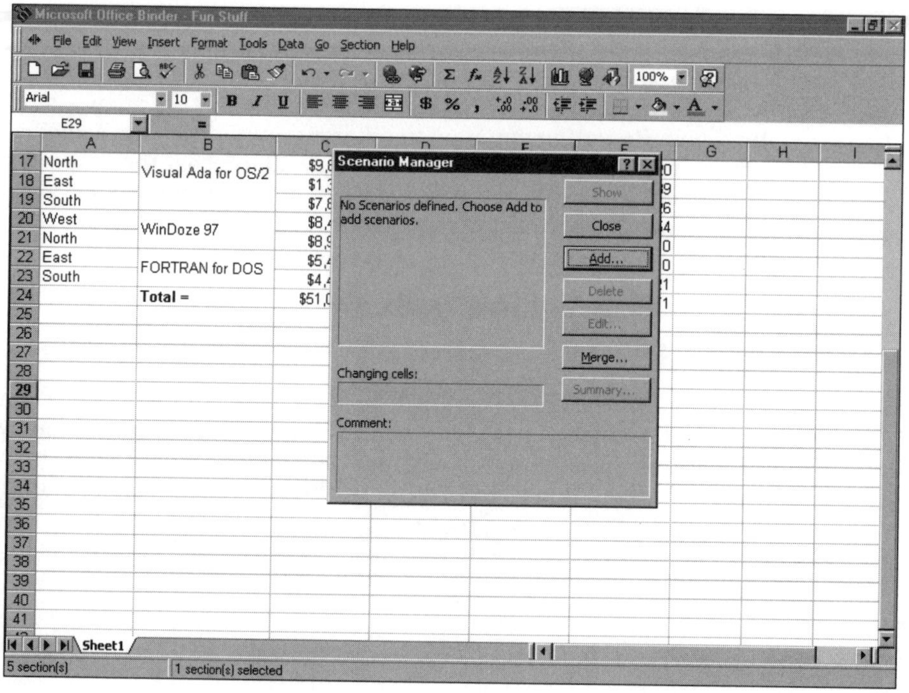

Figure 14-4: The Scenario Manager dialog box.

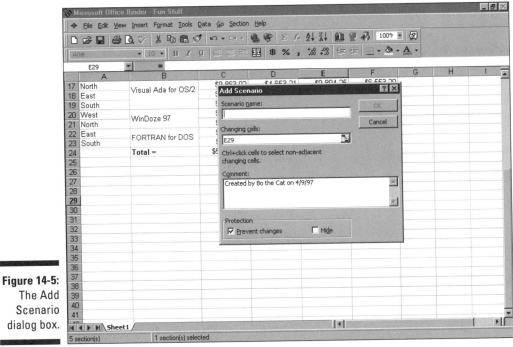

Figure 14-5:
The Add
Scenario
dialog box.

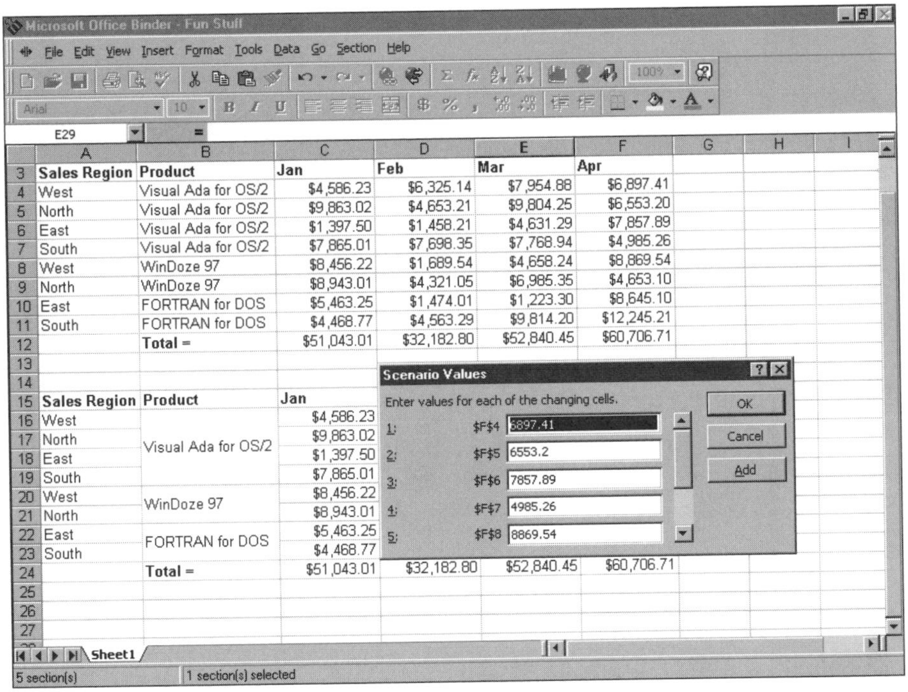

Figure 14-6:
The
Scenario
Values
dialog box.

Viewing a scenario

After you create two or more scenarios, you can view them and see how the different numbers may affect the rest of your worksheet.

To view your scenarios, follow these steps:

1. **Choose Tools⇨Scenarios.**

   The Scenario Manager dialog box appears (refer to Figure 14-4).

2. **Click on the scenario name that you want to view and then click on Show, as shown in Figure 14-7.**

3. **Click on Close.**

   Excel 97 shows you how the numbers stored in your chosen scenario affect the rest of your worksheet.

Editing a scenario

A scenario contains numbers that you can always change later, just in case your first guess was wrong or you eventually got more accurate numbers. If something like that happens, just edit your scenario and plug in your new numbers. Another reason to edit your scenario is to increase or decrease the number of changing cells in a scenario.

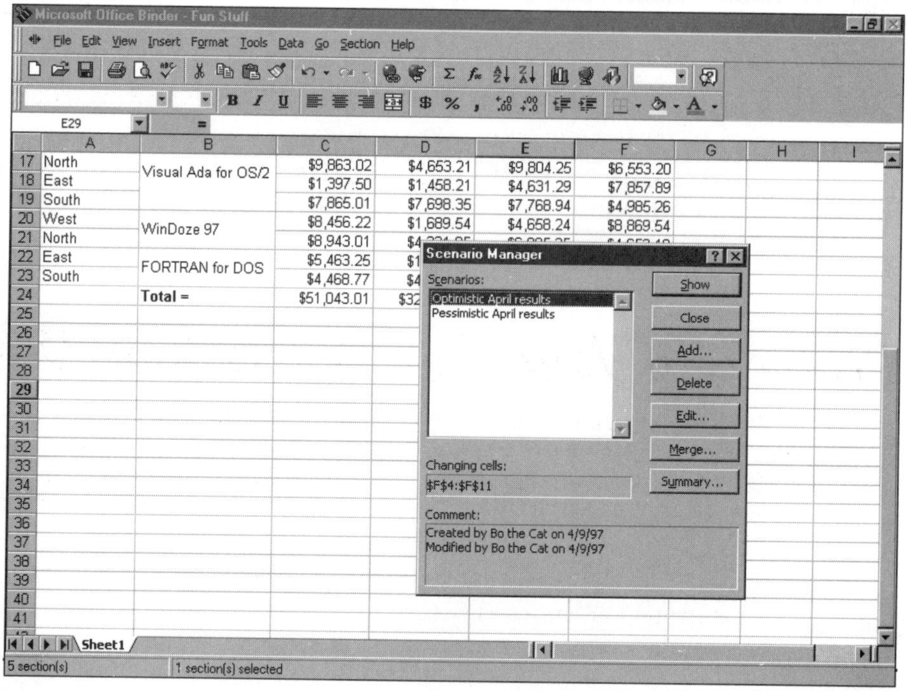

Figure 14-7: The Scenario Manager dialog box listing different scenarios from which to choose.

To edit a scenario, follow these steps:

1. **Choose Tools⇨Scenarios.**

   The Scenario Manager dialog box appears (refer to Figure 14-7).

2. **Click on the scenario name that you want to edit and then click on Edit.**

   The Edit Scenario dialog box appears.

3. **Type a new scenario name in the Scenario name box.**

4. **Click in the Changing cells box, highlight the cells that you want your scenario to change, and click on OK.**

5. **Type the new values for your scenario's changing cells and then click on OK.**

6. **Click on Close.**

Deleting a scenario

Scenarios are great for playing around with different numbers, but you probably won't want to keep your scenarios around forever. When you no longer need a scenario, get rid of it to prevent confusion later on.

If you delete a scenario, you cannot undelete it. Make sure that you really want to delete a scenario because when it's gone, it's gone for good.

To delete a scenario, follow these steps:

1. **Choose Tools⇨Scenarios. The Scenario Manager dialog box appears (refer to Figure 14-7).**

2. **Click on the scenario name that you want to delete and then click on Delete.**

3. **Click on Close.**

Protecting Your Worksheets from Others

If you plan to share your Excel 97 files with others, you probably don't want people to type different values, edit your labels, or mess around with your formulas. To keep others from messing up your carefully crafted worksheets, Excel 97 gives you two ways to protect them from modification:

✔ Protect individual sheets

✔ Protect an entire workbook

A workbook consists of one or more sheets. If you protect only one sheet in your workbook, other people can still modify the other sheets.

When you protect an individual sheet, no one can modify the contents of that sheet. When you protect an entire workbook, no one can add or delete a sheet in the workbook. People can still edit the contents of your individual sheets, however. If you want complete protection from modifications, protect both your individual sheets and your entire workbook.

Protecting your work

Protecting your work is a good idea whenever you plan to let anyone else look at your Excel 97 files.

To protect a sheet or workbook, follow these steps:

1. **Choose Tools⇨Protection and then one of the following:**

   - **Protect Sheet:** Protects an individual sheet in a workbook

   - **Protect Workbook:** Protects all sheets in a workbook

   - **Protect and Share Workbook (not available within an Office binder):** Tracks editing changes but won't allow anyone (but you) to remove or accept editing changes

   The Protect Sheet, Protect Workbook, or Protect and Share Workbook dialog box appears.

2. **Type a password in the Password box to password-protect your sheet or workbook.**

   Typing a password is optional but I highly recommend it. If you don't type a password, anyone can use the Unprotect command to unprotect your work and modify your worksheet. Ideally, you'll pick a password that's easy for you to remember but difficult for someone else to guess. For example, to use your name as a password wouldn't be smart (although doing so might keep your boss from guessing it). A combination of letters and numbers may be best, such as the initials of your name mixed with your favorite numbers, such as S6A6T6A6N.

3. **Click on OK.**

   The Confirm Password dialog box appears, asking you to type your password again.

4. **Type your password again and then click on OK.**

If you have multiple sheets in a workbook, you can protect each sheet with a different password. Then you can share your passwords with other people so that only certain people can edit specific sheets.

If you password-protect your sheet or workbook and forget your password, you're locked out from editing your own work. The good news is that many third-party programs can crack a protected Excel 97 file and retrieve your password. The bad news is that thieves can use these same programs to find your password and modify your Excel 97 files. So don't expect a simple password to keep out determined intruders.

Unprotecting your work

After you let hordes of other people paw over your work, you can unprotect your files so that you can edit them again.

To unprotect a sheet or workbook, follow these steps:

1. **Choose Tools⇨Protection and then either Unprotect Sheet, Unprotect Workbook, or Unprotect Shared Workbook.**

   An Unprotect Sheet or Unprotect Workbook dialog box appears.

2. **Type your password in the Password box and then click on OK.**

Converting Worksheets into Web Page Tables

Excel 97 can turn your worksheets into Web page tables. If you want more advanced Web page editing capabilities, turn to a special Web page editing program such as Microsoft FrontPage, or pick up a copy of my book *Microsoft Office 97 For Windows For Dummies* (IDG Books Worldwide, Inc.)

To convert a worksheet into a Web page table, follow these steps:

1. **Load the worksheet that you want to convert into a Web page table.**

   If you're using Excel 97 within a binder, choose Section⇨View Outside.

2. **Choose File⇨Save as HTML.**

   Step 1 of the Internet Assistant Wizard dialog box appears, as shown in Figure 14-8.

3. **Click on Add.**

   A dialog box appears, asking which range of cells you want to convert into a Web page table.

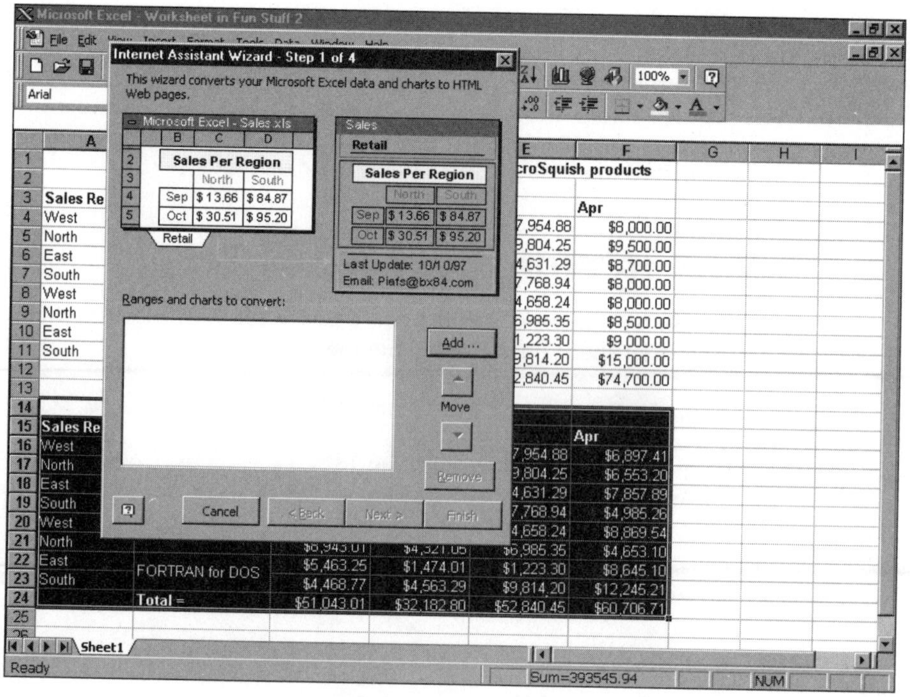

Figure 14-8:
Step 1 of the
Internet
Wizard
dialog box.

4. **Highlight the range of cells that you want to convert and click on OK. Then click on Next.**

   Step 2 of the Internet Assistant Wizard dialog box appears as shown in Figure 14-9, asking whether you want to create a separate Web page or insert your Excel 97 data into an existing Web page.

5. **Click in one of the radio buttons (to create a separate Web page or insert your table into an existing Web page) and click on Next.**

   Step 3 of the Internet Assistant Wizard dialog box appears as shown in Figure 14-10, asking for a header and title.

6. **Type a header, title, and any other information that you want to appear on your Web page and click on Next.**

   The final Internet Assistant Wizard dialog box appears, as shown in Figure 14-11.

7. **Type a filename for your Web page and click on Finish.**

   Excel 97 creates your Web page ready for posting on your Web site, as shown in Figure 14-12.

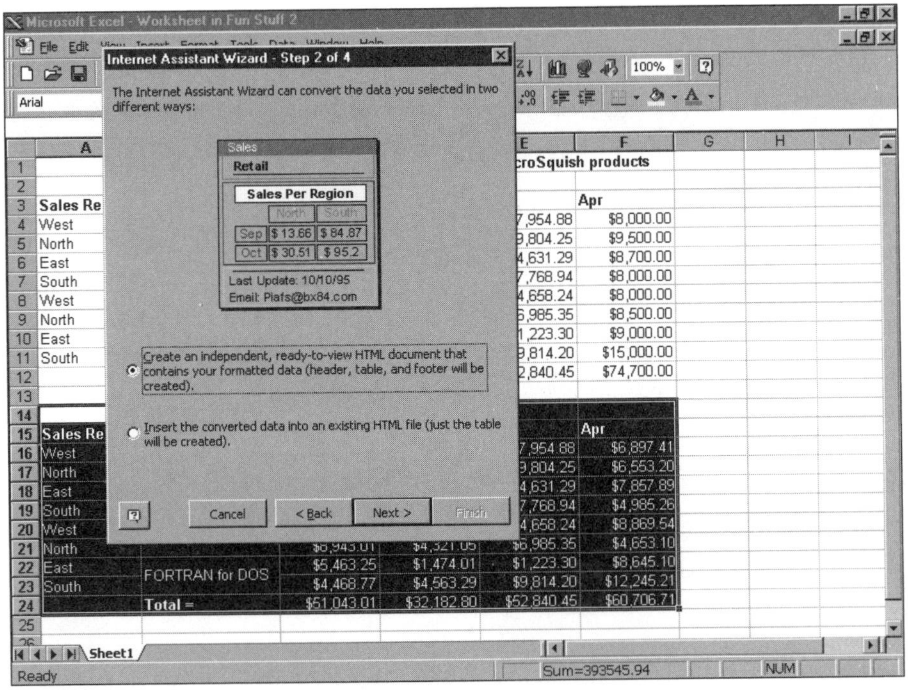

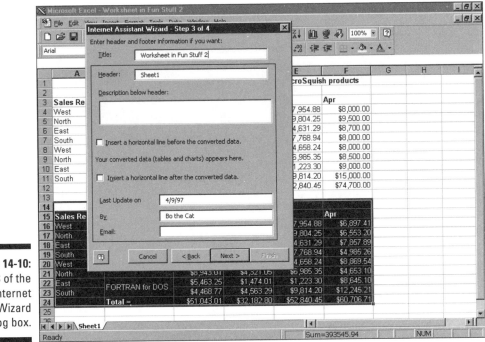

Figure 14-9:
Step 2 of the
Internet
Wizard
dialog box.

Figure 14-10:
Step 3 of the
Internet
Wizard
dialog box.

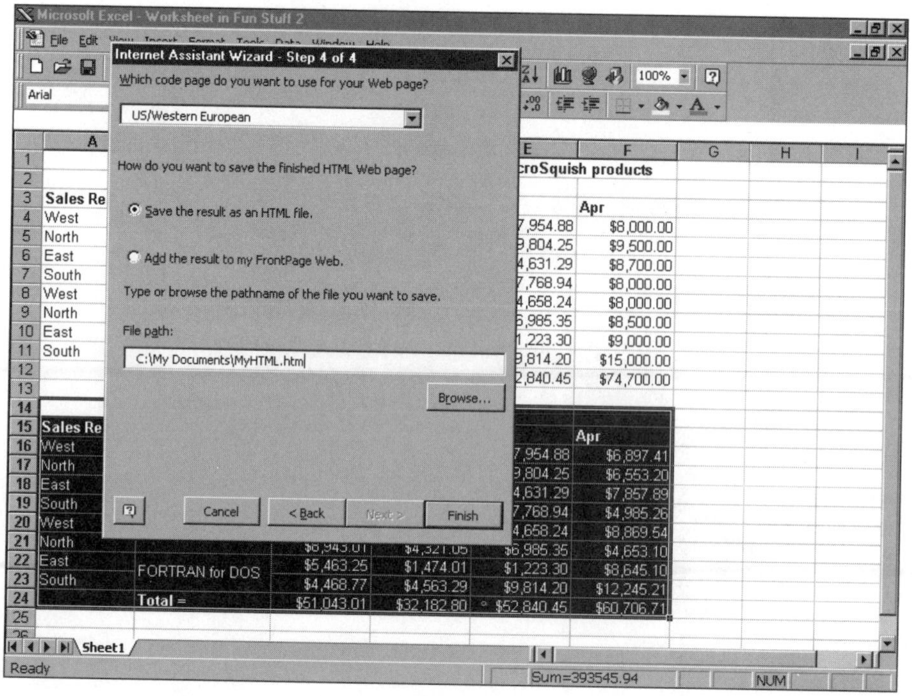

Figure 14-11:
Step 4 of the
Internet
Wizard
dialog box.

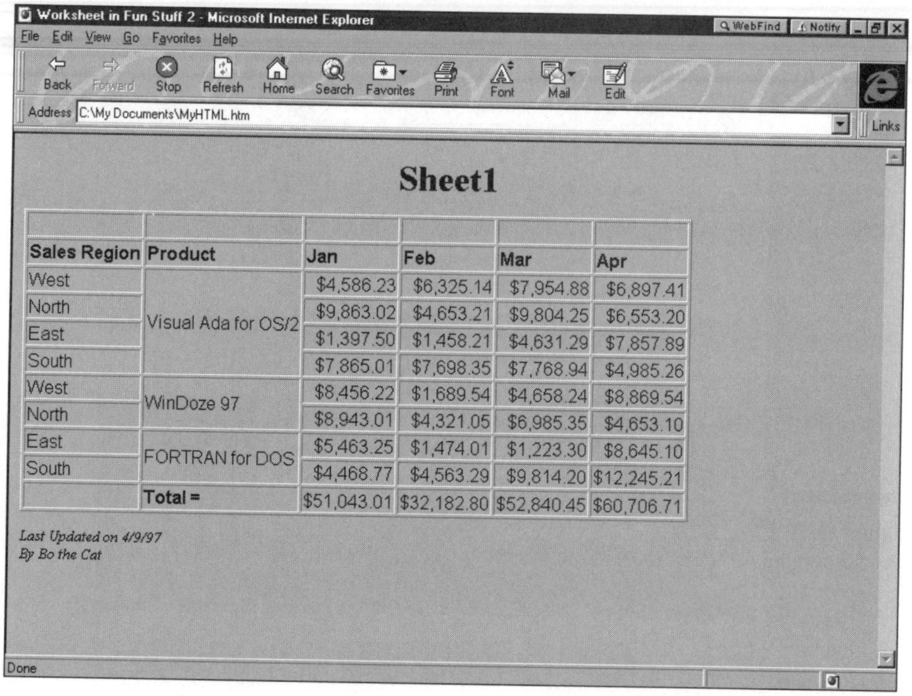

Figure 14-12:
A typical
Excel 97
worksheet
converted
into a Web
page.

Part IV
The Microsoft PowerPoint 97 Dog-and-Pony Show

The 5th Wave   By Rich Tennant

"WELL, SHOOT! THIS EGGPLANT CHART IS JUST AS CONFUSING AS THE BUTTERNUT SQUASH CHART AND THE GOURD CHART. CAN'T YOU JUST MAKE A PIE CHART LIKE EVERYONE ELSE?"

In this part . . .

The Number One fear of most Americans is speaking in public. The Number One fear of most audiences, however, is having their time wasted and being bored to death during a presentation.

Fortunately, Microsoft PowerPoint 97 can tackle both ends of the problem by helping you create dazzling presentations so that you don't have to say a word and your audience doesn't have to do anything but stare mindlessly at your slide show. By learning how to add sound and video, you can give your slide-show presentation that feeling of importance when you may really have nothing of substance to offer.

To help you create and give your slide show presentation, PowerPoint 97 can create notes (so that you know what you're supposed to be talking about at any give time) and handouts (so that your audience doesn't have to take notes themselves, which frees them to daydream instead of paying attention to what you're saying).

With PowerPoint 97 as your presentation tool, you'll never be at a loss for words again. Unless, of course, the power goes out during your presentation.

Chapter 15

Prettying Up Your Presentations

In This Chapter
- ▶ Displaying charts
- ▶ Adding headers and footers
- ▶ Playing with WordArt

*T*he whole purpose of PowerPoint 97 is to present information in a visually pleasing manner so that you can convince others that you're right. To achieve this noble goal, PowerPoint 97 provides several features to help you make your presentations as neat, organized, and pretty as possible. Because nothing is more convincing than facts (even if you have to make them up), PowerPoint 97 enables you to create pie, line, or bar charts that you can plug into a presentation.

Although people like to believe that looks aren't everything, one glance at the paychecks that supermodels receive for posing in a bikini should be enough to convince you otherwise.

Creating and Displaying Charts

PowerPoint 97 allows you to choose from 18 different types of charts, as shown in Figure 15-1. After you've picked the type of chart that you want to display, you also need to specify the actual data to plot on your chosen chart.

Putting a chart on a slide

To be effective, charts need to be fairly large, so you may want to put a chart on a slide all by itself rather than try to cram it on a slide already filled with text and graphics.

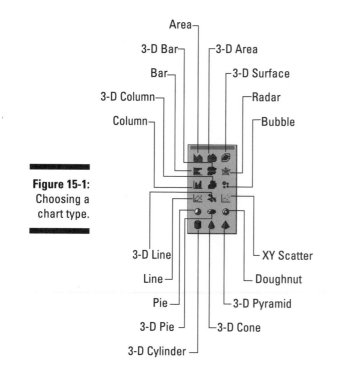

Figure 15-1:
Choosing a
chart type.

To put a chart on a slide, follow these steps:

1. **Display the slide where you want the chart to appear.**

   You may want to create a new slide by pressing Ctrl+M.

2. **Choose Insert⇨Chart or click on the Chart icon on the Standard toolbar.**

   PowerPoint 97 displays a sample chart along with a Datasheet window for storing the data used to plot points on your chart, as shown in Figure 15-2.

3. **Click on the Chart Type icon and choose the chart type that you want (such as a bar chart or 3-D line chart).**

Import File ─┐   ┌─ Chart Type

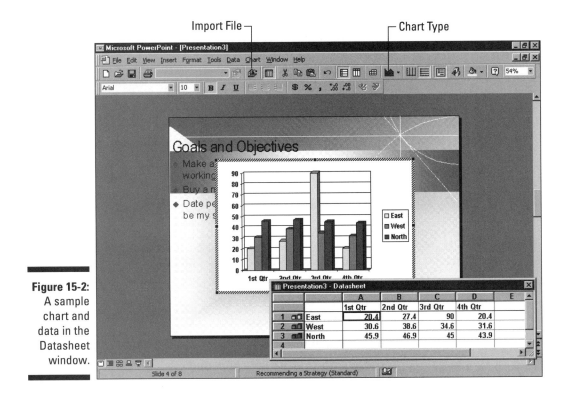

Figure 15-2:
A sample
chart and
data in the
Datasheet
window.

4. **Click in the Datasheet window and type the data that you want to plot on your chosen chart.**

   If you want to use data stored in an Excel 97 worksheet, click on the Import File icon and choose the Excel 97 file you want to use.

5. **Click anywhere outside of the chart.**

   PowerPoint 97 displays your chart on the slide.

Deleting data in the Datasheet window

A Datasheet contains rows and columns of data used to create your chart. You may want to delete or edit data in a particular cell, however.

To delete data in a cell, follow these steps:

1. **Click on the cell that contains the data you want to delete.**

2. **Press Delete.**

To edit data in a cell, follow these steps:

1. **Double-click on the cell containing the data that you want to edit.**

2. **Press the arrow, Backspace, or Del keys to delete characters and type any new numbers or text that you want to add.**

To delete an entire row or column of data, follow these steps:

1. **Click on the gray row or column label containing the data that you want to delete.**

2. **Press Delete.**

Moving your chart

Unless you're really lucky, PowerPoint 97 probably won't put your chart in the exact location where you want it to appear on your slide. To fix this problem, you can move or resize your chart at any time.

To move a chart, follow these steps:

1. **Click anywhere outside of the chart.**

   You can skip this step if the chart borders aren't currently highlighted.

2. **Move the mouse pointer over the chart and click on the left mouse button once.**

   White handles appear around the chart borders, as shown in Figure 15-3.

3. **While holding down the left mouse button, drag the mouse to move the chart to a new location, as shown in Figure 15-3.**

   The new location appears as a dotted line.

4. **Release the left mouse button when you're happy with the chart's new location.**

To resize a chart, follow these steps:

1. **Click anywhere outside of the chart.**

   You can skip this step if the chart borders aren't currently highlighted.

2. **Move the mouse pointer over a white handle.**

   The mouse pointer turns into a double-pointing arrow.

3. **Hold down the left mouse button and drag the mouse to adjust the size of the chart.**

4. **Release the left mouse button when you're happy with the new size of the chart.**

White handles

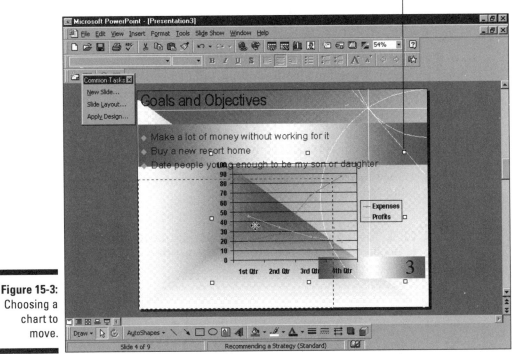

Figure 15-3:
Choosing a
chart to
move.

Editing your chart

Any time after you've created a chart, you may want to alter its appearance by picking a new chart, modifying your chart, or changing the data used to plot the points on your chart.

Picking a new chart

In case you want to pick an entirely new chart (for example, a pie chart rather than a bar chart), you can do so by following these steps:

1. **Move the mouse pointer over the chart and double-click on the left mouse button.**

   Gray borders appear around the chart; the Datasheet window pops up.

2. **Click on the Chart Type icon and choose the chart that you would rather use.**

   You see the same data displayed in the new type of chart.

Modifying your chart

To give you some semblance of control over your charts, you can change the following:

✔ X- and Y-axis gridlines to make your charts easier to read

✔ A chart legend to identify specific points on your chart

✔ Whether to chart data by row or column

✔ Whether to display data on the chart

To modify your chart in any of these ways, follow these steps:

1. **Move the mouse pointer over the chart and double-click on the left mouse button.**

   Gray borders appear around the chart; the Datasheet window pops up.

2. **Click on the Category Axis Gridlines and/or the Value Axis Gridlines icons if you want to display (or hide) gridlines on your chart, as shown in Figure 15-4.**

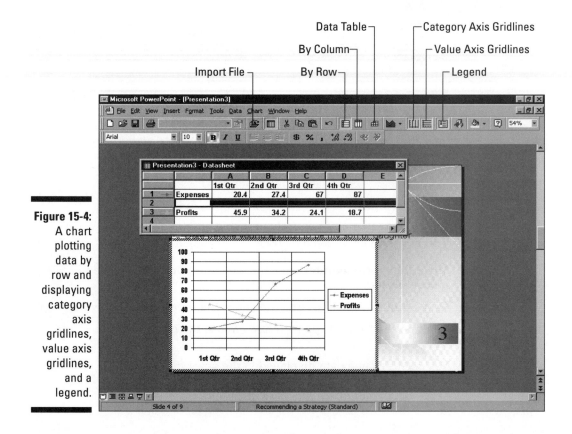

Figure 15-4:
A chart plotting data by row and displaying category axis gridlines, value axis gridlines, and a legend.

3. **Click on the Legend icon if you want to display (or hide) your chart's legend.**

4. **Click on the By Row or By Column icons to define how you want your chart to plot your data.**

5. **Click on the Data Table icon if you want to display your data on the chart, as shown in Figure 15-5.**

Plotting Excel 97 data

Rather than type data to plot in the datasheet, you can just plot data stored in an Excel 97 file instead.

If you want to plot data trapped inside an Office 97 binder, you must first save the data in a separate Excel 97 file.

To plot Excel 97 data, follow these steps:

1. **Move the mouse pointer over the chart and double-click on the left mouse button.**

   Gray borders appear around the chart; the Datasheet window pops up.

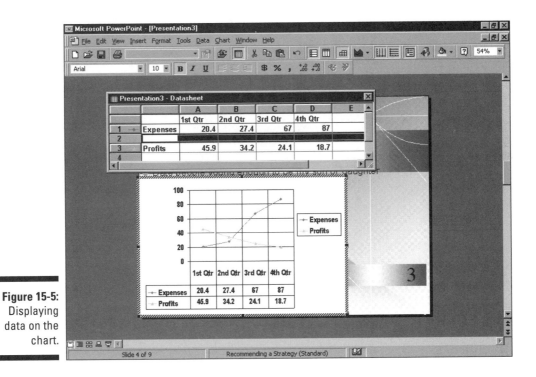

Figure 15-5:
Displaying
data on the
chart.

2. **Click on the Import File icon.**

   An Import File dialog box appears.

3. **Click on the Excel 97 file that you want to use and click on Open.**

   An Import Data Options dialog box appears, as shown in Figure 15-6.

4. **Click on the worksheet name containing the data that you want to plot.**

   You may also want to specify the exact cell range. Click on OK.

Adding Headers and Footers

Headers and footers can display identical text on all your slides. That way, you can always display your company's motto ("We treat everyone equally poorly regardless of race, sex, or age"), slide numbers, or date on every slide of your presentation.

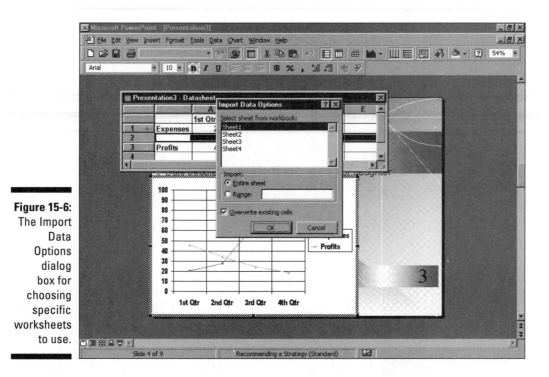

Figure 15-6: The Import Data Options dialog box for choosing specific worksheets to use.

To add a header or footer to your slides, follow these steps:

1. **Choose View➪Header and Footer.**

   The Header and Footer dialog box appears.

2. **Click on the Slide tab (see Figure 15-7).**

3. **Click in the Date and time check box (so that a check mark appears) if you want to display the date and time.**

4. **Click in the Update automatically radio button (and then click on the Update automatically list box to choose a time and date style to display) or click in the Fixed radio button and type any text.**

5. **Click in the Slide number check box (so that a check mark appears) to display the current slide number.**

6. **Click in the Footer check box (so that a check mark appears) and type any text.**

7. **Click Apply to All (to display your choices on all slides) or Apply (to display your choices on the currently displayed slide).**

8. **Click on the Notes and Handouts tab and repeat Steps 3 – 7.**

9. **Click on Apply to All.**

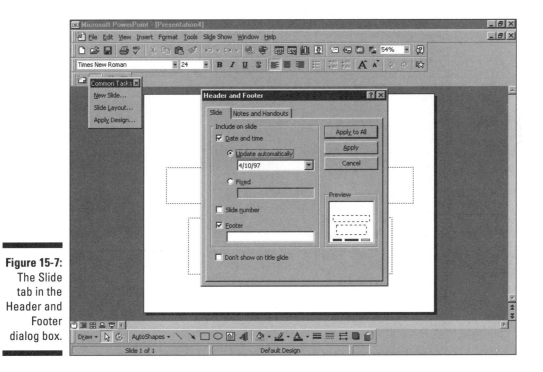

Figure 15-7:
The Slide tab in the Header and Footer dialog box.

Playing with WordArt

To give you yet another way to display text on a slide, PowerPoint 97 enables you to use WordArt, through which you can display text in a variety of odd shapes, as shown in Figure 15-8. WordArt serves no functional purpose other than to let you express your creativity and goof around at your computer while pretending to be hard at work creating an important PowerPoint 97 presentation.

Creating WordArt

To create WordArt, follow these steps:

1. **Choose View⇨Toolbars and then Drawing.**

   (If a check mark already appears in front of the Drawing toolbar, skip this step.) The Drawing toolbar appears, as shown in Figure 15-9.

2. **Click on the Insert WordArt icon on the Drawing toolbar.**

   The WordArt Gallery appears, as shown in Figure 15-10.

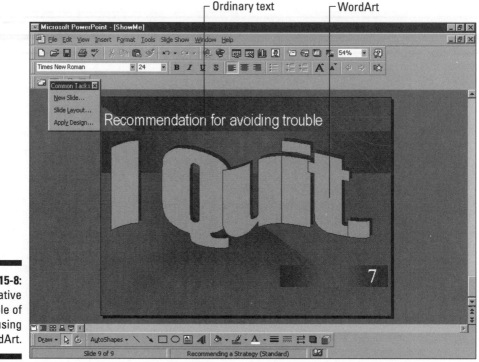

Figure 15-8:
A creative example of using WordArt.

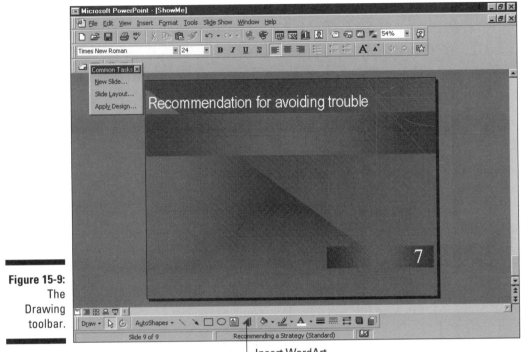

Figure 15-9:
The
Drawing
toolbar.

Insert WordArt

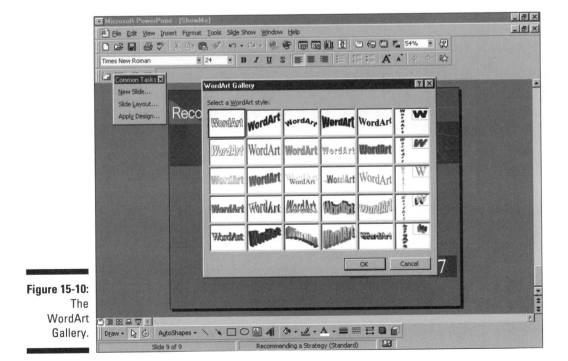

Figure 15-10:
The
WordArt
Gallery.

3. Click on the WordArt style that you want to use and click on OK.

An Edit WordArt Text dialog box appears, as shown in Figure 15-11.

4. Type your text and click on OK.

Any changes that you make to the font, size, bold, or italics affect all your WordArt text. PowerPoint 97 displays your WordArt on the current slide.

Editing WordArt

After you've created some WordArt, you might want to modify it by changing its shape, color, or text just to express your creativity or give you something to do for a few minutes or so.

Editing the WordArt text

No matter how wonderful your WordArt may look, the whole point of using WordArt is to display text. To edit WordArt text, follow these steps:

1. Click on the WordArt that you want to edit.

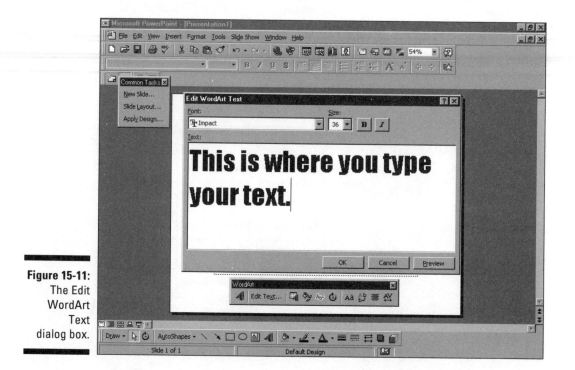

Figure 15-11:
The Edit
WordArt
Text
dialog box.

2. Choose <u>V</u>iew⇨<u>T</u>oolbars⇨WordArt.

(If a check mark already appears in front of WordArt, skip this step.)
The WordArt toolbar appears, as shown in Figure 15-12.

3. Click on the WordArt Edit Te<u>x</u>t button on the WordArt toolbar.

The Edit WordArt Text dialog box appears (refer to Figure 15-11).

4. Edit your text and click on OK when you're done.

Changing the shape of WordArt

After you've typed text to display as WordArt, you may want to change its
shape so that the WordArt appears as a wavy line, a triangle, or a square. To
change the shape of WordArt, follow these steps:

1. Click on the WordArt whose shape you want to change.

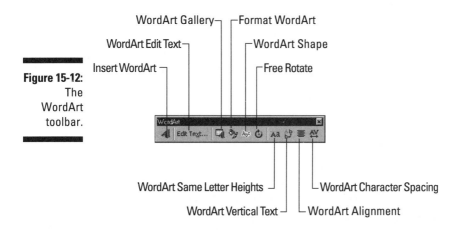

Figure 15-12:
The
WordArt
toolbar.

2. **Choose View⇨Toolbars⇨WordArt.**

(If a check mark already appears in front of WordArt, skip this step.) The WordArt toolbar appears (refer to Figure 15-12).

3. **Click on the WordArt Shape icon on the WordArt toolbar.**

A pop-up menu of different shapes appears for you to choose from, as shown in Figure 15-13.

4. **Click on the shape that you want to use.**

Rotating WordArt

Rotating WordArt lets you (what else?) rotate your WordArt so that it can appear in different angles. To rotate WordArt, follow these steps:

1. **Click on the WordArt whose shape you want to change.**

2. **Choose View⇨Toolbars⇨WordArt.**

(If a check mark already appears in front of WordArt, skip this step.) The WordArt toolbar appears (refer to Figure 15-12).

3. **Click on the Free Rotate icon on the WordArt toolbar.**

PowerPoint 97 displays green dots on each corner of your WordArt, as shown in Figure 15-14.

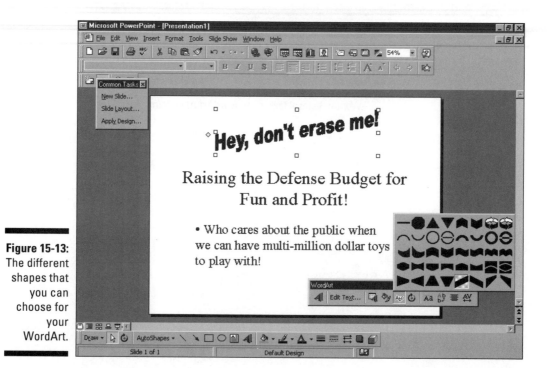

Figure 15-13:
The different
shapes that
you can
choose for
your
WordArt.

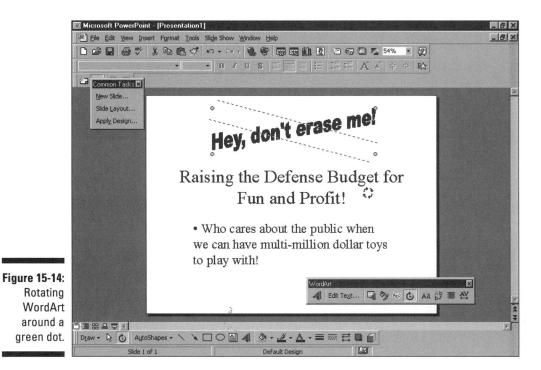

Figure 15-14:
Rotating
WordArt
around a
green dot.

4. **Move the mouse pointer over one of the green dots, hold down the left mouse button, and drag the mouse.**

   PowerPoint 97 displays the new location of your WordArt as two parallel dotted lines (refer to Figure 15-14).

5. **Release the left mouse button when you're happy with the new position of your WordArt.**

Changing the appearance of characters in WordArt

For those who must have absolute control over the appearance of the text that appears in WordArt, PowerPoint 97 lets you adjust the height, spacing, and alignment of your text or decide whether text appears vertically.

To change the appearance of text, follow these steps:

1. **Click on the WordArt whose characters you want to modify.**

2. **Choose View➪Toolbars➪WordArt.**

   (If a check mark already appears in front of WordArt, skip this step.) The WordArt toolbar appears (refer to Figure 15-12).

3. Click on one of the following icons on the WordArt toolbar:

- WordArt Same Letter Heights

- WordArt Vertical Text

- WordArt Alignment

- WordArt Character Spacing

Figure 15-15 shows what WordArt looks like as vertical text and with all letters the same height.

Changing the text color of your WordArt

To get really creative, you can change the color of your WordArt so that text appears in bright orange or hard-to-see yellow. You can change three parts of your WordArt text:

✔ The text color

✔ The text border color (the color of the line that defines the outline of each character)

✔ The text border line style (the line appearance that defines the outline of each character)

Figure 15-15: WordArt appearing in different ways.

To change the color of your WordArt, follow these steps:

1. **Click on the WordArt that you want to modify.**

2. **Choose View⇨Toolbars⇨WordArt.**

   (If a check mark already appears in front of WordArt, skip this step.)
   The WordArt toolbar appears (refer to Figure 15-12).

3. **Click on the Format WordArt icon on the WordArt toolbar.**

   The Format WordArt dialog box appears.

4. **Click on the Colors and Lines tab, as shown in Figure 15-16.**

5. **Click in the Color list box in the Fill group and choose the color to appear inside your WordArt characters.**

6. **Click in the Color list box in the Line group and choose the color to appear on the border of your text.**

7. **Click in the Dashed list box in the Line group and choose a line style to appear as the border of your text.**

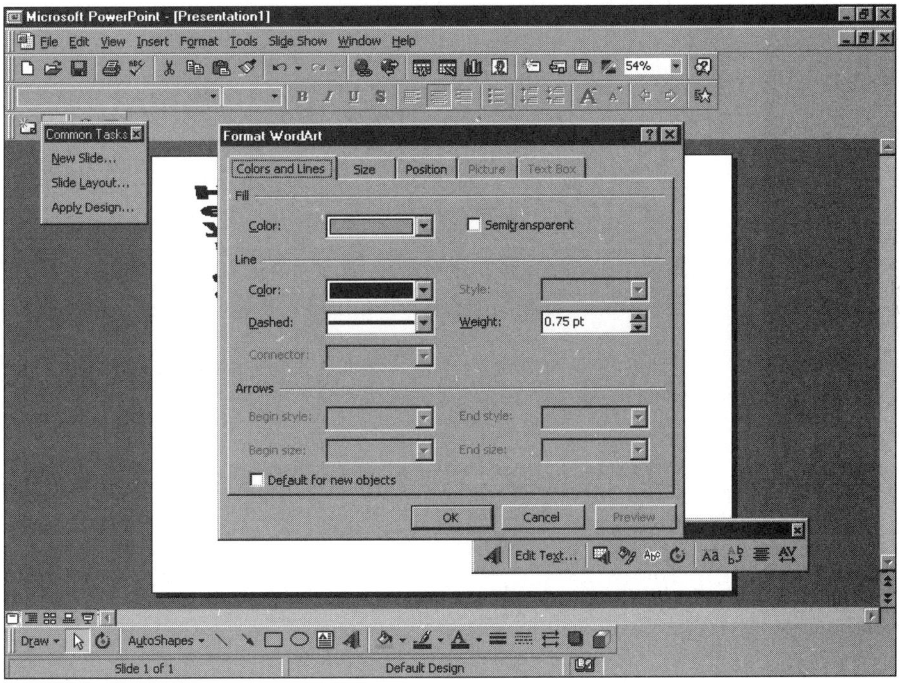

Figure 15-16:
The Format
WordArt
dialog box.

8. **Click in the <u>W</u>eight list box and choose a point size for the border of your text.**

9. **Click on OK.**

You can also use the Format WordArt dialog box to define the position, height, and rotation angle of your WordArt by clicking on the Size or Position tabs of the Format WordArt dialog box.

Deleting WordArt

In case you want to get rid of your WordArt, follow these steps:

1. **Click on the WordArt that you want to delete.**

2. **Press Delete.**

If you accidentally delete WordArt, press Ctrl+Z to retrieve it right away.

Chapter 16

Making Notes and Handouts

*I*n addition to helping you make slides, PowerPoint 97 enables you to create notes and handouts. *Notes* are for your benefit so that you can jot down ideas, statistics, or alibis that you can see while you're making a presentation. *Handouts* let you pass out printed copies of your presentation so that members of your audience can jot down their ideas or questions.

By creating notes to yourself, you can avoid looking foolish during that all-important business meeting that most people won't pay attention to anyway. By creating handouts, you can give your audience members something to remember (or throw away) after they leave your presentation.

Making a Generic Notes Page

Before writing any notes or handouts, take some time to design their layout. Then you can ensure that your notes and handouts look consistent (even if the text that's written on them may not make any sense).

PowerPoint 97 provides a Note Master that enables you to design a uniform layout and appearance for your notes. A note typically contains one slide along with any explanatory text underneath it. By printing your notes and keeping them nearby while you're giving a presentation, you can make sure that you don't forget any relevant points.

Because your notes will likely be seen only by you, you can be as wildly creative and outrageous or as sparse and minimal as you want, without worrying about annoying other people.

The purpose of the Notes Master Page is to design the layout appearance for all of your notes but not the actual notes themselves.

To design the Note Master, follow these steps:

1. **Choose View⇨Master⇨Notes Master.**

   PowerPoint 97 displays your notes page, as shown in Figure 16-1.

2. **Choose View⇨Zoom.**

   The Zoom dialog box appears, as shown in Figure 16-2.

3. **Click on a radio button to choose a resolution (such as 100%) and then click on OK.**

4. **Draw any borders, lines, or shapes that you want to insert on all your notes pages.**

5. **Highlight and format any text styles, such as the Master text style or the Second level style, as shown in Figure 16-3.**

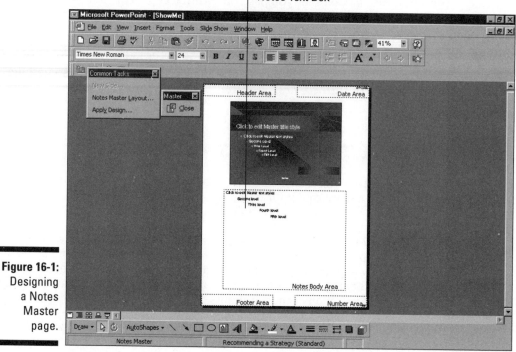

Figure 16-1: Designing a Notes Master page.

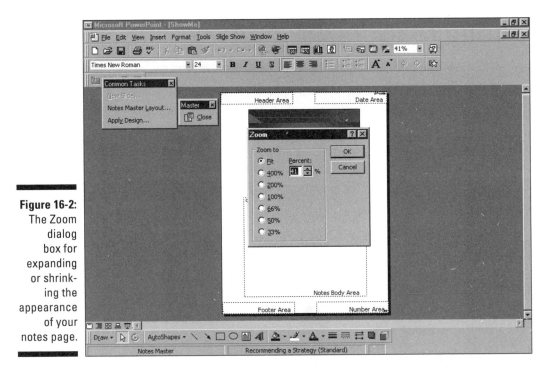

Figure 16-2:
The Zoom dialog box for expanding or shrinking the appearance of your notes page.

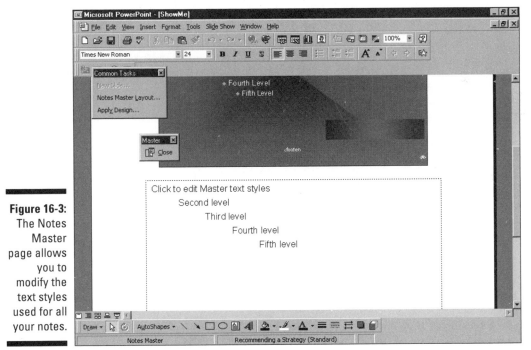

Figure 16-3:
The Notes Master page allows you to modify the text styles used for all your notes.

Jotting Down Notes for Posterity

Because you're the only one who will see your notes, you can write anything on them that you want (points that you want to make during your presentation, stories or statistics to support a particular slide, or tasteless jokes to keep yourself amused while you're giving a presentation to a captive audience).

You can create a separate notes page for each slide in your presentation either before you present your PowerPoint 97 slides to an audience (so that you can jot down notes ahead of time) or during your presentation (so that you can write comments from audience members who are paying attention).

Creating notes for yourself

To create a note before giving a presentation, follow these steps

1. Choose <u>V</u>iew⇨<u>N</u>otes Pages.

PowerPoint displays the current slide on a notes page, as shown in Figure 16-4.

Text Box ⎤   Demote ⎤ ⎡ Promote

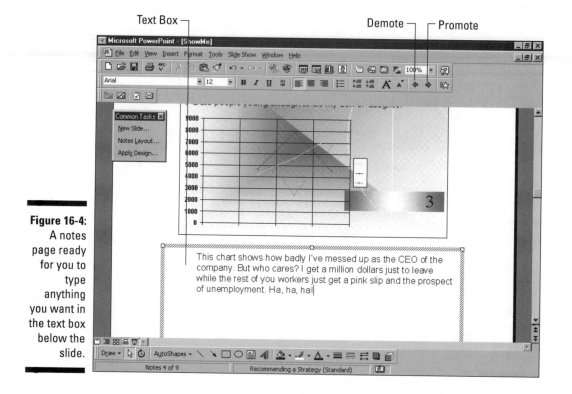

Figure 16-4:
A notes page ready for you to type anything you want in the text box below the slide.

This chart shows how badly I've messed up as the CEO of the company. But who cares? I get a million dollars just to leave while the rest of you workers just get a pink slip and the prospect of unemployment. Ha, ha, ha!

2. **Choose <u>V</u>iew⇨<u>Z</u>oom.**

   The Zoom dialog box appears (refer to Figure 16-2).

3. **Click on a radio button (such as <u>1</u>00%) to change the resolution of your notes page so that you can really see something, and then click on OK.**

   PowerPoint displays your notes page so that you can see what you're writing.

4. **Click in the notes page text box and type any ideas, stories, statistics, or funny jokes that you want.**

5. **Highlight any text and click on the Promote or Demote icons if you want to indent blocks of text.**

Writing notes during a presentation

The notes page is also a great place to jot down any comments, questions, or ideas that you may get from the audience. For example, you may show a slide proving that your company really isn't going bankrupt, and then someone will ask for facts. Rather than jot down this request on a separate piece of paper, you can jot it on your notes page. That way, you won't risk losing any audience comments (unless, of course, you lose your computer).

When you're writing comments during a presentation, you can store them in one of three places:

✔ On the notes page of the currently displayed slide

✔ On a temporary page called the Meeting Minutes page

✔ As a separate slide titled Action Items

Typing comments on the note page

While you're giving a presentation, you may come up with an idea that you want to save on your notes page. To type a comment on a note page during a presentation, follow these steps:

1. **Click on the right mouse button.**

   A pop-up menu appears.

2. **Click on Spea<u>k</u>er Notes.**

   The Speaker Notes dialog box appears.

3. **Type any text that you want to include on your notes page and click on Close.**

Typing meeting minutes

Every boring meeting that won't affect society one bit usually demands that someone keep track of the meeting minutes. To type meeting minutes during a presentation, follow these steps:

1. **Click on the right mouse button.**

   A pop-up menu appears.

2. **Click on Meeting Minder.**

   The Meeting Minder dialog box appears.

3. **Click on the Meeting Minutes tab (see Figure 16-5).**

4. **Type any text that you want to save as part of your meeting minutes.**

5. **Click on Export.**

   A Meeting Minder Export dialog box appears.

6. **Click on Export Now.**

   PowerPoint 97 immediately saves your meeting minutes as a separate Word 97 document.

If you click on the Schedule button in Step 5, you can store your text as an Outlook 97 appointment.

Figure 16-5:
The Meeting Minutes tab in the Meeting Minder dialog box.

Creating a list of action items

While you're giving a presentation, some bozo (your boss, for example) will probably want to know what type of action he or she can assign someone else to do. For these types of unwelcome comments, PowerPoint 97 provides a special Action Items text box. To type text in the Action Items box during a presentation, follow these steps:

1. **Click on the right mouse button.**

   A pop-up menu appears.

2. **Click on Meeting Minder.**

   The Meeting Minder dialog box appears.

3. **Click on the Actions Items tab, as shown in Figure 16-6.**

4. **Type a task description in the Description text box.**

5. **Type the name of a person assigned to the task in the Assigned To text box.**

6. **Click on Add.**

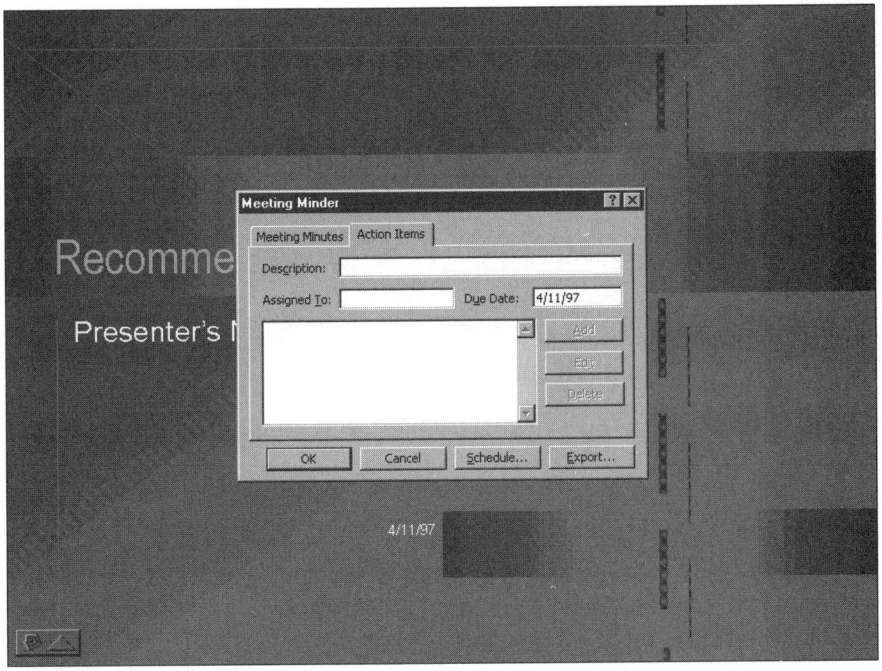

Figure 16-6: The Action Items tab in the Meeting Minder dialog box.

7. Click on Export.

A Meeting Minder Export dialog box appears.

8. Click on Export Now.

PowerPoint 97 immediately saves your meeting minutes as a separate Word 97 document.

If you click on the Schedule button in Step 6, you can store your text as an Outlook 97 appointment.

Printing your notes pages

After you write and save text on your notes pages, you may want to print them so that you don't have to turn on your computer every time you want to read them. To print your notes pages, follow these steps:

1. Choose File⇨Print (or choose Section⇨Print if you're using PowerPoint 97 within a binder).

The Print dialog box appears.

2. Click on the Print what list box and then choose Notes Pages.

3. Click on OK.

Providing Distracting Handouts for Your Audience

Unlike notes, handouts are meant for others to see. Rather than expect others to memorize your slides or take notes, audience members can walk away with printed copies of every slide in your presentation.

To print handouts of your slides, follow these steps:

1. Choose File⇨Print (or choose Section⇨Print if you're using PowerPoint 97 within a binder).

The Print dialog box appears.

2. Click on the Print what list box and then choose one of the following:

- Handouts (2 slides per page)
- Handouts (3 slides per page)
- Handouts (6 slides per page)

3. Click on OK.

Chapter 17
Adding Video and Sound Effects

Most business presentations tend to be dry, dull, and utterly useless. Although the information presented may be valuable, the presentation itself resembles nothing more exciting than watching someone fumble with poorly drawn charts and graphs.

To avoid having your presentations fall into this trap of dullness, PowerPoint 97 gives you the chance to spice up your slide shows with video and sound. By adding sound to your presentations, you can wake up your audience with a siren or a crowing rooster. By adding video, you can make your presentations more visually interesting to watch, much like a Saturday morning cartoon.

Playing Videos in a Presentation

Because most people would rather watch TV than read or listen to the radio, adding video can give your PowerPoint 97 presentations that extra bit of stimulus necessary to keep a roomful of executives interested in what you're trying to say. To make your presentations visually interesting, PowerPoint 97 can play any video file stored in the AVI file format.

You could create your own AVI video files with the proper equipment and software, but most people wouldn't want to go through all that trouble. As a shortcut, Office 97 provides several AVI files on the Office 97 CD.

You can also find many AVI video files on the Internet or your favorite online service, such as America Online.

Adding video files

To add a video file to a slide, follow these steps:

1. **Insert the Office 97 CD in your CD-ROM drive.**

2. **Choose Insert⇨Movies and Sounds and choose one of the following:**

   - **Movie from Gallery:** Allows you to add an AVI video file stored in the Microsoft Clip Gallery

   - **Movie from File:** Allows you to add an AVI file stored anywhere on your hard disk, floppy disk, or CD

   If you choose Movie from Gallery, a Microsoft Clip Gallery dialog box appears, as shown in Figure 17-1. If you choose Movie from File, an Insert Movie dialog box appears where you can choose the specific AVI file that you want to use.

3. **Click on a video file and click Play.**

   PowerPoint 97 shows you what the video file looks like (see Figure 17-2).

4. **Click on Insert.**

   PowerPoint displays your chosen video file on the current slide.

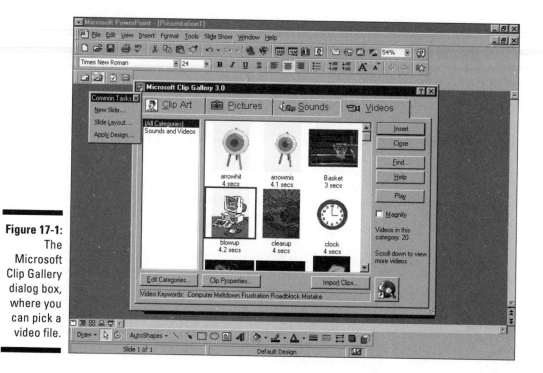

Figure 17-1:
The Microsoft Clip Gallery dialog box, where you can pick a video file.

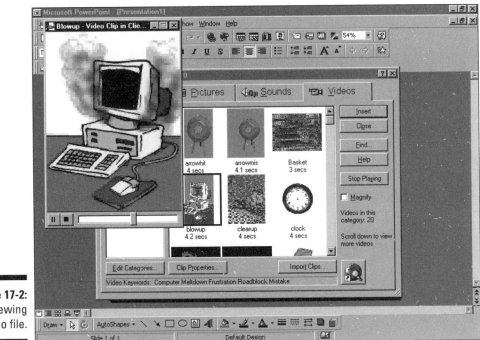

Figure 17-2:
Previewing
a video file.

To adjust the size or location of the video icon, choose one of the following:

1. **Move the mouse pointer over the video icon, hold down the left mouse button, and drag the mouse to move the video icon.**

2. **Move the mouse pointer over a white handle around the edge of the video icon until the mouse pointer turns into a double-pointing arrow, hold down the left mouse button, and drag the mouse to resize the video icon.**

3. **Double-click on the video icon to see how it will look on your slide.**

The Office 97 CD contains more AVI files stored in the D:\Books\Mm directory (assuming that the Office 97 CD is in the D drive). The TO57662a file is really cool because it shows a suspension bridge swaying in the wind before collapsing into the river below.

Adding Sounds to a Slide

Sound effects can highlight an important point, wake up your audience, or just provide additional stimulus to keep your audience wondering what sound or video file you'll show next.

PowerPoint 97 can use sound files (stored in the WAV file format) from four different sources:

✔ The Microsoft Clip Gallery

✔ Any WAV file stored on your hard disk, floppy disk, or CD

✔ Songs from an audio CD, such as your favorite Beatles, Aerosmith, or U2 album

✔ WAV files that you've recorded yourself

To record your own WAV sound files, you need the proper equipment, such as a microphone and sound recording software. Just yelling at your computer won't be enough to record a sound file no matter how loudly you scream.

Adding sound files

To add a sound file to your slide, follow these steps:

1. Insert the Office 97 CD in your CD-ROM drive.

2. Choose Insert⇨Movies and Sounds and choose one of the following:

- **Sound from Gallery:** Allows you to add a WAV sound file stored in the Microsoft Clip Gallery

- **Sound from File:** Allows you to add a WAV file stored anywhere on your hard disk, floppy disk, or CD

If you choose Sound from Gallery, a Microsoft Clip Gallery dialog box appears, as shown in Figure 17-3. If you choose Sound from File, an Insert Sound dialog box appears where you can choose the specific WAV file that you want to use.

3. Click on a sound file and click on Play.

PowerPoint 97 plays your chosen sound file so that you can judge whether you really want to use it.

4. Click on Insert.

PowerPoint displays your chosen sound file as a tiny icon on the current slide.

To adjust the size or location of the sound icon, choose one of the following:

1. Move the mouse pointer over the sound file, hold down the left mouse button, and drag the mouse to move the sound icon.

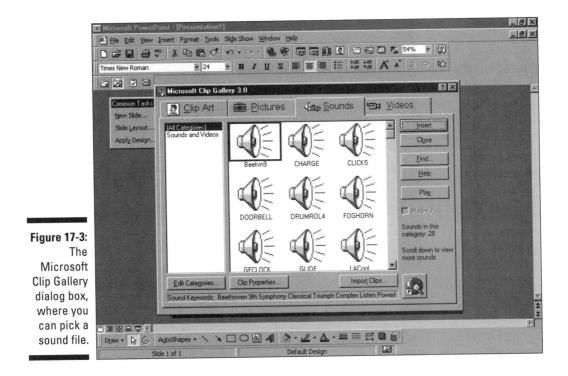

Figure 17-3:
The
Microsoft
Clip Gallery
dialog box,
where you
can pick a
sound file.

2. **Move the mouse pointer over a white handle around the edge of the sound icon until the mouse pointer turns into a double-pointing arrow, hold down the left mouse button, and drag the mouse to resize the sound icon.**

3. **Double-click on the sound file to play it on your slide.**

Playing songs from an audio CD

Rather than use WAV sound files, you might be more interested in playing songs directly off audio CDs instead. In this way, you can play your favorite songs during your presentation to emphasize the point you're making, to provide pleasant background music so that you don't have to keep talking, or to send a subtle message to your audience (such as playing the song, "Take This Job and Shove It").

To play an audio CD track to a slide, follow these steps:

1. **Insert your audio CD in your CD-ROM drive.**

2. **Choose Insert➪Movies and Sounds➪Play CD Audio Track.**

   The Play Options dialog box appears, as shown in Figure 17-4.

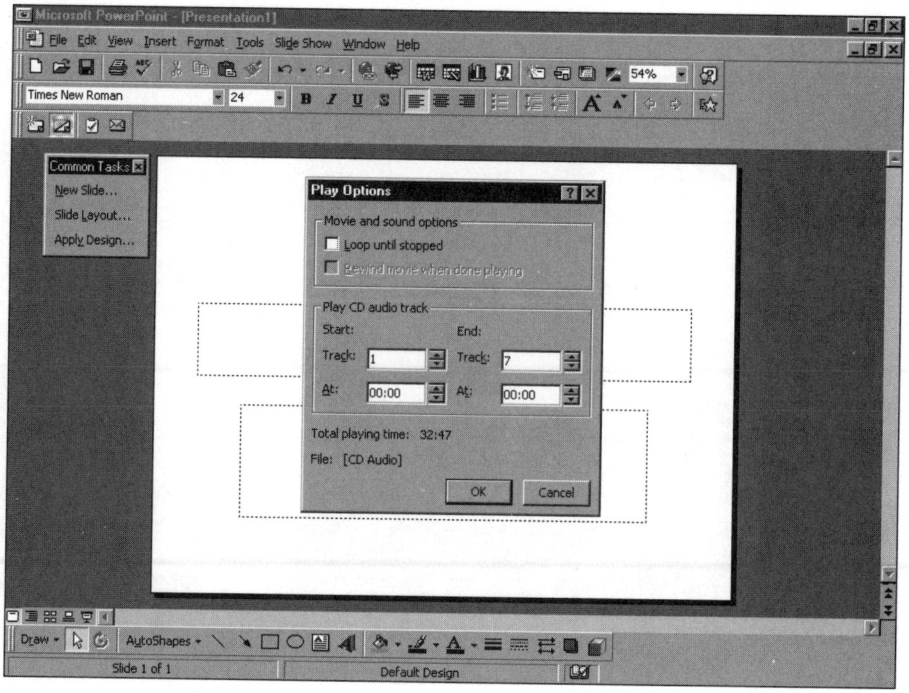

Figure 17-4:
The Play
Options
dialog box
for playing
a song
from an
audio CD.

3. **Click in the Track list box (under the Start group) to define the first audio track to play.**

4. **Click in the Track list box (under the End group) to define the last audio track to play.**

5. **Click in the At list box (under the Start group) to define what part of the song you want to start playing.**

   If you want to start the song at the beginning, choose 00:00.

6. **Click in the At list box (under the End group) to define what part of the song you want to stop playing.**

   If you want to stop at the end of the song, don't change the time listed in the At list box.

7. **Click on OK.**

   PowerPoint 97 displays a CD icon on the current slide.

   To adjust the size or location of the audio CD file, choose one of the following:

   • Move the mouse pointer over the audio CD icon, hold down the left mouse button, and drag the mouse to move the audio CD icon.

- Move the mouse pointer over a white handle around the edge of the audio CD icon until the mouse pointer turns into a double-pointing arrow, hold down the left mouse button, and drag the mouse to resize the audio CD icon.

  8. Double-click on the audio CD icon to play it on your slide.

Deleting Sound and Video Files

If you want to delete a sound or video file from a slide, follow these steps:

1. Click on the sound or video file so that white handles appear around its edges.

2. Press Delete.

When you delete a sound or video file from a slide, the file still physically exists in its original location.

Part V

Getting Connected with Microsoft Outlook 97

The 5th Wave   By Rich Tennant

"IT'S JUST UNTIL THE SYSTEM IS BACK UP AND RUNNING."

In this part . . .

Time is money, which means that if you use your time wisely, you can make more money than people who squander their hours every day until they're left wondering why they're not getting anything important done in their lives.

To become one of those few people who track their activities during the day, learn to use Outlook 97 to help you monitor your time and jot down any sudden inspirational ideas that hit you on the spur of the moment.

By using Outlook 97, you can take responsibility for your own life and pursue the goal of your dreams, which immediately puts you in the minority of the population who know what they want out of life.

Chapter 18

Tips for Using Outlook 97

● ●

In This Chapter

▶ Loading Outlook 97 at startup

▶ Creating an AutoSignature file

▶ Organizing your hard disk

▶ Archiving old Outlook 97 data

● ●

*B*elieve it or not, you can actually run your entire computer from within Outlook 97: You can load and run other programs (such as Word 97 or Lotus 1-2-3) and create directories or delete files. So browse through this chapter and look for tips that help you use Outlook 97 more effectively.

Loading Outlook 97 Automatically

Outlook 97 allows you to read and send e-mail, organize your daily tasks, plan appointments in advance, or jot down notes, but none of these features are any good unless you load Outlook 97 first. Unfortunately, the time and trouble necessary to load Outlook 97 may be just enough of an obstacle to keep you from using Outlook 97 as effectively as you really can.

To fix this problem and remove one more excuse for not organizing your time, your computer, and your information, you can make Outlook 97 load automatically as soon as you turn on your computer.

To load Outlook 97 automatically, follow these steps:

1. **Click on the Start button on the Windows 95 taskbar and choose Settings⇨Taskbar.**

2. **Click on the Start Menu Programs tab.**

3. **Click on Add and then Browse.**

4. **Double-click on Microsoft Outlook.**

   You may have to look inside the /Program Files/Microsoft Office folders first.

5. Click on Next and then double-click on the StartUp folder.

6. Click on Finish and then OK.

The next time you start (or restart) your computer, Outlook 97 loads automatically.

You can have Windows 95 load any program automatically if you click on that program name in Step 4 instead of clicking on Microsoft Outlook.

If you don't want Outlook 97 to load automatically any more (because it takes too much time), you can stop Outlook 97 from loading by following these steps:

1. Click on the Start button on the Windows 95 taskbar and choose Settings⇨Taskbar.

2. Click on the Start Menu Programs tab.

3. Click on Remove.

4. Click on Microsoft Outlook in the Startup folder and click on Remove.

5. Click on Close and then OK.

Making a Signature File

When you send e-mail, you may like to type your name, company name, and phone number at the end of your e-mail message just so that someone can get in touch with you. Information that you want to appear at the end of your e-mail messages is called a *signature file* and consists of text that you create ahead of time.

A typical signature file might appear as follows:

```
George Orwell
Big Brother Computer Stores
"Where we know what's best for you!"
E-mail: bigbrother@1984.gov
Voice: (123) 123-4567
```

By creating and adding a signature file to all your e-mail messages, you can personalize your messages while providing valuable contact information simultaneously.

To create a signature file for your e-mail, follow these steps:

1. **Choose Go⬄Inbox.**

2. **Choose Tools⬄AutoSignature.**

   An AutoSignature dialog box appears (see Figure 18-1).

3. **Click in the Add this signature to the end of new messages check box so that a check mark appears.**

4. **Click on Font.**

   A Font dialog box appears, in which you can choose the font, point size, and styles (underline or italics) that you want to use.

5. **Click on OK.**

6. **Click on Paragraph.**

   A Paragraph dialog box appears, as shown in Figure 18-2.

7. **Click in the Left, Center, or Right radio button and click on OK.**

8. **Type your text in the text box and click on OK when you're done.**

   Any new messages that you write from now on will automatically contain your signature file at the end of the message.

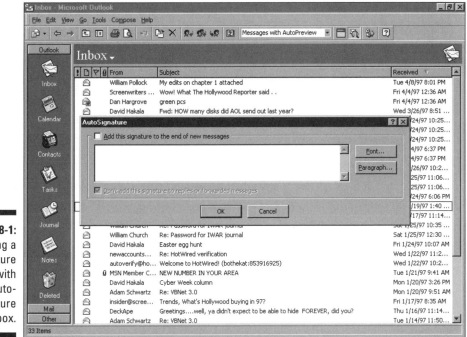

Figure 18-1: Creating a signature file with the Auto-Signature dialog box.

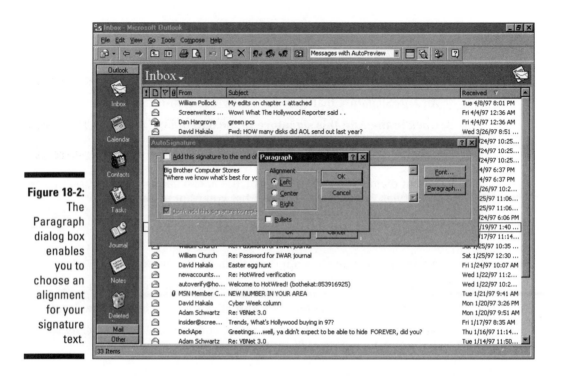

Figure 18-2:
The
Paragraph
dialog box
enables
you to
choose an
alignment
for your
signature
text.

Organizing Files and Folders on Your Hard Disk

Surprisingly, Outlook 97 allows you to view folders and files to help you organize the information on your hard disk.

To view your computer's files and folders, follow these steps:

1. Choose View⇨Outlook Bar.

If a check mark already appears in front of Outlook Bar, skip this step.

2. Click on the Other panel in the Outlook bar.

3. Click on the My Computer icon.

Outlook 97 shows all the drives on your computer, as shown in Figure 18-3.

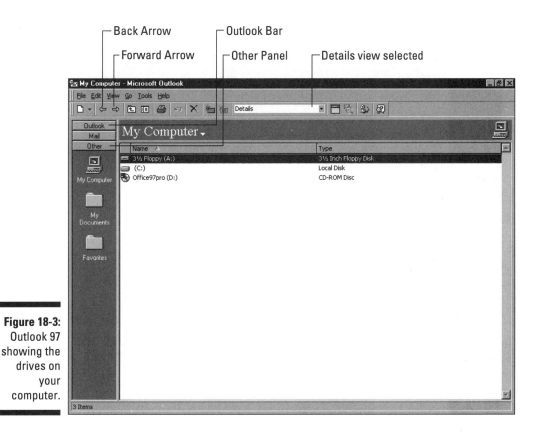

Figure 18-3:
Outlook 97
showing the
drives on
your
computer.

4. Choose View➪Current View and choose one of the following:

- **Icons:** Displays folders as icons just like a Macintosh computer, as shown in Figure 18-4

- **Details:** Displays folders as tiny icons (see Figure 18-3)

- **By Type:** Displays folders as text (see Figure 18-5)

Navigating within a folder

To open (and close) a folder, follow these steps:

1. Double-click on the folder.

Outlook 97 opens that folder and displays its contents (which could be more folders or files), as shown in Figure 18-6.

2. Click on the Back arrow on the Outlook 97 standard toolbar to close the folder.

Icons view selected

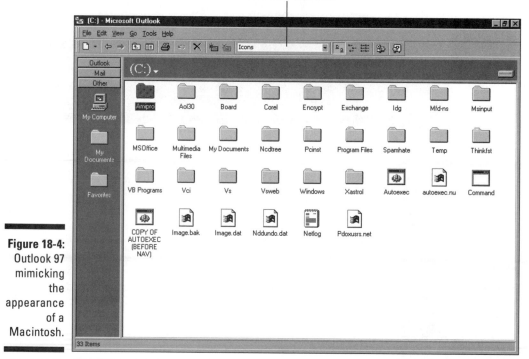

Figure 18-4:
Outlook 97
mimicking
the
appearance
of a
Macintosh.

Rather than dig through multiple folders repeatedly, you can display your most frequently used folders on the Outlook bar. To put a folder on the Outlook bar, move the mouse pointer over the folder, click on the right mouse button, and click on Add to Outlook bar.

Creating a new folder

If you want to create a new folder, follow these steps:

1. **Choose File⇨New⇨Folder or press Ctrl+Shift+E.**

   A Create New Folder dialog box appears, as shown in Figure 18-7.

2. **Type a new name for your folder in the Name box and click on OK.**

You can move folders or files into a folder by dragging that folder or file into its destination folder.

By Type view selected

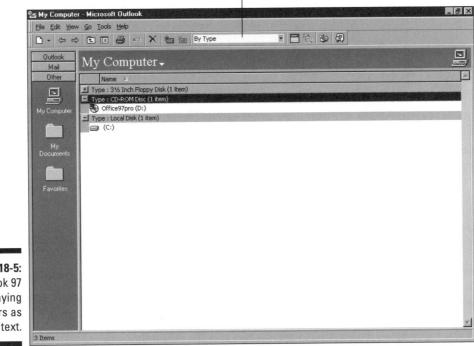

Figure 18-5:
Outlook 97
displaying
folders as
boring text.

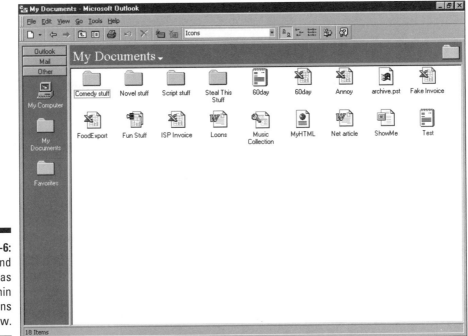

Figure 18-6:
Folders and
files as
seen within
the Icons
view.

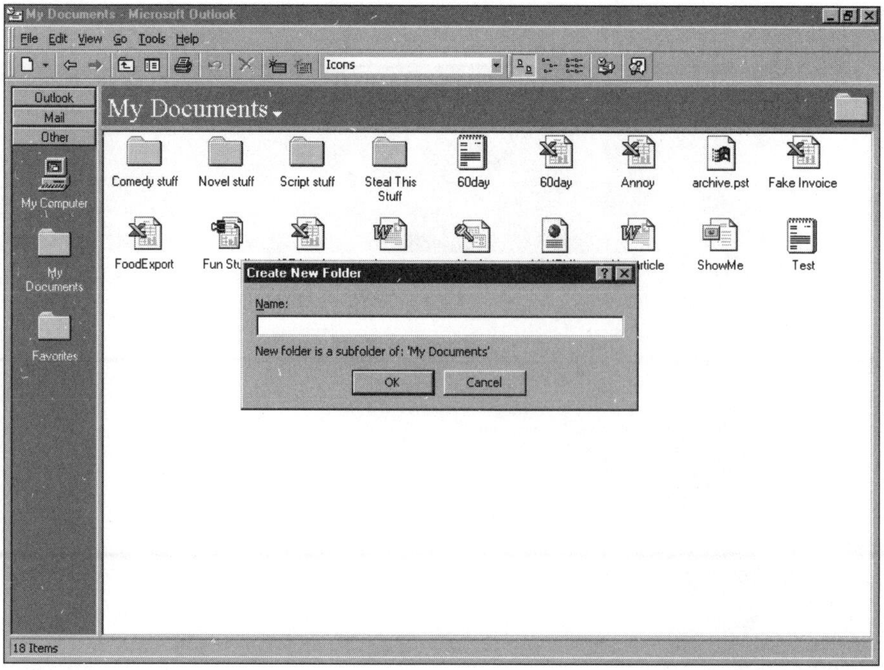

Figure 18-7:
The Create
New Folder
dialog box
for creating
a new
folder on
your hard or
floppy disk.

Deleting and renaming a folder or file

Because Outlook 97 can mimic the Windows Explorer program, you'll be pleased to know that you can delete or rename a folder or file at any time.

To delete a folder or file, follow these steps:

1. **Move the mouse pointer over the folder or file that you want to delete and click on the right mouse button.**

2. **Choose Delete.**

   A dialog box appears, asking whether you really want to delete your folder or file.

3. **Click on Yes.**

To rename a folder or file, follow these steps:

1. **Move the mouse pointer over the folder or file that you want to rename and click on the right mouse button.**

2. **Choose Rename.**

   A Rename dialog box appears.

3. **Type a new name for your folder or file in the New name box and click on OK.**

Launching a file

Besides enabling you to edit, rename, or delete files, Outlook 97 also allows you to launch the program that created that file (provided that you have that program on your hard disk in the first place).

To load a file plus the program that created it (such as Excel 97), follow these steps:

1. **Double-click on the file that you want to edit.**

   Outlook 97 obediently loads the program that created the file and displays your file contents.

2. **Choose File⇨Exit from the program menu that loaded in Step 1 (such as Excel 97).**

   Outlook 97 cheerfully appears once more, ready to do your bidding again.

Saving Old Outlook 97 Data

The more you use Outlook 97, the more information you're going to wind up saving. After a while, Outlook 97 may start to get as cluttered as your closet or garage. Rather than delete your Outlook 97 data, you can save it in a compressed file format. That way, you can keep your information for good without taking up a lot of space in the meantime.

Archiving old information

After a few months or so, you might want to archive your old journal entries or e-mail messages so that you can still keep them without filling up your journal window with old information.

Delete any data that you know you won't ever want to save again. This keeps your archive file smaller and easier to load in the future.

To archive Outlook 97 data, follow these steps:

1. **Choose File⇨Archive.**

   An Archive dialog box appears, as shown in Figure 18-8.

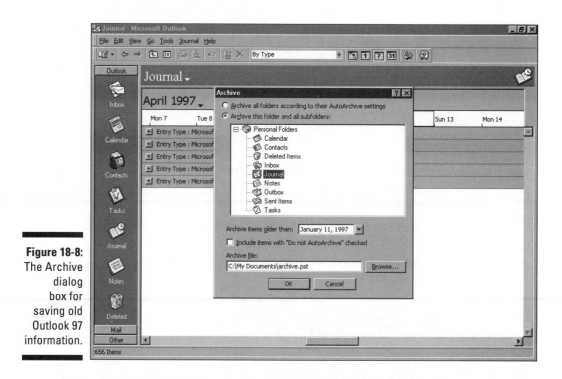

Figure 18-8:
The Archive
dialog
box for
saving old
Outlook 97
information.

2. **Click on the type of information that you want to save (such as Journal or Tasks).**

3. **Click in the Archive items older than list box and choose a cutoff date.**

   The date that you choose (such as January 12) tells Outlook 97 to archive everything up until that cutoff date.

4. **Click on OK.**

   Outlook 97 obediently clears up old information and stores it in an archive file.

If you accidentally delete your archive file, kiss all your old data good-bye for good.

Retrieving archived entries

After you've archived old information from Outlook 97, you might need to retrieve it again at a later date. To retrieve archived data, follow these steps:

1. **Choose File⇨Import and Export.**

   The Import and Export Wizard dialog box appears (see Figure 18-9).

2. **Click on Import from a personal folder file (*.pst) and click on Next.**

   An Import Personal Folders dialog box appears, as shown in Figure 18-10.

3. **Click on the Browse button.**

   A Connect to Personal Folders dialog box appears.

4. **Click on the archive file from which you want to retrieve data and click on Open.**

5. **Click on Next.**

   Another Import Personal Folders dialog box appears, asking what category of data you want to retrieve (such as Journal or Deleted Items).

6. **Click on the category from which you want to retrieve data (such as Meetings or Journal) and click on Finish.**

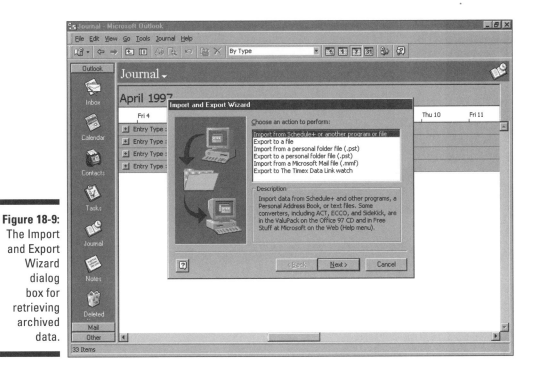

Figure 18-9:
The Import and Export Wizard dialog box for retrieving archived data.

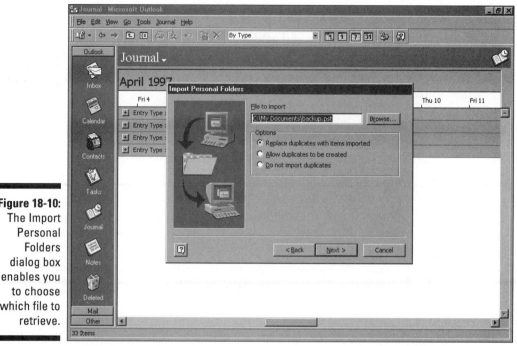

Figure 18-10:
The Import
Personal
Folders
dialog box
enables you
to choose
which file to
retrieve.

Chapter 19

Jotting Down a Journal and Notes

● ●

In This Chapter

▶ Storing a journal

▶ Adding and deleting Journal entries

▶ Creating and viewing notes

▶ Editing and printing notes

● ●

*M*icrosoft Outlook 97 is designed to organize your information so that you can be more productive (just as soon as you spend enough time figuring out how to use Outlook 97 in the first place). To help achieve its noble goal of organizing your information, Outlook 97 provides two neat features that you probably won't find in any other personal information organizer: self-stick notes and a journal.

The self-stick notes feature allows you to jot down ideas as they occur to you. A journal lets you keep track of what you've done so that you can identify how you've been spending your time.

Jotting Down Notes

Usually, when you come up with an idea, you have to scramble for a piece of paper. If you happen to be sitting in front of your computer when you have an idea, you can store your thoughts directly in Outlook 97 instead.

To ensure that Outlook 97 is available for writing notes, load Outlook 97 and then minimize it. That way, when you want to jot down a note in Outlook 97, you won't have to wait for Outlook 97 to load.

Creating a note within Outlook 97

When you want to create a note, follow these steps:

1. **Choose Go▷Notes.**

   The Notes window of Outlook 97 appears, as shown in Figure 19-1.

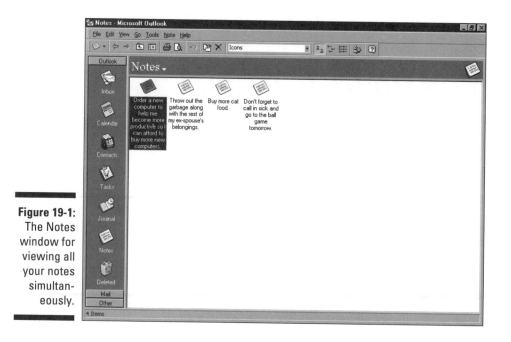

Figure 19-1:
The Notes
window for
viewing all
your notes
simultan-
eously.

2. Press Ctrl+N to create a new note.

A blank note window appears, as shown in Figure 19-2.

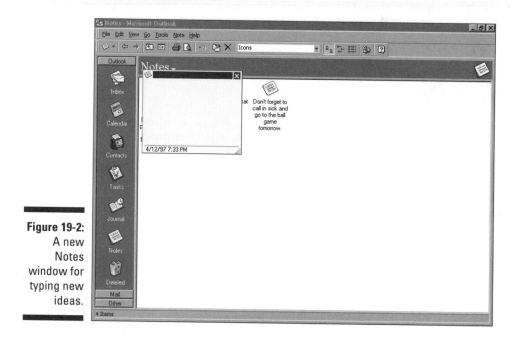

Figure 19-2:
A new
Notes
window for
typing new
ideas.

3. **Type your ideas in the note window and click on the close box of the note window when you're done.**

Creating a note while using other programs

Because you probably won't be staring at Outlook 97 every time you come up with an idea worth saving, you may want to type a note while using another program, such as Word 97 or Excel 97.

To write a note while using another program, follow these steps:

1. **Load Outlook 97.**

2. **Choose Go⇨Notes.**

   The Outlook 97 Notes window appears (refer to Figure 19-1).

3. **Double-click on an existing note window or press Ctrl+N to display a blank note window.**

4. **Click on another program name (such as Microsoft Word) on the Windows 95 taskbar to switch to that other program.**

   Notice that the note window also appears on the Windows 95 taskbar, as shown in Figure 19-3.

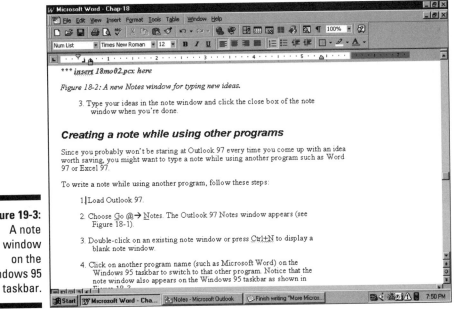

Figure 19-3:
A note window on the Windows 95 taskbar.

5. Click on the note window on the Windows 95 taskbar to display the note on the screen.

If you move the mouse pointer over the title bar of the note window, hold down the left mouse button, and drag the mouse, you can move the note window to one corner of the screen.

6. Click in the control box (the icon that appears in the upper-left corner of the note window).

A pop-up menu appears (see Figure 19-4).

7. Choose New Note.

A new note window appears.

8. Type your idea in the new note window.

9. Click anywhere outside the note window to return to your original program (such as Word 97).

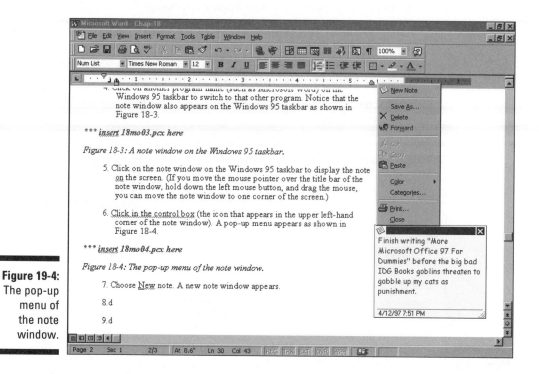

Figure 19-4:
The pop-up menu of the note window.

If you click in the close box of the note window, the note window no longer appears on the Windows 95 taskbar. Closing all note windows that you don't want to view is a good idea to keep your Windows 95 taskbar from looking cluttered.

Viewing your notes

If you wind up writing lots of notes to yourself, you may find your notes cluttering up your screen. To help you organize your notes, Outlook 97 offers several different views:

✔ Icons — Displays each note as an icon (see Figure 19-1)

✔ Notes List — Displays notes as a list of text, as shown in Figure 19-5

✔ Last Seven Days — Displays only those notes that you created in the last seven days as a list of text

✔ By category — Groups notes according to categories that you have assigned to your notes

✔ By color — Groups notes by color

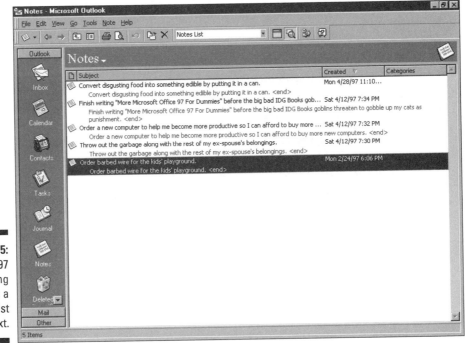

Figure 19-5: Outlook 97 displaying notes as a boring list of text.

To choose a different way to view your notes, follow these steps:

1. **Choose View⇨Current View.**

2. **Choose one of the following:**

   • Icons

   • Notes List

   • Last Seven Days

   • By category

   • By color

Defining categories for your notes

Rather than dump all your notes on the screen at once, take a little bit of time to define categories for your notes. By using categories, you can keep your business-related notes separate from your personal notes.

To define a category for a note, follow these steps:

1. **Choose Go⇨Notes.**

2. **Click on a note that you want to organize by a category.**

3. **Click on the right mouse button.**

   A pop-up menu appears.

4. **Choose Categories.**

   A Categories dialog box appears, as shown in Figure 19-6.

5. **Click in one or more check boxes of the category (or categories) that you want for your note.**

6. **Click on OK.**

Choosing different colors for your notes

As an alternative to organizing your notes by categories, you may find it easier to just organize your notes by color instead. That way you can tell at a glance which are your work-related notes (pink), personal notes (yellow), or goal-related notes (green). Outlook 97 gives you the choice of five different colors:

✔ Blue

✔ Green

✔ Pink

✔ Yellow

✔ White

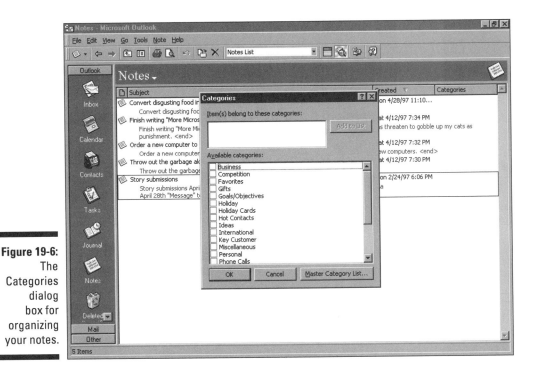

Figure 19-6:
The
Categories
dialog
box for
organizing
your notes.

To choose a color for a note, follow these steps:

1. **Choose Go⇨Notes.**

2. **Click on a note that you want to organize by a category.**

3. **Click on the right mouse button.**

    A pop-up menu appears.

4. **Choose Colors and then one of the following:**

    - Blue
    - Green
    - Pink
    - Yellow
    - White

Editing your notes

If you need to edit the contents of a note, follow these steps:

1. **Switch to Outlook 97.**

2. **Choose Go⇨Notes.**

    The Notes window appears.

3. **Double-click on the note that you want to edit.**

    The note window appears.

4. **Click anywhere inside the note and use the arrow, Backspace, or Del keys to edit your note.**

If the note that you want to edit appears in the Windows 95 taskbar, just click on it to make it appear and then click anywhere inside the note to edit it.

Printing your notes

A note might contain something important that you'll want to print on paper, just in case you don't trust your computer's hard disk to save your data indefinitely. To print a note, follow these steps:

1. **Switch to Outlook 97.**

2. **Choose Go⇨Notes.**

    The Notes window appears.

3. **Click on the note that you want to print.**

4. **Choose File⇨Print or press Ctrl+P.**

    A Print dialog box appears.

5. **Click on OK.**

If the note that you want to print appears in the Windows 95 taskbar, just click on it to make it appear, click on the control box in the note window, and choose Print.

Deleting a note

Chances are good that you won't want to keep your notes around for the rest of your life (or even until next month). To delete a note, follow these steps:

1. **Switch to Outlook 97.**

2. **Choose Go⇨Notes.**

    The Notes window appears.

3. **Click on the note that you want to delete.**

4. **Choose Edit⇨Delete or press Ctrl+D.**

If the note that you want to delete appears in the Windows 95 taskbar, just click on it to make it appear, click in the control box in the note window, and choose Delete.

Tracking Time with a Journal

The Outlook 97 journal lets you track your activities so that you can see what you did in the past. By reviewing your journal, you can find out what day you made an important phone call or the last time you sent e-mail to your parents.

Outlook 97 can record the following:

✔ When you access any Office 97 file (such as Word 97 or PowerPoint 97)

✔ When you send e-mail and to whom

✔ When you request or cancel a meeting

✔ When you request or cancel a task

Customizing your journal

To tell Outlook 97 what types of activities you want to record, follow these steps:

1. **Choose Tools⇨Options.**

2. **Click on the Journal tab (see Figure 19-7).**

3. **Click in the check box of the activity that you want to track, such as E-mail message or Task request.**

4. **Click on OK.**

From this point on, Outlook 97 automatically tracks the activities that you chose in Step 3.

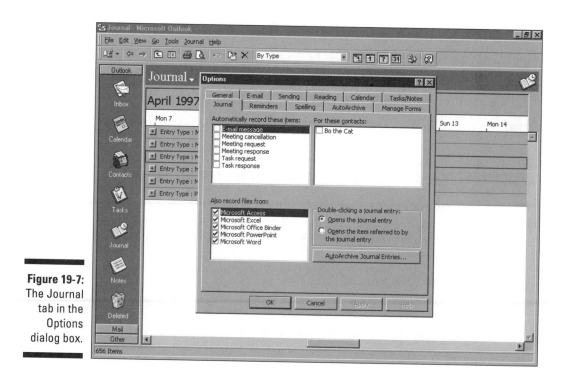

Figure 19-7:
The Journal
tab in the
Options
dialog box.

Viewing your journal

Outlook organizes your journal entries by categories, such as phone calls you've made, e-mail you've sent, or how many Word 97 files you've accessed.

To take a look at your journal entries, follow these steps:

1. **Choose Go⇨Journal.**

   The Journal window appears, listing your journal categories.

2. **Click on the plus sign of a journal entry to view all your entries organized by date and time, as shown in Figure 19-8.**

Manually adding a journal entry

Rather than wait for Outlook 97 to record your journal entries automatically, you may want to add a journal entry yourself. This can be useful if you've told Outlook 97 not to automatically record when you send e-mail, but you have an important e-mail message that you want to record just this once.

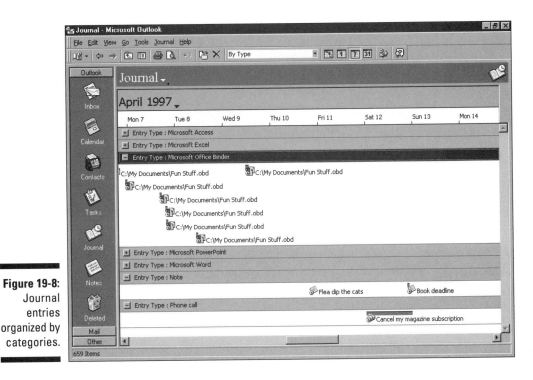

Figure 19-8:
Journal
entries
organized by
categories.

To add a journal entry to Outlook 97, follow these steps:

1. **Choose Go⇨Journal.**

   The Journal window appears, listing your journal categories.

2. **Choose Journal⇨New Journal Entry or press Ctrl+N.**

   A Journal Entry window appears, as shown in Figure 19-9.

3. **Click in the Subject text box and type a brief description of your journal entry.**

   The text appears in the Journal window when you expand on a journal category, such as Phone call or Note.

4. **Click in the Entry type list box and choose a type, such as Meeting or Task.**

5. **Click in the Start time list box and choose a date and time.**

   Click on the Start Timer command button if you want to start timing a task. When you want to stop timing the task, click on the Pause Timer command button.

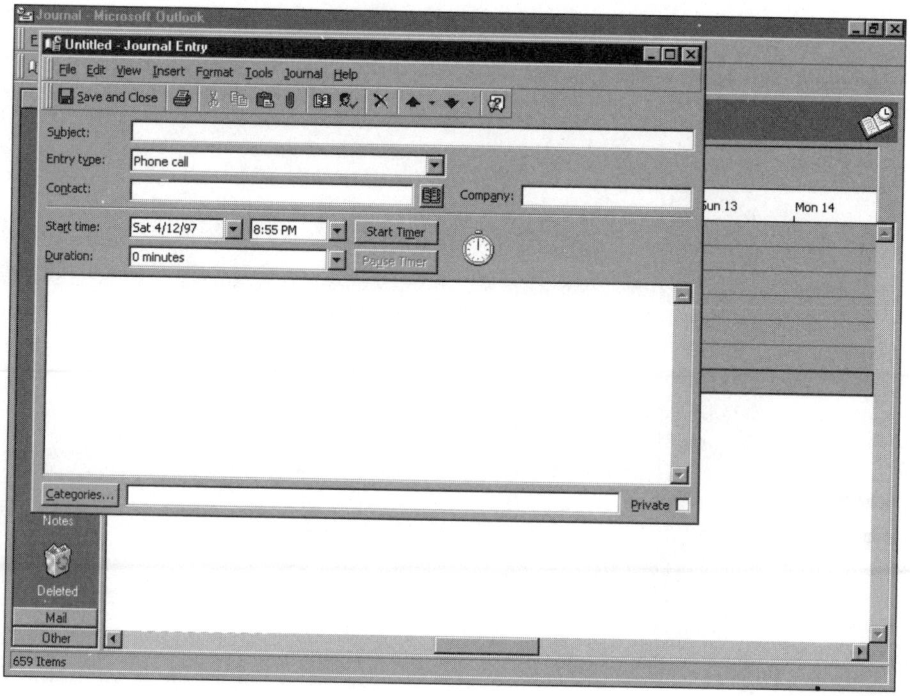

Figure 19-9:
The Journal
Entry
window.

6. **In the text box at the bottom of the window, type any additional description that you want to include for your journal.**

7. **Click on the Save and Close button (right underneath the File menu title).**

If you click on the Start Timer button in Step 5 and then switch to another task (such as making a phone call or attending a meeting), you can see the exact amount of time that you've spent (or wasted) at a particular task. Be careful when using this feature or you may find yourself wasting a lot more time during the day than you might have otherwise.

Printing a journal entry

You might want to get a printed copy of a particular journal entry. That way, you can show your boss (in black and white) just how much time you've been wasting attending meetings designed to teach you how to spend your time more productively.

To print a journal entry, follow these steps:

1. **Choose Go⇨Journal.**

   The Journal window appears.

2. **Click in the plus sign of the journal categories displayed in the Journal window.**

   Your entries in that category appear underneath.

3. **Click on the journal entry that you want to print and choose File⇨Print or press Ctrl+P.**

   A Print dialog box appears.

4. **Click on OK.**

Deleting a journal entry

You probably don't want to keep track of your journal entries forever. To delete a journal entry (and clear up a little bit of space on your hard disk), follow these steps:

1. **Choose Go⇨Journal.**

   The Journal window appears.

2. **Click in the plus sign of the journal categories containing the entry that you want to delete.**

3. **Click on the journal entry that you want to delete and choose Edit⇨Delete or press Ctrl+D.**

If you delete a journal entry by mistake, you can retrieve it right away by pressing Ctrl+Z.

To delete an entire journal category (such as Phone call or Task) along with any entries stored inside, follow these steps:

1. **Choose Go⇨Journal.**

   The Journal window appears.

2. **Click on the journal category that you want to delete.**

3. **Choose Edit⇨Delete or press Ctrl+D.**

   A dialog box appears, asking whether you really want to delete your journal category plus any entries stored inside of it.

4. **Click on OK.**

If you delete a journal category accidentally, don't panic. You can recover the category plus all entries stored inside by pressing Ctrl+Z right away.

Part VI

Storing Stuff in Microsoft Access 97

The 5th Wave   By Rich Tennant

In this part . . .

The Professional edition of Microsoft Office 97 comes with Microsoft Access 97, the most popular relational database program in the world. If you don't have the slightest idea what a relational database is, don't worry. Just remember that Access 97 is a database that lets you store and retrieve information ranging from names and addresses to part numbers and inventory bar codes.

This part of the book shows you how to automate Access 97 and customize it for your own purposes. Need a specialized program for tracking information, but you don't feel like shelling out hundreds of dollars to buy one? Then find out how to customize and program Access 97 to make it obey your commands.

Who knows? With enough practice, you can find out enough about programming Access 97 to start creating your own custom programs to sell or give away. And then you can get a better job, thanks to the power of Access 97.

Chapter 20

Creating Databases from Scratch

● ●

In This Chapter

▶ Designing tables

▶ Creating new forms with a wizard

▶ Editing tables and forms

● ●

*A*ccess 97 gives you two ways to create a database: Use an existing database design or create your own databases from scratch. If you use an existing database design, you may find that the database needs modifying before you can use it. In most cases, modifying an existing database is easier than creating a new database (just as copying somebody else's homework is usually easier than thinking for yourself).

But if you want absolute control over the design of your database, you must be able to create your own databases. Although creating a database from scratch may be more complicated and time-consuming than using someone else's, database creation can be an art in itself and allows you to create custom databases for your job, business, or personal life (in case you really enjoy creating databases).

Creating a New Database

The two most important parts of a database are its tables and forms. Tables define the type of data that you're storing (such as names, phone numbers, blood type, and so on). Unfortunately, tables display data in rows and columns, making them look as inviting to read as the stock exchange listing in *The Wall Street Journal*.

To make data entry and viewing easier, you also need forms. A form simply provides a user interface for accessing your data. You don't *need* to use forms; they exist solely to make viewing and editing the data as simple to use as Windows 95 itself (which may not be saying much, but at least you get the idea).

To create a new database, follow these steps:

1. **Choose File⇨New Database or press Ctrl+N.**

   A New window appears, as shown in Figure 20-1.

2. **Click on the General tab, click on the Blank Database icon, and click on OK.**

   (If you click on the Databases tab, instead of the General tab, you can create a new database based on an existing database design.) A File New Database dialog box appears.

3. **Type a name for your database, click on the folder where you want to store your database, and click on Create.**

   A completely blank database window appears, daring you to do something useful.

If you start Access 97, a Microsoft Access dialog box appears on the screen immediately after Access 97 loads. Just click on the Blank Database radio button and click on OK; then follow Steps 2 and 3 above.

Designing a database

Corporations pay fortunes to programmers who can design databases, so don't expect to become a database expert overnight. Essentially, designing a database means taking the time to understand what type of information you'll need to save and retrieve in the future and how you want to organize your data to make access as simple as possible.

Even though this preparation work may sound easy, it can get fairly complicated in a hurry if you're designing a database for a company that needs to track many different kinds of information, such as inventory, part numbers, customer addresses, shipping dates, and delivery dates.

Designing a database properly is like laying the foundation for a home. Do it right, and the home can last for years. Do it wrong, and you'll probably have to rip out the entire foundation and start all over again — which is something that large corporations hate doing, especially if it means paying their programmers overtime.

So, before rushing right into designing your database, first take some time to plan your database on paper. That way, you can erase, rewrite, and scribble all you want without wasting valuable time on your computer. To help you design your database correctly, ask yourself the following:

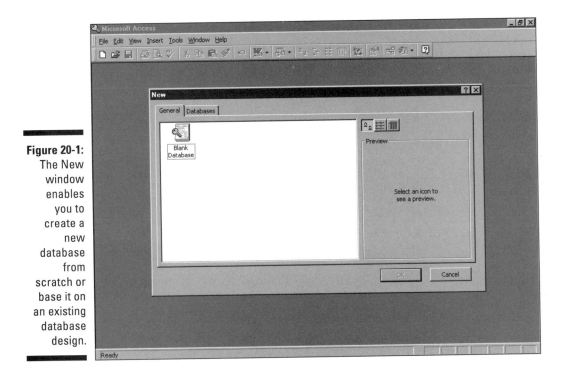

Figure 20-1:
The New
window
enables
you to
create a
new
database
from
scratch or
base it on
an existing
database
design.

✔ **What type of information do I need to save and retrieve?**

Answering this question helps you determine what fields your database needs. (*Fields* are simply categories containing one type of data, such as a name or address.)

✔ **Which information should logically be grouped together?**

The answer to this question helps you decide how to organize fields into tables.

✔ **How do I want to display my information for typing new data and for retrieving existing data?**

Making this decision helps you design your database forms for displaying data on the screen.

Many Ph.D.s in computer science spend years studying optimum database designs, so don't feel bad if you have trouble designing a database the first time. Like any skill, database design improves with practice, so feel free to practice at your job, where you can get paid overtime to fix any mistakes while learning at the same time.

Creating database tables

The simplest database has just one table. For example, if you want to create a database just to store names and phone numbers, your database may consist of a single table with just two fields, called NAME and PHONE.

A *database table* is nothing more than a container for your data.

To create a database table, make sure that the Database window appears and then follow these steps:

1. **Click on the Tables tab and then click on <u>N</u>ew.**

   A New Table dialog box appears, as shown in Figure 20-2.

2. **Click on Table Wizard and then click on OK.**

   A Table Wizard dialog box appears, as shown in Figure 20-3.

3. **Click on the Business or Personal radio button and then click on whichever table in the Sample Tables list box most closely resembles the type of data you want to store in your own table.**

   As its name implies, the Business radio button displays sample tables typically used in business, such as a Mailing List or Contacts. The Personal radio button displays sample tables typically used at home, such as Recipes and Exercise Log.

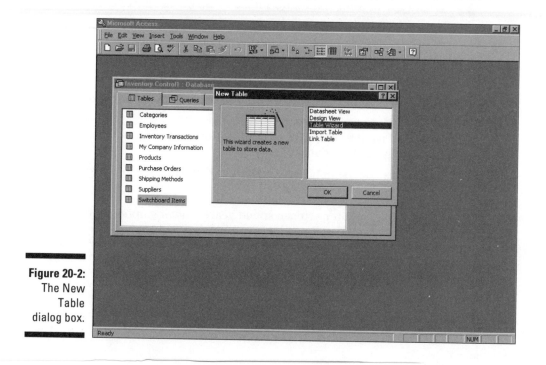

Figure 20-2:
The New
Table
dialog box.

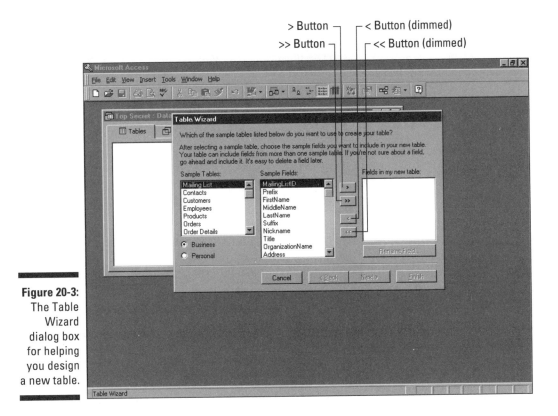

Figure 20-3:
The Table
Wizard
dialog box
for helping
you design
a new table.

4. **Click on a field in the Sample Fields list box.**

   Choose the field that most closely resembles the field you want to use in your own table, such as First Name.

5. **Click on the > button.**

   Repeat Steps 3, 4, and 5 for each field that you want to add to your table. Note that the > button moves one field at a time into the Fields in my new table list box. The >> button moves all fields into the Fields in my new table list box. The < button moves one field at a time out of the Fields in my new table list box. The << button moves all fields out of the Fields in my new table list box. (Figure 20-3 identifies each of these buttons.)

6. **Click on Next.**

   Another Table Wizard dialog box appears, asking what name you want to give your table.

7. **Type a name for your table (up to 64 characters in length) and click on Next.**

   A final Table Wizard dialog box appears.

8. Click on Finish.

Access 97 displays your finished (but empty) table. At this point, you can start typing in the data that you want to store in your newly created database table.

Creating a form

A form provides a window that displays information from your database. Although you don't have to use a form for your database, a form can make viewing and editing your data much easier than trying to hunt for it within the row-and-column format of a database table.

To create a form that displays the information trapped in a table, make sure that the Database window is showing and then follow these steps:

1. Click on the Forms tab and then click on New.

A New Form dialog box appears, as shown in Figure 20-4.

2. Click on Form Wizard.

3. Click on the list box that appears directly above the OK button and choose a table; then click on OK.

A Form Wizard dialog box appears, as shown in Figure 20-5.

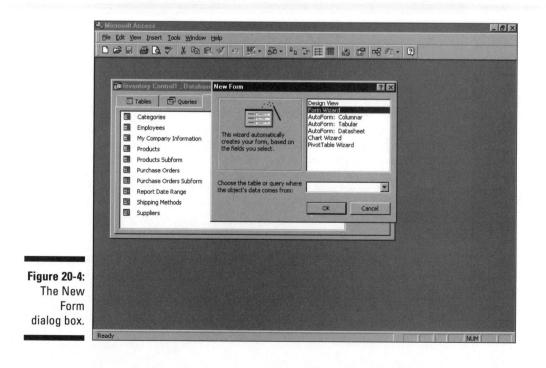

Figure 20-4:
The New Form dialog box.

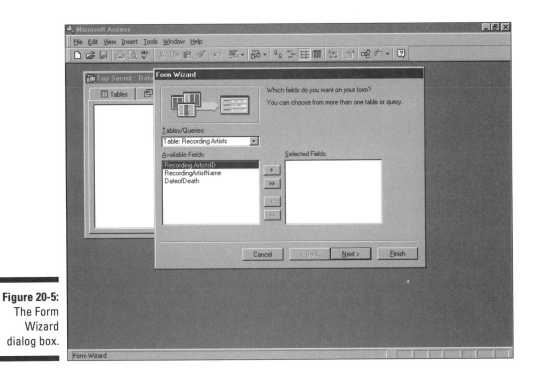

Figure 20-5:
The Form
Wizard
dialog box.

4. **In the Available Fields list box, click on the field that you want to display on your form and then click on the > button.**

5. **Repeat Step 4 for each field that you want to add to your form; then click on Next.**

   Another Form Wizard dialog box appears, asking you to choose a layout, as shown in Figure 20-6.

6. **Click on a radio button (such as Columnar or Tabular) and then click on Next.**

   Still another Form Wizard dialog box appears, asking for a form style to use, as shown in Figure 20-7.

7. **Click on the pattern you want to use (such as International or Standard) and then click on Next.**

   Still another annoying Form Wizard dialog box appears, bugging you for a title to give your form, as shown in Figure 20-8.

8. **Type a name for your form and then click on Finish.**

   Access 97 displays your form, ready for you to start typing data, as shown in Figure 20-9.

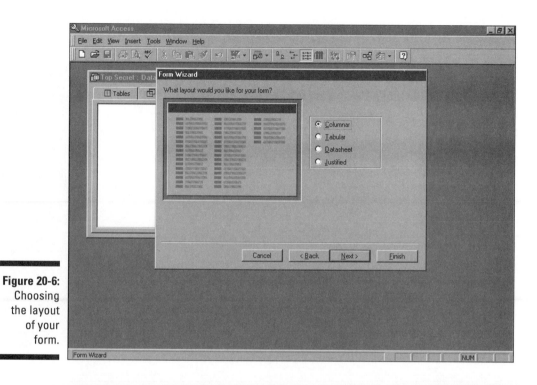

Figure 20-6:
Choosing
the layout
of your
form.

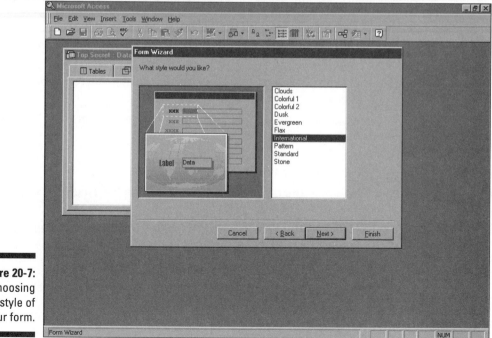

Figure 20-7:
Choosing
the style of
your form.

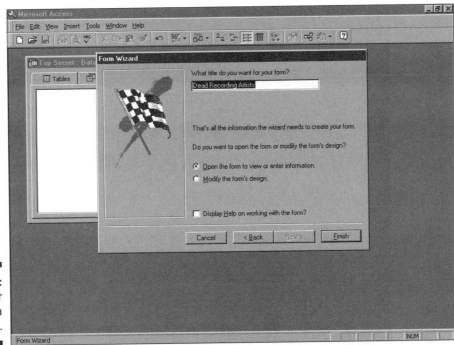

Figure 20-8:
Giving your
form a
name.

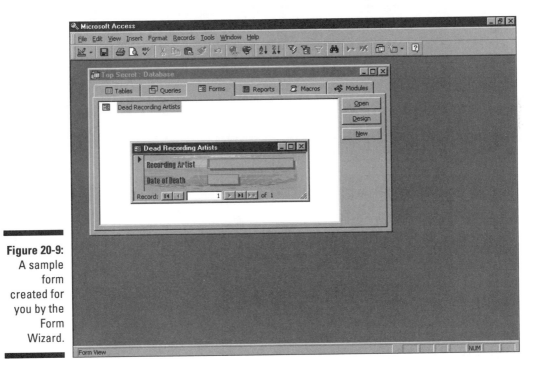

Figure 20-9:
A sample
form
created for
you by the
Form
Wizard.

Editing Tables and Forms

No matter how carefully you design your tables and forms ahead of time, you may need to edit the tables or forms at a later date. Editing a table or form can be as simple as correcting a spelling mistake for a field (such as typing NMAE instead of NAME) or as drastic as deleting existing fields or adding entirely new ones.

Modifying fields within a table

To edit the fields of a table, make sure that the Database window appears and then follow these steps:

1. **Click on the Tables tab, click on the table you want to edit, and then click on Design.**

   Access 97 displays the fields that make up your table, as shown in Figure 20-10.

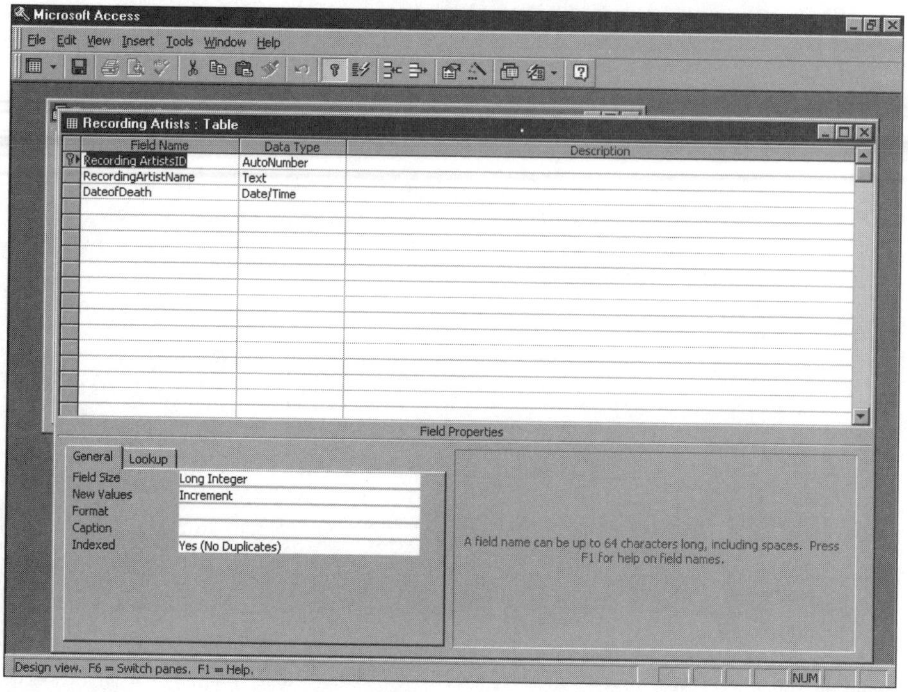

Figure 20-10:
Modifying
the fields of
a table.

2. **Click on the field that you want to edit.**

   Access 97 displays the properties of your chosen field at the bottom of the Table window.

3. **Click in the field property that you want to modify (such as the Caption).**

   Some field properties automatically display a list box, forcing you to choose from a limited list of options.

4. **Repeat Step 3 for each field that you want to edit.**

Click on the close box of the Table window when you're done.

Deleting a field

If you delete a field, you also delete any information stored in that field. So delete a field only if you can afford to lose all the data stored in that field, as well.

To delete a field, make sure that the Database window appears and follow these steps:

1. **Click on the Tables tab, click on the table you want to edit, and then click on <u>D</u>esign.**

   Access 97 displays the fields that make up your table (refer to Figure 20-10).

2. **Click on the field that you want to delete.**

3. **Choose <u>E</u>dit⇨Delete <u>R</u>ows.**

   A dialog box appears, warning that you are about to permanently delete your field and the data stored inside that field.

4. **Click on <u>Y</u>es (or <u>N</u>o, if you decide to save your field at the last minute).**

Adding a new field

After you've designed your database and have had a chance to use it, you may suddenly realize that you need to store additional information on your database. Rather than toss out your entire database, you can just add a new field to a table.

When you add a new field to a table, the field doesn't automatically contain any data. So if your database consists of one million names and addresses, and you suddenly add a new field to store Social Security numbers, the Social Security field will be blank for all one million existing names and addresses. Have fun typing.

To add a new field to a table, make sure that the Database window is showing and follow these steps:

1. Click on the Tables tab, click on the table you want to edit, and then click on Design.

Access 97 displays the fields that make up your table (refer to Figure 20-10).

2. Click on the first blank row directly below the existing field names.

As an alternative, click on any field and then choose Insert⇨Rows to sandwich a new field in between two existing fields.

3. Click in the Field Name column, type a name for your field, and then press Tab.

By default, Access 97 chooses Text in the Data Type column.

4. Click on the Data Type list box and choose a data type (such as Text or Currency).

Data Types are the kind of information the field can hold, such as numbers, text, or dates.

5. Click on the close box of the Table window.

A dialog box appears, asking whether you want to save your changes.

6. Click on Yes.

Depending on the data type that you choose (such as Date or Currency), you may need to define additional field properties after Step 4, such as format, field size, and default value. Although Access 97 defines default values for field properties, be aware that these default values may not be suitable for your fields.

Editing a Form

A form can display one or more fields on the screen so that you can view and edit the data easily. Because a form acts as the user interface to your data, you may want to move fields around, add pictures to your form, or resize fields.

Just remember that any changes you make to a form are purely decorative. Design a form properly, and people may find using your database fun and easy. Design a poorly organized and hideously colored form, and people may not be able to use your database at all, even though you may have done nothing more than change colors of the form to an eye-popping fluorescent orange.

To edit a form, make sure that the Database window is showing and then follow these steps:

1. **Click on the Forms tab.**

2. **Click on the form that you want to edit and then click on <u>D</u>esign.**

   Access 97 displays your chosen form along with the Access 97 Toolbox, as shown in Figure 20-11.

At this point you're ready to delete fields, add new fields, or modify an existing field.

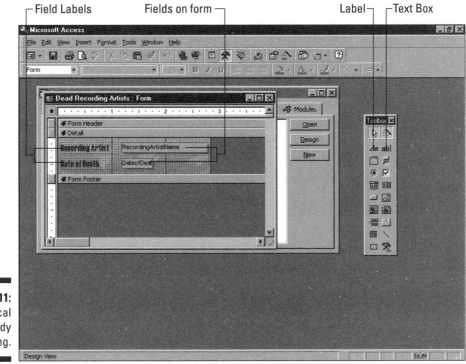

Figure 20-11:
A typical
form ready
for editing.

Moving or resizing a field

Fields consist of two parts: a field label and a field. The field label contains text that identifies what the field contains, such as Name, Age, Address, or Part Number. The field appears on a form as a box where someone can type in information.

Sometimes, a field may be too small or located in the wrong place on the screen. To fix these problems, you can move a field or resize it to make it smaller or larger.

To move a field on a form, make sure that you have displayed your chosen form and then follow these steps:

1. **Move the mouse pointer over the gray field that you want to move.**

2. **Hold down the left (primary) mouse button and drag the mouse.**

   Access 97 displays handles around your chosen field and field label and turns the mouse pointer into a black hand.

3. **Release the mouse button when the field is in a new location that you can live with.**

If you want to move a field label without moving a field (or vice versa), make sure that you have displayed your chosen form and then follow these steps:

1. **Move the mouse pointer over the upper-left corner handle over the field label (or field) that you want to move and click on the left mouse button.**

   The mouse pointer turns into a black hand with one finger (not *that* finger) pointing straight up.

2. **Hold down the left (primary) mouse button and drag the mouse.**

3. **Release the mouse button when you're happy with the new location of the field label or field.**

To resize a field, make sure that you have displayed your chosen form and then follow these steps:

1. **Move the mouse pointer over the gray field that you want to resize and click on the left (primary) mouse button.**

   Gray handles appear around your chosen field and field label.

2. **Move the mouse pointer over a gray handle until the mouse pointer turns into a double-pointing arrow.**

3. **Hold down the left (primary) mouse button and drag the mouse to change the size of the field.**

4. **Release the left mouse button when you're happy with the new size of your field.**

Deleting a field

If you don't want a form to display certain information, just delete that field from your form.

Deleting a field from a form simply changes the way that your form displays data on the screen; it does not delete any data stored in the database itself.

To delete a field from a form, make sure that you have displayed your chosen form and then follow these steps:

1. **Move the mouse pointer over the field that you want to delete.**

2. **Choose Edit⇨Delete or press Delete.**

   Access 97 meekly deletes both your field label and its accompanying gray field at the same time.

If you delete a field and its field label by mistake, press Ctrl+Z right away to retrieve them.

Adding a new field to a form

If you added a new field to a table, chances are good that you'll want to display this new field data on a form, as well.

To add a new field to a form, make sure that you have displayed your chosen form and then follow these steps:

1. **Click on the Text Box tool on the Toolbox.**

2. **Move the mouse pointer over the form.**

   The mouse pointer turns into a crosshair with a miniature text box underneath.

3. **Hold down the left (primary) mouse button, drag the mouse to the desired position, and then release the left mouse button.**

   Your newly drawn field appears, as shown in Figure 20-12.

4. **Move the mouse pointer over the label of your newly created field and click on the right mouse button.**

   A pop-up menu appears.

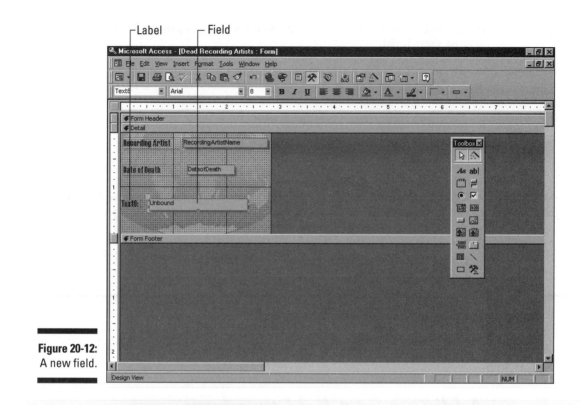

Figure 20-12:
A new field.

5. **Choose Properties.**

   A Label dialog box appears.

6. **Click on the Format tab, as shown in Figure 20-13.**

7. **Click in the Caption box and type text for your label (such as Name or E-mail address).**

8. **Click on the close box of the Label dialog box.**

9. **Move the mouse pointer over your newly created field and click on the right (secondary) mouse button.**

   A pop-up menu appears.

10. **Choose Properties.**

    A Text Box dialog box appears.

11. **Click on the Data tab, as shown in Figure 20-14.**

12. **Click on the Control Source list box and choose a field.**

13. **Click on the close box of the Text Box dialog box.**

You may need to resize or move your newly created field so that it displays all the data simultaneously.

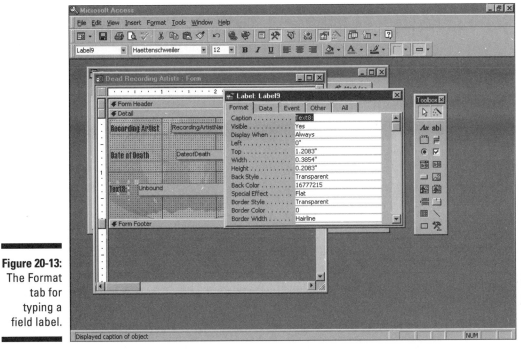

Figure 20-13:
The Format
tab for
typing a
field label.

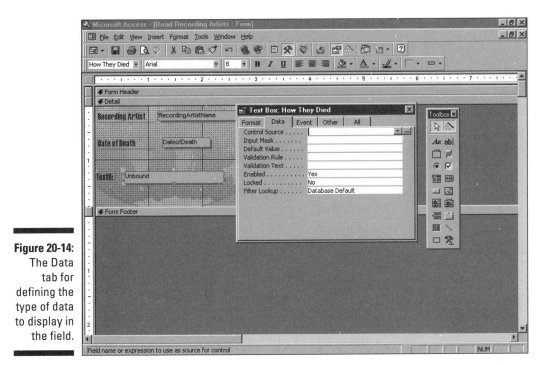

Figure 20-14:
The Data
tab for
defining the
type of data
to display in
the field.

Adding a label to a form

Every field should have a label to identify the type of data it displays, and you can add additional labels at any time, as well.

Labels contain text that never changes. Fields display information stored in a database, which can change depending on the particular database record you're currently viewing.

To add a label to a form, make sure that you have displayed your chosen form and then follow these steps:

1. **Click on the Label tool on the Toolbox.**

2. **Move the mouse pointer over the form, hold down the left (primary) mouse button, and drag the mouse to draw the label on the form.**

3. **Release the left mouse button when you're happy with the size of the label.**

   Access 97 displays your blank label on the form, as shown in Figure 20-15.

4. **Type the text you want your label to display and then click anywhere outside of the label.**

   Access 97 displays your label on the form.

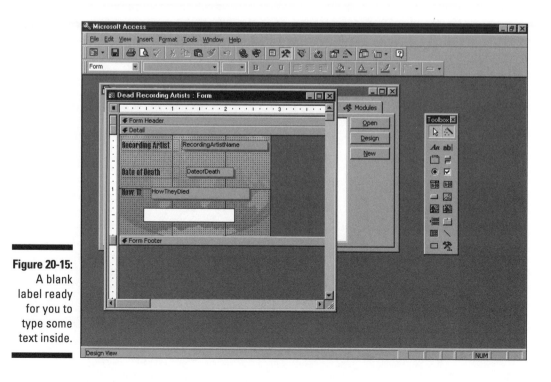

Figure 20-15:
A blank label ready for you to type some text inside.

Chapter 21

Automating Microsoft Access 97

• •

In This Chapter

▶ Creating macros to carry out boring or repetitive tasks

▶ Using command buttons to make Access perform tasks

▶ Programming Visual Basic to automate Access

• •

*W*hy should you work any harder than you have to when you have a $2,000 computer (or a summer intern willing to work for minimum wage) ready to do your work for you automatically? Computers are supposed to make our lives easier, so you'll be happy to know that you can automate Access 97 — to a limited degree. You can focus on your important work and let Access 97 worry about the trivial details, such as typing state abbreviations and part-number codes.

Depending on how much freedom you want to give Access 97, you can use three items to automate Access 97:

✔ Macros

✔ Command buttons

✔ A real-life programming language: Visual Basic

Which one should you choose? If you just want to automate Access 97 for your personal use, create a macro or a command button. If you plan to automate Access 97 for others, use a command button or Visual Basic. If you need to create something really complicated that requires writing your own program, Visual Basic is your only choice.

Making Macros

A macro acts like a tape recorder. First, you record your keystrokes. Then you can "play back" those same keystrokes at the touch of a button. Macros enable you to perform repetitive or complicated tasks only one time and then tell Access 97, "Remember that really long series of keystrokes that I asked you to record three months ago? I want you to perform those keystrokes all over again while I go out to lunch."

Creating a macro

At its simplest level, a macro can automatically type text (such as the word *Massachusetts*) for you or perform an action (such as opening a form and printing it). Access 97 allows you to create macros that can perform all types of tasks; here are two common macro uses:

- ✔ Simulate someone typing at the keyboard
- ✔ Choose a command from the Access 97 pull-down menus

Simulating someone typing at the keyboard

Macros that simulate a person typing at a keyboard are most useful for getting Access 97 to type long, repetitive text for you so that you don't have to do it yourself. For example, if you have to type a long-winded name, such as *The American Corporation for the Creation of Political Dishonesty,* over and over again, you're liable to slowly go mad at your computer.

Although you can choose to shorten the phrase to something simpler (such as *Congress*), another option is to use a macro to do the typing for you, instead. Such a task is perfectly suited for your computer, because computers can't lose their minds — they're perfectly happy to perform dull, repetitive tasks day in and day out.

To create a macro that simulates typing at the keyboard, follow these steps:

1. **Choose Window⇨Database and click on the Macros tab.**

2. **Click on New.**

   A Macro window appears.

3. **Click on the gray downward-pointing arrow in the Action list box and choose SendKeys, as shown in Figure 21-1.**

   An Action Arguments section appears at the bottom of the Macro window.

4. **Click in the Keystrokes box and type the text that you want the macro to type for you.**

   You can type as many as 256 characters.

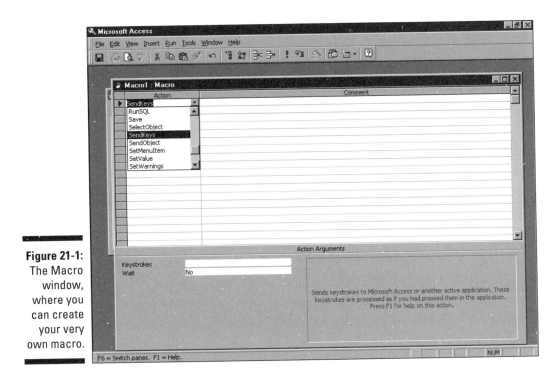

Figure 21-1:
The Macro window, where you can create your very own macro.

5. **Click on the Wait list box and choose Yes or No.**

   The Wait option forces your macro to pause. Choose Yes only if your macro types text too rapidly for your database to handle.

6. **Click on the close box in the Macro window.**

   A dialog box appears, asking whether you want to save your macro.

7. **Click on Yes.**

   A Save As dialog box appears, asking you to give your macro a name.

8. **Type a name in the Macro Name box (up to 64 characters in length) and click on OK.**

You can always rename a macro from within the Database window by right-clicking over the macro, choosing Rename, and then typing a new name.

Choosing an Access menu command

Sometimes, you may need a macro that can choose one or more Access menu commands for you so that you don't have to waste time choosing them yourself. If you want to transfer your Access data to an Excel worksheet, for example, you must choose Tools➪OfficeLinks➪Analyze It With MS Excel. Clumsy? Yes, so let an Access macro do the work for you instead.

To create a macro that chooses menu commands, follow these steps:

1. **Choose Window⇨Database and click on the Macros tab.**

2. **Click on New.**

   A Macro window appears (refer to Figure 21-1).

3. **Click on the gray downward-pointing arrow in the Action list box and choose RunCommand.**

   Access 97 displays a Command list box in the Action Argument portion of the Macro window.

4. **Click in the Command list box and choose the command that you want to run, such as Undo, Save As, or Find.**

5. **Click on the close box in the Macro window.**

   A dialog box appears, asking whether you want to save your macro.

6. **Click on Yes.**

   A Save As dialog box appears, asking you to give your macro a name.

7. **Type a name in the Macro Name box (up to 64 characters in length) and click on OK.**

Running a macro

A macro is no good unless you plan to use it once in a while. To give you as much flexibility as possible when it comes to running your macro, you can run a macro either by choosing a command and typing in the macro's name or by assigning a specific keystroke (such as Ctrl+3) to the macro and then pressing that keystroke when you want the macro to run.

Some macros, such as those that simulate someone typing at the keyboard, require the cursor to be in a specific location before you run them. If you run a macro with the cursor in the wrong location, the macro may run anyway — blissfully unaware that it is typing data in the wrong place.

Running a macro by choosing its name

Access can't read your mind; it has no idea which macro you may want to run. You have to use its menus to tell it, "Hey, stupid! Run the macro named XXX right now."

To run a macro by name, follow these steps:

1. **Choose Tools⇨Macro⇨Run Macro.**

   The Run Macro dialog box appears, as shown in Figure 21-2.

2. **Click on the Macro Name list box and choose the macro that you want to run.**

3. **Click on OK.**

Running a macro by pressing a keystroke combination

Although you can always run a macro by choosing it by name, you may find it more convenient to assign a keystroke combination to the macro. Then you can quickly type the keystroke combination (such as Ctrl+2), and the macro runs right away.

The main drawback to running a macro by using a keystroke combination is that you have to remember which keystroke combination you assigned to your macro. Table 21-1 lists some of the more common types of keystrokes that you can assign to a macro.

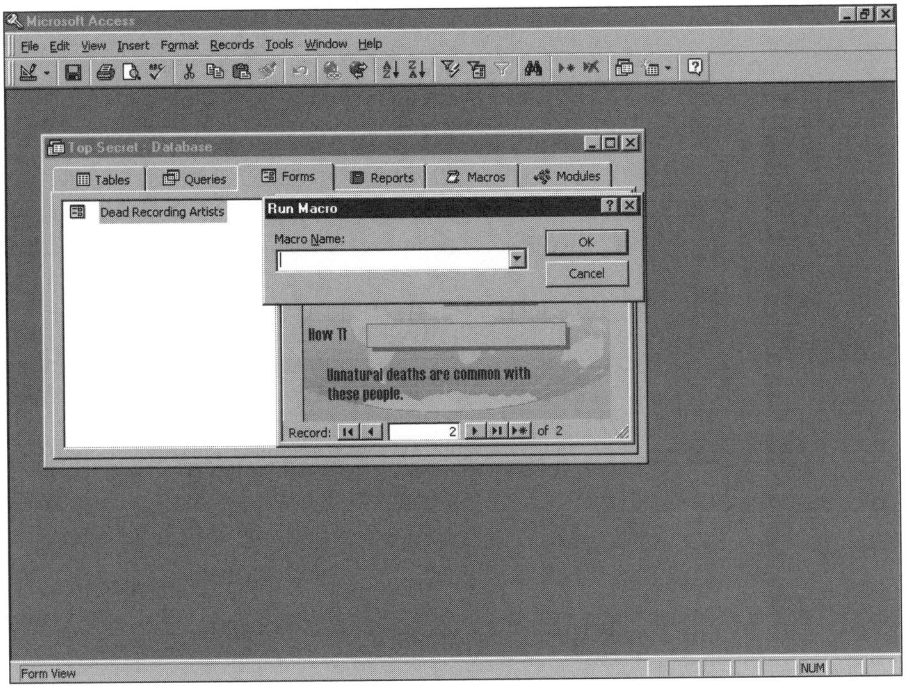

Figure 21-2:
The Run Macro dialog box.

Table 21-1	Common Types of Keystrokes Assigned to Macros	
Keystroke Combination	*Example*	*How Access Interprets the Keystroke*
Ctrl+letter key	Ctrl+Q	^Q
Ctrl+number key	Ctrl+5	^5
Any function key	F11	{F11}
Ctrl+any function key	Ctrl+F12	^{F12}
Shift+any function key	Shift+F4	+{F4}

Every macro that you assign to a unique keystroke combination must be stored in the macro group called AutoKeys. The AutoKeys macro group simply stores all your macros that run when you press their unique keystroke combination. You must separate each macro in its own row within the AutoKeys Macro window.

To assign a keystroke combination to the AutoKeys macro group, follow these steps:

1. **Choose <u>W</u>indow⇨Database and click on the Macros tab.**

2. **Click on <u>N</u>ew.**

   The Macro window appears.

3. **Click on the Macro Names icon in the Macro toolbar.**

   The Macro Name column magically appears (see Figure 21-3).

4. **Click in the Macro Name column and type the keystroke combination that you want to assign, such as ^4 for Ctrl+4 or +{F3} for Shift+F3.**

   Refer to Table 21-1 for examples of how to tell Access what keystroke combinations to use.

5. **Click in the Action column, click on the gray downward-pointing arrow, and choose an option for your macro (such as Spelling or SendKeys).**

   The Action column defines what you want the macro to do, such as type text or run a menu command. For example, if you choose SendKeys, you need to type the text to store in the macro.

6. **Click on the close box in the Macro window.**

   A dialog box appears, asking whether you want to save your macro.

7. **Click on <u>Y</u>es.**

   A Save As dialog box appears.

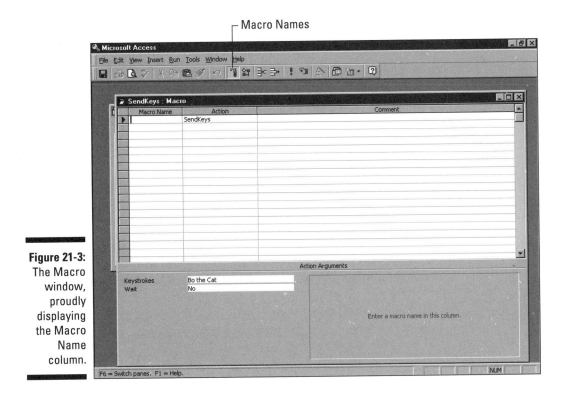

Figure 21-3:
The Macro
window,
proudly
displaying
the Macro
Name
column.

8. Type AutoKeys in the Macro Name box and click on OK.

Your macro is ready to use.

Telling a macro to run automatically

Instead of typing in a macro's name or pressing its unique keystroke combination, you have the option to make a macro run automatically after you update data in a field or the moment you click on a field. By having a macro run automatically, you don't have to waste a precious second or two giving the command to run the macro yourself.

To make a macro run automatically, you need to define two things:

✔ The macro that you want to run

✔ The event that causes the macro to run

An *event* is simply any action that someone takes in an Access 97 field, such as updating the data, clicking the mouse, or moving the cursor out of the field.

To set up a macro to run automatically, follow these steps:

1. **Choose <u>W</u>indow⇨Database and click on the Forms tab.**

2. **Click on the form that you want to use and then click on <u>D</u>esign.**

3. **Click on the field that you want to control the macro and then click on the right (secondary) mouse button.**

   A pop-up menu appears.

4. **Choose <u>P</u>roperties.**

   A Text Box dialog box appears.

5. **Click on the Event tab, as shown in Figure 21-4.**

6. **Click in an event box (such as On Click or On Enter) and click on the downward-pointing arrow.**

   A list of macro names appears.

7. **Click on the macro that you want to run when the event you specified occurs.**

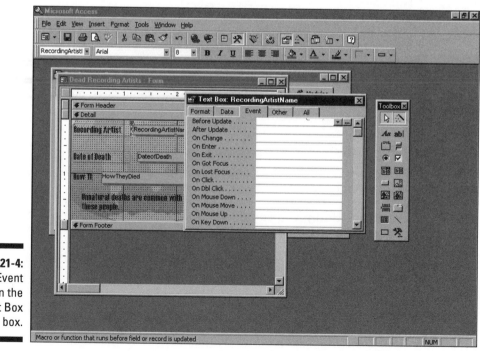

Figure 21-4:
The Event
tab in the
Text Box
dialog box.

8. **Click on the close box of the Text Box dialog box.**

9. **Click on the close box of the Form window.**

    A dialog box appears, asking whether you want to save your changes.

10. **Click on Yes.**

The next time that anyone uses the form you chose in Step 2 and performs the event that you chose in Step 6, the macro that you chose in Step 7 runs.

Deleting a macro

No matter how useful a macro may be, a time may come when you want to delete it. To delete a macro, follow these steps

1. **Choose Window⇨Database and click on the Macros tab.**

2. **Point to the macro that you want to delete and click on the right mouse button.**

    A pop-up menu appears.

3. **Click on Delete.**

    A dialog box appears, asking whether you really want to delete your macro.

4. **Click on Yes.**

If you delete a macro by mistake, immediately press Ctrl+Z to make Access 97 recover the macro for you. Otherwise, you have to re-create it from scratch.

Using Command Buttons

Command buttons are nothing more than little boxes on-screen that you can click on to cause something to happen. The moment that you click on a command button, Access 97 performs a function, such as printing a record, deleting a record, or running a macro. On a form, you can choose a command by clicking on the command button instead of wading through pull-down menus and looking for the command you need.

Creating a command button

Although you can clutter a form with as many command buttons as you want, you should use them sparingly and arrange them neatly so that they look nice and are easy to use.

You can create a command button only while Access 97 is in Form design view. Chapter 20 provides more information about editing within the Form design view.

To create a command button, follow these steps:

1. **Choose <u>W</u>indow⇨Database and click on the Forms tab.**

2. **Click on the form that you want to use and then click on <u>D</u>esign.**

3. **Click on the Command Button tool on the Toolbox, as shown in Figure 21-5.**

4. **Move the mouse pointer to the location on the form where you want to place your command button; then hold down the left mouse button, drag the mouse to draw your command button, and release the mouse button.**

   Access draws your command button and displays the Command Button Wizard dialog box, as shown in Figure 21-6.

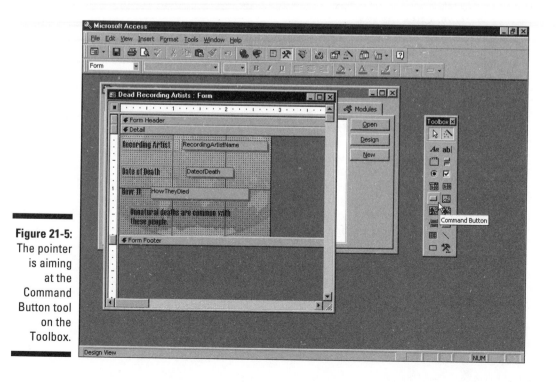

Figure 21-5: The pointer is aiming at the Command Button tool on the Toolbox.

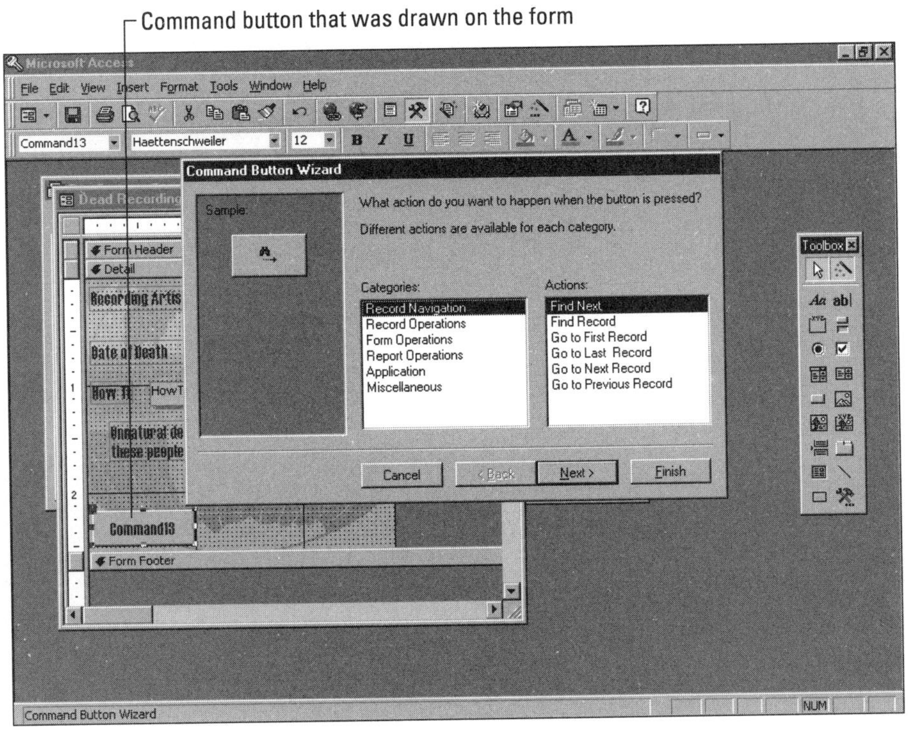

Command button that was drawn on the form

Figure 21-6:
The
Command
Button
Wizard
dialog box.

5. Click on a category in the Categories list box.

The Categories list box organizes actions by their function, such as Record Navigation or Report Operations. If you want your command button to navigate through your database records, you would click on Record Navigation.

6. Click on an action in the Actions list box.

The Actions list box lets you choose the specific action you want your command button to follow, such as Go to First Record or Print a Form.

7. Click on Next.

Another Command Button Wizard dialog box appears (as shown in Figure 21-7), this time asking whether you want text or a picture on your command button.

8. Click on the Text or the Picture radio button and type the text or choose the picture that you want to appear on your command button.

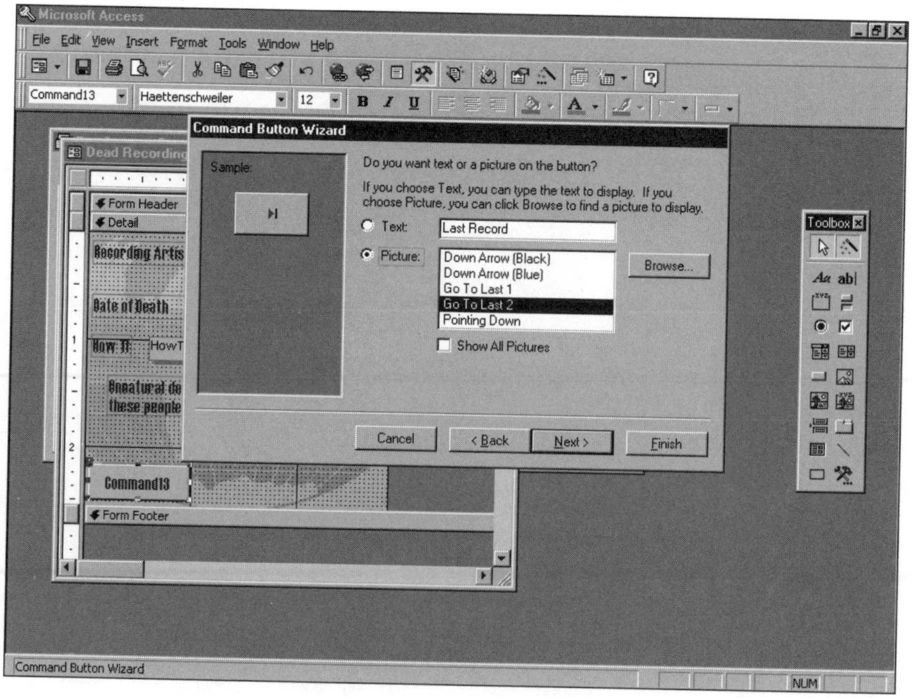

Figure 21-7:
The
Command
Button
Wizard
dialog box
for adding
text or
picture to a
command
button.

Text can provide a written description of what your command button can do. Pictures can provide a visual description (hopefully) of what your command button can do. If you click in the Show All Pictures check box, you can choose from a variety of pictures stored in the Access 97 directory. If you want to display a picture you've created yourself, click on the Browse command button.

9. **Click on Next.**

A third Command Button Wizard dialog box appears, asking you to name your command button, as shown in Figure 21-8. Although you can name your command buttons anything (even after your dog or cat), you should choose a descriptive name. That way if you have dozens of different command buttons, you can find, edit, and modify a specific command button more easily in the future.

10. **Type a name and click on Finish.**

Access displays the command button on your form.

11. **Click on the close box in the Form design window.**

A dialog box appears, asking whether you want to save your changes.

12. **Click on Yes.**

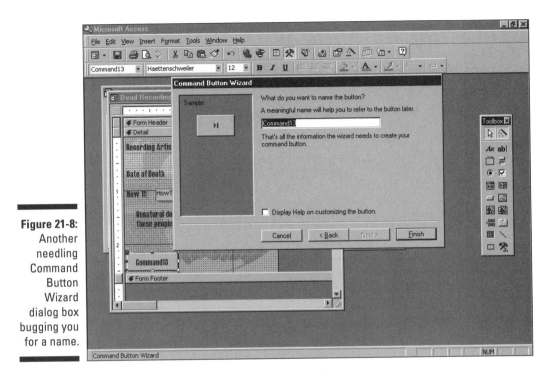

Figure 21-8:
Another
needling
Command
Button
Wizard
dialog box
bugging you
for a name.

Deleting a command button

Because you can always add a command button to a form, it makes sense
that you can also delete a command button at any time.

To delete a command button, follow these steps:

1. **Choose Window⇨Database and click on the Forms tab.**

2. **Click on the form that contains the command button you want to
   delete and then click on Design.**

3. **Click on the command button that you want to delete.**

   Access displays gray handles around the command button.

4. **Press Delete.**

   The command button disappears.

If you delete a command button by mistake, press Ctrl+Z right away to bring
it back again. Otherwise, you'll have to create it all over again starting with
Step 1.

Real Programming with Visual Basic

Visual Basic is a full-blown programming language. In fact, many people have created commercial-quality programs using Visual Basic and even sold these programs for thousands of dollars. For the ultimate in power and flexibility (not to mention frustration and tedium), Visual Basic is the most powerful way to automate Access 97.

Visual Basic programming can get fairly detailed and complicated. If the idea of programming a computer turns your stomach, you might want to skip the rest of this chapter.

Although you can create super-complicated programs using Visual Basic, most Visual Basic programs consist of two parts:

- **Command buttons:** Buttons that make it easy for someone to use your database without using a single Access menu command. Figure 21-9 shows command buttons that allow a user to perform various tasks at the click of a button.

- **Event procedures:** Actual instructions, written in Visual Basic, that tell your command buttons what to do when someone clicks on them. Without an event procedure, a command button looks nice but doesn't do anything useful (much like your boss or co-workers).

The two faces of Visual Basic

Microsoft sells a language compiler, also called Visual Basic, which enables you to write general-purpose programs, such as games, utilities, or even databases. If you want to write different types of programs, you must buy a separate copy of Visual Basic.

If you only want to use Visual Basic to write custom databases, it's easier (not to mention cheaper, especially if you already own a copy of Access 97) just to use the version of Visual Basic that Microsoft includes inside Access 97.

So when people mention "Visual Basic," they could be talking about Visual Basic (the language compiler that you have to buy separately) or Visual Basic for Applications (abbreviated as VBA), which is the programming language that comes free inside Access 97.

When the term *Visual Basic* appears in this book, it refers to the version of Visual Basic inside Access 97.

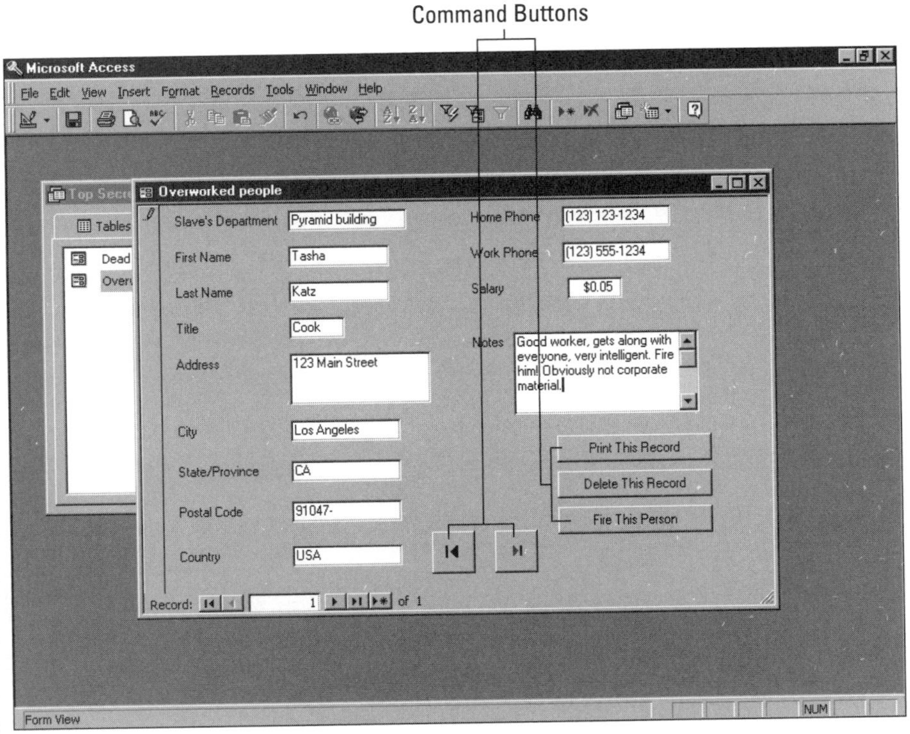

Command Buttons

Figure 21-9:
Typical
command
buttons on
a form.

Creating a command button (for Visual Basic)

When you create a command button, the Command Button Wizard normally sticks its nose in the way and guides you through the creation of your command button by presenting a series of dialog boxes. The Command Button Wizard can be helpful, but it can get in the way if you want to write a Visual Basic event procedure to control your command button instead.

To create a command button so that you can write a Visual Basic event procedure, follow these steps:

1. **Choose <u>W</u>indow⇨Database and click on the Forms tab.**

2. **Click on the form that you want to use and then click on <u>D</u>esign.**

3. **Click on the Control Wizards tool on the Toolbox so that it doesn't appear pressed in, as shown in Figure 21-10.**

   If the Control Wizards tool is already deselected (does not appear pressed in), skip this step.

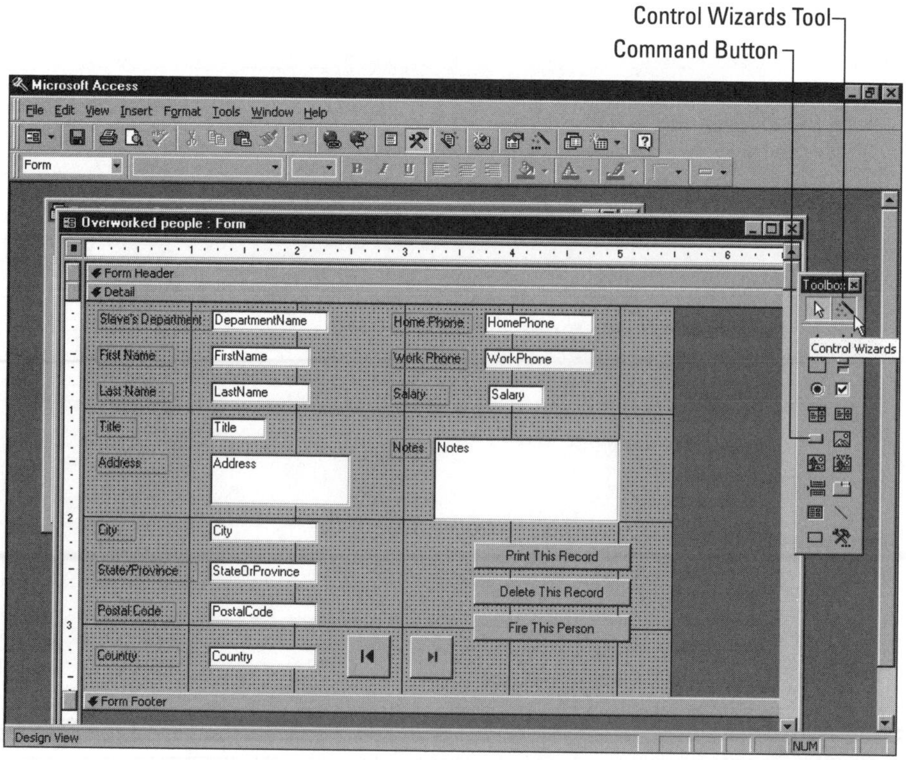

Control Wizards Tool
Command Button

Figure 21-10:
Turning off
the Control
Wizard with
the Control
Wizards tool
on the
Toolbox.

4. Click on the Command Button tool on the Toolbox.

5. Move the mouse pointer to the location at which you want to place your command button; then hold down the left mouse button, drag the mouse to draw your command button, and release the mouse button.

Access draws your command button.

What can command buttons do?

The command buttons you create on a form won't do anything until you write event procedures that tell them what to do when someone clicks on them. Some common Visual Basic commands that you may assign to a command button include the following:

✔ Assign a string or value to another object, such as a text box

✔ Display a message box

✔ Perform a calculation

Assigning another object a string or value

If you want to change the contents of a field (also known as an *object*), you can use Visual Basic to stuff a text string or number into that field. To do so, you must know the name of the field and the text or number that you want to put into it, such as:

```
PostalCode = "92102"
```

This Visual Basic command says, Take the text string "92102" and store it in a field named PostalCode. Of course, to make this command work, you have to type it within an event procedure of a command button. An *event procedure* is an action that occurs to a command button, such as clicking on it.

If you put the text string "92102" into the PostalCode field of a database, when the user clicks on a command button named cmdZip, the complete event procedure would look like the following:

```
Private Sub cmdZip_Click()
  PostalCode = "92102"
End Sub
```

If you had a command button named cmdZip and you clicked on it, Access 97 would look for an object called PostalCode and replace its contents with the text string "92102". The section "Writing an event procedure" later in this chapter explains more about writing Visual Basic commands for command buttons.

Displaying a message box

When a user clicks on a command button, Access 97 can display a message box. To create a message box, you must specify the message that you want displayed and the title of the message box. Figure 21-11 shows the message box that the following Visual Basic code creates:

```
Private Sub cmdZip_Click()
  MsgBox "Delete everything?", , "Warning!!!"
End Sub
```

In the example just listed, the word "MsgBox" tells Visual Basic to display a message dialog box. The string "Delete everything?" appears inside the dialog box while the string "Warning!!!" appears as the title bar of the dialog box. If you want Access 97 to display an icon inside the dialog box, you could insert VbCritical, VbQuestion, VbExclamation, or VbInformation in between the two commas. If you don't type anything in between the two commas, the dialog box won't display an icon.

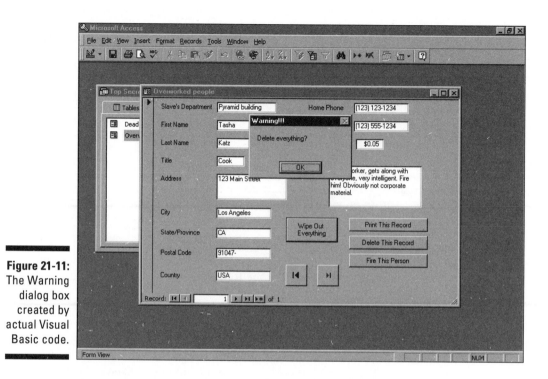

Figure 21-11:
The Warning
dialog box
created by
actual Visual
Basic code.

Performing a calculation

Visual Basic can perform simple addition, subtraction, multiplication, or division by using numbers stored in one or more objects. Table 21-2 shows typical commands for performing a calculation.

Table 21-2	**Common Visual Basic Mathematical Operators**	
Operation	*Operator*	*Real-Life Visual Basic Example*
Addition	+	Total = SalesTax + ProductCost
Subtraction	–	TakeHomePay = Salary – IncomeTax
Multiplication	*	Rabbits = Parents * Days
Division	/	Government = Conservatives/Liberals

The joy of Visual Basic programming

Visual Basic includes all sorts of commands that enable you to create arrays, perform conditional execution by using If-Then statements, and manipulate the information stored in your Access 97 database. If the thought of learning what these terms mean makes your head spin, feel free to skip over the rest of the chapter and forget all about Visual Basic programming.

What can Visual Basic do for you and why should you bother learning how to use it? Access 97 is great for storing information, but unless you know the right commands to choose from its pull-down menus, the information you stored in your Access 97 databases just sits there.

You can use Visual Basic to create your own programs that store and retrieve information, such as a mail-order management program, an inventory-tracking program, a church-management program, a political contribution tracking program, or any other type of program that requires storing lots of different information.

Visual Basic essentially enables you to turn your Access 97 databases into custom programs. If you have ever wished that you had a special program to help you store, track, and organize information, writing your own Visual Basic program in Access 97 may be just what you need.

Writing an event procedure

An *event procedure* is nothing more than one or more Visual Basic commands that tell a command button what to do when a certain event occurs, such as when someone clicks on the command button.

To write an event procedure for a command button that you've already created, follow these steps:

1. **Point to the command button for which you want to write an event procedure.**

2. **Click on the right mouse button.**

   A pop-up menu appears.

3. **Click on Build Event.**

   The Module window appears, as shown in Figure 21-12.

4. **Type your Visual Basic code to perform a task, such as assigning the contents of a field with a string or number or displaying a message box.**

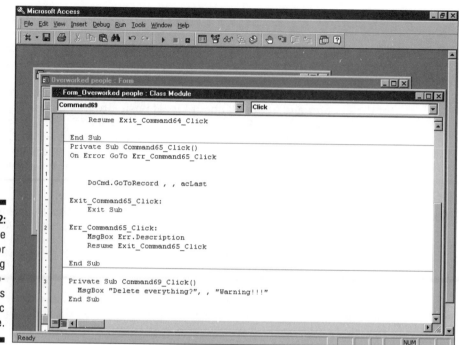

Figure 21-12:
The Module
window for
creating
honest-to-
goodness
Visual Basic
code.

The type and variety of Visual Basic code that you can type in this step
is nearly infinite. Learning Visual Basic programming can be a job in
itself, so you'll have to learn more about Visual Basic programming if
you want to create fancy, custom Access 97 databases.

5. **Click on the close box in the Module window.**

6. **Click on the close box in the Form design window.**

   A dialog box appears, asking whether you want to save your changes.

7. **Click on Yes.**

Obviously, this brief introduction to the Visual Basic programming language
barely scratches the surface of how to program Access 97. If you're intrigued
and want to learn more about Visual Basic programming, pick up a copy of
Access 97 Programming For Windows For Dummies by Rob Krumm (published
by IDG Books Worldwide, Inc.).

Chapter 22

Sharing Your
Microsoft Access 97 Databases

· ·

In This Chapter

▶ Converting databases to and from Access to use information with other programs

▶ Creating a start-up form to provide information to people who use your database

▶ Using a password to protect your work

· ·

*M*icrosoft Access 97 is rapidly becoming the most popular database program running under Windows. Unfortunately, many people who own Access 97 have no idea how to use it, and even more people don't own Access 97 but use a rival database program with a weird name, such as dBASE, FileMaker Pro, Alpha Five, or Paradox. (Believe it or not, because some people even store data in their spreadsheets, Access can convert Lotus 1-2-3 or Excel files into Access 97 database files. Will wonders never cease?)

What happens if you spend hours creating an Access 97 database that contains valuable names and addresses, but you want to give the list to a coworker who uses another database program? You *can* type all the information into the other database program, but that defeats the entire purpose of using a computer. Or you can take the easy way out and convert your Access 97 database into another database file format.

This capability works backward, too. Suppose that your company used to store data in a program such as dBASE but has since switched to Access 97. Go ahead and create your Access 97 database and let Access 97 do the hard work of converting your ancient dBASE files into a real honest-to-goodness Access 97 database.

To make Access 97 as powerful as powerful can be, Microsoft made sure that Access 97 can share your valuable data with other people no matter which program or computer they may be using. The goal is to convince the global population to eventually switch to Microsoft products and take over the world in the name of Bill Gates.

Many rival database programs are actually dBASE clones in disguise, which means that they create and store data in dBASE file formats, just as the original dBASE program does. The most popular dBASE clone programs include FoxPro, Clipper, Approach, and Alpha Five.

Converting Databases to (And from) Access

Access 97 can work with rival database files in three ways. It can

- Convert a foreign database file into an Access 97 database
- Link a foreign database file to an Access 97 database
- Convert an Access 97 database into another file format

Converting a rival database file format (such as a file created in dBASE, Paradox, Approach, or FoxPro) into a real Access 97 database file is handy if you plan to use Access 97 as your sole database program.

Linking database files into Access 97 is useful when you want to use Access 97 along with another database program, such as dBASE or FoxPro.

Converting an Access 97 database to another file format is handy when you want to give your data to someone who uses a different database program. Because two separate copies of the data then exist (one copy in Access 97 and a second copy in a rival database file format, such as dBASE), this method is best if you're abandoning Access 97 and switching to a rival program, such as Paradox.

A long time ago, dBASE was the most popular database program in the world. As a result, nearly every database program can create dBASE files. When you convert database files into Access 97 from a different program, try converting your files into dBASE format first and then converting those dBASE files into Access 97 as explained in the "Converting Access 97 databases into another file format" section later in this chapter.

Identifying your database files

If you have a database file but have no idea which program created it, just look at its file extension, as shown in this table:

File Extension	Database File Type
DBF	dBASE
PB	Paradox
WKS, WK1, WK2, WK3	Lotus 1-2-3
XLS	Excel

Just remember that dBASE comes in different versions: dBASE III Plus, dBASE IV, and dBASE 5. If you have a file that doesn't have any of these file extensions, chances are good that it's stored in a proprietary file format created by an obscure database, such as PFS:File, Nutshell, or DataPerfect. In these cases, you'll have to convert the database to a dBASE file first before converting it into an Access 97 database.

Turning foreign files into an Access database

The easiest way to share database files is, obviously, to force everyone to abandon rival database programs and switch to Access 97 instead. To help you support Microsoft's apparent quest for world software domination, Access 97 can turn foreign database files into a genuine Access 97 database. That way, you never have to use any other database program for the rest of your life.

To convert a foreign database file into an Access 97 database, follow these steps:

1. **Choose File⇨New Database.**

   The New dialog box appears. (Skip to Step 4 if you want to convert a foreign database file into an existing Access database.)

2. **Click on the General tab, click on the Blank Database icon, and then click on OK.**

   The File New Database dialog box appears.

3. **Type a name for your database in the File name box and click on Create.**

   Access displays a blank Database window.

4. **Choose File⇨Get External Data⇨Import.**

   The Import dialog box appears, as shown in Figure 22-1.

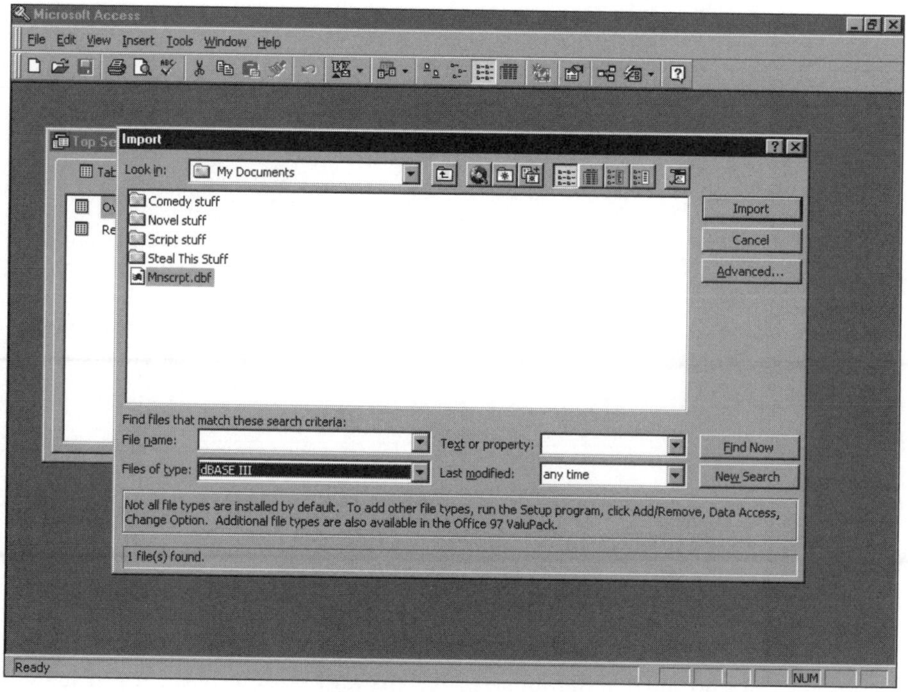

Figure 22-1:
The Import dialog box for converting a foreign database into an Access 97 database.

5. **Click on the File of type list box and choose the file format that you want to convert.**

For example, if you have a dBASE III file, choose dBASE III. A list of files that match your criteria appears.

6. **Click on the file that you want to convert and then click on Import. (You may have to switch directories depending on where the file is located, such as on a floppy drive or in a specific directory on your hard drive.)**

Access 97 displays your newly converted database file as a database table.

7. **Click on Close.**

Access 97 displays your newly converted database in the Database window.

Linking foreign files to Access 97

Having the option to convert foreign database files into Access 97 is great if you never plan to use a rival database again. However, if a stubborn coworker insists on using dBASE while you're using Access 97, you can compromise and just link the dBASE file to Access 97 without converting it. That way, you can share a dBASE file with others without having to endure the torture of learning to use the dBASE program.

The disadvantage of this approach, of course, is that rather than have a single Access 97 file to worry about, you must worry about keeping track of separate dBASE (or Paradox or Lotus 1-2-3) files as well.

If you absolutely must keep data stored in its original file format yet still use it in Access 97, however, linking a foreign database file to Access 97 is easier than giving up Access 97 and switching to another database program.

To link a foreign database file to Access 97, follow these steps:

1. **Choose File⇨New Database.**

   The New dialog box appears. (Skip to Step 4 if you want to convert a foreign database file into an existing Access 97 database.)

2. **Click on the General tab, click on the Blank Database icon, and then click on OK.**

   The New Database dialog box appears.

3. **Type a name for your database in the File name box and then click on Create.**

   Access displays a blank Database window.

4. **Choose File⇨Get External Data⇨Link Tables.**

   The Link dialog box appears.

5. **Click on the File of type list box and choose the file format that you want to link.**

   If you have a Paradox file, for example, choose Paradox. A list of files that match your criteria appears.

6. **Click on the file you want to convert and then click on Link.**

   The Select Index Files dialog box appears.

7. **Click on the index file that accompanies the file you chose in Step 6 and then click on Select.**

   Note: Not all database files have an accompanying index file. An index file helps organize data trapped in a database file.

8. **Click on Close.**

   Access displays your newly linked database in the Database window, shown in Figure 22-2.

Linked dBASE table   Linked Paradox table

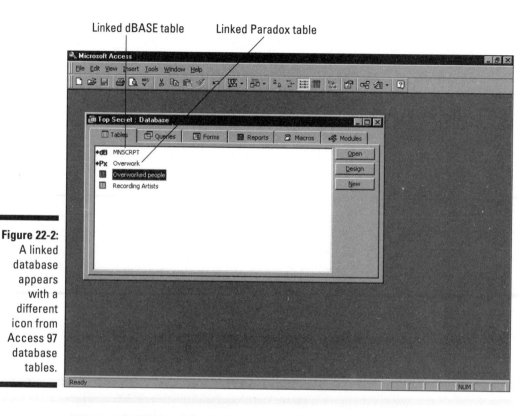

Figure 22-2:
A linked
database
appears
with a
different
icon from
Access 97
database
tables.

Converting Access 97 databases into another file format

Although you use Access 97, your friends may use a rival database program. If you've created a wonderful mailing list of people who are easy to con and you want to share this data with your friends, you may have to convert your Access 97 files into another file format, such as dBASE or Paradox.

Converting an Access 97 database to a different file format creates two copies of the same data stored in two separate files. If you update one file, Access 97 has no way of updating the second file as well. This means that you could inadvertently modify both files with different data, which means that neither file can be completely accurate and up to date.

To convert your Access 97 databases into a different file format, follow these steps:

1. **Open an Access 97 database, click on the Tables tab, and click on the database table that you want to convert.**

2. **Choose File⇨Save As/Export.**

   The Save As dialog box appears.

3. **Click on the radio button labeled To an External File or Database and then click on OK.**

   The Save Table dialog box appears.

4. **Click on the Save as type list box and choose a file format, such as Paradox 5 or Microsoft Excel 7, in which to save the design of your form.**

5. **Click on Export.**

   Access 97 cheerfully converts your chosen Access 97 file into a foreign file format.

Creating a Switchboard Form

To help make your database easier for others to use, you can create a *Switchboard form.* The Switchboard form acts like a group of menu buttons the user can click on to view, edit, or print data, for example.

If you create a database using the Database Wizard, Access 97 thoughtfully creates a Switchboard form that provides a simple one-click menu to access your database forms. However, if you create a database from scratch, you have to create a Switchboard form yourself.

Making a Switchboard form

To create a Switchboard form, follow these steps:

1. **Choose Tools⇨Add-Ins⇨Switchboard Manager.**

   A dialog box appears, asking whether you want to create a switchboard.

2. **Click on Yes.**

   The Switchboard Manager dialog box appears, as shown in Figure 22-3.

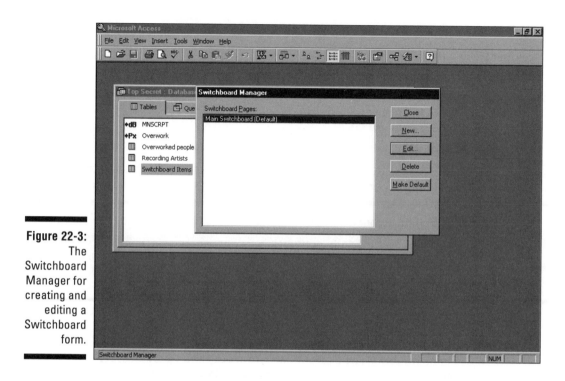

Figure 22-3:
The
Switchboard
Manager for
creating and
editing a
Switchboard
form.

3. **Click on Edit.**

   The Edit Switchboard Page dialog box appears.

4. **Click in the Switchboard Name box and type a name for your Switchboard form.**

5. **Click on New.**

   The Edit Switchboard Item dialog box appears, as shown in Figure 22-4.

6. **Type the text that you want to appear next to the first Switchboard button in the Text box.**

7. **Click in the Command list box and choose a command (such as Open Form In Edit Mode or Exit Application).**

   Depending on which command you chose, Access 97 displays another list box below the Command list box.

8. **Click in this second list box that appears below the Command list box and choose an option.**

   For example, if you clicked on Open Form In Edit Mode in the Command box in Step 7, click on the name of the form that you want to open in the Form box.

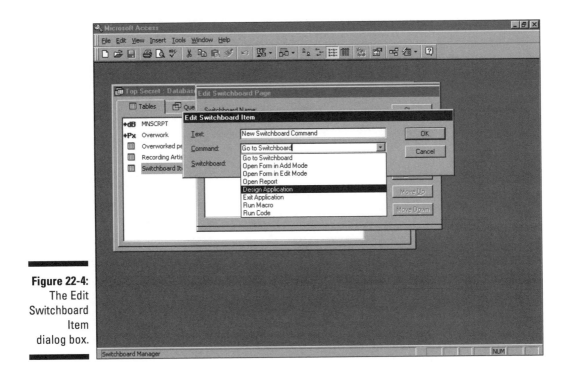

Figure 22-4:
The Edit
Switchboard
Item
dialog box.

9. **Click on OK.**

10. **Repeat Steps 5–9 for each item that you want to add to your Switchboard.**

11. **Click on Close twice.**

Figure 22-5 shows a typical Switchboard form.

Making your Switchboard form appear

After designing your Switchboard form, the final step is to make your Switchboard form appear as soon as you or someone else opens the database.

To make your Switchboard form appear immediately after you load the database, follow these steps:

1. **Choose Tools⇨Startup.**

A Startup dialog box appears, as shown in Figure 22-6.

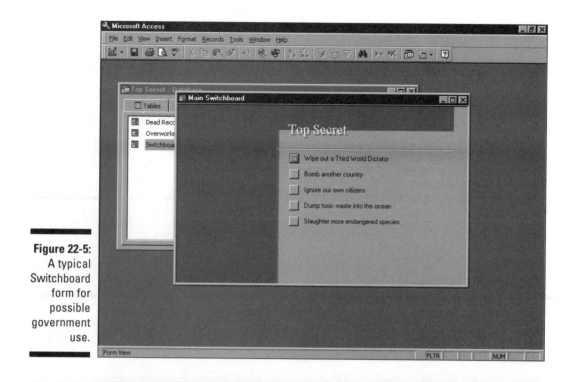

Figure 22-5:
A typical
Switchboard
form for
possible
government
use.

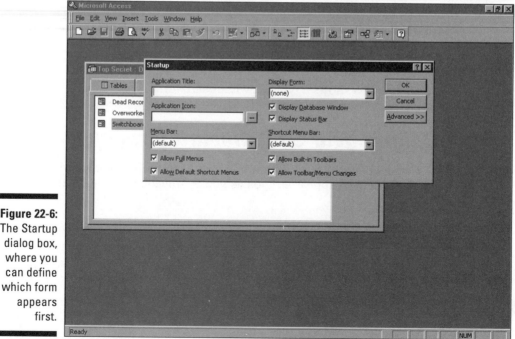

Figure 22-6:
The Startup
dialog box,
where you
can define
which form
appears
first.

2. **Click in the Display Form list box and then click on your Switch-board form name.**

3. **Click on OK.**

   From now on, every time someone opens your database, the Switch-board form appears first.

Password-Protecting Your Valuable Work

What if you store valuable data that could get a president impeached if someone discovered it? In that case, you may want to take the additional precaution of password-protecting your database. Anyone trying to view the information stored in a password-protected database must first supply the correct password.

Password-protecting your database can be both helpful and troublesome. If you forget your password, you won't be able to use your database, either. Worse, if someone steals your password without your knowledge, your database may be wide open to prying eyes while you blissfully think that it's safe. The moral? Don't rely entirely on passwords to protect your data.

Selling and distributing your Access 97 databases

If you create databases for everyone else all the time, you may notice one problem: For other people to be able to use your database, they also need a copy of Access 97 on their computers.

If you would rather not install copies of Access 97 on computers that belong to people who have no idea how to use Access, a better solution exists. Why not turn your Access 97 databases into real programs?

With a copy of the Access Developer's Toolkit, you can turn your databases into programs that you can distribute for free or for profit.

As another alternative, get a copy of the Visual Basic compiler (it's separate from the version of Visual Basic included in Access 97). The combination of Visual Basic and Access 97 allows you to create databases in Access 97 and then use Visual Basic to design the look of your program.

With a little creativity and a lot of luck, you may be able to use Access 97 to create the next best-selling program that will earn you millions, give you the chance to quit your job, and enable you to start your own software company that can compete with Microsoft.

Creating a password

Passwords can be as long as 14 characters and are case-sensitive, which means that NUGGET is a completely different password from Nugget. To make your password as confusing (and thus hard to guess) as possible, mix together numbers and uppercase and lowercase letters, such as NZ8sy4.

The more difficult your password is to guess, the more difficult it is for you to remember — so be careful when you choose a password.

To password-protect a database, follow these steps:

1. **Choose File⇨Close.**

   Skip this step if the database is already closed.

2. **Choose File⇨Open Database.**

   The Open dialog box appears, as shown in Figure 22-7.

3. **Click on the Exclusive check box so that a check mark appears in it.**

4. **Click on the database that you want to password-protect and then click on Open.**

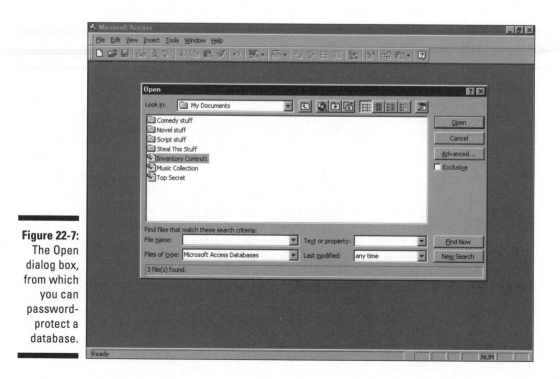

Figure 22-7:
The Open dialog box, from which you can password-protect a database.

5. **Choose Tools⇨Security⇨Set Database Password.**

   The Set Database Password dialog box appears, as shown in Figure 22-8.

6. **Type your password in the Password text box.**

   Access displays your password as a series of asterisks, just in case a spy is snooping over your shoulder.

7. **Type your password again in the Verify text box and click on OK.**

8. **Choose File⇨Close.**

Opening a password-protected database

To open a password-protected database, follow these steps:

1. **Choose File⇨Open.**

   The Open dialog box appears.

2. **Click on the database that you want to open and then click on Open.**

   The Password Required dialog box pops up, as shown in Figure 22-9.

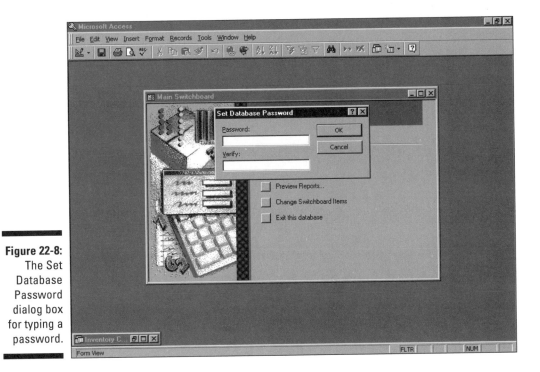

Figure 22-8:
The Set
Database
Password
dialog box
for typing a
password.

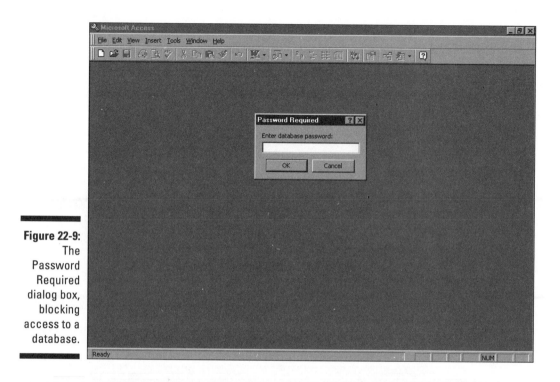

Figure 22-9:
The
Password
Required
dialog box,
blocking
access to a
database.

3. Type the password in the Enter database password text box and then click on OK.

If the password is correct, Access 97 obediently opens the database for you to edit, modify, or view to your heart's delight.

Removing a password

Passwords can be useful, but they can also be a nuisance. If you don't have anything worth stealing or if you just don't care about losing your data, you can remove a password so that Access 97 doesn't continue asking you for one every time you try to open a password-protected database.

To remove a password from a database, follow these steps:

1. Choose File⇔Open.

The Open dialog box appears.

2. Click on the Exclusive check box so that a check mark appears in it.

3. **Click on the database that you want to open and then click on Open.**

   The Password Required dialog box pops up (refer to Figure 22-9).

4. **Type your password in the Enter database password text box and then click on OK.**

5. **Choose Tools⇨Security⇨Unset Database Password.**

   The Unset Database Password dialog box appears.

6. **Type the database password in the Password text box and then click on OK.**

   Your database is now free of annoying passwords and is wide open to corporate spies, undercover government agents, your boss, the janitor, and any annoying coworkers who care to examine your work.

Putting Access 97 Databases on the Web

If you have gobs of fascinating data trapped in an Access 97 database, you may want to display it as a Web page for everyone to see. That way, you won't have to waste time giving everyone copies of your database on a floppy disk.

To convert an Access 97 database into a Web page, follow these steps:

1. **Start Access 97 and open a database that you want to convert into a Web page.**

2. **Choose File⇨Save as HTML.**

   The Publish to the Web Wizard dialog box appears.

3. **Click on Next.**

   Another Publish to the Web Wizard dialog box appears, as shown in Figure 22-10.

4. **Click on the Table, Query, Form, Report, or All Objects tab and then click in the check boxes of the items that you want to convert into a Web page.**

5. **Click on Next.**

   Another dialog box appears, asking whether you want to use an existing document as a template. A template allows Access 97 to create a Web page based on the design of an existing Web page.

6. **Click on Next.**

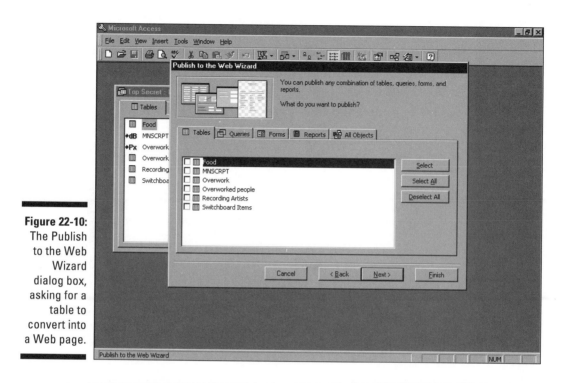

Figure 22-10:
The Publish
to the Web
Wizard
dialog box,
asking for a
table to
convert into
a Web page.

Another dialog box appears, asking what type of Web pages you want to create. Unless you know what you're doing, creating Static HTML is best. Creating dynamic Web pages means that the Web page changes if the information in the database changes. Although convenient, this automatic updating also requires more work on your part to make it happen.

7. Click on Next.

Another dialog box appears, asking where you want to store your Web pages.

8. Type a filename and directory and click on Next.

Yet another dialog box appears, asking whether you want Access 97 to create a home page to link all your other Web pages together. A *home page* can act like a main menu so users can view different Web pages with a click of the mouse.

9. Click on the Yes, I want to create a home page check box (if that's what you want to do) and then click on Next.

A final dialog box appears, asking whether you want to save the Web page in a Web publication profile, which will make designing your Web pages from the same data much easier. If you want to create a Web publication profile, click in the Yes, I want to save Wizard answers to a Web publication profile check box. Otherwise, just skip to Step 10.

10. Click on Finish.

Your Web pages are now ready for posting on a Web server. Figure 22-11 shows a typical Access 97 database table converted into a Web page.

Once you've created your Web pages, you'll need to post them on a Web server so other people can view them. You can post your Web pages through America Online, CompuServe, SpryNet, EarthLink, or whatever Internet provider you use. The procedures for posting Web pages varies from one Internet provider to another, so contact them for more information on how to do it.

Figure 22-11: What an Access 97 database table looks like as a Web page, as seen within Microsoft Internet Explorer.

Worksheet in Fun Stuff 2 - Microsoft Internet Explorer

File　Edit　View　Go　Favorites　Help

Back　Forward　Stop　Refresh　Home　Search　Favorites　Print　Font　Mail　Edit

Address C:\My Documents\MyHTML.htm

Sheet1

Sales Region	Product	Jan	Feb	Mar	Apr
West		$4,586.23	$6,325.14	$7,954.88	$6,897.41
North	Visual Ada for OS/2	$9,863.02	$4,653.21	$9,804.25	$6,553.20
East		$1,397.50	$1,458.21	$4,631.29	$7,857.89
South		$7,865.01	$7,698.35	$7,768.94	$4,985.26
West	WinDoze 97	$8,456.22	$1,689.54	$4,658.24	$8,869.54
North		$8,943.01	$4,321.05	$6,985.35	$4,653.10
East	FORTRAN for DOS	$5,463.25	$1,474.01	$1,223.30	$8,645.10
South		$4,468.77	$4,563.29	$9,814.20	$12,245.21
	Total =	$51,043.01	$32,182.80	$52,840.45	$60,706.71

Last Updated on 4/9/97
By Bo the Cat

Done

Appendix

Getting Free Microsoft Stuff from the Internet

• •

*T*he world of computers changes so rapidly that not even Microsoft can anticipate the future (although it often tries to manipulate it the best it can). In its best attempt to keep its customers from slipping too far behind the industry trends, Microsoft constantly offers loads of free programs, bug fixes, add-ons, and sample files on its Web site (http:/www.microsoft.com).

Much of the Microsoft Web site (see the Microsoft home page in Figure A-1) contains news, press releases, job openings (in case you want to bail out of your current position), and information about programs that most Microsoft Office 97 users would never care about in a million years. (Do you really care about the compilation speed advantages between Visual Basic, Visual C++, and Visual J++?)

But if you're willing to dig through the Microsoft Web site, you can find the following information:

- Additional clip art, sound, and graphics files
- Microsoft Camcorder
- Sample macros
- File converting programs (so you can translate WordPerfect or Lotus 1-2-3 files into Office 97 files)
- Technical support information
- Bug fixes
- Tutorials and lessons for using Office 97
- Program viewers
- Beta software (so you can try upcoming Microsoft products and get hooked on them before they're available in your favorite computer store)

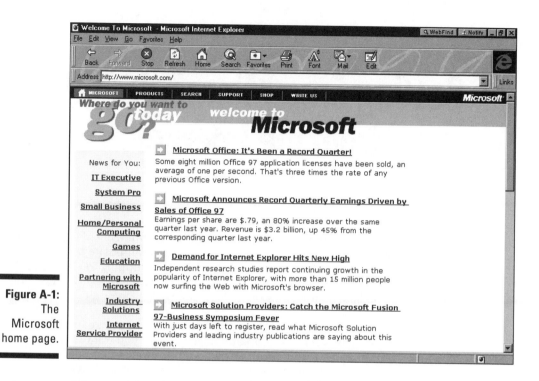

Figure A-1:
The
Microsoft
home page.

Bear in mind that the types and number of files that Microsoft offers keep growing. This appendix lists just a few free files that you may want to consider downloading (if you have an Internet account, that is).

What the Heck is a Program Viewer?

In a perfect world (from Microsoft's point of view), every computer user in the world would buy a copy of Microsoft Office 97, and people would use only Microsoft software. Unfortunately for Bill Gates and Microsoft stockholders, some people still haven't parted with their cash and bought a copy of Office 97.

So what happens to good Microsoft customers who use Office 97 but need to share files with people who don't own Office 97? As a clumsy solution, you could print all your documents and force the other person to type them all on their own computer (as punishment for not buying Microsoft Office 97).

Or you could convert your files, such as Word 97 documents, into another word processor file format, such as WordPerfect, WordPro, or ClarisWorks. However, any time that you convert a file into another file format, you risk messing up the document somehow, such as by losing formatting.

A better solution is to use a Microsoft _program viewer,_ which is a special program that can view and print a Word 97, Excel 97, or PowerPoint 97 file, but can't edit it.

The whole purpose of a program viewer is to let you share your files with someone else without resorting to converting your files into another file format. So the next time you want to share an Excel 97 file with somebody, give that person your Excel 97 file along with the free Excel 97 program viewer. (Likewise, if you need to share a Word 97 file, give away the Word 97 program viewer, and if you need to share a PowerPoint 97 file, give away the PowerPoint 97 program viewer.)

Using the Microsoft Camcorder

As another way for you to share information, Microsoft offers a free program called the Microsoft Camcorder. Like an ordinary camcorder, the Microsoft Camcorder can create "movies" of whatever you do on the computer screen.

For example, if you want to show someone how to create a macro in Word 97, don't bother writing down tedious instructions. Instead, load the Microsoft Camcorder program and record your keystrokes and mouse movements on the screen.

Then give your Camcorder file to others so that they can "play back" your file on their own computers. Whatever you recorded on your computer now appears on their computer as if you had tape-recorded your entire session.

By using the Microsoft Camcorder, you can show people how to use Office 97 without physically looking over their shoulders, pointing at the computer screen, and growing bored out of your mind in the process.

Think of the Microsoft Camcorder as a screen recorder and VCR for your computer. Now imagine some weird stuff that you can display on your computer and think how much fun it would be to record it in a file and pass it around the office for everyone to see while pretending to be hard at work in front of their computer screens.

Getting Technical Support

If you're still stumped by some of the less-than-intuitive features of Office 97, feel free to use this book as a weapon and throw it at your computer. Even though doing so won't help solve any problems, releasing intense emotional stress at the expense of an inanimate object once in a while feels pretty good.

Fortunately, the Microsoft Web site also offers an entire list of technical support resources for you to tap into. Some of the more popular help resources include:

- ✔ **A list of frequently asked questions (FAQs):** The Frequently Asked Questions section simply provides answers to common problems that people experience when using Office 97. By browsing through this list, you can find an answer to a problem that thousands of others have suffered through before.

- ✔ **Newsgroup links:** The Internet offers a handful of newsgroups in which people all over the world discuss problems and offer solutions to a variety of Microsoft Office 97 topics. If you'd rather write a message and hope that a total stranger (who could be on the other side of the planet) has an answer, try using an Office 97-related newsgroup.

  Because so many people browse through these Office 97 newsgroups, chances are really good that someone will have an answer to any type of question you may have.

- ✔ **Knowledge Base:** The Microsoft Knowledge Base is a list of known solutions to some of the more obscure problems that you may face while using Microsoft Office 97. If the frequently asked questions list doesn't solve your problem, dig into the Knowledge Base (used by Microsoft's own technicians) to see whether you can find the answer yourself.

- ✔ **Phone numbers:** If all the other technical support resources haven't diverted you from actually calling Microsoft for help, you can try one of Microsoft's technical support hotlines (listed in the Support Options & Phone Numbers section of the Web page). Be prepared to be put on hold until you can reach a live technical support person, but if all else fails, at least you know that you can call Microsoft directly and get your questions answered.

Index